STRAVINSKY AND HIS WORLD

For Brian Cherney
for introducing me to the music of Igor Stravinsky

STRAVINSKY
AND HIS WORLD

EDITED BY TAMARA LEVITZ

PRINCETON UNIVERSITY PRESS
PRINCETON AND OXFORD

Published by Princeton University Press, 41 William Street,
Princeton, New Jersey 08540
In the United Kingdom: Princeton University Press,
6 Oxford Street, Woodstock, Oxfordshire OX20 1TW
press.princeton.edu

Library of Congress Control Number: 2013937053

ISBN: 978-0-691-15987-4 (cloth)
ISBN: 978-0-691-15988-1 (paperback)

British Library Cataloging-in-Publication Data is available

This publication has been produced by the Bard College Publications Office:
Ginger Shore, Project Director
Karen Walker Spencer, Designer
Anita van de Ven, Cover Design
Text edited by Paul De Angelis and Erin Clermont
Music typeset by Don Giller

This publication has been underwritten in part by grants from
Furthermore, a program of the J. M. Kaplan Fund and Helen and Roger Alcaly.

Printed on acid-free paper. ∞

Printed in the United States of America.

1 3 5 7 9 10 8 6 4 2

Contents

Preface and Acknowledgments

Stravinsky liked to boast to journalists about his worldwide success as a composer. During a chatty interview with Rafael Moragas in Barcelona in 1925, included in this volume, he described in a bemused fashion how two thousand old ladies had honored him at an event in Philadelphia by attempting to kiss his hand. He had put a halt to the proceedings by announcing through a megaphone that he needed his precious limb to conduct future concerts, and that they would have to stop. In spite of the playful annoyance he expressed in telling the story, he clearly relished the adulation.

Fame shaped Stravinsky's career. His ascent to international stardom began for all intents and purposes in May 1913, when Serge Diaghilev, impresario of the Ballets Russes, orchestrated a riot at the premiere of *The Rite of Spring*—a marketing ploy that made Stravinsky an overnight sensation and that proved so successful that it continues to be used to draw audiences to performances of the work today. From the moment that Diaghilev conflated aesthetic appreciation and capitalist desire by transforming the premiere of *The Rite of Spring* into scandal, Stravinsky's music stood in the shadow of his celebrity—his compositional innovations paling in comparison to the symbolic, commercial power of his brand.

Stravinsky's celebrity was no exception in the history of modernism. On the contrary, as Jonathan Goldman argues, celebrity and modernism were mutually constitutive, both serving the goal of reaffirming the centrality of the individual in mass society in the early twentieth century. In *Modernism Is the Literature of Celebrity*, Goldman explains how Oscar Wilde inaugurated modernist celebrity culture in the 1880s, by turning his extraordinary self-production as a psychological subject into an object or stereotype to be admired by the masses—and this shortly after the world's first legal trademarked image, the red triangle on Bass Ale, was registered in England. Modernist writers followed suit, mobilizing the technologies of consumer culture to promote their writings and themselves in the decades that followed. James Joyce, Gertrude Stein, and others fetishized authorship, transforming their signatures into brands, and making style a basis for objectifying themselves as inimitable individuals. The knowledge of their complicity with celebrity culture allows Goldman and others to explode myths about the great divide between modernism and popular culture, and about the modernist artist as isolated, disinterested Romantic genius.

Stravinsky adopted Wilde's culture of the dandy, stylizing himself as an object of desire for the concert-going public while, behind the scenes, flaunting his conspicuous consumption and aristocratic buying habits. After 1913, he was almost always on display: posing for photographs (a medium crucial to the development of modern celebrity), marketing his work in an astonishing number

Figure 1. Stravinsky in Haarlem, the Netherlands, 1930.

of almost daily interviews in multiple languages (leading Richard Taruskin to conclude in an article in the *New York Times* in 2008 that Stravinsky lived "in a perpetual state of interview"), and calculating how to reproduce and disseminate his works using the most advanced technological means. Friends—among them Arthur Lourié, Pyotr Suvchinsky, Walter Nouvel, Alexis Kall, and Robert Craft—served as Stravinsky's unofficial public relations agents, mediating his contact with the outside world and ghostwriting press releases and publications. Craft dedicated his career to consolidating Stravinsky's celebrity during his lifetime, and to perpetuating it in publications and recordings after his death.

Stravinsky designed his words, images, and sounds to sell his celebrity by manufacturing musical need. In his own words, quoted in this volume, "music should be desire, not habit." A photograph from 1930 (see Figure 1) suggests how adept Stravinsky was at molding his own image to arouse the right response; it captures Stravinsky in a moment of jovial relaxation before the camera—a mood he rarely conveyed in his official publicity materials. A second photograph snapped by Stravinsky's lover Vera Sudeikina in Nice in 1924 displays the great composer as an object of desire: the unmade bed and empty bottle of wine on the bedside table reflected in the mirror suggest an erotic interlude, while the large cross revealed under the composer's loosely unbuttoned pajamas point toward both religious passion and a faith that rendered all his pleasures guilty

Figure 2. Stravinsky in Nice, 1924.

ones (see Figure 2). Vera's photographs appear to offer access to Stravinsky's intimate universe—the "man behind the mask" as Stravinsky scholars like to say. But the fact that she and Craft published so many of them in luxury editions after Stravinsky's death—for example, in *Igor and Vera Stravinsky: A Photograph Album, 1921–1971*—suggests that, far from revealing an authentic reality about the composer, they too are designed to sell his image. Such private photographs highlight Stravinsky's charisma, dogma, class, earthiness, passion, licentiousness, and virility—qualities the press had associated with Stravinsky and his music since *The Rite of Spring*. These photographs perpetuate the very traits that have enabled Stravinsky to maintain his celebrity for over a century.

Yet Stravinsky's fame has sat uncomfortably with music scholars. Biographers and critics struggle to abandon deeply-held beliefs about modernist composers as exceptional individuals who express sincerely inner psychological states through word and music, and whose authentic dedication to their art allow them to escape the demands of the market. Such beliefs have led some of Stravinsky's biographers to mistrust the trappings of his fame—whether his commercial successes or the publicity machine that has generated them—and others to adopt a Cold War hermeneutics of suspicion that has led to conspiratorial theories about the composer's innate yet denied Russianness, or about his secret rightwing political agendas.

Stravinsky's fame has also posed a compelling intellectual problem for the community of music theorists who have led the way in Stravinsky research for over half a century. Although many theorists hint at the aesthetics of celebrity in Stravinsky's music by appealing to the metaphor of the "mask" in analyzing it, they shy away from experimenting with analytical approaches that address how modernist commodity culture shapes listening practices. Rather than contemplate what happens to musical meaning when compositions begin to circulate globally as products of celebrity, they omit from their analyses any reminder of such exchange.

Such repression of economic and social origin is evident in the hermeneutic tradition that has arisen around one of Stravinsky's most iconic pieces, the *Symphonies d'instruments à vent*—discussed, almost as a common thread, in several essays throughout this book. In 1962 Edward T. Cone used this piece to define Stravinsky's method of stratification in a classic article in the inaugural issue of *Perspectives of New Music*, initiating a prestigious subfield of scholarship preoccupied solely with interpreting how Stravinsky created compositional coherence and aural continuity in music characterized by blatant narrative discontinuity. Over three decades later, Richard Taruskin launched an alternative campaign for the *Symphonies* by suggesting in *Stravinsky and the Russian Traditions* that its form resembled that of the *Panikhida*, or Russian Orthodox memorial service, which Stravinsky drew on to express his grief over the recently deceased Claude Debussy. The compulsiveness with which Stravinsky scholars (myself included) have cultivated these two interpretive traditions—even in articles and books that have nothing to do with the *Symphonies*— reflects how frantic we have been to restore to Stravinsky the expressive subjectivity of a nineteenth-century musical genius. And yet our efforts have been doomed to fail, because they ignore how drastically celebrity disrupts the classic aesthetics upon which such models of expressive subjectivity depend, and how fundamental the discontinuity of scandal is to Stravinsky's music. Scandal accompanied both the *Symphonies*'s disastrous premiere under Serge Koussevitzky in London in 1921 and the extensive public relations campaign that followed, during which critics invented the infamous (and infamously ill-defined) term "neoclassicism." In the *Symphonies* Stravinsky acknowledges the demands of his newfound celebrity by composing scandalous musical objects—mythologies about music in Roland Barthes's sense—transforming the art of composition into aural spectacle.

The essays in this collection build on the rich international traditions of Stravinsky research and analysis, yet also push those traditions in new directions by addressing some of the issues about biography and analysis raised above. Gretchen Horlacher invites readers to hear Stravinsky's music in new ways by inventing a compelling analytical approach to explore change within sameness as it relates to existential states. Viewing Stravinsky's life from the perspective of his celebrity led me to reevaluate the term "neoclassicism," and to reassess the historic relevance of the many interviews he gave throughout his life. I decided to include here a small collection of interviews from Spanish-speaking newspapers. Whereas Robert Craft and others have tended to isolate statements from these interviews with the goal of proving Stravinsky's essential beliefs as a transhistorical subject, Leonora Saavedra and I present the interviews here in their entirety, accompanied by a scholarly apparatus that links them to their contingent historical circumstances and highlights their temporal specificity. Tatiana Baranova Monighetti valorizes a new kind of evidence—the surface traces Stravinsky left on his Russian library. And Valérie Dufour sheds light on how to interpret ghostwriting—the type of public relations communication most closely associated with Stravinsky's celebrity—in an essay on the genesis of the *Poétique musicale*. Her essay and others in this collection give evidence that some of Stravinsky's publicity agents, and especially Robert Craft, inadvertently misrepresented Stravinsky by mistranslating sources, publishing incomplete and erroneous editions, and by misconstruing historical evidence. Finally, Klára Móricz explores Stravinsky's relationship to Arthur Lourié—an important friend and one-time promoter who expressed in his music a sincere subjectivity at odds with that constituted by Stravinsky in his.

In his study of modernist celebrity, Jonathan Goldman remarks that Oscar Wilde first developed his version of celebrity while on tour in the United States in 1882; fame, he suggests, can result from acknowledgment in unfamiliar contexts. One of the main themes of this book concerns the ways in which Stravinsky, after 1917, represented himself and was represented as a Russian exile. The authors in this volume express very different, even opposing, opinions on this subject, their views depending on their geographical location and own relation to home. The richness of perspectives provided by this international roster of scholars allows the reader to view exile from multiple perspectives, as if refracted through a prism. Jonathan Cross explores how Stravinsky expressed his feelings about exile in the music he performed when he returned to Russia in 1962, while the collection of letters exchanged by Stravinsky, Maria Yudina, and Pyotr Suvchinsky that are included in this volume document the same trip from a more ambivalent and hardened perspective. Leon Botstein explores exile as style in a highly original comparison of Stravinsky and Vladimir Nabokov; Svetlana Savenko offers an insider view on Stravinsky's lasting connection to Russia; and I thematize the composer's strong sense of belonging in Los Angeles, using photographs as documentary evidence. Finally, a collection of documents on *Mavra* details the national conflict that arose when Stravinsky began to assimilate in France after 1920, and the struggle over representation that resulted.

In editing this volume, I have often looked back for inspiration to two of the essay collections on Stravinsky in English I find most beautiful: Jann Pasler's *Confronting Stravinsky* from 1986 and Jonathan Cross's *Cambridge Companion to Stravinsky* from 2003. *Stravinsky and His World* gives evidence of the road travelled in

Stravinsky scholarship since these volumes appeared, of shifting priorities in the scholarly community, and of the timeliness of formulating new questions about his life and works.

* * *

I would like to express my deepest gratitude to Leon Botstein for the opportunity to serve as scholar in residence for the Bard Festival 2013, and as the editor of this collection. My involvement in the Bard Festival has proven to be one of the most gratifying intellectual and musical experiences of my life, and I attribute my happiness to Botstein's visionary leadership, the dialogical culture at Bard, and the brilliant production team and board of directors who organize the festival. Christopher Gibbs's unique psychological insight and rare capacity to conceptualize a project and guide it to completion were key to the success of this volume; I am grateful to him beyond words for his support and advice. I owe as well a tremendous debt to Paul De Angelis, the editorial genius behind the Bard series. Most scholars can only dream of ever working with such a supremely talented editor; I thank him for that great honor, and for being my editorial Rock of Gibraltar during the production process. The team at Bard showed me what can be achieved when experts working at the top of their game collaborate toward a common goal; I have deeply valued the chance to work with each of them. I owe a very special thank you to Project Director Ginger Shore, whose artistic talent and expertise made possible the exquisite aesthetic in evidence in this book. I felt very fortunate to have been able to discuss every aspect of the illustrations and photographs with her, and I will carry her words and advice with me for the rest of my life. Irene Zedlacher, the executive director of the Bard Music Festival, worked miracles behind the scenes, recognizing and solving every problem that came our way before it could even materialize; I am deeply grateful to her for her kindness and support. I thank Erin Clermont for impeccable copyediting, Karen Spencer for her beautiful design and composition, and Don Giller for his patience, humor, and talent in setting the musical examples. Finally, it has been a special privilege to benefit from the musical and historical wisdom of artistic codirector Robert Martin, and of members of the festival program committee Byron Adams and Richard Wilson.

Many members of the larger international community of Stravinsky scholars contributed through their active scholarship to the genesis of this book; I regret that more of them could not have been represented here. Richard Taruskin offered invaluable advice at a very early stage in the project; Ulrich Mosch at the Paul Sacher Stiftung shared his deep knowledge of Stravinsky research in the planning stages; and Valérie Dufour showed immense generosity and patience in helping me to select the interviews to be included here, which are intended to complement her own edition of interviews in French, *Confidences sur la musique: Ecrits et entretiens d'Igor*

Stravinksy. I am grateful to Stephen Walsh for providing through his scholarship the basis for this project although I met him only when it was very advanced, and to Tatiana Baranova Monighetti, Natalia Braginskaya, Olga Manulkina, and Svetlana Savenko for sharing ideas and experiences with me, and for welcoming me into the Russian musicological community, fulfilling my dream of bringing current Russian scholarship on Stravinsky into this collection. My greatest debt goes to Maureen Carr, who served as co-organizer of the document section included in this volume throughout the early and middle stages of the book's preparations. I am profoundly grateful to Maureen for our very many long and fruitful conversations, her guidance on documents and sketches, the contacts she provided and friendships she forged, her patience and understanding, and her indefatigable devotion to Stravinsky. Maureen has supported many Stravinsky scholars over the years, and it is my deepest hope that she will know with this book how much she means to all of us, and how important she is to our scholarly community.

An edited collection depends for its success on the expertise, dedication and scholarly commitment of its contributors. In this respect I could not have been more fortunate. I feel immense gratitude toward Tatiana Baranova Monighetti, Jonathan Cross, Valérie Dufour, Gretchen Horlacher, Klára Móricz, Leonora Saavedra, and Svetlana Savenko for the essays they wrote for this collection. I thank them for their patience, conscientiousness, generosity, and scholarly brilliance. For our long discussions, and for their deep commitment to language and openness to collaboration, I thank as well to our outstanding team of translators, which included Bridget Behrmann, Katya Ermolaev, Laurel Fay, Mariel Fiori, Alexandra Grabarchuk, Yasha Klots, Klára Móricz, Philipp Penka, and Boris Wolfson. Alexandra Grabarchuk went beyond the call of duty in her dedication to the many Russian translations she prepared for me behind the scenes; she became my Ukrainian "eyes" and made it possible through her stunningly sensitive attunement to language for me to work with Russian sources. I thank her, Benjamin Court, Gillian Gower, and Andrea Moore as well for jumping in at short notice through the generosity of a Faculty Research Grant from the Academic Senate at UCLA to complete such first-class work on proofreading the manuscript.

A very last, special thank you goes to my family and to those friends who helped this project grow by being there to listen and share it with me: Byron Adams, Nancy Berman, Erin Brooks, Jerome Camal, Ryan Dohoney, and Tim Stowell. The most important thank you of all goes to René, who shares Stravinsky's birthday and whom I married (unknowingly at the time) on the anniversary of the premiere of *The Rite of Spring*, but who probably never imagined he would have to share so much of his life with the great twentieth-century composer. René's support enables the scholarly passion that made this project possible.

A Note on Transliteration and Titles of Works

The transliteration system used in this book is basically the system used for the *New Grove Dictionary of Music and Musicians* (1980) with modifications introduced by Richard Taruskin. Our principal exceptions to the system concern commonly accepted spellings of given and family names and places (Tchaikovsky rather than Chaykovskiy, Alexander instead of Aleksandr) and suffixes (*-sky* rather than *-skiy*). Also, in the case of a paired *i* of which one is stressed we have chosen *ii* over *iyi* in order to retain the far more common spelling of names such as the Mariinsky Theatre and Daniil Kharms. In the bibliographic citations, however, the transliteration system is respected without exception (Igor' Stravinskiy rather than Igor Stravinsky). Surname suffixes are presented intact, and hard and soft signs preserved.

Titles of works are usually provided in the main text in the language in which they were published or are generally known in the West (original titles of the exceptions can be found in the notes). The corresponding English title of a published composition or translation is provided parenthetically in usual title style. Literal English translations for which no published translations or editions exist are given parenthetically with neither italics nor quote marks, with only the first word and proper names capitalized.

Permissions and Credits

Schott Music has graciously given its permission to reprint musical excerpts from the following copyrighted work by Igor Stravinsky:

Ode © Copyright 1947 by Schott Music GmbH & Co. KG. Copyright © renewed. All rights reserved. Used by permission of European American Music Distributors Company, sole U.S. and Canadian agent for Schott Music GmbH & Co. KG. Used in Example 1a (p. 5), Example 2a (p. 6) in "Stravinsky in Exile" by Jonathan Cross.

Boosey & Hawkes has graciously given its permission to reprint musical excerpts from the following copyrighted works by Igor Stravinsky:

Symphonies of Wind Instruments (Symphonies d'instruments à vent) © Copyright 1948, 1952 by Hawkes & Son (London) Ltd. U.S. copyright renewed. Reprinted by permission of Boosey & Hawkes, Inc. Used in Example 1b (p. 5), Example 2b (p. 6) in "Stravinsky in Exile" by Jonathan Cross and Example 3 (p. 115) in "*Symphonies* and *Funeral Games*: Lourié's Critique of Stravinsky's Neoclassicism" by Klára Móricz.

Orpheus © Copyright 1948 by Hawkes & Son (London) Ltd. Reprinted by permission of Boosey & Hawkes, Inc. Used in Example 3a (p. 10) in "Stravinsky in Exile" by Jonathan Cross; and in Example 5 (p. 96), Example 6 (pp. 98–99), and Example 7 (p. 101–2) in "The Futility of Exhortation: Pleading in Stravinsky's *Oedipus Rex* and *Orpheus*" by Gretchen Horlacher.

Apollo (Apollon musagète) © Copyright 1949 by Hawkes & Son (London) Ltd. U.S. copyright renewed. Reprinted by permission of Boosey & Hawkes, Inc. Used in Example 4 (p. 14) in "Stravinsky in Exile" by Jonathan Cross.

Mavra by Igor Stravinsky & Boris Kochno © Copyright 1925 by Hawkes & Son (London) Ltd. Reprinted by permission of Boosey & Hawkes, Inc. Used on pp. 48–49 of Arthur Lourié's essay on *Mavra*.

Oedipus Rex by Igor Stravinsky, Jean Cocteau, and Jean Danielou © Copyright 1949, 1950 by Hawkes & Son (London) Ltd. U.S. copyright renewed. Reprinted by permission of Boosey & Hawkes, Inc. Used in Example 1 (pp. 84–87), Example 2 (pp. 89–90), Example 3 (pp. 91–92), and Example 4 (p. 93) in "The Futility of Exhortation: Pleading in Stravinsky's *Oedipus Rex* and *Orpheus*" by Gretchen Horlacher.

Divertimento © Copyright 1951 by Hawkes & Son (London) Ltd. Reprinted by permission of Boosey & Hawkes, Inc. Used in Example 1 (pp. 166–69) in "Igor the Angeleno: The Mexican Connection" by Tamara Levitz.

The music used in Examples 1 (p. 113), 4 (p. 116), and 5 (p. 117) in "*Symphonies* and *Funeral Games*: Lourié's Critique of Stravinsky's Neoclassicism" by Klára Móricz is from KölnMusik, Öffentlichkeitsarbeit Archiv.

Also, the following copyright holders have graciously granted permission to reprint or reproduce the following copyrighted material:

The Paul Sacher Stiftung, Basel, for Figure 1 (p. viii) and Figure 2 (p. ix) in "Preface and Acknowledgments"; Figure 1 (p. 23) and Figure 2 (p. 26) in "Who Owns *Mavra*: A Transnational Dispute"; Figure 1 (p. 62), Figure 2 (p. 70), and Figure 3 (p. 72) in "Stravinsky's Russian Library" by Tatiana Baranova Monighetti; Figure 2 (p. 106) in "*Symphonies* and *Funeral Games*: Lourié's Critique of Stravinsky's Neoclassicism" by Klára Móricz; Figure 2 (p. 150), Figure 3 (p. 151), Figure 4 (p. 154), Figure 5 (pp. 155–57), Figure 6 (p. 159), Figure 7 (p. 160), Figure 8 (p. 163), and Figure 10 (p. 171) in "Igor the Angeleno: The Mexican Connection" by Tamara Levitz; Figure 1 in "Stravinsky Speaks to the Spanish-Speaking World"; Figure 1 (p. 226) in "The *Poétique musicale*: A Counterpoint

Erich Lessing/Art Resource, New York, for Figure 1 (p. 106) in "*Symphonies* and *Funeral Games*: Lourié's Critique of Stravinsky's Neoclassicism" by Klára Móricz (the painting by Pytor Vassilievich Miturich, housed in the Russian State Museum, St. Petersburg, Russia).

Modernism/modernity for the photograph used in Figure 1 (p. 145) in "Igor the Angeleno: The Mexican Connection" by Tamara Levitz, and originally published as part of "Modernist Networks: Taxco, 1931" by A. Joan Saab, in Volume 18, Number 2, April 2011, pp. 289–307.

The Estate of Jesús Bal y Gay for the photograph taken by him and used in Figure 9 (p. 164) in "Igor the Angeleno: The Mexican Connection" by Tamara Levitz.

Lebrecht Music & Arts. U.K. for Figure 1 (p. 305) in "Stravinsky's Cold War: Letters About the Composer's Return to Russia, 1960–1963."

Rosspen Publishers, Moscow, selected letters of Maria Yudina that appear in "Stravinsky's Cold War: Letters About the Composer's Return to Russia, 1960–1963"; John Stravinsky, for the letters of Pyotr Suvchinsky that appear in the same section.

Cover Caption and Credit: Photograph of Igor Stravinsky, 1913, Foto Gershel, Paris/Paul Sacher Foundation, Basel.

Stravinsky and His World

Stravinsky in Exile

JONATHAN CROSS

The death in New York of Igor Fyodorovich Stravinsky at 5:20 a.m. on 6 April 1971 was already making broadcast headlines by the top of the next hour. The news of the passing of this "towering figure in twentieth-century music" (*The Guardian*), "one of the great, original creative geniuses in the entire history of music" (*Washington Post & Times Herald*), was soon being wired around the world, with commentators lining up in America, Europe, the Soviet Union, and elsewhere to offer their views on the achievements of this most celebrated of composers.[1] It was not just journalists, friends, and artists who had something to say; politicians, too, some of whom had never even met him, were eager to have their voices heard, to claim Stravinsky's legacy for themselves. At his second New York funeral ceremony (the first had been a simple prayer service on the evening of his death) representatives from the political centers of the opposed sides of the Cold War could be found: Michael Whitney Straight, spokesman for U.S. President Richard Nixon, deputy chairman of the National Endowment for the Arts, and one-time KGB spy; and Anatoly Dyuzhev, cultural attaché to the Soviet Embassy in Washington. Stravinsky's widow, Vera, received letters of condolence from the highest authorities. From the Soviet Ministry of Culture, the former Politburo member Yekaterina Furtseva brushed aside earlier decades of official Soviet hostility toward Stravinsky in expressing her sincerest sympathies. And with barely disguised echoes of Beethoven's Ninth came a letter from the White House: "Surely, the power and force of his genius help to make all men brothers and the magnitude of his loss transcends all national boundaries."[2]

The tone adopted by Stravinsky's obituarists certainly helped consolidate a view that persists in certain quarters today, namely that he was the last of the "great composers," that he was a figure of Beethovenian magnitude who spoke "in the purest language of all peoples" (as Wagner wrote of Beethoven).[3] That such universalist claims were being made for Stravinsky even before his body had been interred should hardly surprise us. Throughout much of his life Stravinsky had himself been largely responsible for his representation as a cosmopolitan figure, as someone whose music could speak to all people in a kind of Esperanto that disregarded national boundaries and identities. His own life, indeed, had spanned cultures and continents. Born a Russian into a family of minor Polish nobility, stranded in Switzerland during the First World War, Stravinsky eventually took French, then U.S. citizenship. In 1948 *Time* magazine reported that he liked to be known as a "California composer," and the fifth edition of *Grove's Dictionary of Music and Musicians* (published in 1954) defined him as an "American composer of Russian origin."[4] Yet, in 1962, on his first return to his homeland in almost half a century, he famously declared at a dinner in Moscow hosted by Furtseva that "a man has one birthplace, one fatherland, one country—he can have only one country—and the place of his birth is the most important factor in his life."[5] On this occasion one has to feel that Stravinsky was speaking from the heart.[6] "I've spoken Russian all my life, I think in Russian, my way of expressing myself [*slog*] is Russian. Perhaps this is not immediately apparent in my music, but it is latent there, a part of its hidden nature."[7] Russia had evidently never left him.

One might wonder, then, why Stravinsky chose his brief Ode of 1943 to be the first work he would ever conduct on Russian soil at the opening concert of his Russian tour, on 26 September 1962, in the Great Hall of the Moscow Conservatory. Neither overtly Russian like *The Rite of Spring*, which Robert Craft conducted in the same concert after the Ode, nor self-evidently a showcase example of his most recent music, its sparse textures and understated language were not designed to make a bold impression. *Orpheus* (1947) formed the second half of the program, a similarly subdued work of melancholic mood, framed by the falling harp lines of the weeping Orpheus. It evidently baffled the audience. Craft reports that the performance was "attended with much reading of program notes, coughing, and other signs of restlessness," all of which can clearly be heard on the recording, subsequently released on the Soviet Melodiya label.[8]

The Ode was a product of Stravinsky's difficult early years in the United States. "We are living lately in a state of continuous anxiety because of the tragic news from our poor old Europe," he wrote to Carlos Chávez in 1940, "and I ask myself if these terrible events will not ultimately have repercussions in the new world."[9] Stravinsky still bore the pain of the triple loss of his daughter, first wife, and mother in just seven months in 1938–39, mitigated only by the happiness of now being free to marry his longtime mistress, Vera Sudeikina. His brother Yury died in Leningrad in 1941, just before the start of the terrible blockade of his native city. In a fascinating volte-face for one who had been so vehemently dismissive of Soviet music, Stravinsky listened, apparently moved, on 19 July 1942, to the U.S. broadcast premiere of Shostakovich's Symphony no. 7 in C Major (*Leningrad*) given by Arturo Toscanini and the NBC Symphony Orchestra.[10] He remained deeply concerned for the well-being of his family left behind in Europe, and followed the progress of events assiduously from afar. The vast distance that separated him from his loved ones served only to exaggerate his sense of anxiety and to reinforce his status as an émigré.

The Ode had been commissioned by a fellow Russian émigré, the conductor Serge Koussevitzky in memory of his wife, Natalia, who had died in 1942. Across many decades the Koussevitzkys had been great champions and publishers of Stravinsky's music. However, the passing of Natalia Koussevitzky did not touch Stravinsky; indeed, his attitude toward the couple had always been disingenuous, bordering at times on the contemptible. The tribute to her in the form of the Ode was, as Paul Griffiths writes, more professional than personal.[11] Indeed, in a decidedly impersonal touch, one of the three movements of this "elegiacal chant," the jaunty central "Eclogue," was recycled from the aborted music for a hunting scene in the film of *Jane Eyre*, directed by Robert Stevenson and produced by Orson Welles.[12] The newly composed outer movements, however, have a very different character. The "Eulogy" breathes the same air as the *Symphonies d'instruments à vent* written over twenty years earlier *in memoriam* Claude Debussy. The brass chords that punctuate the opening of the Ode are a pared-down echo of the start of the chorale from the *Symphonies*: a lower neighbor-note melodic motion in the Ode, whose attendant chords are subsets of the *Symphonies* chords (an exact subset in the case of the second chord of the Ode, D–G–A♭–B); further, the excerpts given in Examples 1a and 1b have identical durational proportions.[13]

Example 1a. Stravinsky, "Eulogy," Ode, measure 6.

Example 1b. *Symphonies d'instruments à vent*, 1920 version, rehearsal number 39.

The later moments of sparse chamber scoring seem to anticipate by a decade another short (serial) tribute work, *In Memoriam Dylan Thomas* (1954). The closing movement, "Epitaph," also carries echoes of the *Symphonies*. Compare, for example, the static, turning figures for flutes that frame the Ode's "Epitaph" (mm. 1–2) with the turning flute figure at measure 29 in the *Symphonies* (see Examples 2a and 2b). Note also the slow, *espressivo* falling lines in the "Epitaph" (mm. 2–3) that lend this

Example 2a. Stravinsky, Ode, "Epitaph," opening 3 measures with upbeat.

Example 2b. Stravinsky, *Symphonies d'instruments à vent*, mm. 29–32.

music its lamenting temperament and can be heard to parallel a short linking passage in the *Symphonies* (mm. 21–22).

The marking *espressivo* had been virtually absent from Stravinsky's scores since *Firebird* of 1910.[14] That the principal thematic material of the *Symphonies'* outer movements carries this indication represents an extraordinary shift for a composer who had given his imprimatur to the view that "music is, by its very essence powerless to *express* anything at all," and who, just a couple of years earlier in the Charles Eliot Norton Lectures at Harvard, was posing the question, via his ghostwriters Roland-Manuel and Pyotr Suvchinsky, "Do we not, in truth, ask the impossible of music when we expect it to express feelings, to translate dramatic situations, even to imitate nature?"[15] Of what, then, does Stravinsky's newly rediscovered expressive voice speak? And why at this moment, in 1940s America? Is it merely another mask, a simulacrum of expression, "only an illusion and not a reality," or is it possible that it might just be a momentary sounding of the authentic voice of Stravinsky?[16]

And how does this subjective note sit with the music's distanced character, which has often been noted?[17] In these questions one might start to look for clues as to why Stravinsky decided the Ode and *Orpheus* were well suited to mark his return to his motherland. In the Ode it is, among other means, the reference to Ancient Greek poetic forms that achieves such distance (from the present). Stravinsky had periodically worn the Greek mask since *Oedipus Rex* (1927). In that opera-oratorio he deployed all manner of distancing effects in his desire to build a monumental kind of theater: soloists and chorus are presented in masks; the "dead" Latin language is used; a narrator is employed to reveal the plot in the vernacular before the actual events unfold; the music moves across a landscape of styles that Stravinsky called a *Merzbild* (collage). The more general allusions in the Ode to the music of the eighteenth and nineteenth centuries have a similar effect of keeping the listener at arm's length.

Indeed, Stravinsky had spent much of the preceding twenty years appropriating the language and practices of classical Western European music, and progressively distancing himself from his Russian roots. One motivation might have been a fear of being perceived as provincial or out of step with sophisticated postwar Parisian society. (Having been hidden from view in Switzerland during the war years, *Pulcinella* flamboyantly announced Stravinsky's return to the limelight on 15 May 1920 with a chic and playful modernized classicism that delighted French audiences.) Such borrowing can certainly be read as a concerted effort at assimilation. For the novelist, essayist, and Czech exile Milan Kundera, it was also a sign of Stravinsky's status as an émigré:

> Without a doubt, Stravinsky, like all the others, bore with him the wound of his emigration; without a doubt, his artistic evolution would have taken a different path if he had been able to stay where he was born. In fact, the start of his journey through the history of music coincides roughly with the moment when his native country ceases to exist for him; having understood that no country could replace it, he finds his only homeland in music; this is not just a nice lyrical conceit of mine, I think it in an absolutely concrete way: his only home was music, all of music by all musicians, the very history of music; there he decided to establish himself, to take root, to live; there he ultimately found his only compatriots, his only intimates, his only neighbors, from Pérotin to Webern; it is with them that he began a long conversation, which ended only with his death.
>
> He did all he could to feel at home there: he lingered in each room of that mansion, touched every corner, stroked every piece

of the furniture; he went from the music of ancient folklore to Pergolesi, who gave him *Pulcinella* (1919), to the other Baroque masters, without whom his *Apollon musagète* (1928) would be unimaginable, to Tchaikovsky, whose melodies he transcribes in *Le Baiser de la fée* (1928) to Bach . . . Pérotin and other old polyphonists . . . Monteverdi . . . Hugo Wolf . . . and to the twelve-tone system . . . in which, eventually after Schoenberg's death (1951), he recognized yet another room in his home

His detractors, the defenders of music conceived as expression of feelings, who grew irate at his unbearably discreet "affective activity" and accused him of "poverty of heart," didn't have heart enough themselves to understand the wounded feelings that lay behind his vagabondage through the history of music.[18]

Certainly one can say that the neoclassical aspects of the Ode, as so often in Stravinsky's music after 1920, offer a kind of defense mechanism, keeping his own feelings at a distance. It is fascinating, therefore, that the Ode should also make such clear references to music of strongly Russian (and therefore more personal) character through, among other means, its recollection of the Russian funeral service that Stravinsky used as a model for the *Symphonies d'instruments à vent*. Any memorial piece was likely to summon up memories of the past. Here, in the Ode, through its repetitions, the music seems to articulate a sense of nostalgia, a longing for a Russia more imagined than real that Stravinsky always carried in his itinerant life, symbolized in the icons that hung in his study or the religious pendants that hung round his neck. Feelings of alienation were now more acutely felt as he began to settle in the United States while his family remained at a great distance in war-torn Europe.

What is intriguing is that Stravinsky, on the occasion of his return to Russia in 1962, chose to speak through the Ode to the people of his native country from whom he had been separated for so long. This work, with its echoes of ancient Russia, with its character of mourning, and with its uniquely expressive voice, spoke of distance, loss, and sorrow. Stravinsky was delighted to be back on Russian soil, but it was a place he no longer knew. He did not try to enter his childhood apartment at 66 Kryukov Canal in Leningrad (St. Petersburg), though he did visit his niece Xenia who still lived nearby; he was officially discouraged from visiting his beloved summer home in Ustilug, which in any case had been ransacked and destroyed after the 1917 Revolution. Stravinsky's Russia lived on only in his memory and imagination, in music such as the Ode. Indeed, ever since *Petrushka* and *The Rite of Spring*, Russia for Stravinsky was already a nostalgic construction, though deeply rooted in authentic folk traditions.[19] The dislocated flutes that frame the "Epitaph" of the Ode, turning in endless repetitions, suggest a melancholic, pastoral landscape; their liturgical chanting mourns the loss of innocence. "Modern nostalgia is a mourning for the impossibility of mythical return, for the loss of an enchanted world," observes Svetlana Boym.[20] This surely sounds like Stravinsky's lament for the losses of family and homeland, for the loss of the enchanted world of his childhood. What better work, then, through which to present himself to his fellow countrymen and women? (If only they had been prepared to listen.)

The pastoral was in fact a theme running through all three works in the 1962 Moscow program. An idealized pastoral is present explicitly in the bucolic horn calls of the Ode's "Eclogue." *The Rite of Spring* begins with the imitation on high bassoon of the sound of the reed pipes or *dudki*, an expression of the "sublime rising of nature as it renews itself," but, far from the idyllic rural life, progresses by means of an uncompromising rhythmic language toward the violent "Sacrificial Dance."[21] And the subject of *Orpheus*, in his ability to charm beasts, trees, and even rocks by the power of his music, stands as the exemplar of the pastoral figure across at least three thousand years of European art. Although the pastoral in Stravinsky might, at one level, be read as symbolic of the pure rural life, the enchanted Russia of the imagination, it is nonetheless inseparable from notions of loss. In the celebrated paintings of the 1630s by Nicolas Poussin, shepherds (from Virgil's *Eclogues*) gather round a tombstone bearing the inscription "Et in Arcadia ego" (I [Death] am even in Arcadia). Death is present, too, in all three Stravinsky pastorals. The Ode is a memorial. The *Rite* ends with a dance to the death. *Orpheus* is pure neoclassical pastoral, yet even at the start we encounter Orpheus weeping for the loss of his lover Eurydice. We hear the falling Phrygian lines of his lyre (harp) in a conventional sign of lament, echoing outward into the strings, which linger mournfully over each note. Stravinsky looks back to Orpheus and the classical past, not to repeat it but to reinvent it, turning it to his own modern purpose. Behind the mask lie both a general sense of late-modern uncertainty and a personal sense of loss. The classical mask also betrays exile. "A writer in exile is by and large a retrospective and retroactive being," writes Joseph Brodsky. "Exile slows down one's stylistic evolution, . . . it makes a writer more conservative."[22]

Death stalks *Orpheus*. The myth offered Stravinsky a context in which he could sing laments of loss. In the "Air de Danse" Orpheus sings of the loss of Eurydice. Once again to the accompaniment of the lyre, an obligato line played on two oboes, moving for the most part in rhythmic unison, gives voice to a deeply melancholic lament, the lines intertwined in grief, echoing a Baroque aria. It is quite clearly a reconfiguration of the soprano aria that occurs toward the end of Bach's *St. John Passion*, "Zerfließe, mein Herze, in Fluten der Zähren" (Dissolve, my heart, in floods of tears), which is accompanied by obligato flute and oboe da caccia. Stravinsky uses a similar scoring, the same aria type of the siciliana (usually associated with pastoral scenes and melancholy emotions), the same time signature (predominantly 3/8), and even some of the same figurations. In looking back to Bach, Stravinsky captures something of Bach's *Affekt*, he makes

Example 3a. Stravinsky, "Air de Danse (Orphée)," *Orpheus*, rehearsal number 80.

Example 3b. J. S. Bach, "Zerfließe, mein Herze," *St. John Passion*, opening.

a plea for the idea of Bach's order that he so craved in a turbulent world, but in the fragmentation and stasis of his own music he also highlights the distance between his age and Bach's, articulating the uncertainty and alienation of both the modernist and of one far from home.[23]

The accented melodic decorations in Stravinsky certainly have their origins in Bach, but also in Russian folk music—heard previously in, say, the *dudki* grace notes of *The Rite of Spring* and *Les Noces*. But now they are transformed into poignant expressive gestures. (It is instructive to compare the melody of Example 3a with Example 2a). Such gestures can also be heard in the vocal lines of Stravinsky's next major work, *The Rake's Progress*. It has often been commented that it seemed strange for Stravinsky to have been writing *The Rake* immediately after the Second World War, a work so apparently disengaged from world events. Yet, like *Orpheus*, far from escaping into ancient Greek mythology or eighteenth-century comedy, the opera's (pastoral) subject matter and its musical treatment engage allegorically with personal and collective loss, and articulate a melancholic sense of modernist alienation. It is striking that at the very end of Tom's life in *The Rake*, in his madness, alienated from himself, and believing himself to be Adonis, he invokes Orpheus with a suitably decorated melodic line: "My heart breaks. I feel the chill of death's approaching wing. Orpheus, strike from thy lyre a swan-like music." *Et in Arcadia ego.*

The deaths of the youthful Orpheus and Eurydice took on particular resonance in the violent twentieth century. So many creative artists turned to myth as a way of coming to terms with events that were, literally, unspeakable. One such was Jean Cocteau, who had completed his tragicomic play *Orphée* in 1925, which he read to Stravinsky in September in Nice, and which became the catalyst for their collaboration on *Oedipus Rex*. In 1949, not long after Stravinsky had completed *Orpheus*, Cocteau returned to *Orphée*, reworking it as a much darker film in which Orpheus is a celebrated yet despised poet in post–Second World War Paris. Vivid reminders of the Nazi Occupation are everywhere. Painful memories of recent events are mediated through the ancient story. Stravinsky had begun work on his *Orpheus* within a year of the end of the war. Though the idea for the subject came from another Russian émigré, the choreographer George Balanchine, it would have struck a chord with Stravinsky at that particular time. He was "desperately anxious" to see his children and grandchildren, still at a great distance in Europe, and had understandably been affected by news of the dislocation and deaths of many of his cousins during the war.[24] As in the Ode, it is a sense of distance and restraint that in general characterizes the apparently timeless *Orpheus*. The turning away from violence in this work should not, however, be read as a sign of retreat from the horror of war. In the face of such slaughter, another barbaric *Rite of Spring* would hardly have been possible. The *Rite*, premiered on the eve of the First World War, had glorified the primitive, the erotic, and the violent. Prescient it may have been, but the reality of the two world wars left artists searching for a new order, and the classical past offered an appropriate framework. In *Orpheus* we hear Stravinsky not reveling triumphally in death but reflecting mournfully on it. Even in the second *pas d'action*, in which the "Bacchantes attack Orpheus, seize him and tear him to pieces," the music is disciplined. The mechanical repetitions, ostinatos, and rhythmic energy of the *Rite* are still present, but the violence is now heard with a sense of detachment and stuttering uncertainty, as if trying to make sense of awful events beyond comprehension.

Thus, from behind the Greek masks of two works from his early years in America, it is possible to hear Stravinsky speaking as an émigré. That the Ode and *Orpheus* were presented to his compatriots in 1962 serves to reinforce the sense that Stravinsky wanted to reveal (consciously or otherwise) both how he imagined Russia to be and how he felt about losing it. He may have pretended to the rest of the world, and perhaps even to himself, that he had left "scenes of pagan Russia" behind, but these ostensibly classical works seem to speak otherwise. Their "eccentric, aloof, nostalgic, deliberately untimely" character —to appropriate the words of George Steiner on the émigré Russian writer Vladimir Nabokov—distinguish them as the work of an "extraterritorial."[25] In a general sense, it might be said that these characteristics are signs of Stravinsky's modernism. The "deliberate untimeliness" (the "lateness") of the neoclassical works that continually glance backwards to earlier music and the art of antiquity is, in another sense, utterly timely: these works articulate a sense of distance and alienation that resonates with the tragic, late-modern era. A late style, Edward Said argues after Adorno, is variously characterized by apartness, exile, anachronism, alienation, a melancholic world-weariness, intransigence, difficulty, and unresolved contradiction.[26] Stravinsky's lateness, symbolized both in the adoption of classical forms and subject matter, and in the musical representations of distance, lament, and loss, is certainly a response to his age; but the seemingly contradictory *espressivo* of his works of second emigration can also be understood as an allegorical response to his own, personal losses.

Just as in his early years in the United States, Stravinsky's years first stranded (in 1914) then exiled (after the 1917 Revolution) in Switzerland, were marked by war, separation from what he held dear, and devastating personal loss:

> My profound emotion on reading the news of war, which aroused patriotic feelings and a sense of sadness at being so distant from my country, found some alleviation in the delight with which I steeped myself in Russian folk poems. . . . Overwhelmed by the successive bereavements I had suffered [his beloved *nyanya* Bertha and his brother Gury], I was now also in a position of the utmost pecuniary difficulty. The communist revolution, which had just triumphed in Russia, deprived me of the last resources which had still from time

to time been reaching me from the country, and I found myself, so to speak, face to face with nothing, in a foreign land and right in the middle of the war.[27]

As has been widely discussed, some of his most characteristically Russian music was the product of his first exile, in Switzerland, including *Les Noces*, perhaps Stravinsky's most glorious celebration of Russia, the first ideas for which dated back as far as 1912, but whose final pared-down, stylized ritual (completed in 1923) represented a Russia imagined and reinvented at a great distance.[28]

At the same time Stravinsky was also producing a number of deceptively simple piano pieces, which appeared to have little to do with Russia and far more to do with the francophone culture in which he found himself: the *Valse des fleurs* (1914), for example, or the *Trois Pièces faciles* and *Cinq Pièces faciles* (both 1917). This is a music *dépouillé*, stripped of the complexity and exoticism of the prewar Ballets Russes scores. Many of the movements use parody and humor as a distancing strategy. Sometimes, as in the first of the *Cinq Pièces*, this also results in a sorrowful music. If anything, the music's childlike simplicity exaggerates its mournfulness; its fixed repetitions suggest that the sorrow cannot be overcome. Said has written of the "crippling sorrow of estrangement." "Exile," he observes, is characterized by an "essential sadness [that] can never be surmounted."[29]

In the interwar years Stravinsky moved progressively further away from Russian and toward Western European models—a deliberate act of distancing. Then, toward the end of the 1920s, he turned for the first time to Ancient Greek material. Myth gave order, distanced, and helped to hide the pain of loss. Apollo, above all others, symbolized such order: the ideal Greek youth, variously god of light, truth, healing, music, and poetry. In the wake of the First World War, Olympian order offered solace. What better subject matter, then, for a ballet concerned with purity, poetry, and order than *Apollon musagète*, Apollo leader of the Muses?

Apollon musagète of 1928 (or *Apollo*, as Diaghilev renamed the work) is stripped of any meaningful narrative and expressive content. What is left is a kind of abstract meditation on classical themes, figures, and dances. Music and dance are unified in the expression of pure, classical beauty. Stravinsky himself designated *Apollo* a *ballet blanc*, a term applied in the nineteenth century to scenes in classical ballet where the principal ballerina wore pure white. The music eschews contrast, pares down the scoring to strings, and employs principally diatonic harmony representative of a kind of white-note Hellenism. Griffiths quips that the "Gallic spirit of *Apollo* is a complex superimposition of Lully and Delibes, *Daphnis* and the Ritz."[30] In keeping with the prevailing spirit of Parisian Art Deco, Stravinsky and his choreographer Balanchine turn a Greek god into French chic.

At least, that is what sits on the surface. But the final "Apotheosis" opens a window onto something beyond the merely playful and decorative. At one level,

Example 4. Stravinsky, "Apotheosis," from *Apollon musagète*,
two measures before rehearsal number 100 to end.

an apotheosis at the end of a classical ballet is entirely to be expected, and
there are certainly echoes here of Tchaikovsky's *Sleeping Beauty*. In keeping with
Apollo's scenario, apotheosis suggests the process of transformation into a god,
the release from the earthly toward the divine. This is signaled by the heroic key
of D major and the Baroque fanfare character of what Eric Walter White has

Example 4 continued

dubbed the Olympian theme.[31] Yet, below these conventional signs of triumph and closure, the music pulls in a different direction. Its D major is less certain than it might at first seem, as triads of G major and B minor also circulate freely and simultaneously. The music cannot easily move forward. And, in unexpectedly expressive appoggiaturas, a personal voice begins to emerge from behind the Baroque mask. All this makes the Olympian theme take on a regretful character, as if it is not what it should be, as if something has been lost. Over an unchanging D-pedal, it is a hollow gesture of triumph, soft, at a distance.

Toward the end of the "Apotheosis" a four-note dotted figure is fractured from the Olympian theme—a shard from Lully perhaps, a frozen motive—which starts to repeat obsessively, suggesting lamenting (see Example 4). It is just one of an entirely new, layered texture of repeating figures, all moving at their own speeds, which simply keep turning in a mechanical way. The D major of apotheosis is sidestepped. The music ends on a B-minor triad, but this resolves little, since the conflicting triads of D major and G major remain implicitly in play. Whereas the mechanical in the "Sacrifical Dance" had been dehumanizing, here the mechanical repetitions become a sign of the melancholic, of distance and loss. The music is not violently ripped apart as in *The Rite of Spring*, but slowly attenuates and fades. The Baroque past fragments. The final standing on a B-minor triad might appear to give temporary consolation, but the memory of what has been lost is not wiped away. B minor seems, rather, to point to an absence, not a presence. Not even Apollo can bring healing. The completeness of the Greek ideal is ultimately unreachable. Stravinsky longs for a return to order but cannot attain it. In revising *Apollo* in 1947, he littered the score with additional markings of *ben cantabile* and *espressivo*, which surely only confirms that in retrospect even he recognized the personal voice that had emerged from behind the classical mask.

As Kundera observed, Stravinsky bore with him the wound of his emigration. His itinerant life was etched into the continually shifting musical "homes" he occupied. His personas were carefully chosen—be they of authentic Russia, neoclassical Greece, or all manner of European music from Monteverdi to Boulez—in order to project himself into the cultures in which he found himself. This was the cosmopolitan Stravinsky, the "citizen of the world," who was celebrated at his death. But these were just so many tokens of a world of appearances, which he could change at will, just as easily as he could discard last season's coat for the most up-to-date fashion:

> Rings, gaiters, scarves, half-belts, ties, tiepins, wristwatches, mufflers, fetishes, pinces-nez, monocles, glasses, chain bracelets, describe him badly. Put simply, they prove on the surface that Stravinsky goes out of his way for no one. He composes, dresses himself, and speaks as he wishes.[32]

What interested Kundera, however, was "the wounded feelings that lay behind his vagabondage through the history of music." The music's playful surface, its appropriation of values of order and objectivity, freed from emotion, masked deeper feelings. He attempted to remove himself and his own history from his music, yet the resulting sense of distance symbolized not only a general modernist alienation but also a particular life lived apart. Despite himself, Russia keeps reappearing across his music, marked by musical signs of nostalgia and mourning. This was Stravinsky's wound.

Stravinsky carried the "sorrow of estrangement" wherever he went. The *Symphony of Psalms* (1930)—impersonal, distanced, monumental—opens with a lamenting Phrygian motive in solo horn and cello marked *cantabile, espressivo* (four measures after rehearsal number 2). Later the choir intones collectively in Latin but in the first person, "Quoniam advena ego sum apud te" (For I am a stranger with thee; rehearsal number 10) or in the French that Stravinsky might well have known, "Car je suis un étranger chez toi." Even the Symphony in C (1939–40), Stravinsky's seemingly most uncompromising engagement with the heroic genre of Western tonal music in the most basic key of all, ultimately speaks otherwise. He later declared that it was written during the "most tragic" period of his life, and that without this work he would not have survived those most difficult days.[33] The first movement was completed (in Europe) just a month after his first wife's death. Its opening motto returns in the final movement (written in the U.S.) as a memory, where it forms the melody to the concluding chorale. Aside from the final string chord, it is scored only for wind and brass, and could almost have been lifted straight from the chorale at the end of the *Symphonies d'instruments à vent*. Can we hear the authentic Stravinsky here, far from home, mourning the loss of daughter, wife, and mother via a nostalgic recollection of Russia? It is undeniably a poignant moment. As in *Apollo*, the classical past fails Stravinsky; it refuses to bring him the order he so desires. The Symphony in C was written in sorrow. Though it seeks order, it discovers loss.

We shall probably never find the real Igor Stravinsky. He thwarts access to the true and authentic at every turn. In opting to speak through Russian puppets, ancient Greek masks, Bachian counterpoint, or Mozartian elegance he was constantly searching for the means by which to distance himself from his true self and impose order on his feelings. Yet this distance itself becomes a metaphor for his situation as an émigré, speaking of alienation and apartness. A life lived in the shadow of war, death, pain, and loss leaves its mark. Without doubt, he wholeheartedly embraced the new cultures in which he found himself and made them his home. There is anecdotal evidence to suggest that, in the later 1940s and early 1950s, married to Vera, free for a while from illness and enjoying the warm California weather, Stravinsky was at his happiest. Photographs even caught him smiling. But when we look behind the mask, or when, momentarily, Stravinsky himself lifts the mask, we see the wound left by estrangement. When the memories of Russia resurface, they speak both of a nostalgia and a failure: a yearning to return to a mythical home that exists only in the imagination. The Ode speaks quietly and eloquently of such nostalgia. It should, then, be clear why Stravinsky chose to present it to his fellow Russians in 1962: it speaks of exile.

NOTES

1. Edward Greenfield, "Stravinsky, the Towering Genius," *The Guardian*, 7 April 1971; Paul Hume, "Igor Stravinsky, Genius in World of Music," *Washington Post & Times Herald*, 7 April 1971.

2. Letter from the White House signed by Richard M. Nixon, 6 April 1971, microfilm 249.1, Paul Sacher Stiftung.

3. Wagner, *Beethoven* (Leipzig: E. W. Fritzsch, 1870), 26; quoted and translated by Scott Burnham in *Beethoven Hero* (Princeton: Princeton University Press, 1995), 155.

4. "Music: Master Mechanic," *Time*, 26 July 1948, 29; Rollo H. Myers, "Stravinsky, Igor Feodorovich," in *Grove's Dictionary of Music and Musicians*, ed. Eric Blom, 5th ed. (London: Macmillan, 1954), 5:137.

5. Stravinsky, quoted in Robert Craft, *Stravinsky: Chronicle of a Friendship*, rev. ed. (Nashville: Vanderbilt University Press, 1994), 328. Craft remarks that Stravinsky's words were simultaneously translated "word for often unbelievable word" (327) for Craft by his official Soviet interpreter Alexandra Afonina, who was seated next to him at the dinner. It is highly unlikely that Craft (or, for that matter, Afonina) would have transcribed these words at the time, so Craft's diary record is surely just an impression of what Stravinsky said. Nonetheless, there is no denying how unexpectedly moved Stravinsky was by his return to his motherland. At the end of the first concert he gave in Moscow, Stravinsky told the audience from the concert platform, "You can't imagine how happy I am today." Quoted in Stephen Walsh, *Stravinsky: The Second Exile. France and America, 1934–1971* (London: Jonathan Cape, 2006), 465.

6. "One would doubt that the octogenarian composer had any need to exhibit a feigned devotion to his roots in order to find favor with his hosts. More probably, these words were spoken with sincerity; they were not a mask worn for the occasion." Margarita Mazo, "Stravinsky's 'Les Noces' and Russian Village Wedding Ritual," *Journal of the American Musicological Society* 43/1 (Spring 1990): 100.

7. Stravinsky, "Lyubite muzïku!," *Komsomol'skaya Pravda*, 27 September 1962, quoted in Richard Taruskin, *Stravinsky and the Russian Traditions: A Biography of the Works Through* Mavra (Berkeley: University of California Press, 1996), 1:13.

8. Craft, *Stravinsky: Chronicle of a Friendship*, 323. See *Stravinsky in Moscow 1962*, Melodiya/BMG (1997).

9. Stravinsky to Chávez, 10 June 1940, microfilm 92.1, 1013, Paul Sacher Stiftung. Original in French; translated differently in English by Robert Craft in Vera Stravinsky and Robert Craft, *Stravinsky in Pictures and Documents* (New York: Simon and Schuster, 1978), 555.

10. *Stravinsky in Pictures and Documents*, 348; Stravinsky thereafter critiqued Shostakovich's symphonies, however; see "Stravinsky says that the OSM is magnificent," in "Stravinsky Speaks to the Spanish-Speaking World," in this volume.

11. Paul Griffiths, *Stravinsky* (New York: Schirmer, 1993), 132.

12. The work consistently carries the subtitle "Elegiacal Chant." See, for example, Eric Walter White, *Stravinsky: The Composer and His Works*, 2nd ed. (Berkeley: University of California Press, 1979), 415. Even today the publisher Schott Music lists it with this phrase, though the subtitle is absent from the published score itself. Concerning *Jane Eyre*, see Walsh, *Stravinsky: The Second Exile*, 148. Stravinsky later tried to justify the relevance of this music to Natalia by describing it in a letter to Koussevitzky of 9 July 1943 as a *concert champêtre*, "music at the heart of nature, the principle which Natalia Konstantinovna defended with such passion and which you realized so brilliantly in Tanglewood." See Victor Yuzefovich, "Chronicle of a Non-Friendship: Letters of Stravinsky and Koussevitzky," *Musical Quarterly* 86/4 (Winter 2002): 806

13. Richard Taruskin, in his reading of the *Symphonies* as the *Panikhida*, the Russian Orthodox office of the dead, aligns this music with the *Vechnaya pamyat'*, "eternal remembrance," a litany "delivered (according to an express rubric) 'slowly and quietly'" (*Stravinsky and the Russian Traditions*, 2:1488). In the Ode, too, this music carries similar associations of prayerful petition well suited to a memorial work.

14. Robert Craft writes that "*Orpheus* is his only score after *Firebird* in which the term '*espressivo*' occurs frequently." See Craft, *The Moment of Existence: Music, Literature, and the Arts, 1990–1995* (Nashville: Vanderbilt University Press, 1996), 294. Craft appears to have overlooked the earlier Ode. Also during the 1940s, in part to circumvent copyright issues, Stravinsky was busy revising many of his scores, including that of *Petrushka*, to which in the 1947 version he added numerous markings of *espressivo*. See the discussion in Jenny Tamplin, "Melancholy, Modernism, Memory, Myth: Orpheus in the Twentieth Century," D.Phil. diss., Oxford University, 2011, 72–76.

15. Igor Stravinsky, *An Autobiography* (New York: W. W. Norton, 1936; repr. 1962), 53; and Stravinsky, *Poetics of Music in the Form of Six Lessons*, trans. Arthur Knodel and Ingolf Dahl (Cambridge, MA: Harvard University Press, 1947), 77.

16. Stravinsky, *An Autobiography*, 53.

17. Louis Andriessen and Elmer Schönberger describe it as "soft, distant, introverted music," in *The Apollonian Clockwork: On Stravinsky*, trans. Jeff Hamburg (Oxford: Oxford University Press, 1989), 134. André Boucourechliev calls it "dignified, distanced, austerely linear," in *Stravinsky*, trans. Martin Cooper (London: Gollancz, 1987), 213.

18. Milan Kundera, "Improvisation in Homage to Stravinsky," in *Testaments Betrayed*, trans. Linda Asher (London: Faber and Faber, 1995), 96–98.

19. See Jonathan Cross, "Stravinsky's *Petrushka*: Modernizing the Past, Russianizing the Future; or, How Stravinsky Learned to Be an Exile," in *Twentieth-Century Music and Politics: Essays in Memory of Neil Edmunds*, ed. Pauline Fairclough (Farnham: Ashgate, 2012), 23–35.

20. Svetlana Boym, *The Future of Nostalgia* (New York: Basic Books, 2001), 8.

21. Igor Stravinsky, "Ce que j'ai voulu exprimer dans *Le Sacre du Printemps*," *Montjoie* 8 (29 May 1913); facsimile in François Lesure, *Le Sacre du Printemps: Dossier de Presse* (Geneva: Minkoff, 1980), 13.

22. Joseph Brodsky, "The Condition We Call Exile," in *Altogether Elsewhere: Writers on Exile*, ed. Marc Robinson (San Diego: Harcourt Brace, 1994), 4, 8–9.

23. Stravinsky's *Poetics of Music* is littered with the words *order* and *discipline*. At the outbreak of the Second World War, America offered Stravinsky the prospect of an orderly life in contrast to the chaos of mobilized Paris.

24. See Walsh, *Stravinsky: The Second Exile*, 193. Walsh provides a terrifying catalog of wartime deaths, including the murder of three of Stravinsky's Yelachich cousins with whom he had played as a child (Zhenya, Alyosha, and Nikolay) and the death of a fourth (Ganya) from a German bomb.

25. Steiner argues for Nabokov as we might also wish to argue for Stravinsky, namely that "by virtue of his extraterritoriality [he remains] profoundly of our time, and one of its spokesmen." George Steiner, "Extraterritorial [1969]," in *Extraterritorial: Papers on Literature and the Language Revolution* (New York: Macmillan, 1971), 11.

26. Edward W. Said, *On Late Style: Music and Literature Against the Grain* (London: Bloomsbury, 2006), 17.

27. Stravinsky, *An Autobiography*, 53, 60.

28. Taruskin discusses this subject at length in the first volume of *Stravinsky and the Russian Traditions*.

29. Edward Said, "Reflections on Exile," in *Altogether Elsewhere: Writers on Exile*, 137.

30. Griffiths, *Stravinsky*, 98.

31. White, *Stravinsky*, 342.

32. Jean Cocteau, "Stravinsky dernière heure," *La Revue musicale* 5/2 (1 December 1923): 142–45. The translation, by Bridget Behrmann and Tamara Levitz, is taken from the article published in this volume as part of "Who Owns *Mavra*? A Transnational Dispute."

33. Igor Stravinsky and Robert Craft, *Memories and Commentaries* (London: Faber and Faber, 2002), 188.

Who Owns *Mavra?*
A Transnational Dispute

INTRODUCTION AND NOTES BY TAMARA LEVITZ

Stravinsky first performed his one-act opera buffa *Mavra* in a version for voice and piano at a gala buffet organized by Diaghilev in the ballroom at the Hotel Continental in Paris on 29 March 1922.[1] *Mavra* premiered a little over two months later, on June third at the Paris Opéra as part of the Ballets Russes 1922 season, in which it appeared on an all-Stravinsky program between a repeat performance of Léonide Massine's version of *The Rite of Spring* and Fokine's of *Petrushka*.[2] The premiere was both a failure and a success, as the reviews gathered here show. The generally negative press crushed Stravinsky.[3] *Mavra* remained dear to his heart, and he worked toward realizing performances of it for the rest of his life.

Although *Mavra* played a vital role between the wars in Stravinsky's personal development as a composer, the fraught dialogue resulting from its first unsuccessful performance led to its virtual disappearance from the concert hall, operatic stage, and secondary literature. *Mavra* may have vanished because of the unresolved questions it raises about nation, race, and gender, which have led it to fit uncomfortably within the framework of neoclassicism that has served for decades to define Stravinsky's second-period style. Musicologists have favored Stravinsky's canonic ballet *Pulcinella* as a much more emblematic work of neoclassicism—a broad stylistic category that describes modernist compositions that borrow techniques or styles of music from the past. And yet Richard Taruskin argues that *Pulcinella*'s importance has been grossly exaggerated, and that *Mavra* provides "the true bridge to a Russian émigré's idea of neoclassicism."[4]

I would go a step further than Taruskin and argue that *neoclassicism* may be an altogether misleading word to describe Stravinsky's music between the wars. The reviews gathered here reveal that temporal concerns about musical borrowings in *Mavra* are inextricably linked with questions of geographical dislocation and class and racial confrontation. Whether and how a reviewer emphasizes *Mavra*'s stylistic retrospectivism depends on national, racial, gender, and class allegiance; neoclassicism as style is inseparable from the historical context of transnational dispute. *Mavra* wreaked havoc not because it embodied a legible and stable retrospective style, but because it moved within a tension-ridden musical "translation zone" in which people and objects traveled across multiple languages and nations.[5]

After *Mavra*'s premiere, a critical battle broke out among Russian émigrés (Boris de Schloezer), an older generation of French critics and impressionists (among them Emile Vuillermoz and Maurice Ravel), and a group of eager young composers briefly labeled Les Six (including Milhaud, Poulenc, and their ringleader, Jean Cocteau, as well as the largely sympathetic critics Roland-Manuel, Louis Laloy, and the Belgian Paul Collaer).[6] The battle expanded when Satie, Cocteau, and Dadaist Tristan Tzara brought news of *Mavra* to the United States through their essays in *Vanity Fair*.

As the reviews below show, the juxtaposition of *Mavra* at its premiere with *The Rite of Spring* and *Petrushka* led critics to criticize Stravinsky's lack of continuous development as a composer. Poulenc, Collaer, and Milhaud, eager to experience the absolute presence of modernity, rejected the notion of a composer's organic stylistic evolution as a standard for the work; they mocked older French critics who still championed the prewar French national style of musical impressionism.[7] Collaer praised the irony in *Mavra* as deeply contemporaneous, and associated it with a postwar need for modesty and for singing without emotion, as if joking. "Think of it!" Cocteau wrote when he heard of the debate about *Mavra* but before hearing the work. "Stravinsky bringing the homage of his supreme contribution to the endeavors of Satie and our young musicians. Stravinsky the traitor. Stravinsky the deserter. It would never occur to any of them to think: Stravinsky the Fountain of Jouvence.[8] For no one ever gives the masters credit."[9] When jazz buff Jean Wiéner included *Mavra* in a more contemporary all-Stravinsky program at the end of the year—with his *Symphonies d'instruments à vent*, Concertino, *Petrushka* (for piano solo, performed by Wiéner himself), and the *Pulcinella* Suite—the work was an undisputed success.[10] A concert performance in Brussels in an all-Stravinsky program with a similar program coordinated by Paul Collaer with the Concerts Pro Arte on 14 January 1924 solidified Stravinsky's reputation in Belgium.[11]

For many critics, *Mavra* raised the question of musical assimilation. Stravinsky wrote it during a period when he was realizing he could not return to Russia and was refashioning himself as a European composer in the Russo-Italian tradition of Glinka and Tchaikovsky. Diaghilev had suggested the idea of the opera buffa to Stravinsky while the two of them were in Seville preparing the London revival of Tchaikovsky's *Sleeping Beauty*, two sections of which Diaghilev had reinstated and asked Stravinsky to orchestrate. In October 1921, Stravinsky had written an open letter on Tchaikovsky to the London *Times*, in which he had championed Tchaikovsky's "Latin-Slav" culture.[12] Just weeks before the premiere of *Mavra*, he had written a second open letter on Tchaikovsky in *Le Figaro* to coincide with the Ballets Russes premiere of *Aurora's Wedding*—a one-act divertissement drawn from the unsuccessful *Sleeping Beauty*.[13] Numerous French critics subsequently associated

Figure 1. Stravinsky at the Hotel Bristol in Vienna, 1930.

Mavra with Stravinsky's press campaign to realign himself with Glinka's and Tchaikovsky's classical tradition of Europeanized or Latin-Russian music.[14]

In order to assimilate, Stravinsky felt he had to separate himself from German traditions, and from the neo-nationalist line of Musorgsky, his teacher Rimsky-Korsakov, and the "Mighty Five."[15] He started to think of *Mavra* as "Italo-Russian," and hoped it would be staged with singers wearing Russian peasant clothes but gesturing as in "old Italian opera."[16] In the program note for *Mavra*, drafted in 1934, that opens this selection of documents, Stravinsky expressed open disdain for the "national-ethnographic" element in music cultivated by the Mighty Five, and reiterated his lifelong belief that composers should not try to replicate music produced by the nation's "people"—an inchoate group Stravinsky imbued with a mystic capacity for collective expression. "Stravinsky rejected Russians in blouses and boots," the Swiss conductor Ernest Ansermet commented in hindsight about these events. "He wanted Russians dressed like everybody else, and embracing everybody else's objectives and diversions but in a Russian manner."[17]

Stravinsky's fellow émigrés did not all agree with his form of musical assimilation. Boris de Schloezer's harsh words for Stravinsky's choices in *Mavra* give a small sense of the long-standing disagreement in Russia over the role of the West in the historical genesis of the Russian national soul. De Schloezer expressed concern about the class and racial origins of the Russian sentimental romance Stravinsky tried to emulate in *Mavra*, and deemed the work a "failure."

Members and supporters of Les Six showed little interest in these Russian émigré internal debates. They situated *Mavra* within a different translation zone— that of the Parisian metropolis, where Russian music collided with European art music, music hall, jazz, French traditions, and an international public. *Mavra* belonged in the ambiguous geographical and stylistic space of modernity created by the Ballets Russes premiere of Erik Satie's *Parade* in 1917, and Jean Cocteau's manifesto *Le Coq et l'Arlequin*, in 1918. The little opera buffa appeared inherently transnational: Stravinsky had composed its overture while the Ballets Russes was performing at the Exposition coloniale in Marseilles; its vocal style had been influenced by the Russian sentimental romances sung in the Moscow touring revue *Chauve-Souris*, which at that time was enjoying tremendous success in Paris.[18] Just months before the premiere of *Mavra*, the Dadaist Francis Picabia had praised Stravinsky for his effortless assimilation and for transforming "Russian milk into Isigny cream, which becomes a great dessert with a little sugar." Picabia continued: "Don't view this as a critique, my dear Stravinsky, I love cream, it's the topping on milk!"[19] Six months after the premiere, Boris de Schloezer too began talking about border crossing as essential to Stravinsky's nature and to what he tentatively labeled "neoclassicism" (a term he introduced into critical discourse).[20] Two years later, the Belgian journalist Joseph de Geynst described Stravinsky as "unconcerned with musical dogmas, composing according to his own inspiration and deliberately knocking down the barriers professors erect so willingly on the roads that open up for independent artists."[21]

Within the translation zone of metropolitan Paris, class mattered as much as or more than national identity. Cocteau, Satie, and Tristan Tzara solidified *Mavra*'s class credentials by singing its praises in the high-end fashion magazine *Vanity Fair*.[22] As a sought-after commodity with the fashion appeal of Cubist painting, *Mavra* fit well in the spectacle of conspicuous consumption the magazine staged for the moneyed transnational cultural elite; it appeared as chic and trendy as the *Chauve-Souris*, which had just taken New York City by storm.[23] In the pages of *Vanity Fair*, Georges Auric and Cocteau celebrated Stravinsky as a role model for Les Six, and Tristan Tzara aligned *Mavra* with Dada.[24] Tzara, like Louis Laloy before him, identified *Mavra* spatially with the "simultaneity" in evidence in Sonia

Figure 2: Léopold Survage, scene design for *Mavra*, a detail of which was
reproduced in the official program for the premiere on June 3, 1922.

Delaunay-Terck's "poem dresses" and in Robert Delauney's paintings, and with
the Cubist sets Léopold Survage created for the opera's premiere (see Figure 2).[25]
In this fractured aesthetic space, cultures, classes, genders, and nations collided for
the pleasure of the very few.

Mavra's class pretensions did not escape the attention of revolutionary Russian
poet Vladimir Mayakovsky when he visited Stravinsky with Jean Cocteau in
Paris in 1922. He and Cocteau both compared Stravinsky's creative work to
capitalist production, but from different angles; Mayakovsky called Stravinsky,
perhaps uncharitably, a "Parisianized Russian." Stravinsky found himself unable
to translate Mayakovsky's words—and with them a revolutionary critique of
bourgeois art—for his friend Cocteau.

The national, temporal, and class paradoxes in *Mavra* remained unresolved
because they are inherent to the music itself. Stravinsky had composed gender,
racial, and class conflicts into the music, without taking sides. Roland-Manuel
correctly identified the most bitterly disputing parties in *Mavra* when he described
it as "Russian with an American accent," its lyrical vocal parts in conflict with the
syncopated rhythms of its wind band accompaniment. Stravinsky's practice of
allowing jazz and the Russian sentimental romance to coexist as opposites aligned
him conceptually with the Surrealists, as well as with a circuit of composers

associated with that emerging movement.[26] A survey published in *Littérature* weeks before *Mavra*'s premiere revealed that Surrealist writers identified jazz with Russian music (that is, Stravinsky) and saw both as a potential means of countering French nationalism.[27] The English bandleader Jack Hylton felt the affinities and arranged sections of *Mavra* for his jazz band in 1931.[28] Pierre Lalo remarked that the public loved such lack of coordination, and would happily combine Mozart with Cubism.[29] But Boris de Schloezer deemed Stravinsky's attempt to combine the Italo-Russian style with the "Negro-Russian" syncopations or references to jazz "impossible," his rejection of miscegenation revealing the devastating notions of racial purity at the heart of his Russian musical nationalism. None of them could really resolve the conflict over ethnic and racial boundaries.

Mavra's orchestration was the greatest bone of contention for the disputing parties. Critics either loved or hated it, depending on their allegiances; Erik Satie worshipped its transparency, for example, and celebrated Stravinsky as a liberator of the new generation.[30] But decades later Stravinsky acknowledged that *Mavra*'s orchestration had prevented performances of the work.[31] *Mavra*'s wind band sound had created a deadlock in Franco-Russian musical relations.

By the late 1920s the debate over *Mavra* had faded to a dull roar. After *Mavra* was performed with *Oedipus Rex* in Berlin in 1928, critics tentatively began to assume the opera was "neoclassical," and to forget its fraught racial, class-based, and transnational past.[32] This trend is evident in Arthur Lourié's essay, which coincides with the Berlin performance, and originally included a substantial section on *Oedipus Rex*. In an attempt to stand up to Soviet critics who condemned Stravinsky for his Western materialism, Lourié exaggerated the "purity" of *Mavra*'s Russian blood ties.[33] Although he recognized the work's "paradoxicality," he sublimated its racial conflict by omitting any mention of jazz, and by translating the dialogue over ethnicity into a formal analysis of meter. In a slippery move for someone who had once worked for the Soviets, he blurred *Mavra*'s class distinction by critiquing the "Gypsy" roots of the Russian sentimental romance on which it was based, and then praising Stravinsky for reviving it authentically as musical form. Within a few decades, *Pulcinella* had become *Mavra*'s surrogate, and neoclassicism the stylistic substitute for the ideological conflicts of the 1920s.

Editor's Note: Although the translations in this section attempt to convey as much of the original document as possible, we have corrected mistakes and inconsistencies in punctuation, spelling, and English transliteration of proper names. At the same time, we have respected the transformation of some first names, such as the gallicized "Serge de Diaghilev," where appropriate to their contexts. Egregious errors or typos in the original document have also been noted.

Unpublished Program Note
Mavra
Igor Stravinsky

My opera buffa *Mavra* was composed during the period from summer 1921 through spring 1922 and performed for the first time on 3 June 1922 at the Grand Opéra de Paris through the efforts of Serge de Diaghilev.[34] This opera was staged and performed in concert, at different times and in different countries and cities: Berlin (Otto Klemperer), Paris (Ernest Ansermet), Amsterdam and Brussels (conducted by myself), etc…[35]

I dedicated this work, whose plot was taken from "Domik v Kolomnè" ["The Little House in Kolomna"], a short story in verse that Pushkin wrote in 1830, to the memory of the latter, as well as to the memory of Glinka and Tchaikovsky. This triple dedication will be easily understood by those who recognize the ideological differences between the group of "Five" [Balakirev, Musorgsky, Borodin, Rimsky-Korsakov, and Cui] and Tchaikovsky, whose inspiration was—as it was, in fact, for the "Five"—Pushkin and Glinka. But whereas in their aesthetic the "Five" cultivated only the national-ethnographic element they found in this source—which is fundamentally not *very* far from the spirit of all those films about the old Russia of the czars and boyars—Tchaikovsky, like Dargomyzhsky and other less well-known composers, quietly continued the musical tradition established by Glinka, a tradition that, though using popular Russian *melos*, was not afraid to present it in a Europeanized way: Italianized in Glinka's case, Italianized and Gallicized in Tchaikovsky's work. Neither Glinka nor Tchaikovsky took into account ethnographic and historical accuracy. But what we see with the "Five," as well as with the modern Spanish "folklorists," both painters and musicians, is precisely this naïve but dangerous longing that pushes them to remake an art already created instinctively by a people's genius. A rather sterile and wrongheaded tendency that afflicted a number of artists at the time.

I conceived the score to *Mavra* in opposition to this type of aesthetic, and with the intention of reviving the excellent Russian tradition established definitively by artists such as Pushkin, Glinka, and Tchaikovsky; this should sufficiently explain the dedication.

Paris, 4 Dec. 1934
—*Translated from the French by Bridget Behrmann*

Excelsior (Paris), 12 June 1922
Mavra
Emile Vuillermoz

In what strange times are we living?[36] What ironic destiny compels us to do justice to Wagner on the same day that we are obliged to deplore the current direction of Stravinsky's genius? Why this malicious "reversal" of the time machine? As in *Renard*, Stravinsky wanted to entertain us. *Mavra* is a parody of the lyric ideal of the Second Empire, of bel canto, duets, of runs and cavatinas. The admirable author of *The Rite of Spring* lapses into humor. In my humble opinion he makes a mistake.

This man of genius is not gay. He has nothing of an entertainer. His character is heavy and insistent. The libretto of *Mavra*—in which a hussar out of a colored lithograph disguises himself as a cook to court his beloved—lacks all wit. And the music is of a weight and volume that removes any ironic charm from this "burden."[37] An interminable and monotone *vag-time*[38] accompaniment drowns this entire cheerless score. And this dangerous wager makes apparent in the most unexpected fashion a few singularly instructive truths. One notices, first, that Italian music is not parodied as easily as one thinks. And then one notes that Stravinsky, whose rhythmic genius is prodigious, lacks terribly in melodic invention. We sensed this in his previous works, but this one does not let us doubt it anymore. This great musician should stop indulging in such useless jokes. He still has so many beautiful things to tell us! We have our clowns if we want to "laugh and entertain ourselves socially."[39] They suffice. *Mavra*, which is surely not the masterpiece of old Russian gaiety, is certainly not that of old French gaiety! . . .

—*Translated by Tamara Levitz*

Posledniye novosti (Paris), 22 June 1922
Mavra
Boris de Schloezer

The originality of Stravinsky is that not only doesn't he repeat himself—which is to say little—but that he doesn't even adapt.[40] He doesn't cultivate the treasures he discovers: he leaves subsequent development to his followers and imitators. No sooner has he merely outlined the way, laying just the first track and setting out stakes, than he immediately abandons all the work he has begun and, making a sharp turn, dashes off in a different direction.

There are composers whose path of development appears to us overall as a single, uninterrupted, nearly straight line. It is comparatively easy for us to discern in their activities a certain logic or consistency. One moment seems to follow naturally from another, like effect from cause. Bach, Wagner, and Scriabin were like this. Stravinsky belongs to a different type. His path appears as a sharply jagged line. Consistency—psychological and aesthetic—can undoubtedly be found here, but its internal logic hasn't been detected yet.

The Rite of Spring inaugurated a new epoch in music all by itself; here everything was new. So we waited, of course, for the composer to go even further in the direction he had revealed and begin to exploit his riches systematically. Instead of that we had *The Nightingale*, little pieces for piano, and for clarinet, *L'Histoire du soldat*, *Renard*, and now, *Mavra*. Essentially, almost every one of these pieces is an experiment, a quest, a challenge and a breakthrough at the same time. Heretofore, the composer's pursuits and endeavors have always been crowned with success (we're not talking here about external success). Fortune was always with him.

Stravinsky's original method of composition quite naturally engendered a certain amount of irritation among the public and critics. With each new work by the composer, the listener is obliged to relearn from scratch. One's expectations are always frustrated; there is no preparation at all. One must make a sharp turn and plunge after the artist into the unknown. Great courage and a passion for adventure are required—qualities rarely found.

Mavra induces a similar sense of wonder and anxiety, mixed with irritation. In my opinion, however, *Mavra* is a failure, Stravinsky's first failure. A bold and interesting endeavor can likewise be discerned here, but he chose his goal inauspiciously; to achieve it was altogether impossible.

As the composer himself explained in advance, he wants to return to the roots of Russian music. Not to folk music, however, which so many have exploited — Stravinsky among them—but to the sentimental romance of Alyabyev, Verstovsky,[41] Glinka, Dargomyzhsky, the so-called dilettantes. This art of towns and of country estates is a curious deformation of Italian song, filtered through Russian tastes, through Russian thinking. The influence of Gypsy song [*tsyganskoy pesni*] also made its mark here. A special Russo-Italian style, integral and viable, was created. To a greater or lesser extent it influenced almost all Russian composers, even those who, like Musorgsky, believe that they draw upon national folk resources exclusively. One of the last and most prominent representatives of this trend was Tchaikovsky.

Until now, Stravinsky seemed a complete stranger to this melodic style (judging by his compositions). At first he trod the path of Rimsky-Korsakov. When, after *Firebird*, he broke with Korsakovian aesthetics, it was only in order to subject Russian folksong and folk dance motives to an entirely distinctive recasting. He emphasized particularly their complex, rich rhythms, renouncing a host of textbook methods and formulas—thematic development, for example—which Rimsky-Korsakov, Borodin, and Balakirev had used to compose their symphonies, overtures, and fantasies on Russian themes. In place of the Italo-Russian style (Verstovsky—Glinka—Tchaikovsky) and the Germano-Russian style (Glinka—the Kuchkists[42]—to some extent the very same Tchaikovsky), a third Russian style emerged, the Stravinsky style, which I will call the Negro-Russian [*negro-russkim*], for there is no doubt that music of the so-called primeval races, with their syncopated rhythms, brutal harmonies, and abundance of all kinds of percussion, influenced its creation. But now Stravinsky has tried to revive the Italo-Russian style that had completely degenerated in the hands of Tchaikovsky's epigones.

Let's set aside for now the explanations Stravinsky has given in print.[43] A work of art speaks for itself, and so far we are reckoning only with *Mavra* and can judge by it alone. It seems to us that this synthesis of Italo-Russian and Negro-Russian elements that Stravinsky has attempted to carry out is impossible, but perhaps we are mistaken and *Mavra* is just a chance failure. Until the composer proves the contrary, however, we may question the merits and viability of a style where the sounds and rhythms of the jazz band are combined with Russian and Gypsy romances. Stravinsky did not achieve unity; the constituent elements of his work feud and fight among themselves. The listener's attention bifurcates; one taken with the melodic writing peevishly shrugs off the annoying orchestration—unequivocally dominated by the brass—while one struck by the piquant rhythms and the clumsy yet interesting sonorities seeks in vain an escape from the sentimental singing.

The overall impression is that it is an intriguing counterfeit of a musical joke. It's unlikely, however, that this was what Stravinsky intended. In any event, the joke is boring and goes on far too long. The plot, moreover, is too trivial and negligible; it cannot carry the scene and, under the weight of the opulent theatrical and musical finery, it crumbles to dust.

The performance of the exceedingly challenging vocal parts was excellent (Mss. Slobodskaya, Sadoven, Rozovskaya, Mr. Belina-Skupevsky) and individual episodes—the intriguing duet, for example—made a very pleasing impression. But the orchestra plays too stodgily, insufficiently crisply with respect to rhythm and with altogether excessive expressivity, intolerable even for Stravinsky. Here, just as in *Renard*,[44] nuances are reduced to a minimum or, more precisely, they are not tailored to the tastes and moods of the performers but are dictated entirely by the instrumentation itself, by the spacing and the combination of orchestral timbres.

The costumes by Mr. Survage are charming, but his scenery in no way conjures up the image of behind-the-scenes Petersburg at the turn of the century.

—Translated from the Russian by Laurel E. Fay

L'Eclair (Paris), 5 June 1922
Igor Stravinsky's *Mavra* at the Opéra
Roland-Manuel

Mr. Igor Stravinsky is an uncompromising magician who loathes repeating his spells.[45] A tremendous evolution separates *Petrushka* from *The Firebird,* and *The Rite of Spring* from *Petrushka.* For fifteen years, a cohort of intrepid admirers has followed the Russian musician's giant strides, the defections of exhausted followers largely offset by the support of hotheaded neophytes trying valiantly but in vain to outstrip their tireless trainer while the better part of the public, remaining silent, is obliged to make extraordinary adjustments just not to lose sight of the front of the pack or the steel-muscled athlete stubbornly setting the pace. But here's the surprise: *Mavra* makes it obvious that the race is no longer following the same course. Stravinsky makes a dazzling about-face, leaving his henchmen bogged down in the marshes of "atonality" and "polytonality" while he takes his aesthetic in an unexpected direction. Suddenly the music lovers, who struggled to follow him from a distance with their opera glasses, are offended by the brutal reappearance of this horrifying man who once took Musorgsky and Rimsky-Korsakov as starting points, and today falls without warning into the arms of Mikhail Ivanovich Glinka.

It must be said: the enormous distance separating *The Firebird* from *Renard* is not in any way comparable to the unsettling abyss separating *Renard* from the short lyric fantasy just performed at the Opéra.

Mavra is a kind of bourgeois comedy that Mr. Boris Kochno took from an unfinished Pushkin short story. A handsome hussar disguises himself as a servant girl in order to be close to the young girl who loves him and with whom he is in love. The young girl's mother comes home at an inopportune moment and catches her new maid in the middle of shaving. Curtain. This good-natured plot has been carved up into arias, duets, and ensembles, and Stravinsky has treated them in a vocal style curiously reminiscent of *A Life for the Tsar* and the early works of the admirable Glinka, so clearly tinged with Italianisms. To be honest, this predilection for Italy is not new in the work of the author of *Pulcinella*, but it was not so manifestly obvious before. The startling thing: this very particular vocal style finds no echo in the orchestra. What Stravinsky accomplishes is not just the independence of the statue from its supporting pedestal, but also the absolute heterogeneity of the two. While the voices on stage seem to sing Mr. Kochno's text "in Italian," the orchestra, with its splendidly mechanical sonorities, speaks Russian with a slight American accent due to the use of a special instrumentation that sacrifices strings in favor of woodwinds and brass, and peculiarly, trombones and tubas. The same attention to detail that not long ago controlled *The Nightingale*'s fragile orchestral mechanism presides over the use of these weighty timbres in *Mavra.* Never has Mr. Stravinsky's orchestral factory articulated each sound with more effective precision; never have his marvelous machines yielded a superior dynamic output.

The light American accent I alluded to is made even more noticeable by the use of simple, sharp rhythms that are wildly enamored of syncopation. As for *Mavra*'s harmonic language, it is the sign of a disruptive reaction motivated and legitimated by the atonal or "polytonal" intemperance dominating music today. In *Mavra*, the harmony is *tonal* in a very precise way from the overture to the final scene. But it seems that Stravinsky moves one step back here only to take two steps forward: he reenters the domain of tonality as a free man. Without escaping the boundaries he assigns himself, Stravinsky contrives to juxtapose not just harmonies foreign to one another, but entire tonal functions that are hostile. At times, he makes one tonality mesh with another with an expert brusqueness. The game is daunting, despite its apparent simplicity; as played by Stravinsky, it never becomes arbitrary.

Here then is a work that scrupulously realizes its author's intentions. It remains to be seen if these intentions are still legitimate. I must say truthfully that I am not entirely persuaded. I do not dispute that the singing's artificial Italianism, the divergence between *Mavra*'s vocal and instrumental styles, are deliberate; nevertheless they irritate me. Perhaps soon Mr. Stravinsky, the most infallible artist in the entire world, will force me to admit that my difficulty with the piece has vanished and that the faults were all mine; I will hasten to confess it publicly.

Aside from the orchestral execution, which is occasionally shaky, the performance of *Mavra* is in all respects excellent. Mss. Slobodskaya, Sadoven and Rozovskaya, as well as Mr. Belina-Skupevsky, make a truly magnificent vocal quartet. Whatever one's ideas about Cubism, Mr. Léopold Survage's infinitely ingenious and appealing set—a masterpiece of smiling *bonhomie*—will not fail to charm.

—Translated by Bridget Behrmann

Comoedia (Paris), 5 June 1922
At the Théâtre de l' Opéra: *Mavra*
Louis Laloy

It is a little domestic drama.[46] On the advice of her daughter, and after complaining to a neighbor, the old woman hires a chambermaid, but the advice was treacherous. The chambermaid is none other than a disguised hussar, who sings a duet with the young girl. Returning home unexpectedly, the old woman surprises him in the middle of shaving. She faints, and the neighbor rushes to her aid.

Mr. Kochno has brought this ironic Pushkin story to the stage very skillfully. The irony is emphasized by Mr. Survage's split-level, elevated set, whose *simultanisme* contrasts with the crinoline costumes; and above all, by Mr. Stravinsky's music, which juxtaposes cavatinas with an inverted orchestra: woodwinds and brass multiplied at the expense of the violin and viola, each reduced to a single instrument, and of the cellos and double basses, charged exclusively with the continuo. An extraordinary orchestra that twitters, chirrups, gurgles, screeches, growls, hoots, sobs, guffaws; a fiery orchestra that leaps and rears—yet still contained and directed by a firm hand that turns it aside at will, pacifies it, flatters it, and makes it set off again only to stop it anew, the whole ensemble trembling from a barely perceptible pressure. Never has the musician demonstrated such mastery. Perhaps *The Rite of Spring* put heavier and more massive sounds into action; but here, the tour de force is achieved in an always unstable balance.[47]

—Translated by Bridget Behrmann

Feuilles libres (Paris), June–July 1922
About Igor Stravinsky's *Mavra*
Francis Poulenc

Obviously, the "musical left" is getting musty.[48] This much is certain—*Mavra* confirmed the impression we received from *Parade*, that is, that though a "prewar music criticism" exists, none has yet developed that's adequate for judging today's music.

It's a shame, because Stravinsky's latest works, like Satie's, truly need understanding commentators if they are to be accepted by and explained to the public. At the time of *The Rite*, Vuillermoz's opinion was law. It's not the same today, Mr. Vuillermoz having proved on numerous occasions in the last two years that he belongs to the *past*.

Given that, what does it matter if he finds that Stravinsky "lacks melody"?[49]

Much more serious to see is that younger music critics, with the exception of Mr. Roland-Manuel,[50] no longer *hear* Stravinsky's music. And so Mr. Maurice Bex declares in the 17 June *Revue hebdomadaire* that he finds in *Mavra* only a "torrent of syncopation," "organized disorder," and "sudden leaps that are as agreeable to the ear as the sight of a puppy playing is pleasing to the eye."[51]

It is regrettable that Mr. Bex heard the score so badly, since, on the contrary, it is remarkable for its splendid *logic* and *precision*.

Another critic finds "the orchestration heavy and vulgar," as if the use of a wind band was not a deliberate choice of the author.

How sad to see a work of *Mavra*'s aesthetic importance left to the scalpels of the *normaliens*, musicographers interested only in Mr. So-and-So's *planar* or *polytonal* "tics."[52]

"Among musicians there are pawns and poets," said Satie. "The pawns impose their music on the public and the critics."[53] I did not need *Mavra*, my dear Stravinsky, to be convinced that you are a true poet. This marvelous work only adds to the immense admiration I have had for your work since that day in 1913 when, though then quite young, I was overwhelmed by *The Rite of Spring.*

Ten years have passed and the public now cheers that work, once so vehemently hated. Even more, they beg Stravinsky for a new *Rite*—one even "more modern," more polyphonic—failing to understand that a masterpiece marks the end of a line. But Stravinsky, like Picasso and all fine artists, detests mining a single vein. He changes form and technique with every work. Make no mistake about it: *Mavra* is the beginning of a new manner.

Many people consider *Mavra* a parody of the style of Rossini and Verdi. Nothing could be more wrong. In music, there is an "opera form" just as there is a "sonata form" or "rondeau form." Anybody is free to use these. All Stravinsky did was to renew the tradition of Glinka and Tchaikovsky as, one would hope, our musicians might follow the line of Gounod and Bizet.

There is no doubt Glinka and Tchaikovsky are two great musicians.

Why then reproach Stravinsky for having taken them as models?

In the end, they attack *Mavra*'s harmony in order to reproach Stravinsky for his lack of *originality.* It's amusing to note in this respect how musicians of the post-Debussy generation, intoxicated by "rare harmonies," have become accustomed to considering any resolution of triads banal.

We are in an age of leveling, when all chords appear to be on the same plane.[54] Newness must then be sought in another domain.

In *Mavra*, Stravinsky put all his effort into the system of modulation. Through the horizontal juxtaposition of distant pitches he has obtained a precise, pouncing, and eminently tonal music—a rare quality today. Not one critic has noticed this. You see how eardrums have hardened.

Go on, sirs, red card holders, think before you place your bets; there is still time, otherwise we'll be obliged to request for you two orchestra seats behind the members of the Jockey Club and L'Epatant.[55]

—*Translated by Bridget Behrmann and Tamara Levitz*

Lumière (Antwerp), 1 November 1922
Mavra
Paul Collaer

The genius of Igor Stravinsky is recognized the world over.[56]

When *Firebird* spread its sparkling wings for the first time a dozen years ago, it was immediately understood that a great musician had just made his debut.

Then came *Petrushka*. In two years' time, Stravinsky had made an enormous leap.

For the first time since Romanticism reigned over European art, objectivist thought[57] manifested itself in music. Stravinsky projected music beyond himself, outside his soul. This revolution was of the highest importance. The work asserted itself right away but was understood only a year later—as is always the case for an authentic masterpiece.

1913. *The Rite of Spring*. Really, who is this man who has the remarkable power of changing so completely from one work to the next! After the poem of suffering that is *Petrushka* (barely ironic, despite appearances), here now is Earth's song, the epic of raging elements, panic music.

I have always had the impression that Stravinsky captured the unbearably tense atmosphere that electrified Europe, and was destined to culminate in the horrific carnage from which we are only now emerging.

Still, the public understood nothing of the *Rite*. They shouted, whistled, cried, reacted with the violence particular to the Parisian public. (Let us note in passing that this reactive faculty is one of the main factors contributing to the constant vitality of French art.)

1914. *The Nightingale*. A marvel of grace: poignant emotion in simplicity. But above all, the symptom of a great change. In place of richness and opulence came the spirit of condensation, the ascetic spirit, the notion of the essential.

On to 1922. A supposed decline of the Ballets Russes is generally lamented. Since, of course, one pretends to forget a bit that Serge de Diaghilew staged Satie's *Parade* during the war, and that Derain[58] and Picasso are involved in this work of the Ballets Russes. So everyone complains and then, back to back, *Renard* and *Mavra*. In *Renard*, we see the advent of objectivism, the perfect realization of condensation. The public has had time to get used to *Petrushka*, has followed post-Cubist painters, and now understands the significance of *Renard* well enough. Everyone is very proud to be "up to date." Alas, eight days later, *Mavra* plunges the public back into uncertainty, and this time the critics and musicographers lose their heads. The most stunned of all must have been Stravinsky himself, reading the pile of idiocies and nonsense written about *Mavra* by reputedly intelligent people.

Mavra was not understood because Stravinsky had changed again, and this time the turnaround was quicker and sharper than ever.

Mavra is clear, lucid, and contains nothing disorienting.

The little opéra-comique in question is intellectually contrary and opposed to the preceding works. *Mavra* is subjectively inspired. In it, the author is sentimental.

Stravinsky looked back this time to Glinka, Dargomyzhsky, and Tchaikovsky, to the era of crinolines and romances. Do not think, though, that he amused himself by composing a pastiche, an "in the style of." The musician completely recast the quaint and outmoded opéra-comique. He concentrated its spirit, and what is more, imposed upon it his powerful personality.

The text itself is charming and offers a digest of the entire genre of sentimental opéra-comique.

Written by Boris Kokhno after one of Pushkin's short stories, the story is as follows:

The action takes place in a Russian petit bourgeois interior. A young girl, Parrasia [*sic*],[59] is at the window and sings a romance. Her beloved, a young hussar, appears in the facing window. A little duet begins between them, which leads to the promise of a meeting. The young girl's mother arrives, still emotional after the recent death of her cook. Parassia goes out to find a replacement. While she is away, the mother and a neighbor indulge in their memories of and grief over the deceased. As they chatter, Parassia returns with a new cook, who gives the name "Mavra." She answers their questions with modesty and kindness.

During a quartet shared by these characters, the agreement is made: Mavra is hired. The mother and neighbor exit. Straightaway, Parassia falls into Mavra's arms—the cook is none other than the hussar in disguise.

Later, Parassia rejoins her mother to go to market. Mavra, left alone, dreams only of his happiness and sings of his triumphant love. Yet he becomes worried . . . about shaving. Suddenly the mother enters, sees Mavra shaving and understands that she has been tricked. She feels ill and calls for help; the neighbor runs in, invoking all the saints; Mavra flees as fast as his legs can carry him; and the young girl, stricken, calls desperately: "Vasily! Vasily!"

And that's all. But it's exquisite. You can imagine what the potential of this would be with sets and costumes by Léopold Survage.

So, here we are in total conventionality. There's nothing wrong with it. The conventionality is deliberate, and the authors know perfectly well that one good convention deserves another provided one isn't fooled by them.

1860. A sentimental time. And from the beginning, after an Italian overture sparkling with malice, Stravinsky offers us a romance. It is neither satire nor parody. It is a true romance, and it is, very simply, pretty.

The dialogue follows in the same gracious and touching spirit. Until the sentimental climax. Logically, the victorious hussar should sing his happiness and love in a *grand air*[60] throbbing with passion.

But seriously, can you see a man of our era, given our contemporary mind-set, give himself up to such a display, abandoning himself romantically to his "transports"? We feel emotion as deeply as the Romantics, but we no longer let it out. We let it show through irony; we even hide it with joking. It's a form of modesty.[61] And this is precisely how Stravinsky operates in *Mavra*. After letting the sentiment rise to the moment of the "*grand air*," the hussar starts singing an excellent parody of all the Toscas and all the Pagliaccis. It's under the mask of laughter that he proclaims his passion. And this is profoundly true, profoundly significant of our time. This brusque passage, from sentimentality to the irony that caps it, is one of the reasons the public was perplexed.

After this scene of the *grand air*, the comic spirit definitively dominates *Mavra*. The hussar's flight, the fainting, and the young girl's despair all produce an extremely fast-paced scene, a free-for-all. The music could have here found a new occasion for grandiloquence; certainly Richard Strauss would not have failed to fall into the trap. But Stravinsky found something unheard of, something astonishing for the climactic scene.

In the finale, as everyone, exhausted, talks at once, Stravinsky withdraws from the fray. And while confusion reigns onstage, the orchestra fades out. Instead of letting loose in curses, the orchestra begins a good-natured little fox-trot—discreetly, with a very detached air. "They're arguing up there? Too bad for them. Me, I'm leaving . . . Good night."

Mavra must be seen and heard if its extreme importance is to be understood from an intellectual standpoint. It is more difficult to talk about from a musical standpoint, because the work is not yet published, and hearing such new music only twice is not enough for me to be able to grasp all the details.

Still, after the lyric declamation, here is a return to bel canto. A temporary or a definitive return? Little matter, since the work is here and is a success. And let's not forget that, especially for Stravinsky, a masterpiece is the end of the line. Reduced to a size appropriate for such a subject, the orchestra sings too, without interruption. Melody is solidly affirmed. This orchestra is made up almost exclusively of wind instruments, and achieves Cocteau's ideal of a "sumptuous wind band."[62] This is not, moreover, the only point of contact with the spirit of young French artists to be found in *Mavra*. And perhaps it is that which so unsettles the many critics who cried foul at *Parade*.[63] *Mavra* brings powerful approbation for young French people, painters, writers, and musicians.

Double basses and a few violoncellos play a sort of "basso continuo," over which the woodwinds and strings weave a dense melodic web. It makes a very "big" orchestra, with a very new sonic balance. The thick, loud basses support the woodwinds, which become more and more mobile from the bassoons to the flutes. And way above the human voices, completely supple in their bel canto. There is a continuous progression toward lightness, as in a tree whose solid roots bear the elegant and capricious crown, swaying ceaselessly in the wind.

Stravinsky's rhythmic frenzy is restrained in this score. The rhythm is simpler, heavier, perhaps to show the orchestra's "big" side. However, the dryness that might have resulted is avoided, since the rhythms are for the most part syncopated and give the music a swaying effect born admirably by the vocal parts.

We should applaud without reservation Serge de Diaghilew's Ballets Russes for their unceasing activity. For twelve years, we have owed them the brightest of our artistic joys. Let us wish them the pursuit of their magnificent labors for many years to come, along with the well-earned glory it brings them.

—Translated by Bridget Behrmann

Musikblätter des Anbruch (Vienna), November 1922
Stravinsky's New Stage Works
Darius Milhaud

In the last few months Paris witnessed the premieres of two new stage works by Igor Stravinsky performed by Serge Diaghilew with his Russian Ballet: *Renard* and *Mavra*.[64] Each work of this remarkable musician surprises by being completely different from that which came before it; the technique and orchestration are so wonderfully novel and based on a skillfulness that deviates thoroughly from the construction of the composer's older works. In *Renard* the orchestra consists of about fifteen solo instruments, including a cimbalon,[65] and human voices. The plot is represented onstage through pantomime while the singers in the orchestra sing the roles as if performing in a small opera, with the difference that the dancers onstage perform in their place. Some critics criticized the use of a small group of solo instruments in a hall as big as the Opéra; accustomed to the massive size of the Wagnerian orchestra, they probably did not understand how to listen carefully. Strength of sound is less a question of quantity than quality. The pure tone of a solo violin carries farther than a greater number of violins playing at the same time with each one sounding slightly off-pitch in a different way. One would never accuse a solo violinist giving a concert of having chosen a hall too large. Why not then fifteen soloists rather than the one? In a small orchestra everything is essential, harmonic parts intended as filler don't exist and—given the means are limited to a minimum—everything conventional disappears. The music is fuller and more intense but sounds so unfamiliar that it is only natural that the conservative public hears it without grasping it.

The music for *Renard* is extremely lively. Nothing is lost, the melodies are of a truly arithmetical precision; they proceed and interlock exactly like cogwheels in a machine. The structure of the work is simple, clear, and planned with unerring certainty. The vocal element livens up the score, giving it tone and mood.[66] The clearly marked rhythm, which the percussion discreetly yet perfectly underlines, is complemented by the cimbalon. *Renard* justifies the attempts made lately by many young composers; these musicians are fighting for small orchestras made up of solo instruments, and now, with one of his works, they will be glad to count Stravinsky—whom they follow with admiring attentiveness—as one of their own.

Mavra is a small one-act opera buffa. I was not in Paris when it was premiered, and yet Stravinsky played it for me on the piano and let me read along with the orchestral score.[67] It is a work of bel canto; a hussar sings a serenade and dresses up as a cook in order to live with his beloved. Bitter sentimentality and mourning hide behind the comic aspect of the subject matter. The harmonic writing in this work is primitive and its simplicity disappointed every admirer of Stravinsky for whom *The Rite of Spring* set the standard. However, with such a prolific musician one has to expect that the public that loves a certain work will feel the ground collapse under it with the next. The orchestra of *Mavra* is almost military music: the strings are limited to six double basses, six cellos, a solo viola, and two solo violins. Here we see realized the "rich *orphéon*" of winds and brass that Jean Cocteau called for in *Le Coq et l'Arlequin*.[68] *Mavra* meets perfectly the goals set by the young French school since Erik Satie's *Parade*; in this work their fondest wishes are fulfilled. *Mavra* has probably been so poorly understood and harshly criticized because it cozies up intellectually with the young Parisian musicians. A famous critic loses himself in comments about this "italo-russo-negro-american music," a famous impressionist composer speaks maliciously of a new *Le Domino noir*.[69] But does all this have any meaning? *Mavra* will blossom when the current school is recognized; a school that works hard, and yet is not believed and is looked upon askance, with eyes still dimmed from the contemplation of useless pretenses, or because they have leaned over Rimsky-Korsakov's *Handbook of Instrumentation* for too long,[70] rather than broadening their horizon with Gabriel Parès.[71]

—German by M. M. Frank, translated by Tamara Levitz

Vanity Fair (New York), November 1922
News of the Seven Arts in Europe: A New Comic Opera by
Stravinsky and the Latest Fermentations of Dada
Tristan Tzara

After presenting *The Marriage of Sleeping Beauty* and *The Fox*,[72] both of them ballets, Diaghilev, the director of the Russian Ballet, added to the list of novelties he has offered this year in Paris a comic opera by Igor Stravinsky, *Mavra*. The libretto of this, the latest work of the great Russian composer, is derived from a story by Pushkin, the Russian Victor Hugo, who died in 1837 at the age of thirty-eight. The story is titled "The Little House in Kolomna" (Kolomna is a suburb of Petrograd). The libretto was written by Boris Kokhno, a young Russian author, who made his adaptation from Pushkin under Stravinsky's personal supervision. . . . [73]

Stravinsky's music is young, alert, tragic and also comic. His originality is inexhaustible. This little man, his eyes and features sharpened by a subtle intelligence, is already ranked as one of the great composers. Stravinsky has told me, in speaking of his latest experiments, that he will henceforth require no literary subject for his compositions, that he dreams of an opera without any plot.

The setting of *Mavra* is the work of a talented Russian painter, Léopold Survage, who for many years has been living in France. His decor, in spite of the Cubist element in it, is clearly founded on the style of Louis-Philippe.[74] He has built up a charming picture about a table with a samovar on it and a cat. The armchairs are painted on the wall in frescoed relief; through the window one sees the onion bulb of a Russian church tower. . . . [75]

A New Fashion

The performances of the Russian Ballet are feminine triumphs in the sense that the fair occupants of the boxes and orchestra seats rival each other in wearing the very latest inventions of the great dressmakers. At the first night of *Mavra* the foyer of the Opera House was agog at the dress worn by Madame Sonia Delaunay-Terck, the wife of the Parisian painter Robert Delaunay. The new fashion initiated by Madame Delaunay was a "*robe à poème*." On the panels of her gown, she had had embroidered in bright colors these verses, signed Tzara:[76]

L'ange a glissé sa main
dans la corbeille l'oeil des fruits
il arrête les roues des autos
et le gyroscope vertigineux du coeur humain

The angel has slipped his hand
in the basket the eye of the fruits
he halts the wheels of the motors
and the vertiginous gyroscope of the human heart

This amusing idea will certainly find imitators. Among other advantages, it provides one which will decide more than one pretty woman to adopt it. When a young man is presented to her he will not have to founder about among the commonplaces which usually follow an introduction: he can con over [*sic*] the poem inscribed on her dress and open a discussion on the subject, which is sure to contain an element of the unexpected. . . .

The Modern Art Convention

Erik Satie, that great modern French composer, that kind friend with subtle smile and twinkling eyes, most gay and amusing of men, younger than the youngest despite his years, has been faithful in his affection for the Montparnasse quarter which he once knew as the artistic center of Paris. In truth, many important contributions have come to us from it. There Cubism was born, and there four years ago in a studio in the rue Huyghens, where the Polish painter Kisling gathered his friends about him for artistic evenings, Satie discovered the group of composers now known as "The Six."[77] Satie has still and always gives us in his music that careful irony, that frankness and liberty of manners, and that soft atmosphere which lend Montparnasse its peculiar charm.

A storm, memorable in the annals of modern art, has lately disturbed our life in Paris. A group of artists decided to hold a sort of convention in defense of modern art; unfortunately they at once proved themselves dogmatists of the narrowest kind, with a straitness of view which could not leave us cold.[78] Satie and I organized a meeting of protest which buried the Convention and discredited its members. We issued a little pamphlet, *Le Coeur à barbe*. Contributors: Satie, Ribemont-Dessaignes, Eluard, Péret, Soupault, Fraenkel, and I.[79] The paper on which it was printed was of a vulgar pink: a housewife would not hesitate to wrap a camembert in *Le Coeur à barbe*. The cover looked like a rebus, but was only a haphazard mixture of pictures from catalogues of thirty years ago.

The irony of Satie is biting: he has a power, malicious and almost magic of showing the ridiculous in those who he satirizes.

We await with great interest the appearance of his comic opera *Paul et Virginie*.[80] Derain, who is preparing the scenery, has sought inspiration in the crude decorations of the circus and street fair. It is to be produced in the Théâtre des Champs-Elysées, with all the lavishness and care for which this playhouse is famous.

Izvestia (Moscow), 29 March 1923
Parisian Sketches
Music
Vladimir Mayakovsky

There is an ancient feud between me and music.[81] Burliuk[82] and I became Futurists out of despair: we spent the entire evening at Rachmaninoff's concert at the Assembly of the Nobility[83] and ran off after *Isle of the Dead*, resenting the whole classical carrion.[84]

Rightfully, I expected the same in Paris, and they could drag me to pianistic ravings only by force.

We are going to Stravinsky's. What struck me most was where he lives. It is the Pleyel pianola factory.[85] This perfected pianola is pushing the musician and the piano more and more out of the world market. Interestingly, the first thing one encounters in this factory is not "divine sounds" but real musical creation, including everything from the musicians to the delivery trucks. The courtyard is the body of the factory. It is full of enormous trucks loaded with pianolas ready for dispatch. Further on—a howling, singing, and rumbling three-story building. On the first floor is an enormous hall, glistening with the backs of the pianolas. In odd corners, there are virtuous Parisian couples listening to all sorts of musical trifles played to try out the instruments. The second floor is Paris's most beloved concert hall. It is not only impossible to play there during the workday, but even just to sit there. The heartrending wails of pianolas being tested carry even through closed doors. Here, sometimes bustling and sometimes exuding dignity, is the factory owner, Monsieur Lyon, sporting his order of the Legion d'honneur.[86] And finally, upstairs—the tiny room of the musician, cluttered with pianos and pianolas. It is here he creates his symphonies, hands them in to the factory, and finally, corrects the musical proofs on the pianola. He says enthusiastically of the pianola: "Write, if you please, for eight, sixteen, twenty-two hands!"

Igor Stravinsky

The soul of this business, or at least one of the souls, is the Parisianized Russian, Igor Stravinsky. Musical Russia knows him very well from *Petrushka*, *The Nightingale*, and other works. Paris likewise knows him very well from the productions of S. P. Diaghilev. You see, the pillars of European art are the Spaniard Picasso in painting, and the Russian Stravinsky in music. I did not go to Stravinsky's concert. He played for us at Lyon's. He played "The Nightingale," "The March," "Two Nightingales," "The Nightingale and the Chinese Emperor,"[87] and also his latest works: "The Spanish Etude" for the pianola,[88] *Les Noces*—a ballet with chorus, which will be playing in the spring with Diaghilev—and excerpts from the opera *Mavra*.

I don't dare to judge. This does not make an impression on me. He is considered simultaneously an innovator and a reviver of the Baroque! Nearer to my heart is Prokofiev—from his pre-abroad period;[89] the Prokofiev of impetuous, rough marches.

— *Translated from the Russian by Katya Ermolaev and Alexandra Grabarchuk*

La Revue musicale (Paris), 1 December 1923
The Latest Stravinsky
Jean Cocteau

During a recent interview the Russian poet Mayakovsky and I had, our interpreter was Stravinsky.[90]

The conversation took an unfortunate turn. Not only did we have to run from one language to another, but indeed from one universe to another.

In a country turned completely upside down, literature gets muddled with the rest. Ideas predominate; poets become politicians.

After such a crisis here at home, we must use the rebus in reacting against speech.[91] Over time the rebus disappears, and the struggle turns on points of extreme delicacy, which people who are absent-minded or foreign do not perceive.

This economy, this dynamic reserve, resembles certain machines that retouch zinc plates: a complex monster that operates a tiny milling cutter.

This is why the power of our greatest epochs leaves strangers with an impression of smallness. Imagine the glance thrown by the colossus Mayakovsky at my slingshot!

Stravinsky was still translating. Mayakovsky's face had nothing to teach me; it was the face of a tremendous infant. The real spectacle was our interpreter; he performed a strange task of contraband, trading single idiom for idiom, passing along only what he wanted.

Here the Stravinsky of today lets himself be seen. Fruitlessly he tried to tie together Russian remarks and untie my own; after Mayakovsky left, we found ourselves among compatriots again.

Because for the first time I witness this miracle: a thunderstorm worried only about the devices that will give it shape. Oriental Romanticism (uneasiness, savage jolts) in the service of Latin order.[92]

Genius is no better analyzed than electricity. One has it or one does not. Stravinsky has it; thus he never thinks about it. He never hypnotizes himself with it. He never makes himself dizzy with it. He does not surrender to the danger of stirring his own emotions, of gilding himself or making himself ugly. He channels a brute power and handles it carefully, so that it serves a use in devices ranging from the factory to the flashlight.

Improving, varying the devices must replace the ancient problem of inspiration, of voluntary sublimity, of head-in-your-hands mysticism.

Here is Stravinsky seen head on, in 1923. Let us observe him in profile.

Charm requires perfect tact. One must stand on the edge of the abyss. Almost all graceful artists fall in. Rossini, Tchaikovsky, Weber, Gounod, Chabrier,[93] lean but don't fall. Their deep-rootedness allows them to lean very far.

Mavra performs a balancing act on the edge of the abyss. We think about those clowns who play mandolin on top of a pile of chairs. The pile rocks. It teeters a long time on its tipping point.

How to depict Stravinsky without following this last step? Rings, gaiters, scarves, half-belts, ties, tiepins, wristwatches, mufflers, fetishes, pinces-nez, monocles, glasses, chain bracelets, describe him badly. Put simply, they prove on the surface that Stravinsky goes out of his way for no one. He composes, dresses himself, and speaks as he wishes. When playing the piano, he and the piano adjust into a single unit; when conducting the Octet, he turns his astronomer's back on us to solve this magnificent instrumental calculus made of silver numbers.

From N. A. Rimsky-Korsakov Stravinsky takes methods of order and bends them to his needs. On Rimsky's table, ink bottles, penholders, rulers would betray the bureaucrat. The order at Stravinsky's is alarming. It is the surgeon's instrument case.

This composer is muddled with the work he does. Clothed in it, harnessed to his oeuvre like the old one-man band, peeling off and piling up around him skins of music, he is indistinguishable from his room. To see Stravinsky in Morges, in Leysin, in Paris, at Pleyel's where he lives, is to see the animal in its shell. Pianos, drums, metronomes, cimbaloms, tools for creating staves, American lead sharpeners, music stands, snare and bass drums are its extension. They are the pilot's cabin, the insect's bristling arms shown us by the filmmaker a thousand times bigger than in nature, during mating season.

Of course *The Rite of Spring* uproots me and *Les Noces*—a sports car—carries me off at an incredible speed; but even in *Les Noces,* where the *Rite's* spirit finds its definitive orchestral formula, beauty is still pitched at the gut level. How to forget that the people sitting next to me in the theater, who acclaim it, showed indifference for *Mavra,* written afterward?[94] Their approval irritates me. I feel like I'm watching the musician being applauded on his own cheeks.

Is there anything more admirable than this stern man, of whom the amorous public demands, "Brutalize me, hit me again," and who offers them lace?

Such a pretty gift disconcerts. Blows are better understood.

—Translated by Bridget Behrmann and Tamara Levitz

Vyorstï (Paris), 1928
Mavra
Arthur-Vincent Lourié

1.

In its significance, Stravinsky's second opera, *Mavra,* lies at the core of everything he has produced in recent years.[95] It was composed and premiered in 1922, but it has yet to be appreciated and accepted. *Mavra* provoked the indignation of some, who heard it as a "triviality," and the indifference of others.

For the circle of those close to Stravinsky's music of *The Rite of Spring* era, *Mavra* was intrinsically unacceptable. The habit, even the necessity of discovering "stunning" sonorities in each of his new works had been formed. Among music lovers, what was almost a "tradition" of Stravinsky's style had taken shape. From each of his new works they expected a continuation of the *Rite*, of its elemental force and rebelliousness.[96]

They were perplexed when this all ended, and were unforgiving. The modernists were perplexed, offended by the triviality and "cliché." It may be the opera disappointed the same people who witnessed the first performances of the *Rite* and the rise in its significance. It disappointed those who had seemingly followed Stravinsky's entire journey over the decade separating the *Rite* from *Mavra*. This explains *Mavra*'s failure and the enthusiasm with which *Les Noces* was received a year later—after the unsuccessful *Mavra* it demonstrated a return to the old way.

Mavra proved least comprehensible because in it Stravinsky pursued his new principles resolutely and rigorously. In fact, this new path in his music began much earlier, with *L'Histoire du soldat* and *Pulcinella*. The characteristic features of the new formal texture [*faktura*] that in *Mavra* are embodied with utmost perfection were already laid out in those works.

The one thing that separates *Mavra* from other works of the most recent period is its fundamental connection with Russian art and culture. In contrast to *Mavra*, all the remaining new works by Stravinsky are based on something like a universal style, irrespective of national differences and musical language. In this respect, *Mavra* is an exception. It is first and foremost a national Russian opera, like *A Life for the Tsar* or *Eugene Onegin*. At the same time, it also presents new possibilities for the rebirth of operatic form in the West—if opera is destined to be reborn at all.

2.

The decline of opera in the West is the result of the Wagnerian legacy. The so-called music drama gradually swallowed up the pure operatic forms. Degenerating into pseudo-Romanticism, post-Wagnerian theater with its rhetorical emotionalism destroyed the instrumental plasticity [*plastiku*] of the classical style. For Western opera *Mavra* may become a formal buttress. Notwithstanding *Mavra*'s profoundly Russian character—which fundamentally governs its musical language and lyrico-epic atmosphere—it can and should be grasped from a non-national perspective, thanks to the principles of its construction. The objective value of *Mavra* is in the method of its formal construction. The reason for its obscurity thus far, its "paradoxicality," lurks within this formal method.

Reviving the Russian national opera along its classic lines, as well as making a down payment on a new flowering for the classic form of opera in the West, Stravinsky takes us back to an unadulterated primary source, first and foremost to the operas of Glinka. The path from *A Life for the Tsar* to *Ruslan and Ludmila* is the entire path traversed by Glinka. In its time, *Ruslan* was a logical consequence of *A Life for the Tsar*. And what happened? *A Life for the Tsar* was embraced—relatively speaking—by Russian society mainly thanks to its patriotic topic. To its contemporaries, *Ruslan* was indigestible. They simply kissed off this opera, and for a protracted period. Glinka himself bore witness to the first performance of *Ruslan and Ludmila*, the opera he regarded as his supreme achievement, and which became the basis for all subsequent Russian music in its national ideal:

"When the curtain descended, they began to call for me, but the applause was very tepid and there was stubborn hissing, primarily from the stage and the orchestra. I turned to General Dubelt in the director's box with the question: 'They seem to be hissing. Should I go out for a curtain call?'

'Go on,' the General replied. 'Christ suffered more than you.'"

During Glinka's life, *Ruslan* was not understood at all. It was appreciated ultimately after Glinka's death and became the foundation upon which the edifice of the Russian national music school was erected. *Ruslan* was the covenant embraced by the "Five" during the first period of the existence of the Balakirev circle. But the "Five" never had a clear understanding of the line that extended from Glinka. As a result, the fork they took led Russian music—represented chiefly by the figure of Rimsky-Korsakov—to a pseudo-Russian nationalism nurtured on German scholasticism.

For all the outward appearance of a link with Glinka, his heritage was exposed to elaboration and to apparent formal extension during that period of Russian musical culture. But it was by no means exposed to enhancement and development of the pure line it manifested. In its essence, Glinka's line has still not been extended. Irrespective of this, the attitude of leading Russian musicians of that time was as typical for them as is our attitude to *A Life for the Tsar*. To us, *A Life for the Tsar* is closer now—for the purity of its primitive forms and its musical virgin territory. Notwithstanding the more significant role *Ruslan* played in the past—which we esteem as the perfect embodiment of the Russian musical empire—perhaps it is precisely thanks to its primitivism that we "need" *A Life for the Tsar* more. The same is true of Tchaikovsky; *Eugene Onegin* is closer to us than *The Queen of Spades*, despite the greater formal perfection of the latter. Or with Bach—the *St. John Passion* and not the *St. Matthew Passion*.

Mavra resurrects the broken link with the line of Glinka. It establishes that line on a new basis and captures reflectively the Glinka not of *Ruslan*, but of *A Life for the Tsar*. Irrespective of the role played by *A Life for the Tsar* in the creation of *Mavra*, Glinka's opera still awaits its actual rehabilitation.

Besides Glinka, *Mavra* makes a return to Tchaikovsky, who in this work became the intermediate link between Glinka and Stravinsky. The genealogical line of *Mavra* can be delineated as follows: *from* A Life for the Tsar *through Tchaikovsky to the contemporary canon*. Stravinsky's attitude to Glinka is a matter of the purity of national tradition and a fundamental bond. For all the dissimilarity of their temperaments and tastes, what he holds in common with Tchaikovsky is based on almost familial blood ties.

Aware of his estrangement from musical modernism, glancing back over Russian music of the past, Stravinsky was bound to align himself with Tchaikovsky. It was the natural reaction against obsolete modernism. The affinity with Tchaikovsky, which always existed, was openly revealed only in *Mavra*, later in the Octet. The return to Tchaikovsky, the reevaluation of him that Stravinsky made during the period of *Mavra*'s creation, and the subsequent consolidation of this position, demolished conclusively the onetime and—what's more—moribund ideology of the modernist camp.[97] Several of the leading French musicians found their own Tchaikovsky in Gounod. Having noted the fact, I refrain from comparisons.

The keys to authentic realism—which has become the ideal of our days—were concealed within the music of Tchaikovsky. Stravinsky found and took possession of them. Loving Tchaikovsky, one cannot but fall in love with *Mavra*; it is a vivid remembrance of Tchaikovsky, miraculously resurrected by Stravinsky.

3.

Above all, it is the insignificance of the subject that astonishes in *Mavra*, its deliberate negligibility as it were. For the shortsighted, this want of scenic plot reduces the work to the level of a theatrical skit, to "trifles" of the sort that aren't worth mentioning. But the fact of the matter is that *Mavra*'s subject isn't an anecdote drawn from "The Little House in Kolomna." Its subject matter is a purely musical, formal task. *In its scenic effect, Mavra is built on an anecdote, but it traces back to the national lyrico-epic opera in its musical effect.* This is the reverse of those countless operas based on the most complex of subjects—mythological, historical, symbolic, and so on—that are musically impossible to fathom. In *Mavra* the correlation with the poem is minimal; it is just a point of departure. The plot of *Mavra* is just the springboard for a vault onto a musical trapeze. In this respect it satisfies its intended purpose. With the exception of two lines, nothing remains of Pushkin's octaves in the libretto of Stravinsky's opera:

> We need a kitchen maid. But find one—where?
> Go ask our neighbor. Cheap ones are so rare!

Stravinsky didn't illustrate "The Little House in Kolomna." He created a work that is analogous with Pushkin's in type and method. As it is in "The Little House in Kolomna," so too in *Mavra* the center of gravity is in what is found *alongside of* the plot.

Mavra Overture

In terms of intimate savor, Stravinsky achieved in *Mavra* what he has always admired: the chiaroscuro of Russian urban *melos* and an idiosyncratic drawing-room ambiance [*bïtovoy kolorit*], sung and instrumental, that has always appealed to him. In *Mavra*, he expressed this more pointedly than ever before. But this is a personal moment in his creativity, about which we will not pass judgment now. What is important to us is the integrated character of the composition and the objective value that is manifested in it.

The genetic link to the sources of the origins of Russian opera, and the rejection of everything that had been accepted concerning its evolution is what, first and foremost, is important in *Mavra*. In every artistic epoch, what is rejected is no less representative than what is endorsed. This disavowal of whole stages of past musical history is very significant at the present moment in the work of Stravinsky. An acceptance of *Mavra* mandates first and foremost the elimination from the contemporary agenda of all Wagnerian theater, as well as the Wagnerian music drama as pursued by his successors, headed by Richard Strauss in Europe and Rimsky-Korsakov in Russia.

The primitivism in *Mavra* is intentional. The apparent poverty and deficiency is the result of creative will and artistic consciousness.

Upon closer examination of the score with an "armed eye," and verification with discerning ears, the primitivism of *Mavra* turns out to be the result of a synthesis, without which the birth of the primitive is impossible. In its simplicity,

Mavra harbors Stravinsky's entire past experience and is the consequence of mature mastery.

4.

The musical text in *Mavra* is built on two principles: 1) the element of song, divided into purely lyrical and drawing-room inflections, and 2) an instrumental-plastic element. Meter and rhythm serve coordinating purposes and are of prime importance with regard to the architectonics. In *Mavra*, meter *shapes the motion* of the sonic fabric, a function that is predominantly conveyed by means of the instrumental accompaniment. Rhythm governs *the structure* and the relationship among the aural components of the sung *melos*. When the instrumental component ceases to accompany and becomes independent, rhythm plays the same role with respect to these very brief, purely instrumental moments.

Given its lyrical foundation, overall the opera is very dynamic. The musical current flows continuously—sometimes driving, sometimes evenly—with such clarity that we seem to see the streambed on which it runs through a transparent veil of sound.

The dynamism that was always so typical of Stravinsky is imparted in *Mavra* by the reinforcement of the role of meters. They are like engines and levers in the opera. Meters take on self-sufficient status; they are independent of the rhythmic construction but are brought into interaction with it. In part, they govern the *instrumental color* of the opera and the aspect of its purely *musical* motion, as opposed to the *scenic* motion proper. In *Mavra*, meters and rhythm take on a completely neutral, almost impersonal aspect. Their job is not (as in the past, in the *Rite*, for instance) to develop emotional energy. In *Mavra*, as in other recent works, meter is the force that sets the contours of the sound design in motion. It governs the *shape of the motion*. Rhythm is the variable that establishes the sounding relationships. It governs the *shape of the structure*. Tempo is the connection between them. It is the *speed control*. The emotional dynamic on which he built some of his previous works (the most striking example in this sense is again *The Rite of Spring*) is circumvented. A dynamic that is purely musical—without emotional inspiration—asserts itself. The aim thus established amounts to the attainment of an almost mechanical "detachment." What is acquired is the precision of the driving force of metric elements, their maximal scope and stability.

The musical language of *Mavra* is utterly simple and straightforward. It is governed primarily by the character of its melody. The basis is a tonal (more rarely a modal) diatonic design. There is frequent use of alternating parallel major and minor, and of the juxtaposition of artificial and natural modes. Everything is transformed into purely singing lines, even into drawing-room inflections. Recitative is nowhere to be found. The integrality of the song forms is one of the greatest virtues of this opera. In terms of the technical mastery of its design, the opera is constructed flawlessly.

Without interrupting the flow, the proportions of the sections and musical periods are arranged so that they fit together seamlessly, without any transitional links. Like Chinese lacquer boxes nested one inside another. The spacing between the individual sections is so exact and true that you feel the air passing between them as between two adjacent objects. This is achieved by the skill of producing broad synthetic amalgamations of sound masses and lines and by the ruthless elimination of everything unnecessary for the flow and development of these lines.

In the transitions from one episode to the next in *Mavra*, cadences and final codas are eliminated and replaced by what could be called a system of musical "automatic doors" leading one episode directly into the next. In these moments— sometimes it is an octave, sometimes a third or a seventh—hidden amalgamations occur that resolve traditional musical formulas into the simplest relationship; in the past they dissipated the overall dynamic of the whole with their ornament and flourish. Stravinsky uses this technique to attach consecutive episodes one to another, creating a seamless equilibrium on this transfer circuit.

A mosaic of consecutive musical sections existed in classical opera. In Romantic drama they were more or less fluid. Stravinsky creates a synthetic construct of the whole.

Thanks to the mastery of amalgamation, the texture of the work is perfectly smooth, without disruptions and disparities in sound intensity. The formal method behind it regulates the whole work and controls its temperature precisely. Spontaneous inspiration and vibrant energy are distributed uniformly, like proper blood circulation throughout the body. For all the thoroughgoing severity of its execution, however, the formal method is hidden and, as a whole, the opera registers emotionally without raising the question of how that is accomplished.

5.

In terms of its orchestral color, *Mavra* isn't endowed with independent significance. Its orchestra is the logical extension of instrumental principles common to all Stravinsky's recent compositions. Here we have the same assemblage of timbres and volumes for which the basis is not the sonic coloration (the "savor"), but the weight, density, and permeability of the sonic volumes as well as the caliber of sonic temperatures. An altogether singular charm of instrumental color is created by the female voices "encased" by the brass.

As a Russian opera, *Mavra* showed the West a side of Russian music with which European art had not yet come into contact. Meanwhile, *Mavra* was just a new manifestation of this age-old style. It is the culture of the Russian urban— predominantly Petersburgian—romance. This line, stretching from Glinka and the musicians of his circle, is virtually unknown in the West, as opposed to the line that stretches from Musorgsky. Dargomyzhsky was descended directly from Glinka. He still carried the legacy of that epoch, but it was he who laid the foundation for dramatic music later validated decisively by Musorgsky, who created the dramatic epos on the foundation of folksong creativity. Glinka's domain was the romance and the lyrical song. Both these lines are equally significant for Russian art and it is impossible to understand Russian music while rejecting one of them. Meanwhile, only the work of Musorgsky was introduced to the West and influenced European music. The attitude to Russian music was an enthusiasm for elemental force and, above all, for the new exotic. The more saturated a work was with folk character, the more it impressed. The attitude to Stravinsky did not escape this; he was considered almost Musorgsky's direct successor. If there were grounds for this in his first period (from the *Rite* to *Les Noces*), with *Mavra* Stravinsky introduces a species of Russian music that is utterly new to the West.

As the indispensable basis for a musical composition, folklore is absent in *Mavra*. In its stead, the style of the urban romance is adopted. After Tchaikovsky this style was held in contempt by Russian musicians, who considered it unworthy of "high" art. It was demoted from the artistic foreground to musical works of the second and third ranks.

6.

The background of this style is complicated. Its roots go far back into the past of Russian music. In the first of the known collections of folksongs (eighteenth-century), the gusli player Trutovsky[98] already presented initial examples of the deformation and the commingling of folksong genres with the urban lyrical romance. He detected considerable influences from Italian and French music on the Russian even then. This influence had an impact on popular musical practice. At the same time they appeared in urban life and the lyrical song-romance received independent development—spreading further and further—parallel to the forms of Russian music that had emerged on the basis of folklore. Finally, in Glinka's era, this style of romance became the primary basis of musical creativity. After Glinka it declined steadily, surviving exclusively in the sphere of urban musical practice and the salon. By then, the Gypsy current had attached itself. The apex of the Petersburg-Muscovite romance style is associated with the era of the Russian Empire. After that it became increasingly vulgarized and, at the same time, infiltrated common practice. It became the main musical expression of the urban petty bourgeoisie, analogous to the "vulgar" forms of pseudo-folksongs we are familiar with in the big cities of Europe.

This style is a piquant fusion of elements of the Western (primarily Italo-French) lyrical song, occasionally the German pseudo-classical, with Gypsy and Russian folklore. After Glinka, it passed to Dargomyzhsky, who exhibited it in *Rusalka* but then turned away from it in *The Stone Guest*, the work in which the development of music drama began in Russia. Thereafter, only Tchaikovsky drew upon this source. After him, this style fell out of use by Russian musicians. Having been abandoned in music, by the middle of the nineteenth century the essence of the lyrical romance withdrew into Russian poetry. Such a remarkable poet as

Apollon Grigoryev[99] was wholly nurtured by it. In our time, Alexander Blok was a brilliant exponent of the same essence of the romance. But in music this style was forgotten. Stravinsky recalled it and created *Mavra*.

The main tendency of *Mavra* is its naked candor, in a system of musical ideas that verge at times toward the simplistic. This is what constitutes *Mavra*'s paradoxicality.

Blossoming from those wellsprings of Russian musical life where Russian music was essentially the refined culture of dilettantes, where no trace of professional musical art as we understand it yet existed, for all its magnificent formal mastery and technical polish *Mavra* sparkles through and through with this dilettantism and near ineptitude. In my opinion, this is where its delicate charm and the magic of its appeal reside. At times you do not know whether it is soulful lyricism or an ironic mask. But the whole point of *Mavra* is that you accept it as an entirely unaffected work, you believe in the absolute sincerity of its lyrical pathos. No devotee of this type of work can relegate it to the level of ordinary aesthetic stylization.

In *Mavra* Stravinsky furnished an experience almost *outside professional art*. Striving for an expression of the utmost truth and simplicity, *Mavra* tries not to be professional music at all if, for the purpose stated here, that makes banishment from the professional experience of modernity inevitable. It's a different matter that, having departed from current practice, *Mavra* creates a new practice—its own—powerfully and persuasively, although this is not yet evident to many. Will it be the victor? Can it replace current moribund operatic traditions? Or will it be an isolated episode? This is a question for the future that concerns not only *Mavra*, but also to all of Stravinsky's creative work at the present time.

Paris, May 1927
—*Translated from the Russian by Laurel E. Fay*

NOTES

1. Stravinsky performed *Mavra* with the singers Stefan Belina-Skupevsky, Oda Slobodskaya, Yelena Sadoven, and Zoya Rozovskaya on the second half of a concert program of "Russian Music Outside of the Mighty Five" that Diaghilev had organized to entertain the press and distinguished guests invited to his gala buffet. On the first half of the program, Diaghilev's rehearsal pianist Nikolay Kopeykin accompanied the singers in music by Glinka ("The Lark" arranged for piano by Balakirev; two arias from *Ruslan and Lyudmila*; and the Act 3 quartet from *A Life for the Tsar*), and by Dargomyzhsky and Tchaikovsky (including a chanson from *Snegurochka*). Ernst Ansermet then introduced *Mavra*, which Stravinsky performed at the piano—"with what vehemence!"—as André Rigaud remarked. Gregor Fitelberg conducted and Kopeykin and a "Mademoiselle Krieger" provided a third hand on the piano to manage difficult passages. See André Rigaud, "Une soirée chez M. de Diaghilev: 'Mavra' de M. Stravinsky," *Comoedia*, 31 May 1922, in which Rigaud also lists the distinguished guests who attended this gala. See also Richard Taruskin, *Stravinsky and the Russian Traditions: A Biography of the Works through* Mavra (Berkeley: University of California Press, 1996), 2:1591–92

2. Gregor Fitelberg conducted a brass ensemble, Bronislava Nijinska provided stage directions, and Léopold Survage completed the Cubist sets for the premiere. The cast included the very same singers who had performed at Diaghilev's gala buffet weeks earlier. See the official program of the *Ballets russes à l'Opéra: Mai–Juin 1922*, available online as part of Gallica, the digital library of the Bibliothèque nationale française, http://gallica.bnf.fr/ark:/12148/btv1b8415093j. r=mavra+programme.langEN.

3. See Théodore Stravinsky, *Le Message d'Igor Stravinsky* (Lausanne: Editions de l'Aire, 1980), 103–5.

4. Richard Taruskin, "Parody as Homage," in *Stravinsky's* Pulcinella*: A Facsimile of the Sources and Sketches*, ed. Maureen Carr (Middleton, WI: A-R Editions, 2010), 61. Taruskin argued vigorously for a reevaluation of *Mavra* and its importance to Stravinsky's path as a composer in *Stravinsky and the Russian Traditions*, 2:1501–1603.

5. Emily Apter describes a translation zone, in reference to Guillaume Apollinaire's 1912 poem "Zone," as "a broad intellectual topography that is neither the property of a single nation, nor an amorphous condition associated with postnationalism, but rather a zone of critical engagement that connects the 'l' and the 'n' of transLation and transNation." See Apter, *The Translation Zone: A New Comparative Literature* (Princeton: Princeton University Press, 2006), 5.

6. Henri Collet coined the term "Les Six" as a counterweight to the Russian "Mighty Five" in 1920 to describe a group of young composers gathered around Erik Satie that included Georges Auric, Louis Durey, Arthur Honegger, Francis Poulenc, Darius Milhaud, and Germaine Tailleferre. See Collet, "Les cinq Russes, les six Français et M. Satie," *Comoedia*, 16 January 1920.

7. They directed their anger primarily at Emile Vuillermoz's review of *Mavra*, included here.

8. The Fountain of Youth.

9. Jean Cocteau, "The Comic Spirit in Modern Art: A Note on the Profound Realism of Exaggeration and Caricature," *Vanity Fair* 19/1 (September 1922): 66.

10. This concert took place 26 December1922. See Georges Auric, "La Musique: Du 'Sacre du printemps' à 'Mavra,'" *Les Nouvelles littéraires*, 6 January 1923. Wiéner included "Paracha's Aria" in a second all-Stravinsky concert on 7 November 1923. Ernest Ansermet was disappointed by this performance. See Stravinsky to Ansermet, 31 December 1922, and Ansermet to Stravinsky, 2 January 1923 in *Correspondance Ansermet-Strawinsky (1914–1967)*, ed. Claude Tappolet (Geneva: Georg, 1991), 2:34–36.

11. The program included *Mavra*, the Concertino, *Pulcinella* Suite, and the Octet. See Valérie Dufour, "Paul Collaer et Igor Strawinsky: Lettres inédites au compositeur (1920–1925)," *Revue belge de musicologie* 56 (2002): 107–11.

12. Stravinsky, "The Genius of Tchaikovsky: Stravinsky's Views. 'The Sleeping Beauty,'" trans. Edwin Evans, *Times* (London), 18 October 1921; repr. as "The Sleeping Beauty" in Eric White, *Stravinsky: The Composer and His Works* (1966; 2nd ed., Berkeley: University of California Press, 1979): 573–74; translated as "La Belle au bois dormant: Lettre à Serge de Diaghilew," *Comoedia*, 14 November 1921.

13. *Aurora's Wedding* (in French, *Le Mariage de la belle au bois dormant*) was premiered 18 May 1922 at the Paris Opéra. See Stravinsky, "Une lettre de Stravinsky sur Tchaikovsky," *Figaro*, 18 May 1922; repr. in *La Revue musicale* 3/9 (July 1922): 87.

14. See Stanislas Fumet, "Quelques mots sur…l'évolution d'Igor Stravinsky," *Intransigeant*, 29 June 1922; Pierre Lalo, "La Musique: Ballets Russes," Feuilleton du *Temps*, 30 June 1922; and Louis Schneider, "M. Igor Strawinsky et les Ballets russes," *Revue de France* 2/4 (July–August 1922): 438–39. Schneider compares Stravinsky's public pronouncements to Victor Hugo's manifesto for *Hernani*, and laments that *Mavra* disappointed in light of the expectations these pronouncements had raised.

15. The Mighty Five or Mighty Handful is a term commonly used to designate a group of composers who sought to produce a Russian national style, and that included Mily Balakirev, César Cui, Modest Musorgsky, Nikolay Rimsky-Korsakov, and Alexander Borodin. For a thorough account of Stravinsky's transformation in these years, see Taruskin, *Stravinsky and the Russian Traditions*, 2:1501–1537.

16. Stravinsky to Stefan Strasser in Kiel, 5 October 1925, microfilm 121.1, 1792, Paul Sacher Stiftung (henceforth, PSS).

17. Ernest Ansermet, "'Mavra' de Stravinski," *Le Radio* 13/654 (18 October 1935): 1. Ansermet had intended to write an article on *Mavra* and Tchaikovsky for *La Revue musicale* in 1922, but these plans never materialized. He told Stravinsky it was taking a long time for him to clarify his thoughts. See Ernest Ansermet to Stravinsky, 26 July and 10 September 1922, in *Correspondance Ansermet-Strawinsky (1914–1967)*, 2:11 and 27–28.

18. Nikita Balieff founded *The Bat* (after the Viennese *Die Fledermaus*) in the basement of the Moscow Art Theater in 1908. After the revolution, he established his revue show as *Chauve-Souris* in Paris, and then toured Europe, the United States, and South Africa. See Taruskin, *Stravinsky and the Russian Traditions*, 2:1538–49; and White, *Stravinsky: The Composer and His Works*, 79.

19. Francis Picabia, "Jazz-Band," *Comoedia*, 24 February 1922.

20. Boris de Schloezer, "Igor Stravinsky," *La Revue musicale* 5/2, special issue on Igor Stravinsky (1 December 1923): 97–141.

21. J. D. [J. de Geynst], "Un musicien russe à Bruxelles: Un entretien avec M. Igor Stravinsky," *L'Etoile belge*, 15 January 1924; repr. as "Un entretien avec Igor Stravinsky," *La Patrie Belge* 6/1 (January 1924): 18–19. In this article Stravinsky again aligns himself as a Russian artist with Glinka and Tchaikovsky and praises the latter for his Franco-Russian mixture (*mélange franco-russe*).

22. On *Vanity Fair*'s elite status and importance to music, see Mary Davis, *Classic Chic: Music, Fashion, and Modernism* (Berkeley: University of California Press, 2006), 129–33.

23. *Vanity Fair* highlighted *Chauve-Souris* as the "in" show of 1922 in numerous articles and photo spreads. See, for example, "The Fashions and Pleasures of New York," *Vanity Fair* 18/2 (April 1922): 26, 28.

24. Auric described how Pierre Monteux's concert performance of *The Rite of Spring* in 1914 had endeared Stravinsky to Les Six, and made him "and the other young men there get up on our chairs, with tears streaming down our cheeks, and cheer with maddest enthusiasm." Georges Auric, "Erik Satie and the New Spirit Possessing French Music," *Vanity Fair* 18/5 (July 1922): 104.

25. *Simultanisme* emerged as an artistic trend in France just before World War I and is also associated with the Futurists and Guillaume Apollinaire. Maurice Brillant remarks at length on Survage's Cubist set in "Les Oeuvres et les hommes," *Le Correspondant* 94/1436 (25 July 1922): 364–68; as does "R.-J." in "Au Théâtre de l'Opéra: 'Mavra,'" *Comedia*, 5 June 1922. Several of the reviews collected here were also illustrated with Cubist drawings. Cocteau's article includes his drawing of Stravinsky's music emerging from the piano; Laloy's includes Picasso's drawing of Stravinsky in a chair; and Poulenc's has a Cubist lithograph by Roger de La Fresnaye. Tristan Tzara discusses and includes a reproduction of Robert Delauney's portrait of Stravinsky in "What We Are Doing in Europe: Some Account of the Latest Ballets, Books, Pictures and Literary Scandals of the Continent," *Vanity Fair* 19/1 (September 1922): 68, 100. Stravinsky's friend Ernest Ansermet thought the "cubisme des Galleries La Fayette" of Survage's sets "enchanted" Diaghilev. His reference to the famous Parisian department store Galeries Lafayette points toward his cynicism about the commercial success of Cubist art. See Ernest Ansermet to Stravinsky, 9 September 1923, in *Correspondance Ansermet-Strawinsky (1914–1967)*, 2:68.

26. Surrealism in music defines not a style, but rather an international network of composers with common musical and intellectual interests and ties to Surrealist writers. This network included Francis Poulenc, Alejandro García Caturla, and Kurt Weill, and had one of its epicenters in Belgium around the composer André Souris and the poet-theoretician Paul Nougé and his journal *Correspondance*. For further insight, see Daniel Albright, *Untwisting the Serpent* (Chicago: Chicago University Press, 2000), 244–74, 275–310; Sébastien Arfouilloux, *Que la nuit tombe sur l'orchestre: Surréalisme et musique* (Paris: Fayard, 2009), esp. the bibliography, 519–30; Catherine Miller, *Jean Cocteau, Guillaume Apollinaire, Paul Claudel et le groupe des six: Rencontres poético-musicales autour des mélodies et des chansons* (Liège: Mardaga, 2003); and Robert Wangermée, *André Souris et le complexe d'Orphée: Entre surréalisme et musique sérielle* (Liège: Mardaga, 1995).

27. When asked about their favorite music, Louis Aragon chose Musorgsky; Jacques Baron, Mozart; André Breton, none (*aucun*); Paul Éluard, Grieg; Théodore Fraenkel, ". . ."; Max Morise,

Bach; Benjamin Péret, noise (*le bruit*); Georges Ribemont-Dessaignes, jazz; Jacques Rigaut, blacks (*les nègres*); Philippe Soupault, ragtime; and Roger Vitrac, Stravinsky. See "Quelques préférences," *Littérature* 2, new series (1 April 1922): 1–4. Louis Aragon, André Breton, and Philippe Soupault early on published the lyrics to Stravinsky's *Berceuses de chat* and *Pribaoutki* as "Berceuses de chat" and "Chansons plaisantes" in *Littérature* 10 (December 1919): 5–6, 7–8. The *Berceuses de chat* was also performed in a "surrealist" concert at the Galerie Barbazanges 8 March 1920, with *musique d'ameublement*, Georges Auric's "Adieu New York," Darius Milhaud's "Printemps," and Max Jacob's play *Ruffian toujours, truand jamais*. See Arfouilloux, *Que la nuit tombe sur l'orchestre*, 133.

28. Deborah Mawer, "Jazzing a Classic: Hylton and Stravinsky at the Paris Opéra," *Twentieth-Century Music* 6/2 (September 2009): 155–82.

29. Lalo, "La Musique: Ballets Russes." See also Maurice Brillant, "Les Oeuvres et les hommes."

30. Erik Satie, "Igor Stravinsky: A Tribute to the Great Russian Composer by an Eminent French Confrère," *Vanity Fair* 19/6 (February 1923): 39; 88.

31. In his program note for the Illini Theatre Guild's staging of *Mavra* for the Festival of Contemporary Arts in Lincoln Hall Theatre at the University of Illinois on 27, 28, 29 February and 1 March 1952 Stravinsky lamented that "Mavra has had comparatively few performances so far, due, partly to its extremely difficult score." He notes that for this performance his son Soulima resolved the orchestral dilemma by transcribing the piece for two pianos (microfilm 121.1, 1825–30, PSS).

32. Hans Curjel situated *Mavra* within a neoclassical tradition in his program notes for the performance at the Kroll Opera in Berlin in 1928. See Hans Curjel, "Mavra," *Blätter der Staatsoper und der Städtischen Oper* 8/19 (February 1928): 14.

33. Soviet critics began writing about *Mavra* after Ernest Ansermet performed excerpts of it in Moscow and Leningrad in spring 1928. A few years later, Arnold Alshvang denounced *Mavra* as "typical émigré art, lacking a future" in "Ideinïy put' Stravinskogo" (Stravinsky's ideological path), *Sovetskaya Muzïka* 5 (1933): 90–100; repr. in Viktor Varunts, ed., *I. F. Stravinskiy: Perepiska s russkimi korrespondentami. Materialï k biografii* (Moscow: Kompozitor, 2003), 3: 834–49. Boris Asasfyev gives a very detailed, thoughtful account of *Mavra*'s Russian roots and connection to the Russian petit bourgeoisie, as well as a theoretical analysis of the score in *Kniga o Stravinskom* (Leningrad: Triton, 1929); translated into English by Robert French with a preface by Robert Craft as *A Book about Stravinsky* (Ann Arbor: UMI Research Press, 1982), 197–222.

34. Stravinsky, unidentified typescript, microfilm 121.1,1812, PSS. I believe Stravinsky may have written this program note for the U.S. premiere of *Mavra* with the Philadelphia Grand Opera Company at the Philadelphia Academy of Music, 28 December 1934. Alexander Smallens conducted this performance, and Maria Kurenko performed the role of Parasha. It is also possible that Stravinsky wrote these notes for Ernest Ansermet's performance of *Mavra* with the Orchestre de la Suisse Romande in Geneva, 23 October 1935, or for another occasion.

35. Ernest Ansermet performed *Mavra* as part of the Concerts Jean Wiéner on 26 December 1922 in Paris; Stravinsky replaced Ansermet to conduct a concert version with the Concerts Pro Arte in Brussels on 14 January 1924 ; and Otto Klemperer conducted when *Mavra* was staged with the premiere of *Oedipus Rex* at the Kroll Opera in Berlin on 25 February 1928.

36. Emile Vuillermoz (1878–1960) was Gabriel Fauré's composition student, a friend and champion of Ravel, and one of the most important music and dance critics in France. After *Mavra*, he continued to follow Stravinsky's career and to write insightful reviews of his work. Stravinsky was so irked by this negative review that he taped it into his manuscript score of *Mavra*, now kept at the University of Illinois. See http://www.library.illinois.edu/rbx/archon/?p=collections/controlcard&id=985.

37. Vuillermoz is referring here to the "burden" of the weak libretto.

38. Vuillermoz's wordplay on ragtime and *vague* (wave).

39. "*rire et s'amuser en société*": the quotation marks indicate that Vuillermoz is referring to the French etiquette of entertaining in polite society, revealed in such books as Léo Lelièvre's *L'Art de s'amuser et de rire en société* (Paris: Librairie Populaire, 1911).

40. De Schloezer published two reviews of *Mavra*, this one in Russian and a very similar one in French. He framed the French review of *Mavra* as part of a larger overview article on recent productions by the Ballets Russes. See "La Musique: Les Ballets Russes; Trois créations: *La Belle au bois dormant* de Tchaikovsky, *Renard* et *Mavra* de Stravinsky; Quelques reprises: *Le Sacre du printemps, Pétrouchka, Contes russes, L'Après-midi d'un faune,*" *La Nouvelle Revue française* 9/106 (1 July 1922): 116–18. De Schloezer (1881–1969) was a Russian writer, translator, and musicologist who immigrated to Paris in 1921. In 1923 he published a seminal biography in Russian of his brother-in-law, Alexander Scriabin, and a decade later a monograph in French on Stravinsky, *Igor Stravinsky* (Paris: Claude Aveline, 1929). Stravinsky never forgave him for his review of *Mavra,* and complained frequently about him to friends and family. See Tamara Levitz, *Modernist Mysteries:* Perséphone (New York: Oxford University Press, 2012), 295–316, esp. 307.

41. Alexander Alyabyev (1787–1851) and Aleksey Verstovsky (1799–1862) were early Russian composers of art song.

42. A Kuchkist is somebody who belongs to the kúchka or "little heap"—a term that comes from the phrase *mogúchaya kúchka,* which Vladimir Stasov first used in 1867 to describe the "New Russian School" of composers around Balakirev. This group is commonly called the Mighty Five in English.

43. Schloezer is referring to Stravinsky's "La Belle au bois dormant: Lettre à Serge de Diaghilew," and "Une lettre de Stravinsky sur Tchaikovsky."

44. *Renard* had premiered 18 May 1922 at the Paris Opéra in a program that included Fokine's *Carnaval, Aurora's Wedding, Renard,* and the *Polovtsian Dances,* by that time a classic of the Ballets Russes repertoire. The proximity of its premiere to that of *Mavra* led many critics to compare the two works.

45. French title: "La Quinzaine musicale: "Mavra" d'Igor Stravinsky à l'Opéra—Les Ballets cambodgiens—Les Sakharoff—Concerts divers," *L'Eclair,* 5 June 1922. Alexis Roland Manuel Lévy, known always as Roland-Manuel, (1891–1966) was a French composer and critic and student of Roussel and Ravel. He later became quite close to Stravinsky, and helped him to write his *Poétique musicale.* See Valérie Dufour's article in this volume, "The *Poétique musicale*: A Counterpoint in Three Voices."

46. French title: "Au Théâtre de l'Opéra: 'Mavra': Opéra-Comique en un acte d'après Pouchkine, poème de M. Boris Kokhno, musique de M. Igor Stravinsky," *Comoedia,* 5 June 1922. This article includes three sections: this untitled first section by Laloy is followed by a section on the performance ("L'Interprétation") by Charles Tenroc and one on the sets ("Le Décor") by "R.-J." Louis Laloy (1874–1944) was one of the most important musicologists and music critics in France in the early twentieth century. He supported Stravinsky for decades, and reviewed many performances of his works.

47. Laloy's part of this article ends with an unfortunate typo. The second to last line is repeated by mistake in place of the line that should be there, leading to the creation of the nonsensical sentence: "D'un équilibre toujours insta-du à plusiers reprises, et le sera."

48. French title: "La Musique: A propos de "Mavra" de Igor Strawinsky," *Feuilles libres* 27 (June–July 1922): 223–24. Stravinsky and Poulenc had met in 1918 and became friends around the time of *Mavra*'s premiere. Stravinsky valued this review, which Poulenc sent him.

49. See Vuillermoz on "Mavra" above. Poulenc quotes the words "lacks melody" misleadingly from Vuillermoz's original sentence: "And then one notes that Stravinsky, whose rhythmic genius is prodigious, lacks terribly in melodic invention."

50. See Roland-Manuel's piece above.

51. Maurice Bex, "La Musique. A l'Opéra: Chorégraphies," *Revue hebdomadaire* (17 June 1922): 360–63. Bex's review is more sympathetic to *Mavra* than Poulenc's commentary reveals. Bex uses the expressions "torrent of syncopation" and "such ingeniously organized disorder" (misquoted by Poulenc) to describe *Renard,* not *Mavra.* Poulenc likewise quotes Bex's final sentence deceivingly. In the original, Bex writes: "And yet [*Mavra*] contains lines and even pages of delicate tenderness mixed with sudden leaps of noisy and unbridled joy as agreeable to the ear as the sight of a puppy playing is pleasant to the eye."

52. *Ecoles normales* are elite schools in France. Poulenc's neologisms and comedic tone here are reminiscent of Eric Satie's prose style.

53. Eric Satie, "Ne confondons pas," *Le Coq* 3 (July–August–September, 1920): 6. Satie lists Liszt, Chopin, Schubert, Musorgsky, Debussy, Mozart, Beethoven, and Wagner as poets, and only Rimsky-Korsakov as a pawn.

54. This expression, *sur le même plan*, points toward a harmonic system that abandons the hierarchies and tensions of tonality. Robert Craft translates this passage more fancifully (and incorrectly) in *Stravinsky: Selected Correspondence* (New York: Alfred A. Knopf), 1:158.

55. The Jockey Club and L'Epatant were elite clubs whose aristocratic members had famously attended performances at the Opéra since the nineteenth century. With "red card holders" Poulenc is referring to cards used to bet on horse races.

56. Paul Collaer met Stravinsky in 1920, and became a hugely energetic promoter of his works in Belgium. Collaer later integrated this piece on *Mavra* into the more comprehensive article he prepared for the premiere of the work in the Pro Arte's all-Stravinsky concert on 14 January 1924. See "Igor Strawinsky," *Arts et lettres d'aujourd'hui* 2/2 (13 January 1924): 23–37. Collaer and Stravinsky had a falling out in 1925, when Stravinsky rejected Collaer's monograph on his life and works. See Valérie Dufour, "Paul Collaer et Igor Strawinsky: Lettres inédites au compositeur (1920–1925)," 99–116; and *Stravinski et ses exégètes (1910–1940)* (Brussels: Editions de l'Université de Bruxelles, 2006), 200–201; as well as Paul Collaer, *Correspondance avec des amis musiciens*, ed. Robert Wangermée (Liège: Mardaga, 1996); and *Strawinsky* (Brussels: Edition "Equilibres," 1930).

57. Collaer uses the unusual expression "une pensée d'objectivisme."

58. André Derain was a French fauvist painter who in 1919 designed the sets for the Ballets Russes production of *La Boutique fantastique* (with choreography by Léonide Massine and music by Ottorino Respighi).

59. The character's actual name is Parasha, which means feces.

60. Collaer uses the French historical term *grand air* rather than the word *aria*.

61. Collaer uses the term *pudeur*, which describes a reserved behavior important in French etiquette after World War I.

62. Collaer here quotes part of Jean Cocteau's statement: "We can expect soon an orchestra without the strings' caress. A sumptuous wind band [*un riche orphéon*] of winds, brass, and percussion." See Jean Cocteau, *Le Coq et l'Arlequin: Notes autour de la musique 1918*, preface by Georges Auric (Paris: Editions Stock, 1979), 65.

63. Collaer describes the critics as "*attribés*"—a nonexistent word that is perhaps a typo. He may have intended to use the word "attribués" to qualify the critics as having been assigned to review *Parade*.

64. German title: "Strawinskijs Neue Bühnenwerke," *Musikblätter des Anbruch* 4/17–18 (November 1922): 260–62. M. M. Frank translated this review from Milhaud's French original, which has not survived in his archives and was never published.

65. The German word *Cymbal* is used for cimbalon here.

66. In German: *Kolorit und Stimmung.*

67. Milhaud did hear *Renard* on May 18, but was on vacation horseback riding and enjoying local customs in Saintes-Maries-de-la-Mer, and missed *Mavra*. "So much for *Mavra*," he wrote his friend Paul Collaer, "I prefer my horse and my evenings with the local people, fishermen or bull breeders, at the door of the little café where I am staying." Milhaud to Paul Collaer, 1 June 1922, in Collaer, *Correspondance avec des amis musiciens*, 101.

68. Paul Collaer also mentions Jean Cocteau's *orphéon* in his review of *Mavra*, which Milhaud perhaps read.

69. Milhaud quotes "italo-russo-negro-american music" from Boris de Schloezer's "La Musique: Les Ballets Russes." In his Russian review, given above, Schloezer similarly describes a "synthesis of Italo-Russian and Negro-Russian elements" in *Mavra*. Ravel is the impressionist composer who allegedly referred to *Mavra* as the new *Le Domino noir* (a reference to the popular opéra-comique by Daniel Auber from 1837). Barbara Kelly claims Ravel said this in a Spanish interview with André Révész, but Ravel does not mention *Mavra* there (see "El gran músico

Mauricio Ravel habla de su arte," *ABC*, 1 May 1924). Ravel did later criticize *Mavra* in a 1931 interview with José Bruyr (in *Le Guide du concert*, 16 October 1931), and there is much evidence he did not like it. See Barbara Kelly, *Tradition and Style in the Works of Darius Milhaud 1912–1939* (Aldershot: Ashgate, 1988), 15.

70. The section of this article starting with "The music for *Renard* is extremely lively" and ending here was translated anonymously into English as "Milhaud on Stravinsky," *The Musical Times* 64/959 (1 January 1923): 40. This excerpt omits part of the text, including Milhaud's reference to Boris de Schloezer and Ravel, and the last line about Gabriel Parès.

71. Gabriel Parès (1830–1887) was a well-known composer and military band conductor.

72. The text reprinted here was published in *Vanity Fair* 19/3 (November 1922): 51, 88. It is illustrated with Henri Rousseau's *The Snake Charmer*. The two ballets Tzara is referring to are Tchaikovsky's *Aurora's Wedding* and Stravinsky's *Renard*, performed on 18 May 1922 at the Paris Opéra.

73. I omit here Tzara's retelling of the story of *Mavra*.

74. "Louis-Philippe" describes a furniture style popular during the reign of that French king from 1830 to 1848. The style is characterized by dark wood and dressers with tulip-shaped, curved top drawers.

75. I omit here Tzara's praise for Stefan Belina-Skupevsky's and Oda Slobodskaya's performances in *Mavra*, as well as the subsection "Modernism in Hungary," in which Tzara reviews the Surrealist, Cubist, and Dadaist content of the Hungarian journal *Ma*. I also later omit his discussion of the painter Max Ernst, new "Dadaist" books, and Henri Rousseau.

76. Sonia Delaunay and Tristan Tzara began creating *robes poèmes* or "poem dresses" in 1921. Delaunay extended onto the human body the theory of *simultanisme* or "simultaneity" that she and her husband, Robert, had earlier explored in painting by juxtaposing blocks of color and words on cloth and by visualizing the dynamic rhythmic experience of modernity in women's fashion. In 1923 Delaunay established her own printing shop, Atelier simultane (1923–34), to realize her fashions.

77. In 1917, the painter Moïse Kisling and the writer Blaise Cendrars planted the seed for the formation of a musical circle around Erik Satie in a series of organized concerts at 6 rue Huyghens, where music by Erik Satie, Arthur Honegger, Georges Auric, and Louis Durey was performed, and paintings by Picasso, Juan Gris, and others were exhibited.

78. Tzara is referring to the *Congress for the Determination of the Directives and Defense of the Modern Spirit*, organized by André Breton in Paris in January 1922 with the goal of rejecting reliance on the past in art in open defiance of Jean Cocteau's "call to order" in *Le Coq et l'Arlequin*. This congress led to the split between Tzara and Breton, and between the Dadaists and the Surrealists.

79. *Le Coeur à barbe* (The bearded heart) was the only issue of a "transparent newspaper" published by Tristan Tzara in April 1922 in reply to André Breton's attacks in "Après Dada," *Comœdia*, 3 March 1922. It contains brief texts by Paul Eluard, Georges Ribemont-Dessaignes, Erik Satie, Philippe Soupault, Théodore Fraenkel, Benjamin Péret, and others who critiqued André Breton and also mocked those who said Cubism was dead. The rift between Tzara and Breton led to the official launch of Surrealism with André Breton's *Surrealist Manifesto* in 1924.

80. Erik Satie worked on the opéra-comique *Paul et Virginie* (libretto by Jean Cocteau and Raymond Radiguet) between August 1920 and 1923. He did not complete the opera and it is now lost.

81. Russian title: "Parizhskiye ocherki," *Izvestiya*, 29 March 1923. The Russian Futurist poet Vladimir Mayakovsky (1893–1930) had traveled to Paris in November 1922. I am very grateful to Maureen Carr, whose idea it was to include Mayakovsky and Cocteau in this section.

82. David Burliuk (1882–1967) was Ukrainian and a seminal figure in the Russian Futurist movement. He gave Futurist performances throughout the Soviet Union with Mayakovsky and Vasily Kamensky from December 1913 to April 1914.

83. The Assembly of Nobility was a self-governing body of the Russian aristocracy. The Moscow clubhouse of the assembly, called the House of Unions after 1917, had a concert hall with excellent acoustics, which today is called Column Hall.

84. Rachmaninoff composed the symphonic poem *Isle of the Dead*, op. 29, in 1908, inspired by Arnold Böcklin's famous painting of the same name. Here Mayakovsky is being cynical about the class premises of classical music.

85. Stravinsky had been given a studio in the Pleyel piano factory in February 1921, possibly as part of his five-year contract with the company, which began in May 1920. He kept the studio until 1933.

86. Gustave Lyon (1857–1936) took over management of the Pleyel factory in 1887. He was known for his research into acoustics and inventions (including the double piano) and became a *chevalier* of the Légion d'honneur in 1889.

87. These are excerpts from *The Nightingale*.

88. Etude for pianola.

89. Mayakovsky is referring to the period before Prokofiev left Russia in 1918.

90. French title: "Stravinsky dernière heure," *La Revue musicale* 5/2 (1 December 1923): 142–45. This essay is accompanied by a drawing with the caption "Igor Stravinsky playing *The Rite of Spring* drawn by Jean Cocteau in 1913."

91. Cocteau refers here to a shift in discourse in countries ravaged by crisis or revolution, when the pictorial symbolism of the rebus becomes capable of countering official speech. Tzara uses the rebus in *Le Coeur à barbe.*

92. Cocteau refers to the percussion instruments that surround Stravinsky in his Pleyel studio as *appareils* (devices or appliances), thereby drawing a connection between art music and mechanical means of production. The "thunderstorm" is the creative idea in Stravinsky's mind that will be given shape by these instruments. "Oriental Romanticism" describes the style of works like *The Rite of Spring*, the exuberance of which Stravinsky reins in after World War I with neoclassical rules

93. Here Cocteau added the footnote, "Today, Francis Poulenc."

94. *Les Noces* was premiered at the Théâtre de la Gaîté in Paris on 13 June 1923. Although premiered after *Mavra*, it was composed earlier.

95. Russian title: "Dve Operï Stravinskogo," *Vyorstï* 3 (1928): 109–26. This article originally had two sections: one, translated here, on *Mavra*, and the other on *Oedipus Rex*. Boris de Schloezer translated the part on *Oedipus Rex* into French as "Oedipus Rex de Strawinsky," *La Revue musicale* 8/8 (August 1927): 240–53. It appeared in German to coincide with the performance at the Kroll Opera as "Oedipus Rex: Opera-Oratorium nach Sophokles von Igor Strawinsky," *Blätter der Staatsoper und der Städtischen Oper* 8/19 (February 1928): 9–13.

96. Lourié does not seem fully aware that *Mavra* received its premiere with *The Rite of Spring* and *Petrushka*.

97. Lourié's anti-modernism is evident in the two documents that can be found in the section in this volume titled "Lourié's Eurasianist and Neo-Thomist Responses to the Crisis of Art." His attitude toward modernism—and with it, we can assume, Les Six—differed significantly from Stravinsky's. Lourié's understanding of modernism was strongly influenced by Jacques Maritain, and centered on rejecting art that was divorced from human experience (and hence from religious purpose as he interpreted it). Stravinsky, in contrast, primarily disliked only the term "modernism," which he felt unnecessarily emphasized the new and gave an inadequate frame to cultural production in his time. Here Lourié appears to reject the very composers Stravinsky remained friends with throughout the 1930s, including Francis Poulenc. Richard Taruskin views this differently, however, seeing Lourié's and Stravinsky's relationships to modernism as basically interchangeable in *Stravinsky and the Russian Traditions*, 2:1584–91.

98. Vasily Trutovsky (1740–1810) was a Ukrainian folksong collector who published the first printed collection of Russian folksongs, *Sobraniye russkikh prostïkh pesen s notami* (1779).

99. Apollon Grigoryev (1822–1864) was a Russian poet and author of romances.

Stravinsky's Russian Library

TATIANA BARANOVA MONIGHETTI

Those who knew Stravinsky well remember him as a passionate, insatiable reader. Photographs depict him reading—on trains and planes, during concert intermissions, lounging in hotels, and in bed before going to sleep. Stravinsky customarily read books with his first wife, Yekaterina, and their children; later, he continued this tradition with his second wife, Vera. He discussed book purchases in his correspondence; Vera, too, mentioned Stravinsky's books in her diary. Stravinsky bought books regularly and in large quantities, and had done so ever since his youth in St. Petersburg. In spite of the losses that may have occurred when he moved from Europe to the United States in 1939 (the number of books he brought with him when he emigrated is unknown), his library in Los Angeles included between nine and ten thousand volumes, most of them in English, fewer in French, and even fewer in Russian. The young librarian Edwin Allen had intended to catalogue them when Stravinsky and Vera moved to a new home in September 1964, but found that because of their large number there was never time to do it.[1] Robert Craft inherited Stravinsky's library after Vera's death in 1982, and sold part of it (approximately 700 books and 1,000 musical scores) to the Paul Sacher Stiftung in 1990.[2] The notes and markings Stravinsky left on these books give lasting evidence of his habits, attitudes, affections, and prejudices.

Stravinsky inherited his passion for books from his father, Fyodor Ignatyevich, an outstanding Russian bass singer at the Mariinsky Theatre in St. Petersburg and a friend of Tchaikovsky's and Dostoevsky's. Fyodor Stravinsky considered book collecting a second calling: he attended meetings for bibliophiles, befriended renowned booksellers, studied rare editions, and, in the last twenty years of his life, built up a unique collection that came to be considered among the best in Russia. His library included thousands of volumes on Russian literature and history, philosophy, religion, law, politics, economics, European history, folklore studies, music, and the fine arts. It also contained bibliographies, encyclopedias, periodicals, scores (including about two hundred operas), and rare first editions.[3] If, as Pyotr Suvchinsky has suggested, the secret of Stravinsky's genius lay in the "mysterious unexpectedness and the marvel of his appearance in the music of Russia and the world," then his father's library probably had a lot to do with that.[4]

Figure 1. Fyodor Stravinsky in his library.

Yet Fyodor's library suffered a tragic fate.[5] After the 1917 Bolshevik Revolution, the Soviet authorities recognized the library as part of their national heritage, and, thanks to the intervention of Arthur Lourié, allowed Fyodor's widow, Anna Kirillovna, to keep it in the family apartment under her supervision.[6] When she emigrated from Russia in 1922, her oldest son Yury (Stravinsky's older brother) took over its supervision. Forced to live with his family in one room of the "communal" apartment, Yury sold off parts of the library. He gave a large collection of about 1,400 engravings to the State Public Saltykov-Shchedrin Library (today the National Library of Russia), sold sheet music to the St. Petersburg State Conservatory Music Library, and offered some items to individual collectors. The Stravinsky family was evacuated from St. Petersburg (Leningrad) during the blockade, and when they returned in 1944 they found the apartment sacked and the library plundered.[7]

Heirlooms

Fyodor Stravinsky died in 1902. One of the greatest legacies he left to his son Igor was his collection of anthologies of Russian folklore. Luckily, Stravinsky saved a few of these anthologies before he knew the rest of his father's library would be lost forever. These volumes, which Stravinsky probably brought to Switzerland in 1914, miraculously survived the Russian Revolution, two wars, and two changes in citizenship. They have fascinated scholars for some time because of the clues they provide to the folk sources he borrowed for his own music, and of the insight they bring to the composer's broader ethnographic interests. They include Ivan Sakharov's *Pesni russkogo naroda* (Songs of the Russian people), 1838–39, and Daniil Kashin's *Russkiye narodnïye pesni sobrannïye i izdannïye dlya peniya i fortepiano* (Russian folksongs collected and edited for voice and piano), 1833–34, as well as Alexander Afanasyev's *Narodnïye russkïye skazki* (Russian folktales), 1873, and *Poēticheskiye vozzreniya slavyan na prirodu* (The Slavs' poetic outlook on nature), 1865–69.[8]

Scholars first became interested in Sakharov's works in the 1980s, when Irina Vershinina discovered that Stravinsky had borrowed the lyrics for his *Podblyudnïe* (*Four Russian Peasant Songs*) from Sakharov's *Skazaniya russkogo naroda* (Legends of the Russian people).[9] Trusting Vershinina's conclusions, many scholars subsequently cited this source as a reference work important to Stravinsky.[10] As Robert Craft noted in 1986, however, the book that Stravinsky actually owned was Sakharov's *Songs of the Russian People*.[11] This much rarer edition of five elegant miniature octavo volumes originally belonged to Stravinsky's father, who had found them valuable enough to bind in expensive leather with press gilding and his initials "ΘC" (FS). These books accompanied Stravinsky throughout his life, and the handwritten annotations in them give evidence that he studied them carefully. Stravinsky added the name "Sakharov" to the initials "I. S." at the end of the preface, corrected the incorrect pagination in the table of contents, and lightly underlined in pencil the song "Ladushka nasha milaya" (Our beloved sweet), which he used in the preliminary scenario of Act II ("At the Bride's") of *Les Noces*.[12] He penciled in the letters "ABAC" next to another song that he used in *Les Noces*, "Ne klich', ne klich', lebedushka" (Don't you cry, swan), hinting at the musical structure he would give the poem.[13]

Stravinsky also placed thin, red silk bookmarks in between the songs "Shchuka" (The pike) and "Ovsen" in the volume 1 section of Sakharov's collection on *Podblyudnïe* or dish-divination songs.[14] He used these in his *Four Russian Peasant Songs* (1914–17). He places similar bookmarks in volumes 3 and 4 for the songs "To Mihayle pesenka" (Song for Mikhalya; likely for use in *Les Noces*) and the lullaby "Bayu bayushki bayu" (Lulla lulla lullaby), the fifth verse of which resembles the fourth of Stravinsky's *Berceuses du chat*, "U kota kota" ("The cat has, he has").[15] These bookmarks and pencil markings leave no doubt that Stravinsky was working with this edition.

Stravinsky left similar traces of his engagement with folksong in his copy of the 1833 edition of Daniil Kashin's *Russian Folk Songs*. This volume contains lyrics and melodies arranged in the sentimental mode of the *rossiyskaya pesnya*, or urban Russian songs, with functional tonal harmony. Stravinsky definitely used Kashin's edition when composing *Mavra*, as Richard Taruskin has demonstrated, but he may also have used it earlier.[16] His annotations reveal his interest not only in the *rossiyskaya pesnya* but also in the lyrics of dance and wedding songs, an older folk genre. That so many of the same titles are marked in pencil in the table of contents of both Kashin's and Sakharov's books shows that Stravinsky compared the songs in them. Taruskin, drawing on Craft's description of an inscription on the first page of this volume, assumes that Stravinsky may have admired it more than he did. That inscription reads: "A very rare book, one of the best collections of Russian songs." Taruskin thought this phrase conveyed "some of the bravado of the *Mavra* period." "As [Stravinsky] knew very well, it was a book his teacher, for one, would have called one of the worst collections, and for the very reasons that made it now so precious to the latter's former pupil."[17] The modest handwritten note, however, neither conveys bravado nor was it likely in Stravinsky's hand. After comparing it with Stravinsky's sweeping autograph on the preceding page, I concluded that it was not Stravinsky, but rather Fyodor or somebody else, perhaps the bookseller, who wrote the note.[18]

The jewels of Stravinsky's folklore collection are Afanasyev's *The Slav's Poetic Outlook on Nature* and the second edition of his *Russian Folktales*—both bibliographic rarities.[19] Taruskin stresses the historical importance for Stravinsky of the first, which Rimsky-Korsakov called "the pantheistic Bible of the Slavonic peoples."[20] As for the second edition of *Russian Folktales*, it became a coveted rarity after Afanasyev's death on account of the new classification system he created for it. The binding for the four volumes of *Folktales* is similar to, though less lavish than, that of Sakharov's *Songs*, including marbled paper, press gilding, and Stravinsky's father's initials "ѲС" (FS). Stravinsky appears to have begun using this book while still in Russia; inscriptions in it date back to the time of the *Firebird*. He left a check mark beside a colorful description of Baba-Yaga arriving in Usïnya-bogatïr, as well as the epic *bïlinas* (epic poems) "Ilya Muromets i Zmey" (Ilya Muromets and the dragon) and "Alyosha Popovich."[21] In volume 4 he marks with a slanted cross the commentaries in the table of contents for "Baba-Yaga," "Koshchey Bessmertnïy" (Deathless Koshchey), "Ivanushka-durachok" (Ivanushka the fool), and "Ivan-durak" (Stupid Ivan).[22] He also adds another conspicuous mark to this book by penciling in the word *zaperdel* (farted) in a line of "Lisa ispovednitsa" (The fox confessor). By filling in the ellipsis introduced by the censors, he transformed the original "Don't you know that Yermak began . . . on an empty stomach?" into "Don't you know that Yermak began farting on an empty stomach?"[23] He retained *zaperdel* in his subsequent sketches for *Renard*, although in the published score it was replaced with *zatreshchal* (crackled).[24]

Marginalia

Stravinsky's marginalia reveal his likes and dislikes, allegiances and disloyalties, and provide a compelling record of his reading process, which was strongly dialogical. His marginalia in Boris Asafyev's 1929 monograph *Kniga o Stravinskom* (*A Book about Stravinsky*, published under Asafyev's pen name Igor Glebov), stand out for their abundance, and have for this reason received tremendous attention in the secondary literature.[25] Yet in spite of this keen interest, no scholar has yet transcribed them accurately.[26] These marginalia have led to confusion about whether Stravinsky approved of Asafyev's monograph; they point toward the ambiguity that such a critical process of reading can bring. Clearly Stravinsky had not appreciated Asafyev's earlier volumes on *Rimsky-Korsakov* (1923) and *The Symphonic Etudes* (1922)—both of which he owned (they are now in the Paul Sacher Stiftung). *The Symphonic Etudes* includes direct criticism of himself. "I read what [Asafyev] wrote on Rimsky and Tchaikovsky," he wrote Ernest Ansermet in 1928, "and I was very surprised to discover that he belongs rather to the André Rimsky and Steinberg clan than to the one opposing that nest of old wasps."[27] Stravinsky made forty-nine comments in the margins of *Kniga o Stravinskom*, many of them harsh. Over half consist of corrections of musical examples, spelling, and titles of works, and about ten express disagreements with Asafyev over fundamental ideological and aesthetic issues. There are also six positive comments—Craft admits to only one and Varunts to two—that touch on such significant issues as the role of accents in music, the accompaniment in *Mavra*, and the plasticity of intonational gestures in instrumental music.[28] Nevertheless, Stravinsky may have been partially flattered by Asafyev's monograph, or at least influenced by the positive impressions it made on his closest friends.[29] The

Russian pianist and musicologist Mikhail Druskin remembered Stravinsky commenting in 1931 that Asafyev "feels my music well." In 1934, Prokofiev reported happily to Asafyev that Stravinsky had answered "Glebov's" when asked which book about himself he considered the best.[30] And yet as an old man he opposed its publication in English—an attitude that led Suvchinsky to believe that he "hated" it, as Suvchinsky wrote in a letter to Maria Yudina.[31]

Stravinsky's marginalia in Modest Tchaikovsky's three-volume biography of his brother Pyotr document Stravinsky's engagement with Russian music, literature, and thought.[32] Stravinsky famously adored Tchaikovsky; in his later years he kept the composer's scores in a special cabinet reserved for his own and Webern's music.[33] He may have been familiar with Modest Tchaikovsky's biography since he was a young man, but he seems to have acquired the copy kept in his library later in life. The book's many previous owners had marked it up, rendering it difficult to determine which pencil marks and comments Stravinsky added himself. The witty remark, "what nonsense, *c'est un lieu commun,*"[34] next to Tolstoy's alleged comment to Tchaikovsky about the pitfalls of sacrificing one's inner convictions to pleasing the public seems to come from Stravinsky, given its similarity to his comments and handwriting elsewhere.[35] Other underlined words, vertical strokes next to passages, and the abbreviation *NB* (nota bene) also seem to originate with Stravinsky, given how closely the passages they highlight are in tune with his own biography and thought. He may have marked the chapter on Tchaikovsky's legal studies, for example, given that his parents, like Tchaikovsky's, had tried to persuade him to study law. Other marks likely made by Stravinsky include those highlighting the lines in which Modest describes Tchaikovsky as "hopeless at mathematics" or as an "incorrigible smoker."[36] Surely Stravinsky marked the passage about his own father, Fyodor, and the sections of the book dealing with Tchaikovsky's religious experience.[37] He also was probably the one who heavily underlined Tchaikovsky's comment that Mozart, Beethoven, Schubert, Mendelssohn, Schumann "composed their immortal works exactly as a shoemaker makes shoes; that is to say, day in, day out, and for most part to order"—the very lines he quotes in his *Chroniques de ma vie* with the added exclamation, rare for him, that "he is so right!"[38] I suspect that even if he didn't mark them all he would have liked passages that describe Tchaikovsky's opinions on Wagner, musical craft, commissions, form, metaphysical inspiration, the creative process, and the quest for compositional solutions—opinions that mirror his own views as expressed through his (and Roland-Manuel and Pyotr Suvchinsky's) *Poétique musicale.*[39]

Ephemera

Ephemera—newspapers tucked away in old books, invitations pressed between pages as temporary bookmarks, and countless other material traces—can offer information on the composer to complement the carefully worded, impeccably structured, ghostwritten essays and books he left to the world. They help solve dilemmas about dating, authorship, or compositional intentions, and offer glimpses into the composer's intimate, human presence. Ephemera offer insight, for example, into Stravinsky's relationship to the Russian poet he loved the most, Alexander Pushkin. Stravinsky had grown up with Pushkin; his father collected Pushkin rarities and knew Pyotr Yefremov, whose eighth edition of Pushkin's works was part of Stravinsky's library.[40] Stravinsky may have inherited these volumes from his father's collection, although it is clear that the marginalia in them belong to neither father nor son. These volumes include Pushkin's "Tucha" ("The Storm Cloud"), upon which Stravinsky set his first song, the first version of "Favn i pastushka" (*The Faun and the Shepherdess*), and "Domik v Kolomnè" ("The Little House in Kolomna"), the short story upon which he based *Mavra*.[41]

And yet it is not only this impressive edition that catches the eye in Stravinsky's library but a small pamphlet by Stravinsky titled "Pushkin: Poetry and Music," written in 1937 for the centennial of Pushkin's death and reprinted in Eric White's classic Stravinsky biography.[42] The Paul Sacher Stiftung owns an unsigned typescript of a French original of this essay with handwritten corrections. But who wrote this article? The answer comes in a letter of 4 January 1937 from Stravinsky's daughter Lyudmila (Mika) and her husband, Yury Mandelshtam. "Tomorrow morning," Mika writes to Stravinsky, "Yura is going to visit Mama and Grandma. There he will meet Irina Terapiano, to whom he will dictate 'his' article, or rather 'your' article on Pushkin. He is sending [the article] with this letter. I think you'll like it since Yura has struck just the right tone he needs when he claims to communicate your opinions." On the left top corner of the letter Yury adds: "I'm sending you here the Pushkin text. The exact date of his death is 23 January in the old style and 10 February by the new calendar. I'll be very happy if this all works. I apologize, Igor Fyodorovich, for the poor typescript. I dictated it to I. K. Terapiano and I didn't have time to have it retyped. She misspelled a few words and even made mistakes, which I had to correct by hand. There was nothing else I could do: in order to send the letter with the *Aquitania*, I have had to send it *telle quelle*. It comforts me that this will serve for translation purposes only, and is not intended for immediate publication. Yu."[43] Busy touring the United States for the third time between December 1936 and April 1937, Stravinsky had leaned on his son-in-law, a professional writer and graduate student at the Sorbonne, to write a laudation for Pushkin. In spite of the fact that he didn't write the essay himself, he must have cared about having his name on it and about celebrating Pushkin's centenary.

Stravinsky's deceptive authorial strategies remained invisible to his contemporaries yet produced a paper trail that allows scholars today to clarify authorship. An omission in the Russian translation of Stravinsky's ghostwritten Pushkin essay offers a lead to solving another mystery of Stravinsky scholarship.[44] This translation was published in the early years of Perestroika, but was probably prepared in the Soviet era, which may explain why its editor, Viktor Varunts, omitted two passages that might have displeased Soviet authorities. The first is the line "Pushkin as the father of the Russian Revolution," and the second is a passage on Marxist commentators of Pushkin that includes a reference to Stravinsky's critique of sociological approaches to Beethoven in *Chroniques de ma vie*. Neither Svetlana Savenko nor Irina Vershinina ever found the source for the piece of Soviet criticism Stravinsky so diligently critiqued in that work, and which was problematic enough to be omitted in the first Russian translation of the *Chroniques* in 1963.[45]

Leafing through Stravinsky's own copy of the second volume of his *Chroniques* (dated by the composer 15 December 1935), I came across a surprising discovery: a folded copy of Ivan Sollertinsky's original article on Beethoven from the Soviet newspaper *Izvestiya*, quoted by the composer in the book.[46] Stravinsky had clearly read this article, identifying it as "*Izvestiya*, 1 May 1935." He also vigorously crossed out a line that he did not cite: "Beethoven is out of favor in the West now. Even the modern musical trendsetter Igor Stravinsky denies him the title of great composer." This piece of random ephemera reveals that Stravinsky's invective against Soviet music criticism may have originated in a personal, gut response to what he considered a public insult.

Ephemera and marginalia not only allow scholars to answer unsolved biographical mysteries, but also offer fascinating insight into Stravinsky's religious faith. A well-worn, pocket-size prayer book signed and dated "Nice, 1926" includes many notes and a piece of graph paper with the handwritten Russian Orthodox prayer one says before taking any action. The handwriting is that of Yekaterina Stravinsky, Igor's first wife.[47] Stravinsky underlined verses in the Book of Job in a Russian Bible acquired around the same time.[48] Stravinsky's confessor in Nice, Nikolay Podosenov, had compared him to Job, "who lost his children, glory and wealth in a flash." Podosenov encouraged him to follow Job's example in condolence letters he sent first after the death of Stravinsky's daughter in December 1938, and of his wife in June 1939.[49] A sheet of paper slipped between the pages of this Bible contains the handwritten Latin text to Stravinsky's *Threni* in the composer's own hand. Stravinsky also read theological and philosophical books including Viktor Nesmelov's *Nauka o cheloveke* (The science of man), and wrote two notes—"Great!" and "Absolutely true," in the sections on doubt in faith and the relationship between religion and scientific thought.[50] Dedications in two books from Stravinsky's library and a tiny note, preserved at Amherst College, attests to Stravinsky's acquaintance with Archbishop Ioann Shakhovskoy—a prominent figure in the Russian Orthodox Church in America.[51] Finally, though Robert Craft claims that Stravinsky stopped attending church in the mid-1950s, and though Vera's and Igor's diaries also stop mentioning communions, prayer services (*moleben*), and funeral services (*panikhida*) at this time, an Orthodox Calendar for 1967 in the Paul Sacher Stiftung with underlined holy days of certain saints, Lent, and Easter hints at Stravinsky's continued Orthodox piety in old age.[52]

Dedications

Many of the Russian books in Stravinsky's library include handwritten dedications. Like Stravinsky's marginalia and carefully preserved newspaper clippings, these books' signings tell a hidden story of human connections through the medium of the printed word. Some of the most moving dedications in Stravinsky's library are by Aleksey Remizov (1877–1957), an astonishing Russian writer whom Stravinsky never met, though Remizov provided materials for *The Firebird*, and in 1914 Stravinsky expressed a wish to collaborate with him.[53] Remizov's highly original works make up a large portion of the Russian section of the library at the Paul Sacher Stiftung. Stravinsky had bought some books in Cambridge, Massachusetts; others were sent from the French publishing house Opleshnik in 1957, at Pyotr Suvchinsky's request.[54] Two of the books include beautiful handwritten dedications by their author.[55] The volume *Tristan i Isol'da: Bova korolevich* (Tristan and Isolde: Bova the prince), contains a dedication Remizov wrote just two days before his death, when he was virtually blind: "To Igor Fyodorovich Stravinsky, my genius of a contemporary, in my world of music, full of sound . . . in this breath of life I preserve my entire life. Aleksey Remizov, 24 July 1957" (see Figure 2).

"I suddenly found Remizov's book on my table," Stravinsky wrote Suvchinsky upon discovering Remizov's inscription. "No one knows how it got there. A miracle. That was *Tristan i Isol'da* with an autograph for me, written in a calligraphic scribble by a poor, blind old man. It's very hard to make out what was written, apart from my own name, of course. That's very disappointing. Most probably he is responding to the gift I sent him on his birthday, which I tried to send with your help. I'm also sending you this letter to ask you to buy me all twelve of his books published by Opleshnik and listed on the last page of the book he sent."[56] Suvchinsky replied that, yes, "poor Remizov is very, very ill. I asked the Opleshnik publishers (they are a small, primitive company) to send you Remizov's books. . . . Remizov received your check some time ago; he was very grateful for it and sent you the book as a gesture of thanks, but he cannot write anymore."[57]

About forty of the books in Stravinsky's library in the Paul Sacher Stiftung were gifts from friends and strangers in the Soviet Union. A few sent their offerings before Stravinsky traveled there in 1962, paving the way emotionally for his return home. The pianist Maria Yudina and conductor Igor Blazhkov played a pivotal role in establishing the exchange of books with Stravinsky, starting in 1959.[58] During this period of intense state propaganda, Soviet citizens valued great classical and modern literature and waited in long lines to purchase it. "It would be unimaginable to think of 'procuring' this volume [of Pasternak I sent you] in an ordinary bookstore," Yudina wrote Suvchinsky in 1961, explaining this situation. "There were thousands of people in line, each signing in when it was their turn. Books were thrown on the market [*vibrasïvali*, Soviet slang for "making rare goods available for purchase"] only a hundred copies at a time,

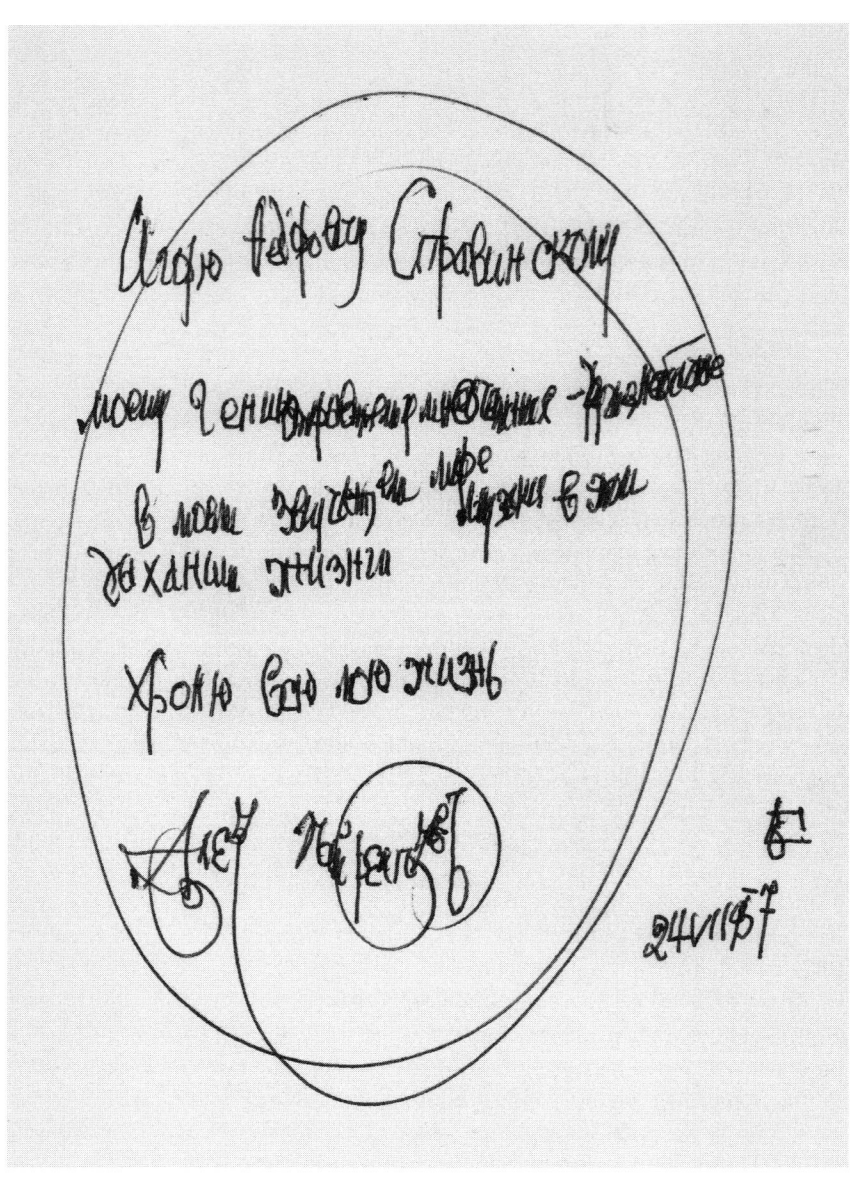

Figure 2. Dedication to Stravinsky, written by the author, in Stravinsky's copy of
Aleksey Remizov's *Tristan i Isol'da: Bova korolevich* (Paris: Opleshnik, 1957).

and each of us, with God's help, procured a copy."[59] It proved equally difficult to send books. Yudina never received the first scores Stravinsky sent and twice tried, unsuccessfully, to send him Vladimir Favorsky's etchings, once through Leonard Bernstein and another time through Van Cliburn.[60] "I think it would be better to send letters and parcels to I. F. directly, or through me," Suvchinsky subsequently warned her. "The truth of the matter is that all these Cliburns and Bernsteins are not friends. Igor Fyodorovich himself is very harsh in his relationships, and very rarely 'befriends' anybody."[61] A year later Suvchinsky warned again: "Do not send valuable books, except with responsible people."[62] Yudina subsequently chose to correspond directly with the composer, who also sent her scores.[63] Indeed, Yudina sent Stravinsky many interesting and rare books, and also encouraged others to send gifts.[64] She understood this as a way of showing gratitude for the music Stravinsky sent her, which she immediately programmed on her concerts.

Through Yudina, Stravinsky came to know current Soviet scholarship, and gained access to Russian sources not necessarily available to him otherwise. Yudina sent him Valerian Bogdanov-Berezovsky's book on his father, for example, which he may have read with great interest if the underlined lines in it are any indication.[65] After receiving Suvchinsky's request to find out which Balmont edition Stravinsky had used for his *Zvezdolikiy* or *Le Roi des étoile*s,[66] Yudina also arranged to send to Stravinsky a copy of it signed by her close friend, the poet's daughter from his first marriage, Nina Bruni-Balmont, and also signed originally by the poet himself.[67]

The channels of communication with friends and family in the Soviet Union opened significantly after Stravinsky's visit there in fall 1962. His family ties were strengthened through his contact with his late brother Yury's daughter Xenia Stravinsky, who subsequently sent him art books. During his visit, friends, family, and strangers bound themselves to him through books, considered material mementos of a past they all shared. Yudina bid him farewell with the gift of a book by Metropolit Moskovskiy Filaret, for example, in which she wrote the sorrowful dedication "Moscow. The sad day of saying good-bye. To our dearest Igor Fyodorovich in memory of two remarkable Russian people. 10 October 62."[68] Besides herself, she was referring to the Russian Orthodox philosopher and theologian Pavel Florensky, who had also signed this book.[69] Sadly, Florensky's autograph was destroyed when the Paul Sacher Stiftung had the book bound in Basel; only a photocopy of it remains.

Welcomed by the highest echelons of the Soviet government after his official visit, Stravinsky ceased to be a *persona non grata*, his work no longer rigidly forbidden as the subject of scholarly inquiry. Friends, but also strangers and former enemies began sending him gifts. After his departure, Blazhkov sent him the first Russian translation of his *Chroniques de ma vie* with a preface by Valerian Bogdanov-Berezovsky.[70] "I am pleased with the Russian translation," he wrote Blazhkov, "but I cannot say the same for Bogdanov-Berezovsky's preface; he is far from empathetic

Figure 3. Stravinsky in his library, photograph signed "Paola Foa 1945."

to my music and to 'the progressive art of the bourgeois West' to which he thinks I belong. There are quite a few Bogdanov-Berezovskys in Soviet Russia, a country that has been free of Stalin for only eleven years."[71] Boris Yarustovsky—a former foe, party functionary, and right-hand man of Tikhon Khrennikov, who made his career in the 1948 campaign against "formalist" composers—sent Stravinsky the monograph he had written, inscribed, "To the renowned creator, from a modest Russian musicologist, this little product of an imperfect mind. October 1964."[72] And a few years later Blazhkov, a loyal friend, sent him Irina Vershinina's *Ranniye baletï Stravinskogo* (Stravinsky's early ballets), which Stravinsky liked and read carefully, as two comments in the margins attest.[73]

After 1962, Stravinsky retained his unfaltering interest in all things Russian. Despite declining health, he eagerly welcomed guests from the Soviet Union.[74] He also regularly bought Soviet books. One, the selected works of Mikhail Lermontov, contains one of the last signatures written in the trembling hand of an old, dying man: "Property of Igor Stravinsky, 7 November 1970."

NOTES

I would like to thank Ulrich Mosch, Carlos Chanfon, Claudia Grzonka, and Johanna Blask at the Paul Sacher Stiftung (hereafter abbreviated as PSS) and Silvie Visinand at the Fondation Théodore Strawinsky for their tremendous assistance. I also thank Richard Taruskin for his support and valuable advice, and Tamara Levitz for her selfless editing.

1. See Edwin Allen, "The Genius and the Goddess," in *Confronting Stravinsky: Man, Musician, and Modernist*, ed. Jann Pasler (Berkeley: University of California Press, 1986), 330.

2. This part of Stravinsky's library is available to the public but has yet to be studied systematically. Robert Craft created a catalogue of fifty-six titles that include Stravinsky's autograph or annotations, but it contains mistakes and inaccuracies. See Craft, "Appendix: Selected Source Material from 'A Catalogue of Books and Music Inscribed to and/or Autographed and Annotated by Igor Stravinsky,'" in Pasler, *Confronting Stravinsky*, 349–57.

3. Stravinsky remembered that his father's library included 7,000 to 8,000 books. See Robert Craft and Igor Stravinsky, *Expositions and Developments* (Berkeley: University of California Press, 1959), 49. Sergey Naumov, the son of a famous bookseller in St. Petersburg, thought the library included 12,000 titles and even more volumes. See *I. F. Stravinskiy: Perepiska s russkimi korrespondentami. Materialï k biografii* (Igor Stravinsky: Russian correspondence. Materials for a biography), ed. Viktor Varunts (Moscow: Kompozitor, 1998), Appendix I, 1:412 (hereafter *SPRK*).

4. Pierre Souvtchinsky and John Warrack, "Stravinsky as a Russian," *Tempo* 81 (Summer 1967): 5.

5. See Abram Gozenpud, "Fyodor Ignat'yevich Stravinskiy: Chelovek i khudozhnik" (Fyodor Stravinsky: Person and artist); and Kseniya Stravinskya, "Chto ya slïshala o moyom dede F. I. Stravinskom" (What I heard about my grandfather, Fyodor Stravinsky)," in *Fyodor Stravinskiy: Stat'i, pis'ma, vospominaniya* (Fyodor Stravinsky: Articles, letters, and memoires), ed. Larisa Kutateladze (Leningrad: Muzïka, 1972), 7–52, 75–81; and Nataliya Braginskaya, "Sledï legendarnoy biblioteki: o klavirakh Berlioza iz biblioteki F. I. Stravinskogo v notnom sobranii Sankt-Peterburgskoy konservatorii" (Traces of a legendary library: Berlioz's vocal scores from Fyodor Stravinsky's collection in the St. Petersburg Conservatory Music Library)," *Opera musicologica* 2/4 (2010): 21–40.

6. *SPRK*, 2:453.

7. Today Yury's descendants still own a few random volumes by Dostoevsky, Goncharov, and Tolstoy, and some arias by Glinka, Tchaikovsky, and Rubinstein. Nataliya Braginskaya discovered in the St. Petersburg State Conservatory two piano scores containing signatures and notes by Fyodor Stravinsky—Hector Berlioz's *La Damnation de Faust* and *Les Troyens*. See Braginskaya, "Sledï legendarnoy biblioteki," 24.

8. Ivan Sakharov, *Pesni russkogo naroda*, 5 vols. (St. Petersburg: V tipografii Sakharova, 1838–39); Daniil Kashin, *Russkiye narodnïye pesni, sobrannïye i izdannïye dlya peniya i fortepiano*, 3 vols. (Moscow: Tipografiya Semena Selivanovskago, 1833–34), kept in the PSS; Aleksander Afanas'yev, *Narodnïye russkiye skazki*, 2nd ed., revised by Koz'ma Soldatenkov, 4 vols. (Moscow: Izdatel'stvo Soldatenkova, 1873); Aleksandr Afanas'yev, *Poèticheskiye vozzreniya slavyan na prirodu*, 3 vols, (Moscow: Izdatel'stvo Soldatenkova, 1865–69). Both works of Afanasyev are kept at the Fondation Théodore Strawinsky. To my disappointment, I did not find either Pyotr Kireyevskiy's *Pesni, sobrannïye P. V. Kireyevskim: Novaya seriya*, vol. 1: *Pesni obryadnïye* (Songs collected by P. V. Kireyevskiy: New series, vol. 1:

Wedding songs) a book very important to Stravinsky, or Tereshchenko's *Bït russkogo naroda* (Manners and customs of the Russian people), 1848. Varunts erroneously lists the latter as part of the collection in the PSS in *SPRK*, 2:275n4.

9. See Vershinina's comments in Igor' Stravinskiy, *Vokal'naya muzïka*, ed. Irina Vershinina (Moscow: Kompozitor, 1988), 2:295.

10. Taruskin cites this source in *Stravinsky and the Russian Traditions: A Biography of the Works through* Mavra (Berkeley: University of California Press, 1996), 2:1138–42, 1341, 1424. See also *SPRK*, 2:275.

11. This edition includes the same content as the *Skazaniya* (Legends), and thus the error of those who cite the latter is not egregious.

12. Sakharov, *Pesni russkogo naroda*, no. 229, 3:331. Taruskin published this scenario in his book but claimed erroneously that this song found its way into the final score at rehearsal number 9. See Taruskin, *Stravinsky and the Russian Traditions*, 2:1341,1424. In fact Stravinsky used another song, "Ne klich', ne klich', lebedushka," in the final score.

13. Sakharov, *Pesni russkogo naroda*, no. 164, 3:152. In the score (rehearsal numbers 9–16), Stravinsky adds another A section in the music and also distributes the lines of the poem differently, creating an ABACA form. Instead of including four lines in section A, two in section B, four in A, and four in C as he originally indicated he might as per the square brackets he jotted next to the poem in Sakharov's book, he set four, two, five, six, and five lines respectively to sections ABACA of the music, inserting an additional eleventh line into the poem himself.

14. Sakharov, *Pesni russkogo naroda*, 1:74. The Russian title "Ovsen," is a nonsense word.

15. Ibid., no.107, 3:174–175; and no.1, 4: 395. See Taruskin, *Stravinsky and the Russian Traditions*, 2:1215–20.

16. Taruskin, *Stravinsky and the Russian Traditions*, 2:1559–60.

17. Ibid., 2:1559. See Craft's original remark in "Selected Source Material," 350.

18. Stravinsky acquired the third folklore collection at the PSS, Matvey Bernard's *Pesni russkogo naroda* (1847; repr., Moscow: Jurgenson, 1886), in a second-hand bookstore in the United States in 1942. See Taruskin, *Stravinsky and the Russian Tradition*, 2:1626–48.

19. Viktor Varunts and Svetlana Savenko claim erroneously that Stravinsky brought another edition of *Narodnïye russkiye skazki* back to Switzerland from Kiev in July 1914. Varunts cites a non-existent edition of this volume (*SPRK*, 2:274), whereas Savenko claims Stravinsky bought Aleksey Gruzinskiy's *Russkie narodnïye skazki A. N. Afanas'yeva* (Moscow: Ivan Sïtin, 1913–14). See Svetlana Savenko, *Mir Stravinskogo* (Moscow: Kompozitor, 2001), 33.

20. Taruskin, *Stravinsky and the Russian Traditions*, 1:568, 880.

21. See "Baba-Yaga," no. 81 in Afanasyev's *Russian Folktales*, 1:375. Stravinsky ticks off "Ilya Muromets i Zmey" and "Alyosha Popovich" twice—in the table of contents of both volumes 3 and 4.

22. Respectively, nos. 58, 93, 224, and 234 in vol. 4 of Afanasyev's *Russian Folktales*.

23. "Sister Fox" is no. 4c in Afansyev's *Russian Folktales*, vol:1, 31. Stravinsky changes "Vedaesh', Ermak . . . natoshchak?" into "Vedaesh', Ermak zaperdel natoshchak?"

24. Taruskin notes that Stravinsky used this word in his sketches and changed it in the published score in *Stravinsky and the Russian Traditions*, 2:1262.

25. Igor' Glebov [Boris Asaf'yev], *Kniga o Stravinskom* (Leningrad: Triton, 1929); translated into English by Robert French as *A Book about Stravinsky* (Ann Arbor: UMI Research Press, 1982), with Robert Craft's "Foreword: Asaf'yev and Stravinsky," vii–xviii, which was reprinted in *Present Perspectives: Critical Writings* (New York: Alfred A. Knopf, 1984), 276–92. See also Valérie Dufour, "Boris Asaf'yev," in *Stravinski et ses exégètes (1910–1940)* (Brussels: Edition de l'Université de Bruxelles, 2006), 33–50; and Viktor Varunts, "Kommentarii k marginaliyam" (Commentaries on the marginalia), *Muzïkal'naya akademiya* 4 (1992): 182–184; *SPRK*, 3:543–45; and Varunts, "Stravinsky protestiert," *Mitteilungen der Paul Sacher Stiftung* 6 (March 1993): 35–37.

26. Varunts misreads a crucial word in Stravinsky's commentary on Asafyev's analysis of his Octet, for example, where the composer writes that "I think such dissections are written for the author's own sake since they convey nothing to others." Varunts, understanding the word *dissections* (*razbori*) as *works* (*raboti*), jumps to the erroneous conclusion that Stravinsky disliked the book in

general. See Varunts, "Kommentarii k marginaliyam," 184; "Stravinsky protestiert," 37; and *SPRK*, 3:545.

27. Stravinsky to Ernest Ansermet, 20 April 1928, in *Correspondance Ansermet-Strawinsky (1914–1967)*, ed. Claude Tappolet (Geneva: Georg Editeur, 1991), 2:147; translated by Robert Craft in *Stravinsky: Selected Correspondence*, ed. Robert Craft (London: Faber & Faber, 1982), 1:191.

28. Asaf'yev, *Kniga o Stravinskom*, 108, 211, 291, 312–313, 323, 327; Asafyev, *A Book about Stravinsky*, 76, 150, 210, 226–227, 234, 237.

29. For positive accounts of Asafyev's monograph, see Nicolas Nabokov to Sergey Prokofiev, 21 February 1930, and Jacques Handshin to Stravinsky, 20 February 1931, in *SPRK*, 3:382 and 420, respectively. See also Pierre Souvtchinsky, "Le Stravinsky d'Igor Glebov," *Musique* 6 (15 March 1930): 250–53.

30. Mikhail Druskin, *Sobraniye sochineniy v semi tomakh*, ed. Lyudmila Kovnatskaya (St. Petersburg: Kompozitor, 2009), 4:493n; Prokofiev to Asafyev, 6 September 1934, quoted in Robert Craft, "Foreword: Asaf'yev and Stravinsky," viii; and Varunts, "Kommentarii k marginaliyam,"184.

31. Pyotr Suvchinsky to Maria Yudina, 26 April 1960, in Mariia Yudina, *V iskusstve radostno bït' vmeste: Perepiska 1959–1961 godov* (It is joyful to be in art together: Correspondence 1959–1961), ed. Anatoliy Kuznetsov (Moscow: Rosspen, 2009), 288. Stravinsky knew that between 1930 and 1940, as the Stalin regime became harsher, Asafyev aligned himself more closely with it.

32. Modest Chaykovskiy, *Zhizn' Petra Il'icha Chaykovskago* (The life and letters of Peter Ilich Tchaikovsky), 2nd ed., 3 vols. (Moscow: Jurgenson, 1903).

33. Allen, "The Genius and the Goddess," 330.

34. "That's a commonplace."

35. Chaykovskiy, *Zhizn' Petra Il'icha Chaykovskago*, 2:28. See also Stravinsky's comments in Asaf'yev, *Kniga o Stravinskom*, 182; and Irina Vershinina, ed., "Pis'ma Stravinskogo k Rerikhu," *Sovetskaya Muzïka* 8 (1966): 63.

36. Chaykovskiy , *Zhizn' Petra Il'icha Chaykovskago*, 1:95, 98.

37. Ibid., 2:185; and 2:49, 467, 471, 631.

38. See Igor Stravinsky, *Chroniques de ma vie* (Paris: Denoël et Steele, 1935), 1:178.

39. Chaykovskiy, *Zhizn' Petra Il'icha Chaykovskago*, 2:117–18, 127, 184, 187, 565; 3:369, 370.

40. Aleksander Pushkin, *Sochineniya*, ed. Pyotr Yefremov, 8th ed., 7 vols. (Moscow: Izd. F. I. Anskago, 1882).

41. Irina Vershinina argues that only the edition from 1887 contains the first version of "Favn i pastushka." See her comments in Stravinskiy, *Vokal'naya muzïka*, 1:191.

42. Igor Stravinsky, *Pushkin: Poetry and Music*, translated from the French manuscript by Gregory Golubeff (New York and Hollywood: Harvey Taylor, 1940); reprinted in Eric White, *Stravinsky: The Composer and His Works* (London: Faber & Faber, 1979), 588–91.

43. Lyudmila Stravinsky and Yury Mandelshtam to Igor Stravinsky, 4 January 1937, microfilm 106.1, p. 1392, PSS. Yekaterina Stravinsky also acknowledges that Yury wrote this pamphlet in a letter to Stravinsky from 3 January 1937, quoted in Robert Craft, *Stravinsky: Glimpses of a Life* (London: St. Martin's, 1992), 123n9.

44. Igor' Stravinskiy, "Pushkin: Poëziya i muzïka," trans. Anatoliy Shaykevich, in *Igor' Stravinskiy: Publitsist i sobesednik*, ed. Viktor Varunts (Moscow: Sovetskiy Kompozitor, 1988), 139–42.

45. See Savenko's note in Stravinskiy, *Khronika: Poëtika* (Moscow: Rosspen, 2004), 160; and Vershinina's note in Igor' Stravinskiy, *Khronika moyey zhizni*, ed. Irina Vershinina (Moscow: Kompozitor, 2005), 281. Stravinsky's critique of Soviet criticism of Beethoven is omitted in *Khronika moyey zhizni*, trans. Lyubov' Yakovleva-Shaporina (Leningrad: Gosudarstvennoye muzïkal'noye izdatel'stvo, 1963), 176. See the omitted fragment in Stravinsky, *Chroniques de ma vie*, 2:65; *An Autobiography* (London: Calder and Boyars, 1975), 116.

46. Ivan Sollertinsky (1902–1944) was a brilliant polyglot and friend of Shostakovich's who was also a contested figure in the Soviet Union. See Lyudmila Grigor'yevna Kovnatskaya, ed., *D. D. Shostakovich: Pis'ma I. I. Sollertinskomu* (St. Petersburg: Izd-vo Kompozitor, 2006).

47. *Pravoslavnïy molitvoslov* (Paris: n.p., 1922). Craft erroneously lists this book as published in Moscow in "Selected Source Material," 349.

48. *Bibliya: Knigi svyashchennogo pisaniya* (Berlin: Izdanie Britanskago i inostrannago bibleyskago obshchestva, 1922).

49 Nikolay Podosenov to Stravinsky, 6 December 1938 and 3/16 June 1939, microfilm 100.1, 2053 and 2068, PSS.

50. Viktor Nesmelov, *Nauka o cheloveke* (Kazan: Tsentral'naya tipografiya, 1905–6), 2:93, 104.

51. Ioann Shakhovskoy was Archbishop of San Francisco, a US representative in the Central Committee of the World Council of Churches, and a gifted writer and poet. He was the brother of Nicolas Nabokov's first wife, Natalie, and lived in Paris and Berlin before moving to the United States in 1946. See Stravinsky's copies of Ioann Shakhovskoy, *Kniga svitetelstv* (New York: Khronika, 1965); and *Kniga liriki* (Paris: Ichthys, 1966); and the note from Stravinsky to Shakhovskoy kept in Series 1, subseries 3, box 15, Archbishop Ioann Shakhovskoy Papers, Center for Russian Culture, Amherst College.

52. *Pravoslavnïy russkiy kalendar' na 1967 god* (Paris: n.p., 1967).

53. See Stravinsky to Alexandre Benois, 11/24 July 1914, in *SPRK*, 2:282. See also *SPRK*, 1:455; and Taruskin, *Stravinsky and the Russian Traditions*, 1:571–76. Stravinsky wrote Remizov's secretary and translator Natalie Reznikoff after his death: "To my great sorrow I did not know Aleksey Mikhailovich Remizov personally." Stravinsky to Natalie Reznikoff, 26 April 1964, quoted in Taruskin, 1:571n35.

54. Stravinsky bought *Vzvikhrennaya Rus'* (Whirling Russia; 1927), *Tri serpa* (Three Sickles; 1929), and *Posolon'* (Follow the sun; 1930) for $1 to $2 in Cambridge.

55. Aleksey Remizov, *Tristan i Isol'da: Bova korolevich* (Paris: Opleshnik, 1957); and *Krug schast'ya: Legendï o tsare Solomone* (The circle of happiness: Legends of King Solomon) (Paris: Opleshnik, 1957).

56. Stravinsky to Suvchinsky, 20 November 1957, microfilm 103.1, 1308, PSS.

57. Suvchinsky to Stravinsky, 25 November 1957, microfilm 103.1, 1309, PSS.

58. Yudina's first letter to Suvchinsky dates from 16 September 1959. Yudina, *V iskusstve radostno bït' vmeste:* 111–12. Blazhkov's first letter to Stravinsky dates from two days later, 18 September 1959, microfilm 87.1, 1347, PSS.

59. Yudina to Suvchinsky, 5 November 1961, reprinted in *V iskusstve radostno bït' vmeste*, 702.

60. On the unreceived scores, see Yudina to Stravinsky, unpublished telegram from 19 February 1960, microfilm 96.1, 1067, PSS. Stravinsky wrote "I never received that" in the margins of a letter from Yudina describing a parcel she had sent through Leonard Bernstein. See Yudina to Stravinsky, 29 April 1960, microfilm 96.1, 1072, PSS; published without Stravinsky's marginal note in *V iskusstve radostno bït' vmeste*, 297. In the same volume, Yudina complains about Van Cliburn's behavior in a letter to Tat'yana Kamendrovskaya, 27–30 September 1961, 676.

61. Suvchinsky to Yudina, 12 September 1960, in *V iskusstve radostno bït' vmeste*, 354.

62. Suvchinsky to Yudina, 23 October 1961, ibid., 673.

63. Yudina describes her correspondence with Stravinsky in a letter to Tat'yana Kamendrovskaya, 11 January 1961, ibid., 438.

64. These include, before 1962, Viktor Lazarev's *Andrey Rublev* (Moscow: Sovetskiy khudozhnik, 1960); Viktor Lazarev's *Feofan Grek i ego shkola* (Theophanus the Greek and his school) (Moscow: Iskusstvo, 1961); and Aleksandr Sokolovskiy's *Starïy Peterburg na knizhnïkh znakakh* (Old St. Petersburg on book plates) (Leningrad: Comintern, 1925).

65. See Stravinsky's copy of Bogdanov-Berezovskiy, *Fyodor Stravinskiy* (Leningrad: Muzgiz, 1951), dated and signed 13 October 1960 by the author.

66. Referred to in English—rarely—as *King of the Stars* or *The Star-Faced One*.

67. Konstantin Bal'mont, *Zelyonïy vertograd: Polnoye sobraniye stikhov* (The green garden: The complete poems) (Moscow: Skorpion, 1911). See Suvchinsky to Yudina, 22 June 1960, and Yudina to Suvchinsky, 25 May 1961, in *V iskusstve radostno bït' vmeste*, 319 and 548, respectively. Balmont's note on the cover, "1920. Spring. Moscow," suggests that he signed it before his emigration on 5 May 1920. The page number of "Zvezdolikiy" is indicated on the cover and two bookmarks, on which Stravinsky has written the titles of the poems "Golub'" (Dove) and "Nezabudochka-tsvetochek (Little forget-me-not), are kept within it.

68. Mitropolit Filaret, *Sbornik mïsley i izrecheniy* (Moscow: Sïnodal'naya, 1897).

69. Pavel Florensky (1882–1937) was a great Russian theologian, priest, philosopher, mathematician, physicist, and martyr. He was arrested in 1928 and 1933 and executed in 1937. Yudina corresponded with him for some time.

70. Stravinskiy, *Khronika moyey zhizni*, copy dated "1 May 1964" that includes an envelope with Blazhkov's return address.

71. Stravinsky to Blazhkov, 22 May 1964, microfilm 87.1, 1372, PSS. Bogdanov-Berezovsky had contributed substantially to rehabilitating Stravinsky's name in the USSR by organizing a ballet production in Leningrad in 1961 and assisting Yudina with Stravinskyana, an exhibition in his celebration during his visit in 1962.

72. Boris Yarustovskiy, *Igor' Stravinskiy: Kratkiy ocherk zhizni i tvorchestva* (Igor Stravinsky: A short summary of his life and creative work) (Moscow: Muzïka, 1964).

73. Irina Vershinina, *Ranniye baletï Stravinskogo* (Moscow: Nauka, 1967), 137, 140. Igor Blazhkov confirmed in an email to me of 3 February 2011 that he mailed this book to Stravinsky.

74. Concerning Yury Grigorovich's visit, see the entry for 11 July 1966 in Vera Arturovna's diary, microfilm 248.1, 812, PSS. On Yevgeniy Yevtushenko's visit on 13 December 1966, see Robert Craft, *Chronicle of a Friendship*, rev. ed. (Nashville: Vanderbilt University Press, 1994), 443–44. And on Maya Plisetskaya's visit on 29 June 1968, see Vera Arturovna's diary entries for 29 and 30 June 1968, microfilm 248.1, 932–33, PSS. Plisetskaya gave Stravinsky a copy of Leonid Zhdanov's *Maya Plisetskaya* (Moscow: Iskusstvo, 1965), and signed it with the date "29 June 1968."

The Futility of Exhortation:
Pleading in Stravinsky's *Oedipus Rex* and *Orpheus*

GRETCHEN HORLACHER

Stravinsky has rarely been kind to his characters in trouble. Finding themselves in situations beyond their control, they are compelled nonetheless to persevere, with little chance of changing their unhappy fates. Be it during his early Russian period, the thirty years he spent writing "neoclassical music," or in his final serial compositions, the composer was frequently attracted to subject matter with a tragic outcome, and especially subjects whose outcomes are known in advance. That is, he chose topics whose sequence of events is driven less by the suspense of surprise than by the fulfillment of destiny. The most famous example is probably the retelling of a Russian folk story in the 1913 ballet *The Rite of Spring*: here a virgin is sacrificed to please the gods and thereby guarantee the fruits of the earth. The ballet is not about the drama of the life of that virgin, but rather a series of ritualistic tableaux that lead to her inevitable demise. More than forty years later, Stravinsky chose a similar kind of tale for his neoclassical *The Rake's Progress*: based on the well-known story of making a deal with the devil, the opera recounts one doomed episode after another. Its central female character, the incredulously gullible Anne Trulove, never stops loving Tom Rakewell in spite of the ridiculous schemes and infidelities with which Nick Shadow (an obviously named devil) tempts him. With Anne by his side, he eventually descends into madness. In both cases we are aware that the fates of the virgin and of Anne are sealed: no one will stop the sacrificial virgin from dancing herself to death. Neither will Anne reconsider or regret her choices in the *Rake*, a fable whose moral is that "the Devil finds a work to do."[1]

The theme of futility—that is, an awareness that strife, supplication, or pleading is both inescapable and ultimately inadequate—pervades Stravinsky's settings of *Oedipus Rex* and *Orpheus*. In the former, an opera-oratorio from 1926–27, Stravinsky retells the classic Greek tragedy of a hero doomed from birth to unwittingly murder his father and marry his mother. Unable to control their fates, Jocasta (both his mother and wife) commits suicide, and Oedipus leaves his community for exile after blinding himself. Stravinsky's setting of *Orpheus* (1947) likewise describes the unsuccessful efforts of the musical hero to retrieve

• 79 •

his lover Eurydice from Hades; although he too strikes a deal with the god of the underworld to restore her to earth, according to the myth, Orpheus must fail to meet the conditions of the deal and she is lost to him forever. These works are not simply explorations of the darker side of life; rather, in choosing topics based on celebrated tragic myths, stories whose endings are determined in advance, Stravinsky compels his audience to pass through a series of deeply disturbing events, as if these accounts bear didactic and moral power: their re-creations are cautionary reminders about the nature of human limitations. We listen and watch not to find out what happens next, but to remind ourselves of the ever-present powers of fate.

How Stravinsky creates works that reveal the unreality of their characters' desires is the subject of this essay. Stravinsky's music has always been characterized by its repetitions of melodic fragments and its layering of those disparate melodies. Less considered is *how* Stravinsky manipulates repeating melodic cells—by adding or deleting a note, or by changing their sequence of pitches, for example—to reveal the inevitability of his characters' fates. By making small variations to a melody already defined by limited pitch content and short duration, Stravinsky is able to represent both the ongoing pleadings of his characters and their underlying futility: though his characters attempt to modify their tunes by reiterating them in a number of guises, these melodies never truly change. Because the underlying essences of those melodies are present even as the characters move through the events of their lives, we know that their fates are sealed: the pleadings of Orpheus will not return his new bride Eurydice from the underworld back to earth, nor will the pleadings of the citizens of Thebes save Oedipus from his own self-mutilation and exile, or his wife's suicide.

The use of varied repetition is ideal for tragic ritual: a compositional style where only very small changes are made to a melody or its accompaniment holds our attention as these variations proceed across time, and their constant presence reminds us that the underlying sequence of events is immutable. In other words, because the variations do not change the essential content of the tune, this method suits the ceremonial retelling of familiar stories: ongoing variations readily represent the sequence of events in a narrative while the inexorable existence of a core motive represents an outcome already known, one that cannot be permanently forestalled. We experience Stravinsky's time world both as sequentially directed and as immutably circular, as are the events of a ritual or a legend.

In both *Orpheus* and *Oedipus*, Stravinsky foretells the outcome of the stories early on; the former begins with Orpheus already mourning the death of his beloved Eurydice, accompanied by a descending bass line almost too "stock" to represent the depth of his grief. (I will return to Stravinsky's special setting of this symbolic musical feature later in this essay.) Both stories involve the predetermined outcome when mortals—even a king or a gifted demigod musician—challenge the gods. In the first scene of *Orpheus*, the mourning musician plays a lament with his back to the audience, letting us know that the death of his treasured Eurydice is the greatest loss he could have experienced. Only then does the ballet begin to tell the story. Similarly, Cocteau (the librettist) and Stravinsky begin *Oedipus* with a narrator, whose role is not to set the scene but rather to forecast its outcome, relieving us of the burden of drama, and even of the memory of the tragic story itself. The narrator *tells* us that Oedipus has been asked to do the impossible: he must contend with "the supernatural powers," that "at the moment of his birth a snare was laid for him," and that we "will see the snare closing."[2] There is no surprise denouement in this play; in fact, the narrator returns at regular intervals to tell us what is about to happen and the audience is enjoined to follow the particular ways in which Stravinsky and Cocteau slowly cause the gods to tighten the noose around the king. In the next section I will demonstrate how the singing of three key characters—Oedipus, his community (the citizens of Thebes that form the oratorio's chorus), and his brother-in-law Creon—reveal the futile nature of Oedipus's struggle.

Oedipus the King

Following the narrator's opening explanation of the plot, the citizens of Thebes begin this opera-oratorio by pleading with Oedipus their king to save them from the plague. This disaster has been interpreted as a punishment from the gods, and because Oedipus is not only their king but also the one who has solved the problem of the Sphinx (in an earlier part of the myth), they beg him to come to their aid. The features of their key melody are particularly Stravinskian: over and over they repeat just three pitches (D♭, C, and B♭), always moving by step, and using only eighth and quarter notes. Within these limitations, their plea for help is hardly grandiose; moreover, they unwittingly set forth a chain of events that will lead to Oedipus's destruction. Figure 1 gives the text and translation for the music of the opening chorus, which begins at rehearsal number 2 after some introductory music. The left side of the figure shows Cocteau's original libretto and its translation into English, and the right side shows Stravinsky's manipulation of the libretto, putting in bold the words Stravinsky chooses to repeat. Notice how many times the chorus implores Oedipus by name.[3]

Examples 1a and 1b lay out the musical setting of the chorus's entreaties and Oedipus's first response to them. Although shown in reduced scoring and an unusual format, all of the choral music and the lower ostinato from rehearsal number 2 through rehearsal number 4 are shown in Example 1a (in other words, one may follow the music by moving through each of the five systems, numbered with Roman numerals, continuously; each of the five systems moves across two pages).[4] In order to follow the ways in which the chorus moves through three pitches, I have broken the chorus melody into five subsections (most of which

COCTEAU'S LIBRETTO, WITH TRANSLATION	STRAVINSKY'S SETTING, WITH WORD REPETITIONS **BOLDED**
Opening choral text:	
1. Kaedit nos pestis. (The plague falls on us.)	Kaedit nos pestis.
2. Theba peste moritur. (Thebes is dying of the plague.)	Theba peste moritur.
3. E peste serva nos. (From the plague preserve us.)	E peste serva nos **serva.**
4. Qua Theba moritur. (For Thebes is dying.)	**E peste** qua Theba moritur.
Beginning of ostinato at rehearsal number 2	
5. Oedipus, adest pestis. (Oedipus, the plague has come.)	Oedipus, **Oedipus,** adest pestis. **Kaedit nos pestis, Oedipus. E peste serva nos, serva, Oedipus.**
6. E peste libera urbem. (Free our city from the plague.)	E peste libera urbem, **Oedipus. E peste qua Theba moritur.**
7. Urbem serva morientem. (Preserve our dying city.)	Urbem serva morientem.

Figure 1. Cocteau's libretto for the opening chorus of *Oedipus Rex* compared with Stravinsky's setting.

follow the breaks in the text), each of which vertically aligns with the place where a key set of pitches, the most stable melodic motive, are sung. The example also shows the ominous ostinato (a short melodic or accompanimental figure that never varies) in the timpani, piano, and harp on two of their three pitches (B♭ and D♭).[5] The most consistent choral melody begins with two D♭'s, and a neighboring of C by B♭ before moving up to D♭ in a recognizable rhythm, and is bracketed in its first appearance in Example 1a. Broken into five segments, the example suggests that the chorus continuously urges Oedipus to act: notice that while each subsection uses the melody as a point of departure, it continues in distinct ways, with slightly different pitch configurations as the text repeats its essential message with varied language. None of these variations stray from the constrained pitch or durational conditions defined earlier. Rather, varied continuations of this tiny melody endow the passage with great determination, putting enormous pressure on Oedipus to fulfill his duties to his citizens.

Against these boundaries the ongoing ostinato pushes forward, repeating almost endlessly without change. These two ways of moving through the passage, taken together, create this section's time world. We feel the pleadings of the chorus both as it repeats just a few pitches and as its demands accumulate: the pull of melodic flow, even with its minimal variation, versus the stasis of ostinato, helps us to understand the desperation of Thebes even as we know that the chorus's pleadings will not change the fate of Oedipus.

Of particular note is the way the chorus sings Oedipus's name in this passage. Because the unchanging ostinato implies an unchanging ⁶⁄₈ meter (one we are likely to maintain counting, despite any notational changes of meter to ⁹⁄₈, as in systems IV and V in Example 1a) we can identify various ways in which Oedipus's name is repeated within the context of perceived strong and weak beats. Notice that the passage begins with three repetitions of the king's name, the first of which is placed in syncopation (a classic 3:2 hemiola) with the ostinato. Other repetitions occur at the end of a system (II), or connect lines of text (shown visually at the end of III and IV). In fact, in this format Example 1a demonstrates that the music surrounding the foundation motive, although confined by pitch and rhythm, provides a constant variation to it. The piteous insistence of the chorus derives in large part from these surreptitious manipulations of the melodic motive. Notice also that choir members singing the upper-bass part (in the middle of the texture) must traverse unmelodious lines, moving torturously through tritone leaps and diminished-triad arpeggiations, harmonizing the main melody in particularly harsh ways.[6]

The parsing of Example 1a demonstrates how the chorus expresses a consistent message in a series of varied entreaties, insisting that Oedipus respond. Notice that the portions of the chorus's melody on staves 2, 3, and 4 are noticeably shorter, and that as the chorus continues, its requests become more specific: in lines six and seven of Cocteau's libretto the chorus asks Oedipus to free the Thebans from the plague and to save their dying city. As the chorus reaches its final line of text—"Urbem serva morientem" (Preserve our dying city)—it finally breaks the circular repetitions of B♭, C, and D♭ in eighths, instead repeating those pitches in a descending cadential gesture from D♭ to the closing B♭ (see the end of system V). Although the chorus breaks off from the fundamental motive, moving instead to other twisted, chromatic melodies, it continues to repeat essentially the same text.

The chorus continues its demands for several more minutes until Oedipus finally sings his four words at rehearsal number 16, given in the same kind of format in Example 1b. Contrasting highly with the compact and countable music of the chorus, the essential shape of Oedipus's repeated melody is an uneven descending line, passing chromatically downward through unpredictable durations. Each of these descents appears in its own system in Example 1b for comparison with one another.

Although we know from the opening narration that Oedipus's responses will be in vain, we may still have enough faith to wonder if his first valiant attempt to assure his citizens will succeed. The elongation of the gesture at system III, beginning with introductory music at the left margin and extending beyond the lengths of the previous two gestures on the right, certainly suggests that he is willing to help the Thebans. These melodies have an operatic quality to them, reminding us that at this point in his compositional career (the so-called neoclassical period, extending from about 1920 through the mid-1950s) Stravinsky often borrowed

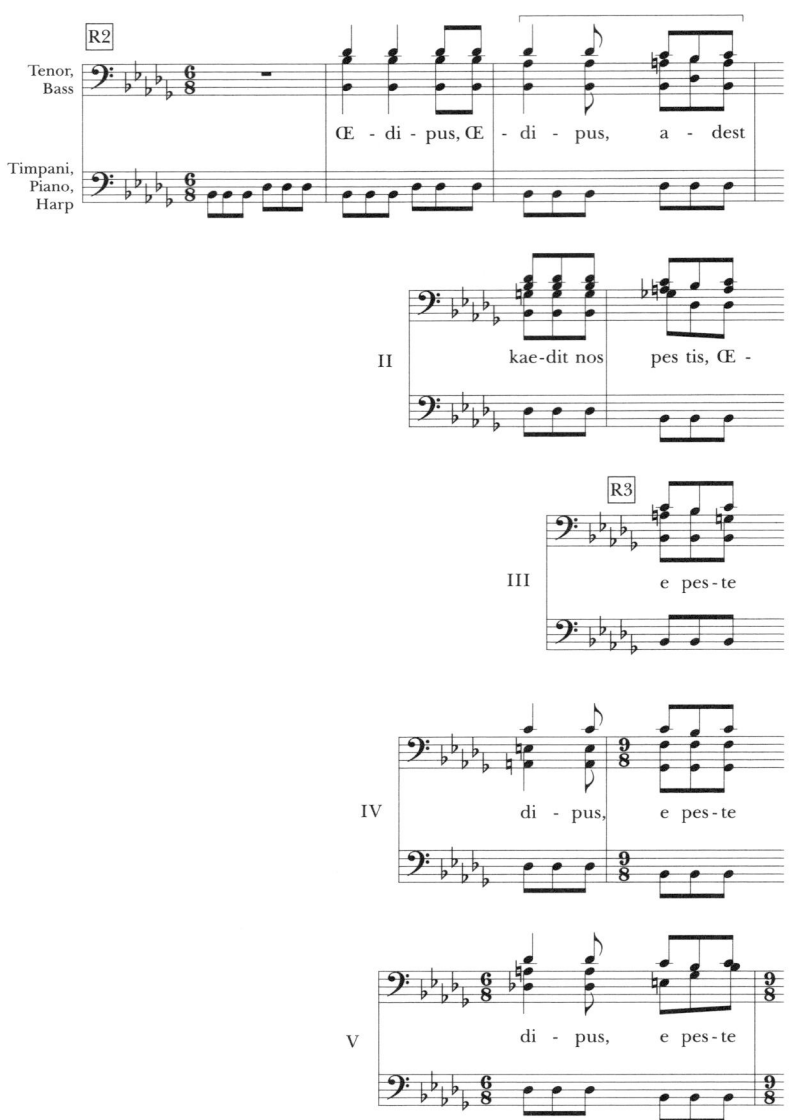

Example 1a. *Oedipus Rex*, ordered succession for the first chorus from
rehearsal number 2 through rehearsal number 4.

Example 1a continued

Example 1b. *Oedipus Rex*, ordered succession of Oedipus's first response from rehearsal number 16 to seven measures after rehearsal number 18.

gestures associated with tonal music (a point made even clearer in the discussion of *Orpheus* below).[7] Oedipus's first two recitative-like melodies begin with what appears to be a virtuosic display of courage, beginning on the dominant-functioning F above the tenors' earlier melody, exceeding their registral reach. But from F he can only descend in a metrically ambiguous and indirect path toward B♭. In his third attempt, given in system III, he reaches higher, beginning a step upward on G, and moving down once more through a minor scale (here based on C). Although Oedipus tries to replace the minor mediant E♭ with a Picardy-like E♮, that melodic extension (in the last two measures of system III) extends up a tritone to F♯, as if he is not in control of his choice of scales. In one last try, shown as a revised repetition of system III on system IV, he descends in failure back down to B. These operatic bursts centered on the "wrong" tonics ironically set the text "Ego clarissimus Oedipus" (I, illustrious—or famous—Oedipus), a text that both the chorus and Oedipus repeat again in the opera, suggesting a grave mismatch between the reality of the situation and Oedipus's own assessment of his powers. Stravinsky's setting of his text reveals a hubris that must be addressed by fate.

Example 1b continued

That Oedipus's response has not been satisfactory is indicated by the return of the chorus's music at rehearsal number 19 (Example 2a). Recapitulating the original D♭–C–B♭, turning figure, the chorus continues to implore him for aid. A comparison with the earlier chorus music (see Example 1a) shows how the singing has become more desperate. In place of the three lines in Example 1a, the chorus nearly constantly reiterates the verb *serva* (preserve us); in place of the five subsections guiding the format of Example 1a we find an extended intonation on D♭ in system I, a contrasting, short petition in system II, and in the third a breathtaking breaking of the D♭ boundary. Even as the chorus sings "Serva nos, clarissime Oedipus" (Preserve us, illustrious Oedipus), reminding Oedipus of his

Example 2a. *Oedipus Rex*, ordered succession for second chorus from
rehearsal number 19 through rehearsal number 20.

own proud self-characterization, it begins to rise up via E♮ (not the E♭ of a B-flat-minor scale) to reach his own earlier F. The substitution of E for E♭ suggests that the chorus is not satisfied he has heard them, or that he can save the Thebans.

Into this scene enters Creon, the brother of Oedipus's mother and wife. As the bearer of truth, and thus the character who will eventually relieve Thebes of the plague, Creon's initial music consists neither of the painful repetitions of the chorus nor the ambiguous chromaticism of Oedipus, both of which invoke the minor mode. Example 2b shows both the chorus music welcoming him and, after

Example 2a continued

the narrator tells the audience that Creon brings the truth from an oracle, Creon's initial response. Despite the narrator's interjection, the harmonic connection between the chorus and Creon—a dominant resolving into a straightforward descent through a C-major triad—contrasts highly with the interactions the chorus has had with Oedipus. Even at this point of the story, Stravinsky makes it clear that Oedipus's preceding song has not been sufficient, and that despite their best efforts, the Thebans' exhortations to Oedipus will not work. Creon's very first words "Respondit Deus" (God will respond) reveal that fate is in control, not Oedipus the King.

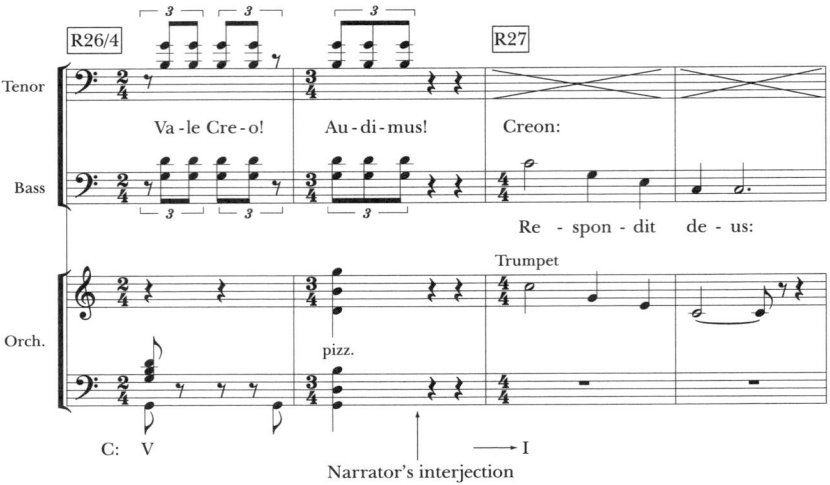

Example 2b. *Oedipus Rex*, Creon's first response, two measures before to two measures after rehearsal number 27.

Oedipus eventually adopts Creon's triadic singing, but not until it is too late. The final two examples for this opera describe Oedipus's "moment of truth," the point at which he finally puts together clues about his past and realizes what he has done. Example 3, an ordered succession for two measures before rehearsal number 167 to 170, shows music derived both from Creon's C-major arpeggiations and the D♭–C–B♭ core motive with which the chorus began (for reasons of space, systems IV and V are shown on the second page, and V has been shown over two systems). The passage begins with an uneasy alternation of D-minor chords (in the strings) and B-minor chords (in the winds), whose clash of F and F♯ prefigures Oedipus's awful realization of his true identity. Choosing the winds' key area to launch his melody in system III (rehearsal number 168), Oedipus repeats almost exactly three statements of a melody combining the limited melody of the opening chorus (here up a half step in the form of B, C♯, and D) and the descending arpeggio of Creon (here as a B-*minor* triad). Drawing together the chorus's appeals for help with the truthful music of Creon, Oedipus puts together the last pieces of the puzzle about his true origins. The lack of variation in the three statements, shown in systems III, IV, and V, suggests that Oedipus finally realizes his fate, and that there is no escape available. Even in his final, climactic melodic melody (at the end of system V) Oedipus cannot descend confidently from chordal root to root (from B to B), but from fifth to fifth, and not through a major triad but a minor one (F♯–D–B–F♯). As a replacement for his earlier chromatic descents, where Oedipus presents himself as the illustrious king, this descending minor triad on the text "Lux facta est" (All now is made clear) focuses not on him, but on the truth that we have known but that he never knew until this moment.

Although this moment is a denouement for Oedipus, it is hardly one for the audience, which has been told that from the start Oedipus's fate will not be to save Thebes, but to bring dishonor and death upon himself and his family. The narrator has informed us in the preceding scene about what is about to transpire:

Example 3. *Oedipus Rex*, ordered succession for Oedipus's realization, rehearsal nos. 167–69.

Example 3 continued

"O, this lofty all-discerning Oedipus: he is in the snare. He alone does not know it. And then the truth strikes him." Oedipus's use of B minor—sitting unhappily at a half step between the B-flat-minor entreaties of the chorus and the C-major truth-seeking of Creon—draw us in not because we are surprised at the truth itself, but rather because we watch him accept the inevitable, and hear the terrible consequences of fate. In the opening chorus (rehearsal numbers 2–4 in Example 1a) minor variations to limited melodies take us through the chorus's time of pleading; the lack of variation in Oedipus's three repetitions (systems III, IV,

Example 4. *Oedipus Rex*, ordered succession for the chorus's farewell to Oedipus, from 6 measures after rehearsal number 202 to the end of the piece.

and V in Example 3) indicate the end of his striving and the beginning of his resignation. This is the time of no change, of acceptance of the truth of the gods.

All that is left is for the chorus also to accept Oedipus's fate, and to bid him farewell. Example 4 shows its final speech to him—"Vale, vale Oedipus, miser Oedipus noster, te amabam, Oedipus. Tibi valedico, Oedipus, tibi valedico" (Farewell Oedipus, our poor Oedipus, I loved you Oedipus. I bid you farewell Oedipus)—as he begins his self-imposed, blind exile. Returning to its original exhortational music, the chorus no longer implores Oedipus for help, nor even invites him to remain in Thebes, but instead mourns its own powerlessness to change Oedipus's fate. Even though the chorus loved him and pities him, it now knows its cries for help were in vain and that it too must accept the decisions of the gods and send him away. Example 4 once again aligns the original choral motive for comparison with its surrounding music; here it appears in a truncated version, transposed down to the pitches of B♭, A, and G. Notice that immediately after the original motive returns, another one immediately follows. Gone are the longer, varied responses of the original chorus. After a single B♭ in system III, a single heart-wrenching new melody, where the chorus sings a rising G-minor scale, culminates not as expected but on the dissonantly chromatic D♭, and stops on the open C, an unresolved scale-degree 4 in this G-minor context.

As shown in system V, the chorus fails to reach a cadence (as it did at the end of Example 1a), and simply dies away on the open B♭. Certainly this recapitulation of the original choral motive clarifies its failure: it no longer reveres Oedipus as its powerful king. After the chorus's final outburst in system III, it simply runs out of steam; its final repetitions in systems IV and V omit the characteristic first B♭ of the motive, and thus the last two statements (on A–G–A–B♭) are incomplete. No longer is the chorus pleading to Oedipus; rather, it sings the sounds of resignation, of an acceptance of the futility of its original cries. As the chorus dismisses its blind hero from Thebes, the ostinato itself also ceases, and its final two lower Gs merely decelerate to an ensuing silence.

Orpheus

Written as a companion piece to the 1928 ballet *Apollo* (in collaboration with choreographer George Balanchine), the ballet *Orpheus* again shows Stravinsky's fascination with casting central characters from Greek tragedy as victims of destiny. The composer commented later in life that he and Balanchine chose its series of dances "with Ovid and a classical dictionary in hand."[8] Although various versions of the story differ in some details, its essential elements are fairly consistent. Orpheus, having one human parent and one supernatural one (in the Stravinsky/Balanchine collaboration, the god Apollo is Orpheus's father), has been endowed with an extraordinary gift of music, especially in his playing of the lyre. When Eurydice, his young bride, dies, Orpheus plays to the community of the Underworld so beautifully that he is allowed to travel there to retrieve her. Like Lot in Genesis, however, he must not look back at his beloved while he leads her back to Earth. But in his anxiety to see her again he does turn back, and all is lost: Eurydice returns permanently to Hades. Like Oedipus, Orpheus is punished for his actions, in this case by the Bacchantes, who dismember him.

This myth is not only about human weakness and the loss of love: like *Oedipus Rex*, *Orpheus* at a very fundamental level underscores the non-negotiable difference between finite human existence and the infinitely powerful world of the gods. Stravinsky's characterization of Orpheus contrasts two irreconcilable conceptions about time: Orpheus is faced with an eternal separation from Eurydice, but through the use of music, which takes place *through* time, he wishes to restore her to his own time world, the world of time's passage. Given the remarkable gift of music, the ultimate temporal art, he seems invincible, and yet being human, the power of his music cannot exceed that of the gods.

In the setting worked out between Stravinsky and Balanchine (published in 1947, near the end of Stravinsky's deep engagement with Baroque and classical music genres) the story's identity as a tragedy is made immediately apparent. We find Orpheus *not* in the nuptial bliss of marrying Eurydice, the way that Monteverdi begins his seminal version of the story in his opera *L'Orfeo*. Rather, Eurydice is already dead at the beginning, and in his first appearance Orpheus is already grieving her death. As we watch only his back, Orpheus plays on his lyre a grief-stricken stepwise descent from E (scale-degree 1) to B (scale-degree 5), recalling the well-known lament figure of Baroque music. In fact, in her valuable study of Stravinsky's treatment of Greek subjects, Maureen Carr has discovered that an original scenario by Stravinsky and Balanchine describes the opening music as a "requiem for Eurydice."[9]

However, as it continues, Stravinsky treats the lament figure uniquely, characterizing Orpheus not only as an exceptional musician, but also foreshadowing his downfall. After its initial descent to B, the melody first returns to E, as if it were to follow the Baroque practice of repeating this "stock" gesture. However, after that fifth pitch, Orpheus interrupts a supposed repetition of the lament, instead leaping down to A, and continuing through a second stepwise tetrachord down to the lower E; the two joined tetrachords create a Phrygian scale, also an emblem of sorrow (see Example 5). Taken together, their completion of the doleful scale signals an ominous continuation, foreshadowing both Orpheus's trip to the Underworld and his ultimate failure; playing this music before he begins his journey frames the temperament of the entire ballet. As the well-known dance critic John Martin observed in his review of the ballet's premiere, the work "is in essence that of a reperforming of a ritual before the tomb of a hero."[10]

Orpheus continues to repeat his descending lament over much of the opening movement. Example 5 demonstrates a parsing of his melody from the opening of

Example 5. *Orpheus*, ordered succession for Orpheus's opening music
to four measures after rehearsal number 1.

the piece to four measures after rehearsal number 1, when the harp (his lyre) comes to an unexpected stop on a low F, an unresolved scale-degree 2 in this Phrygian setting (see the very end of Example 5). As with earlier examples, I have vertically aligned key portions of the melody to point out how Stravinsky manipulates the descending scale in subtle ways; the example does not omit any part of the melody, and may be heard and read continuously. Each new system begins when the higher E occurs (or should occur) on a downbeat, and also includes the gathering accompanimental string parts below Orpheus's tune. It shows how each of the repetitions is ordered into a larger series of varied laments.

Example 5 tracks the first four segments of Orpheus's melody, paying particular attention to the places where he is able to begin on the upper E and where he is able to reach the lower E. In each iteration of Orpheus's melody we may take note both of his growing urgency and the difficulty of his task. At the end of his first iteration (system I), Orpheus attempts to descend entirely through the Phrygian scale without the intervening leap up to E; notice that he does not arrive there (signified by the X at the end of the system). Instead, in a Sisyphean manner, he returns to his original E to begin another descent. The iterations in systems II, III, and IV show similar difficulties in completing the journey downward. In the second, Orpheus reaches the lower E, but at the expense of being able to return to the higher one on time (that is, on the downbeat). Instead he must leap up awkwardly through a dissonant minor seventh to continue his journey downward. System III repeats the difficulties of system I; system IV returns to the opening divided journey, and although it expands its register to reach an E even an octave lower, this journey begins with an enormous leap downward by a minor ninth, and just at the moment when Orpheus could arrive on a very low E, even on a downbeat, he ceases to play, as if he is unable to go on (see the exclamation marks at the end of system IV). Each of these imperfect descents suggests that even Orpheus's music will be unable to save Eurydice. Along the way the accompanying strings also provide early hazardous signs: their initial arrival on the low E (at the end of system I) clashes with Orpheus's F sounding directly above it, and as he continues downward during the second measure of I, they support his A rather than his goal pitch E, placing their lower E in less prominent inner voices. The strings' lower-voice A overlaps into system II, where an additional lower G is added to their harmony. The resulting sonority at rehearsal number 1 (the first bar of system II) is an ambiguously rooted chord; that this harmonic uncertainty evolves as Orpheus misses his target pitch is a symbol of the time world of the ballet as a whole, where mortal efforts are thwarted just when success is within reach.

How does Orpheus continue after the initial defeat that ends Example 5? Example 6 gives the entire movement in a format similar to that of Example 5, aligning in this case a repeating F–G–A–B melody in the first violins (see the brackets beginning in system III). In addition to parsing the movement by

Example 6. *Orpheus*, ordered succession for the entire first movement
to five measures after rehearsal number 3.

phrase, this alignment draws attention to the increasingly important role of the accompanying string and wind parts. Are they signs of hope, or do they complicate Orpheus's song? Two immediate observations will help us to understand how these additional voices interact with Oedipus's melody, both shaping and revealing his fate. Notice first (at the end of system V) that the movement ends *not* on a lower E, but on the problematic A, harmonized here in an unsettling dominant seventh whose doubled rumbling C♯'s can only mean trouble. (Orpheus himself also ends on A, as I will discuss below.) Before the troubling end, however, notice that the majority of these lines move upward, rather than downward, by step. It seems that Orpheus's music has had some effect. At rehearsal number 2 (the last measure given in system III) the score indicates that some friends begin to enter onstage to

Example 6 continued

offer Orpheus presents and to comfort him. Although Orpheus's music continues to descend, the upward motion of the strings continues to accumulate, both in rising stepwise lines and in a growth into the upward registers of the orchestra.

In other words, as upward movement in both lower and upper strings matches Orpheus's downward movement, the movement as a whole expresses a futility tinged with hope. In their earliest ascent, in system II, the upper strings rise tentatively from E as far as A before falling back to a quasi-cadential G. In their next attempt, shown in system III, they reach as far up as B, meeting Orpheus's original tetrachordal descent to that pitch, and winds reinforce the arrival of the B in a higher octave. But that meeting fails spectacularly: just as strings reach up to B Orpheus is not on E but on F, where he is compelled to stop. The subsequent chord in the winds reaches the end of a phrase on a grating doubling of F and B harmonized by a dissonant augmented triad from below. Although the goal pitch arrives at the end of system III, it is neither played by Orpheus nor do the pitches around it sound secure.

The fourth system begins similarly; the strings rise only to A, Oedipus stops on F, and the winds once more intervene with an uncomfortably dissonant harmony (in the first complete bar of system IV). After this second failed intervention, they take a new tack, *descending* from F rather than rising from it (see the second complete measure of IV). Their repetitions have an amazing effect on Orpheus: although he finally achieves the lower E for which he has been striving, he unfortunately continues even further down to D (see the exclamation mark at the end of system IV). The C-rooted chord on which this phrase ends is notably missing its third E, inflected instead by a replacement D.

System V, the last phrase in the movement, shows one final attempt to bring descending and ascending lines into some kind of synchronization. Orpheus once again returns to his original melody as the phrase starts, and manages to move through an entire uninterrupted descent in its third measure. But his success is short-lived: in the final bars of the movement he descends not from the higher E, but from C (circled in the fourth measure of the system). His final melody eventually comes to rest on a decelerated, off-the-beat descent from E to A, the pitch that first challenged his melody in the second measure of the movement. Against this brave, if useless, movement are the upper strings, which refuse to budge beyond A; the upper brackets over the upper violin melody at the start of system V identify a particularly emblematic gesture in that they sound above, and thus weaken, the B to E ascent below them. Their rising motion from B to E is clearly superseded by the newer motion of E up to A and the eventual close by Orpheus himself from E down to A. The replacement of E by A as an alternative goal forecasts the futility of Orpheus's music.

The plaintive slowing down of all parts and the many modally inflected minor triads in system V are final signals that Orpheus's mission is doomed. Even so, the final chord, whose dominant-seventh G has been present in previous measures,

Example 7a. *Orpheus*, scene 3 "Orpheus's Apotheosis," opening nine measures.

Example 7b. Final five measures of scene 3.

compels the music to continue onward: despite all signs thus far, Orpheus is compelled to strive to reunite with Eurydice in one more retelling of this ancient ritual, and thus the ballet moves from prologue to actual dancing. Over the course of the dancing Orpheus does not succeed in returning Eurydice to earth because he must look back; in fact, he rips a bandage from his eyes just before their journey is over, and she falls dead. In the final *pas d'action* (immediately preceding the apotheosis, to be discussed below), Balanchine and Stravinsky create a dance in which Orpheus's failure leads to his hideous dismemberment by the Bacchantes, the female worshippers of the god Bacchus, who are sometimes known for representing that god's destructive power.

Yet, although Orpheus is dead, and his mission unaccomplished, his lyre remains. In a final poignant apotheosis movement, Apollo (Orpheus's reputed father) wrests the lyre from Orpheus's body, whereupon it begins to play its original mournful tune. Examples 7a and 7b reproduce the beginning and end of the final movement, bracketing the reappearance of the tune in its original incarnation from E to E. After its first statement—perhaps an homage to the life of Orpheus—Apollo transforms the melody, sending it upward, this time not in a failed journey from Hades to Earth, but from there to the heavens, where music may continue unimpeded by the fates of those constrained to live on Earth. Moreover, Apollo has inverted the scalar melody from a mournful E-Phrygian footing to a more realistic and sustainable Dorian D. In his hands, the harp melody becomes stable, in fact a near ostinato: it is no longer subject to the vagaries of incompletion found in the first movement, and in its final measures makes one final, unimpeded journey from a lower D to an upper one.

Whereas the opening movement closed on an unusually spaced A-major dominant-seventh chord, the ballet itself comes to an end on a more conventionally spaced D-major seventh suggesting that the music goes on, even if Orpheus is dead. This final movement is an apotheosis in the truest setting of the word: in this setting, it is not Orpheus who has been elevated to divine status, but his music. With human parentage, Orpheus was bound to fail; but music escapes the finite temporality of Earth to sound even in the heavens.

From the start, Stravinsky's Orpheus struggles with two contrasting conceptions of the nature of time: he has lost his beloved to an eternity of separation, but through the use of music, which takes place through time, he wishes to restore Eurydice to his own temporality, to the world of time's passage. Orpheus loses his battle with the time of passage, as we always knew he would. But another conception of time, one associated with infinity, fulfillment, and the world of the gods, supersedes Orpheus's mortality. We are reminded that Greek tragedy takes its origins in ritual, whose essential function is to repeat a given narrative rather than to develop it. Orpheus's exhortations may have been futile, but they give rise to the eternity of music.

Measuring Repetition

In the analyses above I have focused on how Stravinsky's manipulations of repetition evoke particular interpretations of *Oedipus Rex* and *Orpheus*. As modern recapitulations of ancient stories, Stravinsky's settings interpret the myths as ritualistic reiterations of given truths. His emphasis on the "hand of fate," the power of the gods, and the inevitability of human strife arises from his consummate use of repetition, spanning a spectrum of exact replication to melodic and harmonic variation. Each end of the spectrum presents a particular temporal experience: whereas variation from one event to the next creates the painful passage through time of Oedipus and Orpheus, an exact repetition, such as an ostinato, reminds us of, and often reveals to them, their unchangeable fates. In my reading of these two settings, the characters are introduced to us as pawns of destiny; as they may be striving for or against something, we too become pawns, able only to follow and to learn from their experiences.

Of course, not all of Stravinsky's repetitions are symbolic of futility, grief, or the power of fate; his subject matter is not always grim. (I think here especially of the graceful dances in *Apollo*, and their ostinato-driven ascent to the Mount of Parnassus in the ballet's apotheosis.) What is remarkable is that so much may be conveyed by so little. Through the interaction of unchanging ostinato and minimally varied motivic figures we may approach issues central to the human condition. Stravinsky's repetitive techniques here testify to the Aristotelian idea that tragedy, as a form of drama, hearkens back to the structure of ritual: as modern mortal beings, we too are compelled to move through the limitations of earthly time and human limitations. Ultimately, though, as we too will lose our battle with time, Stravinsky's music will live on.[11]

NOTES

1. These are the chorus's final words in the Epilogue of the opera.

2. E. E. Cummings's English translation of the narrator's part as it appears in Stravinsky's score for *Oedipus Rex* (London: Boosey and Hawkes, 1949), x–xi.

3. The English translations of the libretto used here are from Stephen Walsh's *Cambridge Music Handbook for* Oedipus Rex (Cambridge: Cambridge University Press, 1993), 79–91.

4. Ordered succession is a way of representing the formal consequences of Stravinsky's repetitions by vertically aligning key motivic figures. For more information on this analytical method, see my *Building Blocks: Repetition and Continuity in Stravinsky's Music* (New York: Oxford University Press, 2011).

5. Bass ostinatos composed of leaping thirds or fourths are often associated with seriousness of purpose or even grief and disaster in Stravinsky's music. Examples include the thirds bass line in the *Rite*'s "Sacrificial Dance," and the leaping fourths in the opening music of *Symphony of Psalms* and at the end of its last movement.

6. Walsh gives a similar (if not as technical) reading of this passage in the *Cambridge Music Handbook for* Oedipus Rex, 32–33, 36.

7. Walsh suggests that much of *Oedipus Rex* has the quality of an oratorio by Handel, citing a commentary made by Stravinsky's contemporary Arthur Lourié around the time of its first performance. See ibid., 28–30; and Arthur Lourié, "*Oedipus Rex* de Stravinsky," *La Revue musicale* 8/8 (1927): 240–53.

8. Igor Stravinsky and Robert Craft, *Themes and Conclusions* (Berkeley: University of California Press, 1982), 52.

9. See Maureen Carr, *Multiple Masks: Neoclassicism in Stravinsky's Works on Greek Subjects* (Lincoln: University of Nebraska Press, 2002), 240.

10. John Martin, "Stravinsky Work in World Premiere," *New York Times*, 29 April 1948.

11. Daniel Albright describes the Cocteau-Stravinsky setting of *Oedipus* even more bluntly, noting that "Sophocles has Jocasta hang herself; but Stravinsky, a more flagrant sort of mass murderer, kills off the language, the music, even the concept of drama itself. . . . *Oedipus Rex* is indeed a post-mortem opera, a sort of autopsy of a Greek tragedy." See Albright, "Truth and Lies in the Stravinskyan Sense," *Modernist Cultures* 3/1 (Winter 2007): 26.

Symphonies and *Funeral Games*:
Lourié's Critique of Stravinsky's Neoclassicism

KLÁRA MÓRICZ

In their 1989 monograph *The Apollonian Clockwork*, Louis Andriessen and Elmer Schönberger express bewilderment at Stravinsky's high esteem for an obscure figure in music history, the Russian composer Arthur Vincent Lourié:

> Up till now, readers of biographies of Stravinsky have been faced with a *fait accompli* by the presence of Lourié, like a new character that enters out of nowhere half-way through a play. Now that Lourié has received a past—thanks to recent research on the eclipsed Russian musical avant-garde of 1910–30—the sudden entrance and sudden shining role of Lourié in Stravinsky's life becomes, strangely enough, even more of a mystery.[1]

To show the illogicality of such a strong tie between the successful, brilliant Stravinsky, and the forgotten, lackluster Lourié, the authors quote Lourié's seemingly bizarre statement that "our melodic capacity is directly proportional to our capacity for goodness and love" from his 1929 article "An Inquiry into Melody."[2]

Even in recent scholarship, puzzles remain regarding Stravinsky and Lourié's relationship.[3] In this essay I explore Lourié's thoughts on melody, which, I argue, are not only not senseless, as Andriessen and Schönberger suggest, but show him at his most original and thus can help us differentiate between Lourié's and Stravinsky's ideas on music, aesthetics, politics, and ethics. As the date of "An Inquiry into Melody" indicates, the seeds of disagreement were already planted in the late 1920s, when Lourié was still actively promoting Stravinsky's work. The article's implied criticism of Stravinsky reveals not only Lourié's gradual distancing from Stravinsky, but also his close ties to Jacques Maritain, the French neo-Thomist philosopher who had a profound influence on Lourié during his years in exile. I demonstrate Lourié's original approach to melody through a close reading of his *Funeral Games in Honor of Chronos* (1964), a work heavy with references to Stravinsky and thus illustrative of both the similarities and the

Figure 1. Pyotr Miturich, *Portrait of the Composer Arthur Lourié*, 1915.

differences between the composers' views. Analyzing Lourié's *Funeral Games* in the context of his thoughts on melody helps us understand how Lourié, who was for years Stravinsky's right-hand man and who, as Maritain's close friend, played a crucial role in shaping Stravinsky's *homo faber* philosophy, became a critic of the very ideas he had once espoused.[4]

A Forgotten Composer

Lourié's obscurity in emigration marked a sad ending to a career with a promising start. In the 1910s Lourié was associated with St. Petersburg's most cutting-edge artists; as Vladimir Mayakovsky jested: "Tot dur'yo, kto ne znaet Lur'yo" ('Tis a blockhead who doesn't know Lourié).[5] Portraits of the dandyish composer by prominent artists, the most famous one by Pyotr Miturich, testify to his high standing in St. Petersburg's avant-garde circles (see Figure 1).[6] A musician frequently featured in the avant-garde nightclub The Stray Dog, Lourié earned his reputation as a daring musical futurist by experimenting with atonality and quarter tones. His progressive credentials led Anatoly Lunacharsky to appoint him head of the Music Division of the Commissariat for Popular Enlightenment (Narkompros) in the early post-revolutionary years. Like many other intellectuals, in 1922 Lourié left Russia for good. In Paris he befriended Maritain, who inspired his ardent Catholicism and whose conception of art as craftsmanship influenced his and Stravinsky's neoclassical aesthetics.[7] After the composer fled to the United States in 1941, he never regained the momentum lost in Paris. In his last years he found refuge in the Princeton home of his faithful friend Maritain, who did not stop believing that Lourié provided the greatest example of creative inspiration in contemporary music.

In Stravinsky's Shadow

Lourié met Stravinsky on 18 January 1924 in Brussels.[8] They were introduced by Stravinsky's lover and future wife, Vera Sudeikina, who knew Lourié well from their years in St. Petersburg where the two lived together in the early 1920s in a sort of *ménage à quatre* with Sergey Sudeikin and his wife, Olga (at this time Sudeikin and Vera began a relationship that led to their marriage).[9] Shortly after the two composers met, Lourié started to write a book on Stravinsky, for which he produced a series of influential essays that shaped the reception of Stravinsky's music and aesthetics.[10] These articles and the editorial commissions he received on Stravinsky's recommendation provided Lourié with much needed income during his time in Paris. Yet Lourié's friendship with Stravinsky also adversely affected his compositional career. His secretarial role inevitably put him in a subservient position, earning him such dismissive epithets as "Stravinsky's shadow" (composer Nicolas Nabokov), "Stravinsky's *valet de chambre*" (cultural entrepreneur Pyotr Suvchinsky), and "Stravinsky's office boy" (Stravinsky biographer Stephen Walsh).[11]

In 1929 Stravinsky seems to have finally begun to take a serious interest in Lourié's music. Lourié reported the change to Ernest Ansermet on 25 December 1929:

> Something surprising came about after your departure. Igor's attitude toward me has completely changed, by which I mean his attitude regarding my music. He asked me to show him the concerto [*Concerto spirituale*] and approved of it. The change was such that I rubbed my eyes to make sure that it was not a miracle that had come about. He is very sympathetic to the direction I have taken; I see the same problems as he does, and what I write interests him to

such an extent that he remains at the piano for hours examining the manuscript. . . . Vera says that this behavior is entirely exceptional for him and that I can now consider myself his only pupil. Before he left he even "ordered" me to write a symphony. . . . Igor now insists on 100 percent technique from me and he shows himself to be more pedantic than all the professors at the conservatory.[12]

It is conceivable that Stravinsky's recognition that Lourié was capable of far more than being a publicist contributed to his gradual distancing himself from his assistant. No documentary evidence provides a full explanation for why Lourié's relationship with Stravinsky soured. They exchanged only a few letters in the 1930s; in one, from 5 September 1935, Lourié complained to Stravinsky that he "has to make arrangements through others" if he wants to see him.[13] By 1934 Lourié was clearly showing signs of disillusionment with Stravinsky. In a letter to Boris de Schloezer, whom Stravinsky resented because of his negative reviews, Lourié gave vent to his frustration.[14] Since it was a rare occasion that Lourié wrote unguardedly, I quote the letter at length:

> After several months I finally met with Stravinsky. We were both very cautious, which showed that he suspects my opposition, and that is why, although we did not talk about anything serious, he was still glad to see me, because our meeting created at least the facade of the old friendship. The fact that there is no content behind this facade does not seem to concern him. I think he only needs these superficial relationships to neutralize and bind, and thereby paralyze any possible action against him.
>
> He made a sad impression on me. He is pathetic, self-righteous and intolerably bourgeois. He told me about his great friendship with . . . Darius Milhaud. To my surprise he told me that "for tactical reasons, [he tries] to make friends now with all of [his] enemies". . . !? Here are the fruits of "evolution," of the former inflexibility and all the "audacity."[15]

The widening gap between Stravinsky and Lourié may have also been related to their differing political views. Indeed, politics frequently became a cause of disagreement between fellow émigrés during the late 1930s, eventually leading to the disintegration of the Russian émigré community in France. Amid the rising political tensions in Europe some émigrés sought reconciliation with the Soviet regime, while others turned to the extreme right in the hope that fascism or Nazism would be able to defeat Communism. Having little sympathy with the revolution of the lower classes, Stravinsky moved further to the political right after emigration, and thus his aesthetic insistence on "order as a rule and as a law opposed to disorder" gained political overtones.[16] In interviews he openly embraced Mussolini's fascism, and repeatedly announced his enthusiasm for the new political order in Italy. In a 1935 interview for a Roman newspaper Stravinsky asserted: "The Voice of Rome is confused in my spirit with the voice of the Duce. I also say Duce because I feel like a fascist. Today, anyway, pretty much everybody in Europe is a fascist."[17] "I became a French citizen," he said in another Italian interview, "but spiritually I am also a fascist, above all a fascist. Anyway, this is the way everybody thinks in France."[18] Although his sycophantic admiration of Italy's new ruler may have been part of a strategic publicity move in preparation for future Italian performances, there is no doubt that Stravinsky nurtured anti-democratic sentiments. In a 1936 interview in *La Nación* he declared that he was "an anti-parliamentarian."[19]

Unlike Stravinsky, Lourié strongly disliked the rising authoritarian regimes around him. Despite his Catholicism, he never renounced his Communist past, and though he defected and was a critic of Stalinist Russia, he remained unapologetic about his participation in early Bolshevik rule. Born Jewish, he was also personally threatened by the rise of Nazi power. In 1941, the year he fled occupied France, Lourié publicly denounced what he called the "new order": "In all parts of Europe where this new order is now taking form, there may be noted the total eclipse of those values embraced in the concept of 'Humanism.' The mere acceptance of the coming 'Order' seems to free the mind of the moral and intellectual connotations of humanism, at the same time absolving it of any feeling of trespass when abusing the term."[20]

Robert Craft, who took over Lourié's old position as Stravinsky's secretary in 1948, attributed Stravinsky's break with Lourié to Stravinsky's second marriage in 1940, suggesting that the breach was caused by Lourié repeating gossip about Vera Sudeikina, Stravinsky's second wife, to the composer's son Théodore, thus prejudicing him against his father's second marriage.[21] Vladimir Nabokov assumed that Stravinsky simply dropped Lourié, as he dropped most of his former friends who witnessed, in Suvchinsky's words, his *"gaietés parisiennes."*[22] Whatever the cause, by the time they had relocated in the United States the two composers' relationship was openly hostile: cold rejection on Stravinsky's part, resentment mixed with hostility on Lourié's. In a letter to Koussevitzky on 10 February 1948 Lourié gleefully reported that at a rehearsal of Stravinsky's *Symphonies d' instruments à vent* Arturo Toscanini maliciously remarked: "Too bad that it was not Stravinsky who died and Debussy who wrote a symphony in his memory."[23]

Although Stravinsky gradually disappeared from Lourié's life as a friend and confidant, he left a shadowy mark on Lourié's work. Many of Lourié's late works and writings continue the dialogue with Stravinsky that was broken in the late 1930s. Stravinsky's shadow is still perceptible in Lourié's Dionysian self-portrait from the 1940s (see Figure 2). As in Miturich's painting, the composer is sprawled leisurely on a pillow, but instead of posing as a St. Petersburg dandy, he is dressed in classical

Figure 2. Lourié's drawing.

garb and Roman sandals, crowned with laurel, an issue of the Russian-language magazine *Novoye slovo* (New word) spread on his lap. On the composer's right stands a table laid with food, behind it on a hanger a jacket from Saks Fifth Avenue to remind us of the aging Lourié's dandyish habits. The drawing thus combines elements of interwar Paris, with its Russian press and fad for neoclassicism, and Lourié's new surroundings, the United States.[24] At the composer's feet a monkey peruses *Ulysses* by James Joyce, whose poems "Ecce Puer" and "Alone" Lourié set in 1941; on Lourié's left a donkey reads Kierkegaard, whose books Lourié had started to read in English before he even mastered the language and whose philosophy he compared to that of Russian philosopher Vladimir Solovyov.[25] The only musical references on the drawing are the faint outlines of a female singer behind the composer and the barely visible title of Lourié's ill-fated Parisian opera-ballet *Le Festin pendant la peste* (The feast in time of plague), scribbled in the lower-right corner.[26] Significantly, Lourié's *Le Festin* has a Stravinskian resonance: in this opera-ballet Lourié included a dialogue by Petrarch in Charles-Albert Cingria's translation, for which Stravinsky had also once sketched a couple of bars of music.[27]

Symphonies and *Funeral Games*

Lourié continues his dialogue with Stravinsky in *Funeral Games in Honor of Chronos* for three flutes, piano, and cymbals—a work of approximately ten minutes that Lourié completed in 1964.[28] Unperformed in Lourié's lifetime, *Funeral Games* belongs to a series of late works and essays in which Lourié nostalgically revisited his past.[29] He dedicated his *Funeral Games* to the memory of Abbé Roger Bréchard who, like Lourié, was a member of Maritain's circle in Meudon, a suburb southwest of Paris where Jacques and Raïssa Maritain lived from 1923 until their departure to the United States in 1940, and where they held yearly Thomist retreats with forty to three hundred participants.[30]

Lourié prefaces his *Funeral Games* with a Latin epitaph consisting of three lines from Job 28:

> 3. *Tempus posuit tenebris, et universorum finem ipse considerat lapidem quoque caliginis et umbram mortis.*
>
> He has set a time for darkness, and the end of all things he considers, the stone that is in the dark and the shadow of death.
>
> 5. *Terra de qua oriebatur panis in loco suo igne subversa est.*
>
> The land, out of which bread grew in its place, has been overturned with fire.
>
> 11. *Profunda quoque fluviorum scrutatus est, et abscondita in lucem produxit.*
>
> The depth of rivers he has also searched and hidden things he has brought forth to light.

The dedication and the epitaph suggest that Lourié conceived of *Funeral Games* in the tradition of the seventeenth-century French *tombeau*, resurrected in the twentieth century in such pieces as Ravel's *Le Tombeau de Couperin* (1914–17), the six movements of which are dedicated to friends who died in World War I, or *Le Tombeau de Debussy* (1920), a collection of pieces published in a commemorative special issue of *La Revue musicale* for which Stravinsky submitted the chorale of his *Symphonies d'instruments à vent*.[31]

Like *tombeaux*, funeral games in ancient Greece had a commemorative function. In the *Iliad* Achilles honored his friend Patroclus with funeral games that enacted the heroic deeds of the deceased; even the Olympic Games originated as funeral games. Lourié's *Funeral Games*, however, is not only a memorial, but also an intricate dialogue with the past, a celebration and at the same time a critique of Chronos, the mythological embodiment of time in Orphic cosmology and the progenitor of the god Phanes, the creator of the cosmos. Significantly, Phanes is the protagonist of Lourié's Orphic pantomime "The Birth of Eros" in his last opera, *The Blackamoor of Peter the Great* (1948–61), a monumental journey through different historical layers of Russian culture.[32]

Although the dedicatee of *Funeral Games* is Abbé Bréchard and its honoree Chronos, Stravinsky remains its unnamed protagonist. An obvious sign of Stravinsky's shadow in the *Funeral Games* is Lourié's choice of tempi. Like Stravinsky in *Symphonies d'instruments à vent*, Lourié starts *Funeral Games* at ♩ = 72, a tempo that both composers soon change to ♩ = 108. Although less systematically octatonic, Lourié's *Funeral Games* occasionally displays the same octatonic collection that Stravinsky used in his *Symphonies*. Lourié's string-free sound, percussive use of the piano, frequently changing meters, insistent ostinatos with metrically different superimpositions, folklike, hiccupping embellishments, and varied repetition of short motives can be heard as distinctly Stravinskian. Neoclassicism à la Stravinsky's Octet (another piece Lourié arranged for piano in Paris) also left a mark on the piece in the form of contrapuntal textures and large intervals, frequently producing Bachian (or Stravinskian) two-register melodies.

The most striking tribute to Stravinsky comes at the end of *Funeral Games*. Before the last section begins at measure 161, all accidentals disappear, and the music moves slowly in diatonic, white-key purity to its end as if demonstrating the progress from the darkness (*tenebrae*) to light (*lux*) described in the epigraph. Like Stravinsky before him in the *Symphonies d'instruments à vent*, Lourié concludes his piece with a clearly articulated homophonic hymn (see Example 1), reminiscent of the slow and quiet *Vechnaya pamyat'* (Eternal remembrance), the closing part of the *Panikhida*, the Russian Orthodox memorial service.[33] The parallel with Stravinsky's *Symphonies* is not coincidental: Lourié arranged it for piano in 1926 and recognized in its final section "a chorale not of a Western type but closer to the Orthodox practice."[34] The narrow range and stepwise motion of the traditional melody for the *Vechnaya pamyat'* are clearly recognizable in the final hymn of the *Funeral Games* (see Examples 2a–c). Its three-part, falsobordone harmonization, with the melody in the middle voice and the top voice moving in parallel thirds, evokes *kantï*, the "old," "monastic" or "tender" (*umilitel'nïy*) style of singing Orthodox chant. The parallel between Lourié's and Stravinsky's closing sections goes even further: the last twenty measures of Stravinsky's *Symphonies* consist mainly of alterations of E-minor sevenths and D-minor ninth chords (see Example 3); when Lourié repeats his melody in two-octave parallel between the flute and the alto flute at

Example 1. Lourié, *Funeral Games in Honor of Chronos*, mm. 161–76.

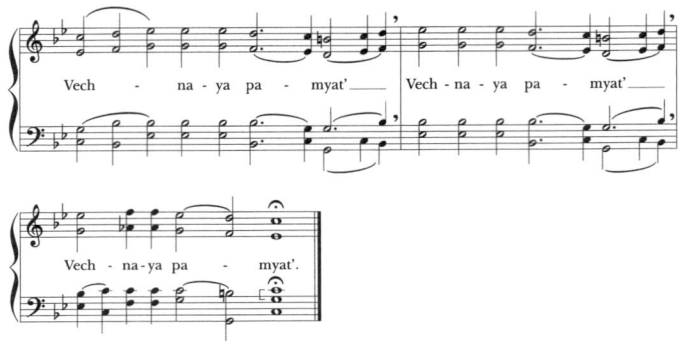

Example 2a. Traditional melody for the *Vechnaya pamyat'*
(from Richard Taruskin, *Stravinsky and the Russian Traditions*, 2:1492).

Example 2b. Lourié's melody.

Example 2c. Stravinsky's melody (from Taruskin, *Stravinsky and the Russian Traditions*, 2:1492).

Example 3. Igor Stravinsky, *Symphonies d'instruments à vent*, arranged for piano
by Arthur Lourié, mm. 275–99.

measure 177, his sole accompaniment is an E-minor seventh chord with an added
C (Example 4). Nor can it be accidental that Lourié's melody starts with precisely
the same three notes (B–C–D) with which Stravinsky's melody ended, or that
Lourié again chose the same tempo marking ($\downarrow$ = 72) as Stravinsky. As Examples
2a–c show, Lourié's *Vechnaya pamyat* is closer to Stravinsky's rendition of the service
than to the traditional tune.

Despite its strong Stravinskian resonances, Lourié's music, apart from a few
sections, sounds decidedly different from Stravinsky's. Its dissonances are less
harsh, its rhythms less exuberant, its performative surface less immediately inviting.
To put it in positive terms, while Stravinsky's stylized dissonances and angular
melodies create ironic distance, Lourié's harmonies and melodies preserve their
warmly expressive potential. The large intervals in Lourié's melodies do not result
in grotesque angularity, but in expressive gestures that demonstrate his belief in
the power and primacy of melody over other elements of music.

Example 4. Lourié, *Funeral Games*, mm. 177–84.

The least Stravinskian passage in Lourié's *Funeral Games* is a short, two-register melody that disrupts the previous metric regularity of the piece. In measure 90 the tempo slows to ♩ = 68 (see Example 5). The melody is preceded by four gong-like sonorities, the last of which is built on notes taken from octatonic Collection I, out of which the piccolo takes all but one note of its expressive melody. With this melody the piccolo assumes an individual voice, soaring above the chromatically descending flute line and the static pedal of the alto flute. Notated in alternating duple and triple meters, Lourié's melody does not conform to a metric pattern: the piccolo's phrase starts on the first beat, then, at its repetition, on the second beat of the bar; its climactic B falls first on the second, then on the first beat,

Example 5. The espressive melody in Lourié, *Funeral Games*, mm. 87–95.

accented by the piano's harmony; its last note is sustained for two beats on its first appearance, and five-and-a-half beats on its second.

The Freedom of Melody

To explain why this melodic passage is so magical, I call Lourié as a witness, citing the very article ridiculed by Andriessen and Schönberger. As Lourié reported to Koussevitzky, the article stirred controversy even before it was published.[35] After its publication Maritain became its champion, quoting from it extensively in his own writings.[36] In the article Lourié argues that melody, unlike harmony and rhythm, is "always irrational in its essence" and remains inaccessible to "the logic of our conscious self." Despite this disclaimer, Lourié does explain melody in rational terms. He sees melody as "the primary moving force and organic essence of art," its primacy deriving from its uncanny ability to "reveal some intimate truth, the genuine psychological and spiritual substance of its maker," or, as Maritain paraphrased it, the maker's "ontological value."[37] "*Melody*," Lourié declares, "*discloses the nature of the subject, not the object.*"[38] And this is precisely why composers, afraid of melody's potentially dangerous revelation, frequently hide behind stylization and irony, the primary function of which, Lourié wrote in a moment of poetic inspiration, is to mask fear.[39] Lourié identified melody's ability to disclose some otherwise inaccessible truth with a moral force—hence his evocation of the human capacity for good in relation to melody in the sentence that Andriessen and Schönberger found so absurd: "Our melodic gift is in direct relation to our capacity for good, not in the sentimental but in the religious sense. . . . Melody in itself is a primary good, a sort of purification through repentance."[40] Allowing melody to rule requires infinite faith and trust from the composer, and a willingness to accept the process of self-discovery, whatever it discloses.

Lourié's concept of melody appeals not to the personal (or, as he writes, "sentimental"), but to the transcendental and religious spheres. As the above example from *Funeral Games* demonstrates, melody can create the illusion of suspended time. "Melody in itself is not connected with any action," Lourié explains, "and does not lead to any action." It "serves no purpose at all. It brings *liberation*," a disruption of logic, "a sense of freedom."[41] This sense of liberation is related to melody's power to abolish "the conditions of space and time," and to free the spirit "from the chains of spatial and temporal limitations." Melody's spiritual potential is unleashed when it disrupts "the sense of [the] spatial and temporal causality of earthly life."[42] In Maritain's explanation, melody "arises from a break in temporal connections"; it is "the pure and direct expression of poetic experience in the composer."[43]

Lourié's ideas about melody may have been inspired by Henri Bergson, whose philosophy was well known in Russia and whose anti-positivist ideas greatly influenced Maritain at the beginning of his career. As Suzanne Guerlac writes, melody, for Bergson, is a figure of duration that "implies a certain mode of organization" and "involves a temporal synthesis of memory that knits temporal dimensions together." Melody performs "the act of temporal synthesis . . . to the extent it binds past, present, and future together in a radically singular way."[44] Bergson's proposed simultaneity of past, present, and future must have been alluring to Lourié who, despite his early Futurist credentials, absorbed much of the Bergsonian time-dissolving poetic practices of St. Petersburg's Acmeist poets— Anna Akhmatova, Osip Mandelshtam, and Nikolay Gumilyov.[45] Whatever the inspiration, in Lourié's mind the liberty of melody seems to have been related to melody's peculiar relation to time. Lourié's *Funeral Games* not only honors Chronos enacting time's heroic deeds but also shows chronos defeated, rendered powerless by melody's irrational yet invincible liberating force.

In Lourié's view the unrestrained nature of melody also had strong erotic connotations. Among the many quotations in the libretto for his opera *The Blackamoor of Peter the Great*, Lourié gives special emphasis to Pushkin's famous lines from *The Stone Guest*: "Of all the happy pleasures life supplies, / To love alone does music yield in sweetness; / But love itself is melody."[46] In Pushkin's play melody signals socially unconstrained love, promoted in *The Blackamoor* by Eros, a statue that comes to life in order to prevent the unnatural, autocratically ordered marriage between Peter the Great's godson, the blackamoor Ibrahim, and Natasha, the young daughter of a Russian nobleman. Lourié unleashes the irrational, explosive force of Eros in the opera, letting him wreak havoc by turning the characters against social customs and authoritarian power. Not coincidentally, Lourié marks the birth of Eros with a rhythmically free-flowing, unaccompanied melody and the destruction of love with a twelve-tone passage as Peter the Great, in yet another instance of defying nature, sends the adulterous Natasha to the convent and marries her lover to the family jester.[47]

Lourié's ideas on the erotic potential of the creative act might have been influenced by Russian philosophers Vladimir Solovyov, Vasily Rozanov, and Nikolay Berdyaev, in whose philosophies love occupies a central place. Maritain likewise confirms the erotic aspect of creation when he describes the sensual perception of material as enabling the intellect to capture physical beauty, which "stirs desire and produces love. . . . Every form of beauty is loved at first for itself, even if later the too frail flesh is caught in the snare. Love in turn produces ecstasy, that is to say, renders the lover beside himself."[48] Significantly, Maritain evokes Eros when he describes what he calls Lourié's "ontological" or, in Kierkegaard's terms, "existential" music:

> "Ontological" music is "erotic" music—here again I am speaking Danish—I mean that it owes its substance to the Eros immanent in being, to that internal weight of desire and regret which moans in all created things, and that is why such music is naturally religious, and does not entirely awaken save under a touch of the love of God.[49]

The erotic resonances of Lourié's concept of melody signal that he took notice of Kierkegaard's thoughts on music's fundamentally sensuous nature. "Music always expresses the immediate in its immediacy," Kierkegaard wrote in his famous essay on Mozart's *Don Giovanni* in *Either/Or*. This immediacy, he continued, is always sensuous, "absolutely lyrical, and in music it erupts in all its lyrical impatience. That is, it is qualified by spirit and therefore is power, life, movement, continual unrest, continual succession. But this unrest, this succession, does not enrich it; it continually remains the same; it does not unfold but incessantly rushes forward as if in a single breath."[50]

It would be hard to find a better way to articulate the quintessentially lyrical moment in Lourié's *Funeral Games* I have discussed above. "If I were to describe this lyricism with a single predicate," Kierkegaard writes, "I would have to say: It sounds—and with this I come back again to the elemental originality of the sensuous as that which in its immediacy manifests itself musically."[51] Or, as Lourié put it in an essay titled "The Noumenal and Phenomenal in Music": "Revelation in art is given by momentary flashes only, in a piercing and acute sensation which is as fast and brief as a sudden glare of lightning." To underline the erotic connotations of such a moment, Lourié uses strongly suggestive language: "Music is a mask worn by chastity. Its chaste condition veils all that cannot be expressed due to modesty and the rules of propriety, i.e.—God, love, conscience, purity, virginity, faith, happiness, heroism, etc."[52] Unlike Kierkegaard, however, Lourié sees in melody not only sensuousness and erotic potential but also moral force. In Maritain's interpretation Lourié judges the nature of melodies according to their capacity to achieve "moral-aesthetic unity."[53]

Dialogue with Stravinsky

If we read Lourié's *Funeral Games* metaphorically as a display of time's defeat and melody's triumph, we can decipher in the composition yet another hidden conversation between Lourié and Stravinsky. Chronos, after all, was the name Stravinsky (more precisely his ghostwriter Suvchinsky) gave to musical time in his *Poétique musicale*.[54] But musical time, Lourié argued in a 1944 essay, should be understood more broadly than the "rhythmic structure of sounding time."[55] It should include the melodic element, which, according to Lourié, was next in line to gain primacy after harmony and rhythm as developed by Scriabin and Stravinsky.

Stravinsky, like Lourié, placed melody at the summit of the hierarchy of the elements of music, but he seemed to want to limit its power, warning against the danger of becoming "beclouded by melody to the point of losing balance" and thus forgetting that "the art of music speaks to us in many voices at once."[56] Art, Stravinsky declared in his *Poétique musicale*, "is contrary to chaos." Suvchinsky believed that Stravinsky's conception of art as order and his adherence to dogma had a paralyzing effect on the composer, preventing him from achieving the liberty that Maritain considered essential in the creative act. Stravinsky's religious (or he could have said compositional) practice, Suvchinsky wrote in 1975, did not reflect "faith of a psychological, lyrical or moral order. For him it was about the discovery (by grace, or maybe by fear?) and the resigned acceptance of a structure, dogma, and reality established for all eternity; being and life existed the way they were; they were practiced in conditions managed by secret and strange laws."[57]

As Tamara Levitz has argued, Stravinsky's resolute devotion to compositional dogma eventually alienated Maritain, who by the mid-1930s judged his music too constrained.[58] Stravinsky, Maritain wrote in 1943, "is obstinately bent on obeying jealously the figures and the operative rules of the nature-like producing will. He fears the eternal laws," and thus his works would hardly escape "sheer craft and athleticism."[59] Lourié's words about the revelatory power of melody and about composers' fear of exposing themselves to it seem applicable to Stravinsky. For Stravinsky, Lourié writes disapprovingly in 1944, "music is play. He is always playing, or, more precisely, he stylizes: people, things, ideas, feelings, and even life itself."[60] Such stylization, we may recall, signaled fear for Lourié, the incapability of exposing oneself to melody's potentially dangerous revelation.[61] By the time Maritain's *Creative Intuition in Art and Poetry* appeared in 1953, the philosopher unapologetically situated Stravinsky among the "great artists who take pleasure in describing themselves as mere engineers in the manufacturing of an artifact of words or sounds." Stravinsky, Maritain wrote, purposefully hides the truth by grudging against the power of inspiration, which, he claims, is irrelevant to real art.[62]

Like Maritain, Lourié related Stravinsky's adherence to dogma to his repression of music's erotic potential. He thought that Stravinsky's *Petrushka* was a "reaction against the erotic mysticism of Scriabin."[63] Discussing *The Rite of Spring* and *Les Noces* Suvchinsky declared that despite "the sap and erotic passion of renewal" of the topics, in these works "the sensual element is transformed, heightened and even totally absorbed by a sort of cosmic will, [which] is implacable and anonymous to such a degree that it becomes mechanical, with the consequences that every whiff, image, or allusion to anything erotic becomes excluded." Consequently, in Suvchinsky's views these potentially erotic works remain "coldly thought out and composed."[64] Lourié seems to have anticipated Suvchinsky's judgment when he described *Les Noces* as "dynamic in a musical sense," but emotionally "saturated with the calmness and 'quietude' of the icon. It is," Lourié summed up, "lacking in ecstasy."[65]

Still full of enthusiasm for Stravinsky in 1926, Lourié did not intend his remarks to be critical. Gradually, however, the sense that Stravinsky's music lacked a certain magic became a thorn in the eyes of Lourié and Maritain. In Stravinsky's music, according to Maritain, the spirit of the work is the composer's dominating intellect and will. "The more he becomes himself, the further he removes himself from magic."[66] In *Apollo* or *Capriccio* "the brilliant poetry depends in its entirety on the made object."[67] In contrast, Maritain states, in Lourié's music magic, which the philosopher defined as the Plotinian notion of grace, "rises from the shadows of the human depths" and "crosses the threshold of supernatural orison."[68] "Magic in music," in Lourié's own definition, "is not an artificially irrational order" but "a breach of the law of gravitation or elevation without the aid of a motor."[69] "The quality of magic," Maritain writes, suggests "a completely free element, a kind of separate 'grace' superior to the poetry of the work as engaged or absorbed in the meaning and substance of the work." Magic is a "free *surplus* of poetry . . . an inexhaustible intuitive emotion, diffuse in the composer's entire subjectivity, which has not been 'caught' in the actuation of the free creativity of the spirit engendering the work through the instrumentality of art, and which, however, passes into music that has a magical quality." This "surplus, the inexhaustible intuitive emotion" passes "through creative intuition . . . as a free element, a free 'spirit,' which *overflows* the creative intuition through which it passes, and immediately moves and permeates, as a grace in addition, the working activity, without the composer's having the least awareness of it."[70]

Like Lourié's melody, Maritain's surplus is free. It disrupts "the sense of spatial and temporal causality," and "gives the impression of belonging to the category of the eternal."[71] Taking the lead from Lourié, Henri-Irénée Marrou, one of the composer's Catholic admirers, argued that melody exists "solely in memory"; its existence is "completely spiritual and free of the inexorable passage of duration."[72]

Lourié's *Funeral Games* has many functions: it honors the dead by imitating the actions of fallen heroes, and, like the funeral games in honor of Patroclus in Homer's *Iliad*, provides a farewell to previous characters. In this context Stravinsky's actions are recalled only as actions of a fallen hero, fallen, not like Abbé Bréchard, the dedicatee of the piece, heroically, in combat against the Germans in 1940, but like someone who had turned from a friend into an enemy. The closing hymn of Lourié's *Funeral Games* transcends Chronos by turning to the eternal truth of Christianity, which, in its immutability, indivisibility, and simultaneity, was for him, as for Thomas Aquinas and his promoter Maritain, the affirmation of the existence of God.

At the end of *Funeral Games* the piccolo, which presented Lourié's irresistible, free melody, all but disappears, taking with it its shadow companion, the flute. For the first iteration of the concluding hymn at measure 161 only the alto flute remains, moving, initially, in parallel octaves with the upper part of the piano left hand. At the repetition of the hymn's third line at measure 177, the flute returns to double the alto flute an octave higher (see Example 4). The piccolo also resumes here, its role reduced now to an additional color in the piano's bell-like punctuations. Instead of being the agent of free-flowing melody, the piccolo serves a higher purpose in the hymn, its sensuous immediacy giving way to the eternity of spirituality. It is as if Lourié, by a magician's (or professional ideologue's) sleight of hand exchanged Kierkegaard's sensuous immediacy with Maritain's religious immutability as music's absolute subject. In his concept of melody Lourié thus combined what Kierkegaard presented as different modes of life—the aesthetic (sensuous) and the ethical— under the category of religion, which in Kierkegaard's philosophy overturns the sensuous stage.

Lourié's *Funeral Games* is religious music in which neoclassicism and its cathartic function are transformed into Christian transcendence, Stravinsky's chronos is defeated, and sensuous immediacy is converted into the eternity of religious belief. Yet as the similarity of the ending of Lourié's *Funeral Games* to the Russian funeral service, the *vechnaya pamyat'* (eternal memory), reminds us, on a more personal level the eternity achieved at the end of the piece remains the eternity of memory in which the past lives on, boundless and completely oblivious to the approaching end of human time. The enigma of Lourié may be solved if we listen carefully to his ephemeral yet powerful melodies, which, as Schönberger and Andriessen suggest, are incongruent with Stravinsky's aesthetics. Not because Lourié's ideas about melody are senseless, but because in their creative freedom, sensuous immediacy, moral revelation, and magical potential, Lourié's melodies contradict Stravinsky's ascetic dogma.

NOTES

1. Louis Andriessen and Elmer Schönberger, *The Apollonian Clockwork: On Stravinsky*, trans. Jeff Hamburg (New York: Oxford University Press, 1989), 93.

2. Ibid., 92. Arthur Lourié, "An Inquiry into Melody," *Modern Music* 7/1 (December–January 1929–30): 3–11.

3. Recent scholarship on the relationship between Stravinsky and Lourié includes Valérie Dufour, "Néo-gothique et néo-classique: Arthur Lourié et Jacques Maritain, aux origines idéologiques du conflit Stravinski-Schoenberg," in *Musique, art et religion dans l'entre-deux-guerres*, ed. Sylvain Caron and Michel Duchesneau (Paris: Symétrie, 2009), 31–41; Larisa Kazanskaya, "Lur'ye i Stravinskiy: 'V teni geniya?'" (Lourié and Stravinsky: In the shadow of a genius?), *Muzikal'naya akademiya* 2 (2010): 102–6; Tamara Levitz, *Modernist Mysteries*: Perséphone (New York: Oxford University Press, 2012), 117–81, 290–395; and Richard Taruskin, "Turania Revisited, with Lourié as my Guide," in *Funeral Games in Honor of Arthur Lourié*, ed. Klára Móricz and Simon Morrison (Oxford University Press, forthcoming).

4. Andriessen and Schönberger, *The Apollonian Clockwork*, 94.

5. Mayakovsky's jest derives from the Russian possessive adjective *duriy* (from *durak*, fool), occurring here in the neuter singular from the fixed expression *dur'yo gnezdo* (a nest of fools), used to describe a blockhead or a stupid, clueless person. Mayakovsky alters the stress of Lourié's name in Russian (Lur'YE to Lur'YO) to accommodate the rhyme. The shift in vowel from -'*ye* to -'*yo* at the end of a noun also suggests a familiar, folk, or conversational tone.

6. The poet Anna Akhmatova, Lourié's onetime lover, recalled Miturich's painting along with portraits of such illustrious artists as Vsevolod Meyerhold, Anna Pavlova, and Stravinsky in *Zapisnïye knizhki Annï Akhmatovoy (1958–1966)* (Notebooks of Anna Akhmatova, 1958–1966) (Turin: Giulio Einaudi Editore, 1996), 174.

7. The Jewish Lourié converted to Catholicism on 4 June 1913 before he married his first wife, the Polish Catholic Yadviga Tsïbulskaya.

8. Kazanskaya, "Lur'ye i Stravinskiy," 104.

9. Lourié was already connected to the Stravinsky family: from 1919 on he lived in the apartment of Stravinsky's mother, Anna Kirillovna, and as a commissar helped her to emigrate. Ibid., 103–4.

10. Lourié never completed the book. The articles, in chronological order, are: "La Sonate pour piano de Strawinsky," *La Revue musicale* 6/10 (1 August 1925): 100–104; "Muzïka Stravinskogo," *Vyorstï* 1 (1926): 119–35; "Oedipus-Rex," *La Revue musicale* 8/8 (1 June 1927): 240–53; "A propos

de l'*Apollon* d'Igor Strawinsky," *Musique* 1 (1928): 117–19; "Dve operï Stravinskogo," *Vyorstï* 3 (1928): 225–27; "Neogothic and Neoclassic," *Modern Music* 5/3 (March–April 1928): 3–8; "Krizis iskusstva," *Yevraziya* 4 (1928): 8, and *Yevraziya* 8 (12 January 1929): 8; "Strawinsky à Bruxelles," *Cahiers de Belgique* 3 (December 1930): 330–32; and "Le Capriccio de Strawinsky," *La Revue musicale* 11/103 (April 1930): 353–55.

11. Nicolas Nabokov, *Bagázh: Memoirs of a Russian Cosmopolitan* (New York: Atheneum, 1975), 166; Suvchinsky quoted in Igor Stravinsky and Robert Craft, *Retrospectives and Conclusions* (New York: Alfred A. Knopf, 1969), 194; and Stephen Walsh, *Stravinsky: The Second Exile: France and America, 1934–1971* (Berkeley: University of California Press, 2008), 384.

12. Lourié to Ernest Ansermet, 25 December 1929 (Fonds Ansermet, Bibliothèque publique et universitaire de Genève, Msmus 184), quoted in Katerina Levidou, "The Encounter of Neoclassicism with Eurasianism in Interwar Paris," D. Phil. diss., Oxford University, 2008, 156–57. Translation after Levidou.

13. Lourié to Stravinsky, 5 September 1935, in *Igor' Stravinskiy: Perepiska s russkimi korrespondentami. Materialï k biografii* (Russian correspondence: Materials for a biography), ed. Viktor Varunts (Moscow: Kompozitor, 2003), 3:584.

14. On the negative reviews, see Levitz, *Modernist Mysteries*, 307.

15. Lourié to Boris de Schloezer, 13 October 1934, Collection Boris de Schloezer, Bibliothèque Louis Notari, Monaco.

16. Igor Stravinsky, *Poetics of Music in the Form of Six Lessons*, trans. Arthur Knodel and Ingolf Dahl (New York: Vintage Books, 1947), 17.

17. "Un musicista interpretato da se stesso: Igor Strawinsky e la sua estetica," *Il Piccolo*, 27 May 1935, quoted in Levitz, *Modernist Mysteries*, 335.

18. Renzo Giacomelli, "Cronaca teatrale: Intervista con Igor Strawinski," *Il Resto del carlino*, 22 May 1935, quoted in ibid., 335.

19. "I am an anti-parliamentarian. I can't stand it like a horse can't put up with the camel." From "Igor Strawinski nos habla de las orientacones futuras de la música y de su arte," *La Nación* (Buenos Aires), 25 April 1936, quoted in Levitz, *Modernist Mysteries*, 337.

20. Lourié, "Notes on the 'New Order,'" *Modern Music* 19/1 (November–December 1941): 3.

21. Robert Craft, *Stravinsky: Glimpses of a Life* (New York: St. Martin's, 1993), 136.

22. Correspondence between Vladimir Nabokov and Mstislav Dobuzhinskiy, in *Zvezda* 10 (1998), quoted in Kazanskaya, "Lur' ye i Stravinskiy," 106. For Suvchinsky's remark see Craft, *Retrospectives and Conclusions*, 193.

23. Lourié to Koussevitzky, 10 February 1948, folder 2, box 40, Koussevitzky Collection, Library of Congress.

24. For Stravinsky's preoccupation with Greek topics see Maureen Carr, *Multiple Masks: Neoclassicism in Stravinsky's Worlds on Greek Subjects* (Lincoln: University of Nebraska Press, 2002).

25. Lourié's diary entries, 25 November 1945 and 15 August 1951, file 8, Lourié Collection, Paul Sacher Stiftung, Basel, Switzerland. Special thanks to Olesya Bobrik, editor of the 4-volume collected writings of Lourié, for sharing these entries with me.

26. Details of the aborted performance are documented in an unsigned and undated document and the 1938–39 correspondence between Jacques Rouché, director of the Opéra, and Lourié in the archives of the Bibliothèque Musée de l'Opéra, Bibliothèque Nationale de France.

27. See Carr, *Multiple Masks*, 194 and 339n87.

28. On 28 February 1964, Lourié reported the completion of *Funeral Games* to Maritain. Lourié to Maritain, 28 February 1964, Centre d'Archives du Cercle d'Etudes Jacques et Raïssa Maritain, Kolbsheim, France.

29. These writings include "Cheshuya v nevode (Pamyati M. A. Kuzmina)" (Scales in the Seine [In memory of M. A. Kuzmin]), *Vozdushnïye puti* (Arial ways) 2 (1961): 186–214; "Detskiy ray" (Children's paradise), *Vozdushnïye puti* 3 (1963): 161–72; and "Ol'ga Afanas'yeva Glebova-Sudeykina," *Vozdushnïye puti* 5 (1967): 139–45. Lourié conceived of his opera *The Blackamoor of Peter the Great* as "a monument of Russian culture, the Russian people and Russian history." See Lourié to Anna Akhmatova, 25 March 1963, quoted and translated in Caryl Emerson, "Arthur Vincent

Lourié's *The Blackamoor of Peter the Great*: Pushkin's Exotic Ancestor as Twentieth–Century Opera," in *Under the Sky of My Africa: Alexander Pushkin and Blackness*, ed. Catherine Theimer Nepomnyashchy, Nicole Svobodny, and Ludmilla A. Trigos (Evanston, IL: Northwestern University Press, 2006), 332.

30. Diverse luminaries such as Jean Cocteau, Charles du Bos; philosophers Emmanuel Mounier, Gabriel Marcel, and Nikolay Berdyaev; Russian composer Nicolas Nabokov; Italian Futurist painter Gino Severini; and Stravinsky were drawn to Maritain's circle. About the Maritains' Meudon years see Judith Suther, *Raissa Maritain: Pilgrim, Poet, Exile* (New York: Fordham University Press, 1990), 52–64. Lourié's dedication in the score, in French, reads: "In memory of Lieutenant Abbé Roger Bréchard fallen in France in June 1940."

31. See Stravinsky, "Fragment des *Symphonies pour instruments à vent*, à la mémoire de C. A. Debussy," *La Revue musicale* 1/2 (1 December 1920), supplement.

32. About Lourié's *Blackamoor* see Móricz, "Decadent Truncation," *Cambridge Opera Journal* 20/2 (July 2008): 181-213; and "Retrieving What Time Destroys: The Palimpsests of Akhmatova's *Poem Without a Hero* and Lourié's *The Blackamoor of Peter the Great*," in Móricz and Morrison, eds., *Funeral Games in Honor of Arthur Lourié*.

33. About the parallels between the *Panikhida* service and Stravinsky's *Symphonies d'instruments à vent* see Richard Taruskin, *Stravinsky and the Russian Traditions* (Berkeley: University of Californa Press, 1996), 2:1486–99.

34. Lur'ye, "Muzïka Stravinskogo," 131. See Igor Stravinsky, *Symphonies d'instruments à vent, à la mémoire de Claude Debussy*, arranged for piano by Arthur Lourié (Paris: Edition Russe de Musique, 1926).

35. Lourié to Koussevitzky, 8 December 1929, folder 2, box 40, Koussevitzky Collection, Library of Congress.

36. Jacques Maritain, "Sur la musique d'Arthur Lourié," in Jacques and Raïssa Maritain, *Oeuvres complètes* (Paris: Editions Saint–Paul/Freibourg: Editions Universitaires, 1982), 6:1060–66; and Jacques Maritain, *Creative Intuition in Art and Poetry* (New York: Pantheon Books, 1953). For an in-depth analysis of Maritain's influence on Lourié, see Caryl Emerson, "Jacques Maritain and the Catholic Muse in Lourié's Post-Petersburg Worlds," in Móricz and Morrison, eds., *Funeral Games in Honor of Arthur Lourié*.

37. Maritain, "Sur la musique d'Arthur Lourié," 1065.

38. Lourié, "An Inquiry into Melody," 4. Lourié's emphasis.

39. "Indeed, today the artist hides all that he cannot overcome or master under the veil of irony; but then, irony is, above all, the mask of fear." Arthur Lourié, "Oedipus-Rex," 252.

40. Lourié, "An Inquiry into Melody," 5–6.

41. Ibid., 9, italics original.

42. Ibid., 6.

43. Maritain, "Sur la musique d'Arthur Lourié," 1064; and Maritain, *Creative Intuition in Art and Poetry*, 253.

44. Suzanne Guerlac, *Thinking in Time: An Introduction to Henri Bergson* (Ithaca, NY, and London: Cornell University Press, 2006), 66–67.

45. About the influence of Bergson's philosophy on Russian Modernism, see Hilary L. Fink, *Bergson and Russian Modernism 1900–1930* (Evanston, IL: Northwestern University Press, 1999). About Lourié's and the Acmeists' conception of time, see my "Retrieving What Time Destroys."

46. Alexander Pushkin, *The Stone Guest*, in *Boris Godunov and Other Dramatic Works*, trans. James E. Falen (New York: Oxford University Press, 2007), 141–42. About the literary sources of the opera's libretto see Móricz, "Decadent Truncation."

47. For a different interpretation of melody in the *Blackamoor*, see Emerson, "Jacques Maritain and the Catholic Muse in Lourié's Post-Petersburg Worlds."

48. Jacques Maritain, *Art and Scholasticism with Other Essays*, trans. J. F. Scanlan (New York: Charles Scribner's Sons, 1937), 26–27.

49. Jacques Maritain, "The Freedom of Song" (1935), in *Art and Poetry*, trans. Elva de Pue Matthews (New York: Philosophical Library, 1943), 96–97.

50. Søren Kierkegaard, "The Immediate Erotic Stages or the Musical-Erotic," in *Either/Or*, part 1, ed. Howard V. Hong and Edna H. Hong (Princeton: Princeton University Press, 1987), 71.

51. Ibid.

52. Arthur Lourié, "The Noumenal and Phenomenal in Music," *Third Hour* 8 (1961): 48–49.

53. See Maritain's extensive quotation from the French publication of Lourié's "De la mélodie" (*La Vie intellectuelle* [25 December 1936]: 491–99) in his *Creative Intuition in Art and Poetry*, 253–54. For more about the Kierkegaardian resonances in Maritain and Lourié's aesthetics, see Emerson, "Jacques Maritain and the Catholic Muse in Lourié's Post-Petersburg Worlds."

54. Stravinsky, *Poetics of Music*, 29. Stravinsky quotes from Pierre Souvtchinsky, "La Notion du temps et la musique: Réflexions sur la typologie de la création musicale," *Le Revue musicale* 20/191 (May–June 1939): 70–80.

55. Artur Lur'ye, "Linii evolyutsii russkoy muzïki" (The evolutionary lines of Russian music), *Noviy zhurnal* (New review) 9 (1944): 257–75.

56. Stravinsky, *Poetics of Music*, 40–41.

57. Pierre Souvtchinsky, "Neuf paragraphes (disparates): Stravinsky auprès et au loin," in *Stravinsky: Etudes et témoignages*, ed. François Lesure (Paris: J. C. Lattès, 1982), 26; repr. as "1975: Stravinski auprès et au loin," in *(Re)Lire Souvtchinski: Textes choisis par Eric Humbertclaude* (La Bresse: Eric Humbertclaude, 1990), 194–95. Quoted and translated in Levitz, *Modernist Mysteries*, 160.

58. Ibid., 162.

59. Maritain, "The Freedom of Song," 72. Maritain's "la volonté naturante," which Elva de Pue Matthews translates as "nature-like producing will," might be better understood as "naturing will." The end of the quotation about "sheer craft and athleticism" does not appear in the original French version of the 1935 article.

60. Lur'ye, "Linii evolyutsii russkoy muzïki," 313. He repeats this line exactly in "Igor Stravinski (1944)," in *Profanation et sanctification du temps: Journal musical Saint Pétersbourg–Paris–New York, 1910–1960* (Paris: Desclée de Brouwer, 1966), 74.

61. Lourié, "Oedipus-Rex," 252.

62. Maritain, *Creative Intuition in Art and Poetry*, 62.

63. Lur'ye, "Muzïka Stravinskogo," 186. In an interview Stravinsky himself "spoke clearly against eroticism in music and on this occasion put Scriabin on trial." "Où va la musique moderne: M. Stravinsky juge Wagner un musicien sans importance," *Comoedia*, 25 March 1928, quoted in Levitz, *Modernist Mysteries*, 362n231.

64. Pierre Souvtchinsky, "Igor Strawinsky," *Contrepoints* 2 (February 1946): 24, quoted in Levitz, *Modernist Mysteries*, 363.

65. Lur'ye, "Muzïka Stravinskogo," 191.

66. Maritain, "The Freedom of Song," 102.

67. Ibid.

68. Maritain, *Creative Intuition in Art and Poetry*, 401; and Maritain, "The Freedom of Song," 102.

69. Lourié, "The Noumenal and Phenomenal in Music," 48.

70. Maritain, *Creative Intuition in Art and Poetry*, 401, 402–3, Lourié's emphasis.

71. Lourié, "An Inquiry into Melody," 6; and Maritain's translation of Lourié's article in *Creative Intuition in Art and Poetry*, 253.

72. Henri Davenson [Henri-Irénée Marrou], *Traité de la musique selon l'esprit de Saint Augustin* (Neuchâtel: Editions de la Baconnière, 1942), 21.

Arthur Lourié's Eurasianist and Neo-Thomist Responses to the Crisis of Art

INTRODUCTION AND NOTES BY KLÁRA MÓRICZ

Arthur Lourié published his article "Krizis iskusstva" (The crisis of art) in two installments in the fourth and eighth issues of the weekly Eurasianist newspaper *Yevraziya* (Eurasia) in 1928–29. The first installment appeared with Lourié's essay on Rachmaninoff, the second with his report on Otto Klemperer in Paris.[1] Lourié was not only an occasional contributor to the newspaper. From the tenth issue (26 January 1929) his name appeared on the masthead along with such prominent Eurasianists as Lev Karsavin, Dmitry Sviatopolk-Mirsky, and Pyotr Suvchinsky. "The Crisis of Art" is one in a series of essays Lourié published about Stravinsky between 1925 and 1930 in various periodicals, among them *Vyorstï* (Mileposts), another short-lived Eurasianist journal. Unlike *Vyorstï*, which its editors, Sviatopolk-Mirsky, Suvchinsky, and Sergey Efron, intended as a politically independent literary "thick" journal, *Yevraziya* had a strong political angle, which led to a split in the Eurasianist movement.

The Eurasianist movement was launched in Sofia in 1921 by the publication of *Iskhod k Vostoku* (*Exodus to the East*), a collection of ten essays by the movement's four founders, theoretical linguist Prince Nikolay Sergeyevich Trubetskoy, the Orthodox theologian Georges Vasilyevich Florovsky, the economist and geographer Pyotr Nikolayevich Savitsky, and music critic and patron Suvchinsky. Although the movement was never ideologically coherent, its founders agreed on Russia's special place in world history, claiming—as the anonymous preface to *Exodus to the East* stated—that the "Russians and those who belong to the peoples of 'the Russian world' are neither Europeans nor Asians."[2] The special location of Eurasia came with a special mission. According to the motto that appeared on the front page of *Yevraziya*, "The Russia of our time decides the fate of both Europe and Asia. Occupying a sixth of the world, Eurasia is the center and the beginning of a new world culture."[3]

The debate about *Yevraziya* centered on the newspaper's attitude toward the new Soviet state. Against Savitsky's strong opposition, Suvchinsky, who was the moving force in the editorial office, published Marina Tsvetaeva's salutation to Vladimir Mayakovsky in the first issue. Tsvetaeva recalled her last meeting with the poet before her departure from Russia in 1922 and the message he proclaimed to the West: "That truth is over here!" She also quoted her reaction to Mayakovsky's reading his own poems in Paris in 1928: "That strength is over there [in the Soviet Union]!"[4] Many interpreted Tsvetaeva's lines as an endorsement of the Soviet system.[5] Suvchinsky's articles, which Savitsky and other Eurasianists read as apologias for Marxism and Communism, further outraged Savitsky, Trubetskoy, and their allies.[6] To distance themselves from Suvchinsky and his Parisian group's proto-Marxist views, Savitsky published a brochure titled *On the Newspaper* Yevraziya: *The Newspaper* Yevraziya *Is Not an Organ of Eurasianism.*[7]

Lourié became involved with *Yevraziya* through his friendship with Suvchinsky. The composer's presence in the newspaper might have been another irritant for Savitsky, who was uncompromising in his rejection of Communist ideology and must have known that before his emigration Lourié worked for the Soviet People's Commissar Anatoly Lunacharsky. Savitsky suspected that Suvchinsky, whom he accused of having a hand in most of the articles published in *Yevraziya*, was behind Lourié's use of phrases such as "common cause" and "spiritual experience" in "The Crisis of Art."[8] "Common cause" was mystic lay philosopher Nikolay Fyodorov's phrase to describe mankind's shared struggle against death. Savitsky considered Suvchinsky's attempts to bring Fyodorov's ideas into the Eurasianist discourse a deviation; seeing the term used by Lourié strengthened his belief that Suvchinsky was gaining too much control over the movement.[9]

To what extent Suvchinsky dictated Lourié's "The Crisis in Art" is unclear. Based on the article, in which Lourié dismisses the art of both the West and the East (that is, the Soviet Union) as subordinate either to bourgeois values or to Marxist propaganda, Savitsky could hardly have accused Lourié of covert pro-Soviet ideology. As Lourié's reference to Alexander Blok in the article attests, his Eurasianism was still affected by the Russian Symbolists' Scythianism, their anti-European affirmation of Russia's Asian identity, and their enthusiastic embrace of their country's messianistic role in saving a declining West.[10] Like the Eurasianists, Lourié saw the contrast between East and West in terms of their differing attitude toward individualism and would have agreed with Suvchinsky's assessment that the "principle of personal freedoms and individual self-determination, promulgated by every European revolution, has in the course of time turned into a harsh social indifference."[11] The Romantic substitution of art for religion created art for art's sake, Lourié argued, which then turned into art without art: empty, manufactured goods for the entertainment of bourgeois society. Lourié accused the West of replacing spiritual principles with material goods and substituting aesthetic for spiritual experience. Art in Soviet Russia did not fare much better in Lourié's judgment. Subjugated to the social good, art in the new Soviet state became propaganda for the proletariat. Whereas Suvchinsky saw the Russian Revolution as a step toward the Eurasian ideal, Lourié regarded it as a missed opportunity for the creation of a new type of art. In Lourié's opinion, under these circumstances neither the East nor the West could produce genuine, "living" art.

Like the Eurasianists, Lourié looked for a solution in a liminal, in-between area and found it, predictably, in Stravinsky's "supra-individual, impersonal, and supra-emotional" art. With the ease of a professional ideologue, trained under Lunacharsky, Lourié fit Stravinsky into a Eurasianist cast. He depicted Stravinsky as an artist who "turned away from the present with a feeling of nausea" and returned to the past to retrieve from it what he found "resonant not so much with the contemporary canon as with his own personal sensibility." In Lourié's view Stravinsky "entered into conflict with modernity," which Lourié identified with "disequilibrium and disorder," and which Stravinsky, according to Lourié, replaced with an "ideal state of order" and "a durable equilibrium." Stravinsky's victory over chaos and his creation of order in art seem to have satisfied what Suvchinsky described as "a thirst for social stability and a quest for another way of life" among the masses, a quest for a new social order in which "the personal fate of each human being is somehow *guaranteed* by some objective and mandatory authority,"[12] or, as Lourié put it, a quest for a new way in which "a revolutionary dynamic of extreme emancipation" has come "to the stasis of submissive contemplation." And that is why Stravinsky, although he turned his back on the present, could write music that was "a documentary testimony to the historical events of [his] time, in all aspects, whether aesthetic, ethical, political, or social."[13]

What Lourié called "submissive contemplation" gained a specifically religious meaning in his article "Le Problème de la musique religieuse moderne" (The problem of modern religious music), which appeared five years after "The Crisis of Art" in the monthly Catholic journal *L'Art chrétien*. Like *Yevraziya*, *L'Art chrétien* was a new publication, promising to print "only original articles," "illustrated by the most sophisticated modern methods." Among the specialists consulted were professors teaching at Catholic institutions, religious authorities, and curators of museums. Lourié's article was published in the second issue along with Marie Belmon's essay on the fresco, the second part of Dr. Adelheid Heimann's article on the iconography of the Trinity, and Maurice Brillant's article "Joy and Liberty of Catholic Art."[14] Lourié's contribution was not an article but a transcription of an interview the unnamed editors had conducted with Lourié, whom he called "one of today's most prominent young composers" with two recently completed religiously inspired works, the *Sonate liturgique* and the *Concerto spirituale*. Lourié's essay served as an introduction to the question of modern religious music, which would be discussed further in forthcoming issues.[15]

Whereas "The Crisis of Art" bears Suvchinsky's Eurasianist mark, "The Problem of Modern Religious Music" reflects the influence of Jacques Maritain, the most prominent neo-Thomist Catholic thinker of the French *Renouveau catholique*. Lourié met Maritain through Stravinsky in the mid-1920s. Unlike

Stravinsky, whose contact with the philosopher remained sporadic, Lourié, himself a Catholic convert, became a close friend. Jacques and his Russian-Jewish wife, Raissa, had many important musicians in their circle, including, apart from Lourié and Stravinsky, Georges Auric, Roland-Manuel, Erik Satie, and Ricardo Viñes. Only Lourié and Roland-Manuel became engaged in Maritain's rigorous studies of Thomas Aquinas's theology. It was through Roland-Manuel, one of the ghostwriters of Stravinsky's *Poétique musicale*, that Maritain's *Art and Scholasticism* (1920) became a source for Stravinsky's aesthetics. Lourié attended the Maritains' meetings in Meudon, kept up a copious correspondence with them, and ended his life in Maritain's house in Princeton, which Raissa willed to him before her death in 1960.[16]

In "The Problem of Modern Religious Music," Lourié still distinguishes between bourgeois and proletarian art according to the social needs they serve, but he looks for a higher purpose not in Eurasia but in religious faith. Religious art, the neo-Thomist Lourié declares, does not depend on subject matter but on the composer's inspiration and his willingness to subordinate his work to a transcendental cause. As opposed to what Lourié calls "objective" art that serves social goals, such art is "ontological," for it keeps its connection with life and with "the artist's temperament and spiritual experience." Lourié emphasizes that despite its subordination to a "final cause," religious art has to remain free and should obey "no specific laws, for its essence resides in musical language and material, not in style."

The parallels between Lourié's and Maritain's conceptions of religious art are striking. Like Lourié, Maritain defines religious art not as "*ecclesiastical art*, an art specified by an object, an end, and definite rules," but as "art bearing on the face of it the character of Christianity." "Everything," Maritain wrote, "sacred and profane, belongs to it."[17] What Lourié describes as art with a higher goal, Maritain asserts as art "in a state of absolute dependence upon theological wisdom." But this "ultimate control by theology," Maritain, like Lourié, insists, "does not impose any aesthetic genre, any style, any particular technique, on sacred art." Since according to Maritain there is "no style *peculiar* to religious art, there is no *religious technique*," it would be useless "to try to discover a technique, a style, a system of rules or a method of work peculiar to Christian art."[18] Christian art, Maritain would have agreed with Lourié, leaves the artist, as artist, free. Lourié's emphasis on the role of inspiration also originates in Maritain's philosophy. Authentic inspiration, Maritain writes, is "a special impulse of the natural order" proceeding "not from the Muses, but from the living God," and "transcending the limits of reason."[19]

Whereas in "The Crisis of Art" Lourié found the solution to the crisis in Stravinsky's music, here he implicitly offers his own work as an example of spiritual art. Proponents of Maritain's neo-Thomist ideal, such as Henri-Irénée Marrou, a Catholic French historian and an old Parisian friend of Lourié, saw Lourié's music as "essentially religious, spiritual, and mythical because," Marrou writes, "it fulfills our most secret desire for a music that no longer provides earthly nourishment tending to carnal needs and thus it is no longer the voice of Satan."[20] In Maritain's view ontological music, which Lourié identified with religious music, was best represented by Lourié's art, which was "born in the singular roots of being," and which, like ontology, evolved from "metaphysical knowledge . . . at the highest degree of abstractive intuition."[21] Maritain sensed in Lourié's music "the great influx of the soul and inspiration which is renewing music today," recognizing in it the same possibility of spiritual renewal he was initiating in French Catholicism. Like the anonymous editor in *L'Art chrétien*, Maritain singles out Lourié's *Sonate liturgique* as the piece with which "the period opens in which Lourié's art attains its plenitude and verifies in an unimpeachable way the Pauline axiom—where the spirit is, there is liberty." According to Maritain this new liberty is also perceptible in Lourié's *Concerto spirituale*, which, although it is constrained by its transcendental goal, is "free of all traditional form" and thus "rediscovers, together with its essential inspiration, an astonishing spontaneity."[22] If nowhere else, in the Christian philosopher's mind Lourié surpassed his former idol Stravinsky.

The Crisis of Art (1928–29)
Arthur Lourié

1.

It is time to realize, finally, that art in our time, with some exceptions, has become *art without art*.[23] The formula "art for art's sake" (an outdated phrase to which we are nevertheless still bound somehow by anguished memories—marginally, though, and only by nerve endings) was coined by generations of people who had lost their faith in art and replaced it with aesthetic idolatry. Aesthetic experience became a surrogate for spiritual experience a long time ago. In the late nineteenth and early twentieth centuries a large amount of spiritual energy was devoted to this change. Aesthetics, which took the place of authentic spiritual experience, was declared a fundamental virtue. But Wagner, Baudelaire, Nietzsche, Wilde, Scriabin, and Vrubel were neither pranksters nor buffoons.[24] They shaped new mythologies. This was the era of creating magical, artificial worlds. The power of creative and spiritual genius had gone astray and given itself up to the phantom of false self-assertion.

We have to acknowledge these people, however misguided they may have been, because for them artifice became genuine art. They were among the last for whom art was still an expression of spiritual experience. Those who followed them and obliterated their names squandered any hope of remaining on a spiritual path. Over the past ten years art without art, which has been born of emptiness, has surreptitiously spread. It is being created by people and for people who need absolutely nothing. But as soon as art loses its connection to genuine spiritual experience, it becomes a factory of artifacts.

Art is no longer "prophetic"—it has become "material." And that is how things stand both in the West and in Russia. There is "art without art" both here and there, but for different reasons. Western Europe, driven by avarice, is busy manufacturing useless commodities. In Russia, where everything is now viewed from a Marxist angle, art is being compelled to serve the social process. There is no living art, neither here nor there. Whether art belongs to God (along with human life itself, from which it is inseparable) or whether it serves the social process, it is subordinate in equal measure. In either case, art is not a value in itself. But in the former case the subordination is voluntary and imperceptible. It is informed directly by one's personal spiritual experience, and so it is dedicated to the "common cause," that is, to the stewardship of divine grace (*domostroitel'stvo*) and universal concord (*mirostroitel'stvo*).[25] In the latter case the subordination is by force, and spiritual experience, deemed obsolete, is excised.

"In Europe there is life and death" (Blok).[26] Art has lost its soul. In the aesthetics of contemporary Russia, the soul has been exiled from both life and art. It is self-evident that if art is taken to be an elemental force, it can only be an instrument of the transcendent. How this comes to pass and manifests itself is a separate matter, but no other option exists for art. Its submission must be absolutely voluntary. Any other mode of subordination constitutes abuse. When Marxists force art to serve *their* "common cause" (the material reconstruction of the world), they necessarily reject genuine living art. What they officially call art is merely a derivative theory or the propaganda of Marxist ideas in the guise of aesthetics.

This may all be well and good as long as it serves the purpose of "primitive accumulation,"[27] yet all of this lies well beyond the realm of art. And so, appropriated by the ruling class, art in Russia has ceased to be art.

The only difference between the modes of artistic production in Russia and in the West is that the aesthetics of production in Russia is meant ultimately to serve the interests of the proletariat, whereas the aesthetics of production in Europe already serves the bourgeoisie. But the aesthetically untutored proletariat obviously prefers bourgeois production in art, whereas the surfeited bourgeoisie lusts after the proletarian. All this matters not so much for illuminating the individual creative processes of particular artists as for characterizing the order of things and the spirit of the times. If we want to understand what is happening in art right now, we are compelled to address such basic, fundamental matters.

In contrast to the West, Russia's current political and social reality has put forth the issue of proletarian aesthetics. To this day the thesis of proletarian art remains vague; it is a dogmatic premise that exists only in the fog of neo-Marxist dialectics. Its antithesis —"bourgeois," free art—no longer has any practical meaning, since art in Europe no longer issues from the sphere of spiritual experience. This is why proletarian art, lacking a thesis, is unable to arise in reaction to its antithesis. What might in mutual struggle have given rise to new authentic values, amounts only to a sterile draw. Revolutionary pathos, which could have sidestepped theses and antitheses and used its explosive force to bring the art of the proletariat into being, is nowhere to be found. I do not know how contemporary art in the West came to lose its "divine purpose"; nor do I know how the revolution failed to give birth to a revolutionary pathos in art. But there is now a kind of equivalence between these states of affairs, insofar as both here and there art is being animated solely by *method*. In Europe this method is formal—that is, aesthetic. In Russia the method is internal—that is, dialectical. In Europe the method is qualitative (how), while in Russia it is conceptual (what). *But art animated solely by method is art without art.*

Method devours art. Art without art is the same as "art for art's sake," but in its newest, that is, totally barren form. Earlier, aesthetic experience became a surrogate for spiritual experience; now formal experiments are supplanting creativity. The living flesh of art, its matter and substance, is being counterfeited by aimlessly generated new forms.

2.

Both in Russia and in the West the art of the past decade was characterized by a commitment to generating new forms. The only real aesthetic development of that time was methodological experimentation. The dialectical method of transforming matter became both dominant and self-sufficiently hermetic; everything else was sidelined. The dialectic was also a polemic, which guaranteed its relevance. Only polemics had any resonance whatsoever; all else was irrelevant, obsolete. Works of art were not generated in the process of creating something new but almost exclusively through a critical reexamination of the past. This artistic output arose through a violent, willful fusion of the modern with phases from the past, long gone and left behind. Whatever energy could be extracted from the past was used to power the contemporary sensibility of form. In effect, this was a process of elimination, provoked by the realization that the art of the modernist period found itself in a dead end. This reaction did not generate a lively and effective creative force. Its impotence forced it to return time and again to the past, overcoming it and at the same time obliterating the remains of whatever had managed to survive and could have potentially been put to creative use.

For example, returning to Bach in music or Ingres in painting ("liking" or "not liking" them is an entirely separate matter) is at this point simply impossible in any creative endeavor. The very best works of the past decade find their ideological justification in Pascal's words:

> Let them not tell me that I did not say anything new: it is the arrangement of the materials that is new . . . .
>
> I would prefer if they tell me I was using old words. And even if thoughts do not form another set of utterances by being arranged differently, words do form different thoughts by being arranged differently.[28]

Even if the upper crust of contemporary artistic output can occasionally be justified this way, the front lines of aesthetic action witnessed a most vulgar degradation of art, which reduced creative activity to crude imitation and contraption, occasionally spiced with frivolous improvisation.

It was primarily the painting and music of those years that found the most complete expression in the formal dialectical method. Not since the distant classical era has the dialectic of form and material been expressed with such brilliance and forcefulness as it has in the last decade, in Picasso's art and Stravinsky's music. In those years both Picasso's and Stravinsky's art was animated by the ambition to articulate the most systematic, ironclad method of dialectical construction possible. They excluded from the domain of art all that interfered with a pure, formal process, abolishing everything that threatened to destabilize it and become alien to it. Accomplishing this required both of them to obliterate their personal pasts, and that is just what they did. Picasso, however, found a way to reconcile the brown and green-gray canvases of his formal and emotional exaggerations with his new credo of equilibrium, synthesis, and impersonal texture. Stravinsky proceeded more decisively. He rejected his "Sturm und Drang" period and entered into conflict with modernity, which refuses to follow in his footsteps, demanding that he re-embrace his legacy, which he has fully exhausted and annihilated.

Picasso, having broken down pictorial nature practically to its constituent atoms, has brought it to an organized and organic unity. Stravinsky, having laid bare the essence of music, has reined in chaos, clamping it with a steel bit. Both, having begun with ideally expressed disequilibrium and disorder, have brought their musical and painterly equipment into an ideal state of order, returning to visual and auditory material a durable equilibrium and the regularity of a new causality. Departing from a revolutionary dynamic of extreme emancipation, both have come to the stasis of submissive contemplation. Time has come full circle, and, it seems, has to begin anew with the center of artistic activity shifting toward the greatest possible disequilibrium, toward new explosions of creative energy, toward the explosion of a new dynamic that makes possible new advances in the organization of a temporal and spatial system.

In pursuing his creative goals neither Stravinsky nor Picasso belongs in any way to the set of values and practices that I have been calling "art without art." In music and painting this term refers to what in contemporary official, that is, recognized, art is peripheral to these artists' work. Insofar as genuine art necessarily expresses national or universal experience (even when it eschews an ideological connection to it and finds means of expression that sidestep it purely in formal and methodological terms), Stravinsky and Picasso have embodied every aspect of the past decade. The music of Stravinsky and the painting of Picasso are a documentary testimony to the historical events of their time, in all aspects, whether aesthetic, ethical, political, or social. Picasso's designs were not simply a backward glance for the purposes of restoring old art. He established new sets of relationships that ran parallel to old art, without aiming to resurrect it. Picasso's formal method served constructive goals, but at the same time established equivalence between the newly emerging and the old. Picasso's artistic sensibility represents a particular instantiation of the contemporary situation, and, at the same time, is consonant with any genuine pictorial-constructive movement of the past, be it naive barbaric archaism or the geometrical principle in the Italian Renaissance. Stravinsky has turned away from the present with a feeling of nausea. He has, for reasons other than Picasso's, gone back to the past, where he brings back to life that which he finds resonant not so much with the contemporary canon as with his own personal sensibility. His excursions into the past are conditioned not so much by formal-constructive principles like Picasso's as they are by formal and ethical principles. But both of them persistently return to bygone cultures, summoning a whole set of values from the past to renewed existence under the conditions of our contemporary existence. Each accomplishes this in his own way, based on different premises. Therein lies an essential difference between these two artists, even if their names continue to merit being invoked together. Having absorbed all the individual contemporary artistic processes that found themselves, voluntarily or not, drawn into their spheres of influence, Picasso and Stravinsky have used their authority to subjugate painting and music to their experience. This is so because the positions taken by the two artists not only command a vast field of activity in the realms of contemporary art but also radiate into all areas of artistic achievement in the past that can be associated in any way with contemporary art. Of course, here we can generalize only about those particular processes that are already linked by a common thread and can be gathered under the umbrella of the currently prevailing formal-aesthetic conception of art as a formally objectified activity—that is, supra-individual, impersonal, and supra-emotional. For the moment all individualistic processes in modern art remain outside our field of vision. Next to Picasso and Stravinsky one should mention Valéry, whose aesthetic conception in effect lays bare the fundamental tendencies that became firmly established among the leading artists of this direction over the past decade. Valéry leads us into another domain—the realm of poetry and poetics. That deserves a separate discussion.

—*Translated from the Russian by Katya Ermolaev,*
Yasha Klots, Klára Móricz, and Boris Wolfson

The Problem of Modern Religious Music (1934)
Arthur Lourié

We thought it would be interesting to ask one of today's most prominent young composers to articulate for our readers the problem of modern religious music.[29] The author of the Sonate liturgique *and the* Concerto spirituel *[sic] was willing to let us publish these few notes gathered over the course of our conversation.*

The problem posed here from the perspective of a religious aesthetic should be followed by studies of a more technical character. This problem is thus both the introduction to and link between the different subjects Arthur Lourié discusses in greater depth here.

—THE EDITORS

We have been asked to attempt to address the problem of religious music as it presents itself to us from the perspective of its modern reality. Addressing such a broad question compels us to remain in the domain of generalities; otherwise we would find ourselves having to stop all the time to give extreme nuance to the judgments we make on specific cases. We will thus keep to general characteristics, situating ourselves from the start on a religious plane.

Leaving aside the subject of religion itself, we have to look for the aesthetic principles governing the religious genre. Indeed, it is not only a matter of the artist taking on a religious subject; it is through *inspiration* that his music will be a work worthy of being called religious music; we need to return to this often forgotten notion.

The first of these principles is unquestionably the work's free subordination to a final cause. Just as the Christian's life is essentially free and yet ordained to its spiritual purpose, so too religious art cannot find its end in itself and yet remains essentially free.

Thus creation manifests itself in two ways.

On the one hand, we see works that are, so to speak, *manufactured*,[30] because they are isolated from everything that lies outside their own operational rules and the object to be created in itself. These works can be distinguished from one another only by the criterion of quality. For this reason, and for greater ease, we will describe them with the term *objective* art.

In contrast to these works we see others that are a reflection of spiritual life and whose character is essentially ontological. With these works it cannot be a question of *pure music*, of *art for art's sake*, because they are always tightly bound up with life itself, with the artist's temperament and spiritual experience.

The art we have called *objective* may well attempt to tackle religious subjects, but it is not free to do so. Ordained to no transcendental purpose, this art puts itself at the service of social process; and it is in this sense that it is correct to say that there is such a thing as *bourgeois* or *proletarian* art. If the Russian artist is subjected to serving the new collectivity, the artist from other countries undergoes as well an alienation from his liberty that is no less real for being less conscious. The former *must* create an art that captures the spirit of the dictatorship of the proletariat, but the latter *consents* to express through his art profound elements of bourgeois culture. In our opinion, the difference is not essential.

In this way *freedom* plays a key role in defining the nature of religious as well as secular art.

Religious music, for its part, is absolutely free and has no specific laws, for its essence resides in musical language and material, not in style. Styles may vary here depending on momentary conditions, just as in *objective* art. The important thing is not these variations in style, but rather the permanent element through which tradition is imposed. This permanent element is the musical language.

The only living tradition in this case is the tradition of musical language, since in religious music the musical material's role is not to restore old things but to be in constant and direct contact with life, to rediscover life through the artist's spiritual experience. Today, the musician involved in religious art is faced with a formal problem—he has to, first, reestablish the value of modes in themselves. These modes have been neglected and even forgotten in contemporary *atonal* music, which has exaggerated to the extreme the role of chromaticism, considered not as a function but as a substance. By doing this, contemporary music has destroyed the unity of musical language and manufactured a great number of idioms that fail to communicate among themselves.

In contrast, by giving new importance to the mode, by letting it be reborn on new foundations in its in relationship to tonality, one finds the means to separate the poles of attraction between tonality and mode and synthesize their two natures.

Such are the very conditions of musical language by which, we believe, religious music communicates a certain spiritual reality.

The great difficulty is not to turn backward by restoring old forms and modes and by being contented with a scholiast's work. But neither should we fall back into anarchy, which is nothing more than an elementary and scattered form of life.

We must confess that one does not always encounter the strongest trace of religious life in art that presents itself officially as religious art. But whereas in so many other forms of artistic expression, such as poetry or painting, a negative aspect of the work can lead to a sort of reverse witnessing, as for example in Rimbaud or Baudelaire, in music it can only be a question of positive witnessing: by its essence music always affirms Being. It is precisely because it has this character that music can acquire a purifying meaning for the artist, and rise to the heights of religious expression.

It seems that Nietzsche would have known how to address this problem and that it was even the basis of his quarrel with Wagner. "*From what do I suffer,*" he says in *Ecce Homo* ("The Case of Wagner: A Musical Problem"),[31] "*when I suffer from the fate of music? From the fact that music has been stripped of its purifying virtues, of its affirmative character, from the fact that it has become a music of decadence and that it is no longer Dionysus's flute.*" It is not so surprising that the father of Zarathustra understood that Wagner, despite his genius, betrayed this profound meaning of music by making it serve the resurrection of a manufactured mythology.

So we see that the problem of religious music goes back to the very sources of inspiration, and we also see how rich this particular music can be and must be among all other musics; for it molds living material, which seems to us to be the richest and ultimately only true kind.

—Translated from the French by Bridget Behrmann and Tamara Levitz

NOTES

1. Arthur Lourié, "Krizis iskusstva 1" and "O Rakhmaninove" (About Rachmaninoff), *Yevraziya* 4 (15 December 1928): 8; "Krizis iskusstva 2" and "Kontsertï v Parizhe: Otto Klemperer" (Concerts in Paris: Otto Klemperer), *Yevraziya* 8 (26 January 1929): 8. Only one other article by Lourié appeared in *Yevraziya*, on Bartók. See "Béla Bartók," *Yevraziya* 18 (23 March 1929): 8.

2. "Authors' Introduction," in *Exodus to the East: Forebodings and Events, An Affirmation of the Eurasians*, trans. Ilya Vinkovetzky with Catherine Boyle and Kenneth Brostrom, ed. Ilya Vinkovetsky and Charles Schlacks Jr. (Idyllwild, CA.: Charles Schlacks Jr., 1996), 4.

3. The motto is taken from what is commonly referred to as "The Moscow Program," a fifteen-page brochure that appeared as *Yevraziystvo* (Paris: Yevraziyskoye knigoizdatel'stvo, 1927); and in *Yevraziyskaya khronika* 9 (1927): 3–14.

4. Marina Tsvetaeva, "Mayakovskomu," *Yevraziya* 1 (24 November 1928): 8.

5. Simon Karlinsky, *Marina Tsvetaeva: The Woman, Her World and Her Poetry* (Cambridge: Cambridge University Press, 1985), 192.

6. For Savitsky's 1929 memorandum about *Yevraziya* and the circumstances of the split in the Eurasianist movement, see Irina Shevelenko, "K istorii yevraziyskogo raskola 1929 goda," in *Themes and Variations: In Honor of Lazar Fleishman*, ed. Kovistantin Polivaviov, Irina Shevelenko, and Andrey Ustinov, Stanford Slavic Studies 8 (Stanford: Department of Slavic Languages and Literature, 1994), 376–416. For more documents relating to the movement, see Sergey Glebov, *Yevraziystvo mezhdu imperiyey i modernom: istoriya v dokumentakh* (Moscow: Novoye izdatel'stvo, 2009).

7. Russian title: *O gazete 'Yevraziya': Gazeta 'Yevrazia' ne est' yevraziyskiy organ* (Paris, 1927).

8. For Savitzky's criticism of Lourié see his 1929 memorandum in Shevelenko, "K istorii yevraziyskogo raskola 1929 goda," 399. He writes: "In Lourié's [article] the clearly and essentially expressed enthusiasm for the Knowledge of God (or the rebellion against God) and God-creation (or God-destruction) in art are substituted with 'common cause' and with the vaguely defined 'spiritual experience.'"

9. Suvchinsky's group tried to combine Fyodorov's ideas with Marxism. See Stephen Lukashevich, *N. F. Fedorov (1828–1903): A Study in Russian Eupsychian and Utopian Thought* (Cranbury, NJ.: Associated University Presses, 1977), 27.

10. For more about Scythianism see *Russia Between East and West: Scholarly Debates on Eurasianism*, ed. Dmitry Shlapentokh (Leiden: Brill, 2006), esp. Marlène Laruelle's chapter, "The Orient in Russian Thought at the Turn of the Century," 9–38. Lourié quotes Blok's reaction to the Bolsheviks' failed peace negotiations with Germany at Brest-Litovsk from an entry in the poet's diary, 11 January 1918: "If you do not wash away the shame of your wartime patriotism with at least a 'democratic peace,' if you destroy our revolution, then you are no longer Aryans. And we shall open wide the Eastern Gates.... We're barbarians? All right, then. We'll show you what barbarians really are. And our cruel reply, our terrible reply, will be the only answer worthy of man.... Europe (her theme)—*Art and Death*. Russia—life." Aleksandr Blok, *Dnevnik*, ed. Andrey Grishunina (Moscow: Sovetskaya Rossiya, 1989), 261; translated into English by Avril Pyman in "An Introduction to 'The Scythians,'" *Stand* 8/3 (1966–67): 32.

11. Pyotr Suvchinskiy, "Novïy 'zapad,'" *Yevraziya* 2 (1 December 1928): 1–2, quoted and translated in Richard Taruskin, "Eurasia Revisited with Lourié as My Guide," in *Funeral Games in Honor of Arthur Lourié*, ed. Klára Moricz and Simon Morrison (New York: Oxford University Press, forthcoming). For Lourié's anti-individualistic views see ibid., and Lourié's "Neogothic and Neoclassic," *Modern Music* 5/3 (March–April 1928): 3–8.

12. Suvchinskiy, "Novïy 'zapad.'"

13. For a more in-depth analysis of Lourié's article see Taruskin, "Eurasia Revisited with Lourié as My Guide."

14. Marie Belmon, "La Fresque"; Dr. Adelheid Heimann, "L'Iconographie de la Trinité"; and Maurice Brillant, "Joie et liberté de l'art catholique," *L'Art chrétien* 2 (November 1934): 7–18, 19–30, and 35–75, respectively.

15. *L'Art chrétien* 2 (November 1934): 31.

16. For more about Maritain's relationship to Lourié see Mikhail Meylakh and Olesya Bobrik, "Semya Zhaka Mariten i russkiye muzïkantï," *Muzïkal'naya akademiya* 2 (2010): 96–102; and Caryl Emerson, "Jacques Maritain and the Catholic Muse in Lourié's Post-Petersburg Worlds," in Moricz and Morrison, eds., *Funeral Games in Honor of Arthur Lourié*. Emerson explores in depth the neo-Thomist aspects of Lourié's art. Lourié's correspondence with the Maritains, reviews of his concerts, Raissa's notes concerning Lourié's music, and a typescipt of "The Problem of Modern Religious Art" are kept in the Centre d'Archives, Cercle d'Etudes Jacques et Raïssa Maritain, Kolbsheim, France.

17. Jacques Maritain, "Art and Scholasticism," in *Art and Scholasticism, with Other Essays*, trans. J. F. Scanlan (New York: Charles Scribner's Sons, 1937), 68.

18. Jacques Maritain, "Some Reflections Upon Religious Art" (1924), in ibid., 143–47.

19. Maritain, "Art and Scholasticism," 69–71.

20. Henri-Irénée Marrou, "Lourié 1936," in *Crise de notre temps et réflexion chrétienne (de 1930 à 1975)* (Paris: Editions Beauchesne, 1978), 377.

21. Jacques Maritain, "The Freedom of Song" (1935), in *Art and Poetry*, trans. Elva de Pue Matthews (New York: Philosophcal Library, 1943), 97. "If the musical work of Arthur Lourié appears to me so rich in sense, this is because it seems to me that in no other artist today is the creative intuition born at a deeper level" (92).

22. Ibid., 96, 98.

23. Russian title: Artur Lur'ye, "Krizis iskusstva 1–2," *Yevraziya* 4 (15 December 1928): 8; and *Yevraziya* 8 (26 January 1929): 8. Emphasis in original.

24. Mikhail Vrubel (1856–1910), a Russian painter.

25. *Domostroitel'stvo*, literally "building of a house," is a theological term, originating from the Greek *oikonomia* (divine economy, economy of salvation, or stewardship). The term appears in Proverbs 9:1: "Wisdom has built her house, she has set up her seven pillars"; in 1 Peter 4:10: "As each has received a gift, employ it for one another, as good stewards of God's varied grace"; 1 Corinthians 4:1–2: "This is how one should regard us, as servants of Christ and stewards of the mysteries of God. Moreover it is required of stewards that they be found trustworthy"; Ephesians 3:2: "Assuming that you have heard of the stewardship of God's grace that was given to me for you." *Mirostroitel'stvo*, literally "world- or peace-building," refers to the active, human construction of a world full of divine presence; though the words for "world" and "peace" were different in church Slavic, this concept seems to bring them—conceptually—together. Special thanks to Boris Wolfson and Serge Glebov for explaining these terms.

26. Lourié incorrectly quotes from Alexander Blok's diary entry: "Europe (its theme) is art and death. Russia's is life." For a fuller quotation of a different translation of this passage, see n. 10 above.

27. "Primitive accumulation" is Marx's term for an accumulation that is "not the result of the capitalist mode of production, but its starting point." Karl Marx, "The Secret of Primitive Accumulation," in *Capital*, vol. 1, part, 8, chap. 26, paragraph 1.

28. "Qu'on ne dise pas que je n'ai rien dit de nouveau: la disposition des matières est nouvelle. . . . J'aimerais autant qu'on me dit que je me suis servi des mots anciens. Et comme si les mêmes pensées

ne formaient pas un autre corps de discours par une disposition différente aussi bien que les mêmes mots forment d'autres pensées par leur différente dispositions." Blaise Pascal, *Pensées*, art. 7, sec. 9.

29. French title: "Le Problème de la musique religieuse moderne," *L'Art chrétien* (November 1934): 31–34.

30. Lourié uses the term *fabriquer* throughout this essay in direct reference to Maritain's philosophy. The more proper term here would be *made*, but for fluidity we have translated it as *manufactured*.

31. The correct title of part 1, *Ecce Homo* (1889), is "The Case of Wagner: A Musician's Problem." Lourié misquoted this passage, which in the original reads: "From what do I suffer when I suffer from the fate of music? From the fact that music has lost its world-transfiguring, yea-saying character—that it is decadent music and no longer the flute of Dionysus."

Igor the Angeleno: The Mexican Connection

TAMARA LEVITZ

Stravinsky arrived in New York City aboard the *Manhattan* on 30 September 1939 to begin a series of lectures as the Charles Eliot Norton Professor at Harvard. Within months of his arrival, Carlos Chávez sent a telegram inviting him to conduct the Orquesta Sinfónica de México. If Stravinsky could arrange to travel to Mexico City on his own dime, Chávez explained, adding that the train ride from New York took a mere 72 hours, the Orquesta would pay Stravinsky $1,250 for a two-week visit, 15–28 July 1940.[1] In the weeks that followed, and in their first face-to-face meeting in New York, on 14 March, the two composers solidified the details. The first concert would include Cherubini's *Anacreonte* Overture, Tchaikovsky's Symphony no. 2, Stravinsky's *Petrushka* Suite, and his Divertimento.[2] The second would include Stravinsky's *Apollon musagète*, a repeat performance of the Divertimento, *Jeu de cartes*, and the *Firebird* Suite. Stravinsky agreed to the terms and on 23 April asked for and received double the proposed fee ($2,500).[3] That summer the Orquesta and Stravinsky signed a contract with RCA Victor Mexicana to record the Divertimento with the orchestra for a flat fee of $1,000.[4]

A few months after Stravinsky's successful first visit to Mexico, Chávez wrote apologetically to explain that interference from a local radio station had damaged the recording they had made of the Divertimento and that they would have to record it again. To provide a pretext for Stravinsky's return visit, Chávez invited him for a one-week stay from 14 to 20 July 1941 during which he would conduct the Orquesta in two broadcast concerts and redo the recording.[5] Stravinsky wrote back, suggesting as repertoire his Symphony in C, Capriccio, *Pulcinella* Suite (a premiere in Mexico), and, again, his Divertimento. He urged Chávez to listen to Koussevitzky's recording of the Capriccio with soloist Jesús María Sanromá (which he thought "wasn't bad"), told him he would make a "photostat" of the score for him, and suggested they find a pianist for it in Mexico to bring down costs (Chávez chose Salvador Ochoa).[6] This time the distance to Mexico was not as great: Stravinsky and Vera had arrived in Los Angeles on 9 February and on 6 April had moved into their new home at 1260 North Wetherly Drive.

In spite of the mutual goodwill, it was not effortless for Stravinsky to travel to Mexico; both of his trips—in 1940 and 1941—were hindered by visa difficulties.

In 1940 Ricardo Ortega, the Orquesta's manager, and Stravinsky's lawyers had worked hard to organize for Stravinsky and Vera's six-month visitor visas and reentry permits to the United States with the aid of former Mexican president Adolfo de la Huerta.[7] In spite of these efforts, Stravinsky experienced trouble obtaining a reentry permit. Ortega and Chávez urged Stravinsky to cross the border by train at Ciudad Juárez on the way down—a border crossing Vera described as "miserable, where Mexicans with guitars, babies, and bundles crowd on board. Next to the station is a café, 'Cabellero,' and in front of it in the middle of the street a dead cow."[8] On the way back, Stravinsky had to wrangle with a "very suspicious" border guard in Nogales, Arizona, for three hours as he and Vera reentered the United States as numbers 1053425 and 1053429 under the allowable quota of Russian immigrants permitted by the U.S. Immigration Act of 1924.[9] Several months later Stravinsky told a reporter in Cincinnati about the "red tape" involved and "inconvenience" of traveling to Mexico. "Ah, the convenience," of becoming a U.S. citizen, he had exclaimed in French, "the happiness when I discovered I could be in the quota!"[10] The Stravinskys were not yet U.S. citizens by the time of their next trip to Mexico, however, and the Mexican consulate denied them visas in part because Vera was a "Russian émigré" with nothing more than a Nansen (stateless person's) passport and *titre d'identité et de voyage* for the United States from the French government but no French passport (although she was married to Stravinsky, who had one). Stravinsky also complained to Ortega that the U.S. government was now stipulating that anybody who left the country first pay their taxes for the past six months—and that he wouldn't be able to come unless the Orquesta advanced him $700, which it did.[11] Adolfo de la Huerta again facilitated the couple's passage with an official note filled with high praise.[12] Stravinsky crossed at Ciudad Juárez, requesting from Ortega that a big bottle of water be ready for him at the Reforma Hotel when he and Vera arrived.[13]

The above description of Stravinsky's preparations for his first trips to Mexico challenges the classic image of the composer as suffering in exile during the twenty-eight years he lived in Los Angeles after 1941. Stravinsky appears in this account less as a Russian émigré preoccupied with his homeland than as a savvy cosmopolitan attentive to new markets and willing to jump on a train to Mexico for the purpose of monetary gain within months of arriving on U.S. shores. The story gives credence to the thesis that Stravinsky immigrated to the United States for economic rather than political reasons, seeking financial opportunity lacking in war-torn Europe. He chose to settle in the Hollywood Hills, and to organize his extensive concertizing activities from that location.

The story of Stravinsky's Mexican travels also reveals that he was not primarily a victim—as the standard narrative about his state of exile in the United States can romantically imply—but rather a cosmopolitan celebrity with immense class privilege and extraordinary mobility enabled by networks of friends and associates who provided visas and passports, money, materials (scores, parts, bottles of water), and technologies (trains, photostats, recording companies). Just a year after the U.S. Immigration and Naturalization Service stopped "Mexican repatriation"—an illegal process that led to the deportation of a million or more Mexicans from the United States within a decade—teams of lawyers and representatives of the highest echelons of the Mexican and U.S. government helped Stravinsky secure visas to travel to Mexico City to perform.[14] Those same friends in high places ensured that he could apply for U.S. citizenship within the quota for Eastern Europeans entering from Mexico—privileges extended, as is well known, selectively and in an extremely limited fashion to Eastern European Jews.[15]

In this essay, I pierce the myths surrounding Stravinsky's years in Los Angeles by creating a scrapbook in images and words of his travels in the Spanish-speaking world—a snapshot of the contingent and concrete material circumstances that led to his brief trips to Mexico in 1940 and 1941, on the cusp of his permanent move to Southern California. His visits to Spain, Argentina, and Mexico represent only a small fraction of his experience as a traveling musician between 1916 and 1940—a period during which he performed regularly and had close contacts in over eighteen countries—but these travels to the Spanish-speaking world are particularly neglected. The format of the scrapbook allows me to present coincidental and anecdotal evidence that challenges the transhistorical archetypes— among them "Russian national," "émigré," "cosmopolitan," "serialist," and "last great composer"—that have dominated musicological approaches to the study of Stravinsky's LA years.[16] Photographs and scrapbook memories reveal the depth of Stravinsky's affective bonds with people, places, and things across the Spanish-speaking world; they fill the emotional gap left by the austere modernist *Chroniques de ma vie* he wrote with Walter Nouvel in 1936 and the stony celebrity-infatuated conversations guided by Robert Craft.[17] By favoring the study of these visual and anecdotal traces of Stravinsky's relationships over the identity politics that lead musicologists to peg him as a Russian exile composer, I come closer to understanding, in Adrianne Cavarero's words, *who* he was as a person in his particular uniqueness, rather than *what* he universally symbolized within modernist discourse. A person cannot tell his or her own story, Cavarero argues, but rather always has it *narrated* to him or her by a necessary other in a relationship of desire and love.[18] The self is fundamentally relational, she concludes, constituted by the other; even uniqueness is a gift from the other.[19] Similarly, Stravinsky's uniqueness as a composer unfolded in relation to his friends in the Spanish-speaking world, who exchanged stories with him and mirrored his desires, creating counter-narratives to the mythical label of modernism (which Stravinsky despised).[20]

The literary form of the scrapbook as travelogue also breaks down hegemonic ideas about cosmopolitan identity, forcing acknowledgment of local contexts. Without a relation to the material specificity of home or "quotidian struggle for survival," Homi Bhabha argues, cosmopolitan communities lose the element that provides an "ethical entitlement to, and enactment of, the sense of community," leaving philosophers who are trying to make sense of cosmopolitanism to resort to liberal assumptions about the givenness of commonalities between people around the world, or of an "empathetic self capable of creating global relations that erase local struggles."[21] Bhabha coined the term "vernacular cosmopolitanism" to describe the necessary relationship of imagined or universal global community to local, patriotic, or national interests.

Art historian A. Joan Saab has noted how modern artists' movement between global and local contexts determined how they perceived difference, and how they situated themselves and the products they produced in terms of race, gender, nationality, and class in what she calls "vernacular modernism"—a term related to vernacular cosmopolitanism yet modified to focus on style. Saab analyses a remarkable photograph in which U.S. silver impresario William Spratling poses with the Mexican muralist David Alfaro Siqueiros, the Russian avant-garde film-maker Sergey Eisenstein, and the Mexican filmmaker Chano Urueta in Taxco, Mexico, where Siqueiros was under house arrest for Communist activism after having been released from prison in Mexico City in 1930 (see Figure 1). Spratling had used the commission he earned from selling a mural by Diego Rivera to resuscitate the silver industry in Taxco, Saab explains. He taught locals to create traditional jewelry, thereby transforming the town into a popular tourist and shopping destination. Saab notes that Spratling and Siqueiros wear leather sombreros popular among Mexican cowboys and revolutionaries, and Eisenstein and Urueta wear berets, a symbol of the Parisian bohemian artist. These hats give evidence of their owners' "multiple cultural allegiances," she argues, and of a tension between the local ("Mexican cowboys" or "Parisian bohemians") and the global (modernism), between popular and elite. Such mass-produced material goods as hats circulated in a transnational marketplace that became a "crucial site for the dissemination of what it means to be modern at this moment in time."[22]

Saab's example highlights how easily local contexts transform into tourist attractions, and artistic products into souvenirs, when considered in the light of the circuits of vernacular modernism. It gives evidence of how U.S. industrialists artificially constructed local Mexican cultures for tourist consumption, creating desire for the romance of Mexican peasantry as a substitute for the knowledge of their exploitation of local Mexican resources (silver). Siqueiros, Eisenstein, Urueta, and Spratling used Taxco as an attractive backdrop for the photograph they took from Siqueiros's house, which became an important cosmopolitan meeting place during the period of his house arrest there—a startling example of the convergence of local and global in this period (house arrest and modernist fame). The group's decision to pose with Taxco as their backdrop exemplifies one of the mechanisms by which the modernist cosmopolitan community produced collective modes of perceiving difference. In Brent Hayes Edwards's words, the "color line" shifted when framed from a "world" rather than local view.[23] The hats in this image, like Stravinsky's music when it was later performed in Mexico, cease

Figure 1. William Spratling, David Alfaro Siqueiros, Sergey Eisenstein, and Chano Urueta, meeting in Taxco during Siqueiros's house arrest, 1931.

to function as aesthetic and become exchange objects in the cosmopolitan space. Represented in translation between different cultures, the hats function as signs of national and modern difference rather than as tasteful products in and of themselves. In denial about the inequality between cosmopolitans and locals, spectators imbue these hats with a nostalgic longing that transforms them into souvenirs.

Inserted into this context of vernacular cosmopolitanism, Stravinsky ceases to be a "great composer" and becomes a traveling celebrity musician, his music less defined by style or the score than in relation to the place where it was performed and the unique audiences that received it. The consequences of his itinerant music-making for his approach to composition become nowhere more evident than in the Divertimento—the orchestral suite drawn from *Le Baiser de la fée* (*The Fairy's Kiss*) that Stravinsky conducted eight times in Mexico in 1940 and 1941 and that is the subject of this essay. Cosmopolitanism does not manifest as style in this work, however, as numerous scholars have tried to claim in different contexts in recent studies of modernism. If it did so, I argue, it would become naturalized, and the connection to local day-to-day struggle and minority voices would be lost.[24] Rather, the Divertimento reflects the choices Stravinsky made in programming repertoire for his concerts around the world, and the subsequent transformation of his music from aesthetic object of modernist contemplation to cosmopolitan souvenir.

Although some scholars believe that cosmopolitan negotiations can lead artists to a "critical" stance toward modernism, Stravinsky did not become critical, but rather remained self-serving in his choices and oriented toward his own and others' entertainment and pleasure.[25] The very frivolousness and banality of his endeavors says more about his music's moral value than would any projected intentions about the fundamental moral worth of modernism as a musical project per se. I offer this brief story with the metaphorical title "Igor the Angeleno" as a model for interpreting how Stravinsky's music may have also functioned in Los Angeles in the 1940s, and as a call to arms for scholars to begin studying this period in Stravinsky's life in detail in relation to a desegregated history of music in the local context of that city. The dynamics of vernacular cosmopolitanism may explain why Stravinsky felt so at home in Los Angeles, and why he chose to become an Angeleno.

Nationalism in the Mirror: Stravinsky in Spain

Stravinsky first established his modus operandi for negotiating his experience of local Spanish customs when World War I prevented Diaghilev's Ballets Russes from touring as planned, and the company found its itinerary rerouted to Spain. King Alfonso XIII rescued Diaghilev by inviting the Ballets Russes to stage productions of Stravinsky's *Firebird* and *Petrushka* with Rimsky-Korsakov's *Scheherazade* at the Teatro Real in Madrid from 28 May to 9 June, and to produce a Spanish-themed program that included *Petrushka* and an orchestral excerpt, Glinka's *Summer Night in Madrid,* in San Sebastián that August.[26] Diaghilev's presentation of Russian and Spanish national culture within a modernist framework delighted and infuriated Spanish critics, themselves involved in a profound reexamination of national traditions within the context of their own burgeoning vanguard movement.[27] Famous by reputation for *The Rite of Spring* (which would receive its Spanish premiere only in 1928), Stravinsky became the focus of their attention; reactions to his work were intense and divided. Manuel de Falla and Adolfo Salazar defended Stravinsky in seminal essays that strengthened the bonds between the international and local vanguard, and between Spain, Russia, and France.[28] Salazar, a brilliant twenty-six-year-old Spanish critic and composer who championed Schoenberg, the French Impressionists, and the Russian School, excitedly sent Stravinsky two of the many reviews he wrote about him during his visit.[29] In these reviews, Salazar displayed his insider knowledge of Stravinsky's modernist circle by quoting liberally from French sources, and by describing a private dinner of intimate friends in Madrid at which Stravinsky performed in a four-hand version of the *Rite.*[30] These exchanges and critical confrontations proved decisive: Stravinsky returned to Paris with a refreshed perspective, Spanish audiences and critics having mirrored his nationalism in a way that helped solidify his path toward a more objective musical style.

Stravinsky felt attracted by the foreignness and familiarity of Spain, and found his "new acquaintances" there, among them the Chilean silver mining heiress Eugenia Errázuriz, "very agreeable" as he wrote years later in *Chroniques de ma vie*. Nevertheless, "at the [Spanish] border the smell of frying in oil already became perceptible," he wrote, hinting at his disdain for lower-class cooking habits.[31] The strangeness of Spain dissipated when he visited Toledo and the Escorial, where he experienced not the "horrors of the Inquisition or the cruelties of the days of tyranny" but rather "the profoundly religious temperament of the people and the ardent mysticism of their Catholicism, so similar in its essence to Russian religious feeling and spirit." Although he claimed to find Spanish folk music indistinctive, he spent "whole evenings" frequenting taverns "listening indefinitely to the guitar-ist's prelude-tunings and a deep-voiced singer with interminable breath unfolding her long Arab cantilena with rich fioriture."[32]

Stravinsky responded to his first experience of Spain by writing pieces like "Española" (the second of his *Cinq Pièces faciles*, 1916–17), the Etude for Pianola (1917; published and premiered in 1921 and orchestrated as "Madrid" in his Four Etudes for Orchestra of 1930), and the "Royal March" from *L'Histoire du soldat* (1918; based on a paso doble). In these works he did not imitate a Spanish style but rather, in his own words, "paid tribute" to Spain as Glinka once had in *Summer Night in Madrid* by capturing "the comical nature of the unexpected mixtures exhibited by the mechanical pianos and clatter of out-of-tune instruments on the streets of Madrid and in the little nocturnal taverns"—in other words, the technolo-gies of reproduction that enabled the Spanish tourist industry.[33] By combining modern technology with Spanish urban street sounds in these works, Stravinsky departed radically from Glinka's model of program music with its lush express-ive orchestration, exoticized aural images, stereotypical thematic contrasts, and recognizable Spanish tropes (castanets), instead manifesting in his music the relationship between local impressions and global technology characteristic of vernacular cosmopolitanism.

Stravinsky returned to Spain six times between 1921 and 1936, traveling to Barcelona and Madrid, but leaving no impression of what he thought of the Catalan-Spanish national conflict.[34] After hearing Aurelio Fernández premiere Stravinsky's Three Pieces for Clarinet in April 1921, Salazar announced the advent of neoclassicism (*nuevo clasicisme* [*sic*])— a fiercely debated aesthetic in Spain.[35] Listening to *Petrushka* around the same time, José Ortega y Gasset praised Stravinsky for breaking with the nineteenth-century aesthetics of feeling. "This music is something external to ourselves. It is a distinct object, perfectly located outside ourselves, and in the face of which we feel we are pure contemplators," he wrote.[36] When Stravinsky conducted his much anticipated *Pulcinella* Suite at the Gran Teatre del Liceu in Barcelona on 16 March, and at the Teatro Real in Madrid on 25 March 1924, critics received it within the context of these intellectual debates, and perhaps even in relation to the publication in *El Sol* in January and February 1924 of the first installments of Ortega y Gasset's "The Dehumanization of Art."[37] That spring Salazar confirmed *Pulcinella*'s importance to the Spanish vanguard by comparing it to Falla's *El Retablo de Maese Pedro* in an article for Ortega y Gasset's recently established journal, *Revista de Occidente*.[38] Stravinsky had been assimilated effortlessly into the Spanish cultural elite, becoming for it a symbol of European musical modernity.

By the mid-1920s, Stravinsky was beginning to feel a genuine attachment to the city of Barcelona. In 1924 he established a successful working relationship with Juan Mestres Calvet, director of the Gran Teatre del Liceu in Barcelona, and consolidated his decision to devote his career to performing his own music. Calvet arranged Stravinsky concerts and festivals in Barcelona in 1924, 1925, 1928, and 1936, programming new works each year, and becoming more daring as time went on.[39] Through these repeated visits, Stravinsky established lasting relationships with Catalan friends, who introduced him to folk traditions being reinvented in Barcelona at that time. The psychiatrist Jeroni de Moragas remembered with pride how the Ateneu Barcelonès invited Stravinsky to hear the Cobla Barcelona play *sardanas*—a Catalan round dance—in 1924.[40] "Stravinsky scrutinized the movements of the cobla through his monocle, listened attentively for the new sounds, and every now and then gasped in surprise. . . . He looked at the instruments and wanted to understand how everything worked. . . . When I return to Paris," he told his Spanish hosts, "send me some *sardanas* to study, and send me some popular melodies as well. Then I'll send you the *sardanas* I write."[41] Rafael Moragas likewise describes an evening in Madrid in 1925, when Stravinsky joined Joaquín Turina, Falla, Picasso, and others for a concert given by Ricardo Viñes, after which they retired to a *buñoleria*, or doughnut store, where Turina "succumbed to the canto jondo," and Falla went on what was for him a "binge" by drinking two bottles of Mondariz, a Spanish bottled water that was a luxury item. Falla feared he would anger Stravinsky if he went to bed early, but Stravinsky was too drunk to notice.[42]

Musical Scrapbooks

During his travels to Spain and other countries, Stravinsky began to take many photographs, and upon his return home he organized these meticulously into photo albums. Early albums from the war years document family vacations with Yekaterina and their four children. A later album belonging to Vera Sudeikina provides fond memories of her many trips with him, whereas a stately album from the 1930s presents impressions of Stravinsky's concert tours with his son

Soulima and others.[43] The photographs Stravinsky so carefully pasted into these scrapbooks give evidence of his affluence, and of how he saw the world as a traveler, and the types of tourist attractions he cared about. He photographed friends and family but also countless zoos, and sometimes peasants—for example, in Bucharest in 1930. Yet he and Vera most often photographed means of transportation. As if celebrating the technology that enabled their mobility, they pasted into their albums picture after picture of trains and boats; frequently Stravinsky stands beaming next to an expensive car. These photographs reveal Stravinsky's passion for collecting and arranging material manifestations of his experience as a means of keeping memories present: as voraciously as he snapped photographs, he purchased souvenirs in all the places he visited.

Stravinsky's photo albums capture not only material memory but also the affective content of past experience. From his early years touring with Diaghilev, Stravinsky understood music making as an expression of intimate friendship—a way of coping he invented when as a lonely child alienated from his parents he bonded with his gay younger brother Gury, who died of typhoid fever on military service in Romania in 1916 (see Figure 2). His albums document his intimate relationship to Gury, his love affair with Vera, and the intense camaraderie and male bonding with travel companions from Picasso to Charles-Ferdinand Ramuz. They are striking for their intensity of affect. As Stravinsky got older, it became ever more important to him to tour with close companions, whether the Russian-American Jewish violinist and student of Fritz Kreisler, Samuel Dushkin, or his son Soulima.[44] In later life, he traveled always in the company of Robert Craft. He appeared to choose these companions not for their musical talent per se, but for their trustworthiness and degree of intimate connection to him. They gave him a sense of permanence and home amidst the whirlwind of his world travels.

Stravinsky's photo albums and itineraries reveal that he was almost always either on tour, commuting between his family home in Southern France and his mistress Vera in Paris, or vacationing with one or the other; his schedule left little time to establish roots. His state of exile and the closing of the Russian border had led to a loss of financial security, and he needed to tour incessantly to make ends meet. This compulsive traveling affected how he understood nations and musical nationalisms, which he came to see as somewhat interchangeable. By the 1930s he considered himself neither Russian nor cosmopolitan, but as "global" or, simply, "Stravinsky"—composer of the "Chinese March" in *Le Chant du rossignol*, the Spanish-inflected Etude for Pianola, *Pulcinella*, and later, *Four Norwegian Moods*.[45] He saw these works as qualitatively distinct from the "picturesque in music" that he associated with Ravel, Rimsky-Korsakov, Villa-Lobos, and others, and defined his own musical brand as beyond local definition.[46] Music was not national but universal, as he later told a reporter in Caracas. It was "just music, plain and simple."[47] His aristocratic privilege had given him access to a global range of musical practices, and it all belonged to him.

Figure 2. Gury Stravinsky (in foreground) with an unidentified man, Romania, 1916.

To make a living while on tour, Stravinsky frequently had to perform his "greatest hits"—the Russian ballets of his early years—in a format that could be rehearsed and performed quickly with orchestras of any caliber. He programmed most often not the "neoclassicism as style" for which he had become famous in the 1920s and for which he has found a place of honor in the history books of musical

Figure 3. Stravinsky's personal photograph "mit Samuel Dushkin," n. d., ca. early 1930s

modernism, but rather commercial repertoire that included old warhorses like the *Pulcinella*, *Firebird*, and *Petrushka* suites and the Divertimento. These works were the products he gave international audiences in return for the souvenirs and folk entertainments his hosts always offered him on his travels. After 1931, he performed them in arrangements for violin and piano with Samuel Dushkin.

Although Robert Craft felt that "all [these arrangements] together are scarcely worth the shortest *original* composition [by Stravinsky]," they are the compositions Stravinsky probably performed most in the 1930s.[48]

Stravinsky and Dushkin became fast friends and intimate travel partners, performing about seventy concerts together between 1931 and 1937 (see Figure 3). Stravinsky composed his *Duo concertante* and Violin Concerto for Dushkin and allowed him to collaborate in the composing process. "I love you, I admire you, and I am grateful to you, and I ask you not to hate me if I ask you to let the trumpets play more softly or *en sourdine* in spots!" Dushkin wrote in 1931 about the Violin Concerto, indicating how well he understood how to charm Stravinsky into agreeing with him.[49] They performed together in France, Italy, England, Spain, and Germany, and when concerts started to dry up there after 1933, undertook extensive tours of the United States in 1935 and 1937. Reactions ranged from enthusiasm in Manchester, through disappointment in Lyon, to boredom in Los Angeles.[50]

A concert program from a recital Stravinsky and Dushkin gave at the Residencia de Estudiantes in Madrid on 21 November 1933 provides insight into their usual choice and ordering of repertoire within the Spanish context, and also of the way in which popular hits from the international concert circuit infiltrated local modernist contexts.[51] The Residencia was a unique educational institution that had been founded in 1910 with the goal of nurturing a specialized intellectual elite in Spain, inspired in part by the philosophy of its close associate, Ortega y Gasset. It offered selected students boarding and a comprehensive education that combined tradition and modernity within an international framework. The musicologist and resident Jesús Bal y Gay organized musical activities in the 1930s, following a cultural agenda similar to that of Adolfo Salazar (a frequent guest there). "The most intelligent of our aristocracy and the most aristocratic of our intelligentsia" were gathered in the Residencia, Jesús Bal y Gay later remembered, highlighting the exclusivity of its cultural circle.[52] On 11 June 1931 the Sociedad de Cursos y Conferencias of the Residencia staged the Madrid premiere of *L'Histoire du soldat*. Two years later, on 21 November 1933, Stravinsky and Dushkin performed there a selection of some of Stravinsky's most beloved tunes arranged and programmed for greatest dramatic effect (see program on facing page).[53]

Stravinsky and Dushkin display bravura, impeccable collaboration, and sensational showmanship on the recordings they had made of most of this repertoire in Paris earlier that year.[55] The two relished performing these musical scrapbooks, the order and content of which they varied incessantly, sometimes adding excerpts from the Violin Concerto, or the Divertimento, which Stravinsky transcribed for his friend in 1932.

But the tours also became depressing. In January 1936, Stravinsky told Dushkin that the tours were no longer giving him enough "moral and material guarantees" to make them worthwhile. He also found nothing interesting in his symphonic

1.

Suite italienne

2.

Duo concertante

Intermission

3.

Pastorale, "Marche chinoise," and "Chants du rossignol" from *Le Rossignol,*
Scherzo and Berceuse from *Firebird,* and the "Danse russe" from *Petrushka.*

4.

Suite from *L'Histoire du soldat* (with Aurelio Fernández on clarinet)[54]

programs, which included "always the same thing—*Firebird* and *Petrushka!*" He
felt this was not good for his moral health.[56] He spoke of his upcoming tour to
Argentina, and of his hope that another U.S. tour with Dushkin in 1937 would be
different. But when that tour ended a year and a half or so later he told Dushkin
candidly that they had not made enough money and that the whole enterprise
was bad for Dushkin's career.[57] Although they performed together after this date,
they never toured again. At the same time, the Spanish Civil War had ended
Stravinsky's concertizing career in Spain and the activities of the Residencia:
many notable former residents were killed while others went into exile in France
and the United States, though most went to Argentina and Mexico.

Dancing on the Volcano: Argentina 1936

Stravinsky's frenetic concertizing schedule and high-class international socializing
took on a morally questionable character after the Spanish Civil War started and a
European war seemed imminent. His privilege caused him to appear increasingly
out of touch. In April 1936, months before the civil war broke out, Stravinsky traveled to Argentina with Soulima aboard the German luxury ocean liner *Cap Arcona.*
He documented the voyage in his photo album with a large professional photograph of Soulima and himself dining with the ship's captain, Richard Niejahr,
as well as snapshots of other boats and the stopover they made in Rio de Janeiro.
Athos Palma, director of the Teatro Colón in Buenos Aires, had invited them to
perform in an impressive festival of old favorites and new works that included full
ballet productions of *Petrushka* and *The Firebird* as well as Nijinska's *Le Baiser de la*

Figure 4. Stravinsky and Victoria Ocampo, from
Stravinsky's photo album, Argentina, spring 1936.

fée, piano concerts with Soulima, and the Argentinian premiere of *Perséphone* with
Victoria Ocampo in the lead role. Just as King Adolfo XIII of Spain had saved
the Ballets Russes by inviting them to Spain during World War I, the Argentinean
cultural elite rescued Stravinsky from a dismal European season by inviting him to
Buenos Aires on the eve of the Spanish Civil War. In each case, conflict forced the
most active cultural agents in the European metropolis into the periphery, revers-
ing the relationships between both.[58] The tour was on the whole a success, in spite
of the political scandal caused by Stravinsky's critique of Soviet "materialism" and
(indirectly) the Spanish Left in the interviews he gave upon arrival in Argentina.[59]

During his time in Argentina, Uruguay, and Brazil, Stravinsky established a
deep friendship with Victoria Ocampo, the remarkable Argentine intellectual and
socialite he had met through Ernest Ansermet in 1932 (see Figure 4).[60] Ocampo
was a leading player in a transnational circle of writers invested in promoting the
emerging cultures of the Americas. In 1930 she launched the literary journal *Sur*,
in which she published numerous articles about or related to artistic circles around
Stravinsky. Ocampo played a pivotal role in establishing lines of communication
among intellectuals in the United States, Latin America, and Europe (especially
France, where she lived for extended periods). Friendships were an article of faith
for her. She considered them the antidote to the centralized power of the European
metropolis, and in her autobiography spoke about the importance of love as a
"passion that filled out the entire space of a life for those who were born to feel it."[61]

Figure 5. Snapshots of Victoria Ocampo with Soulima and Igor Stravinsky
from Stravinsky's photo album, Argentina, spring 1936

Ocampo had ties to Stravinsky before they met up in Argentina in 1936. She
had witnessed his major premieres in Paris before the war, and had seen how
people whistled *Firebird* on the Champs d'Elysées afterward.[62] She was also close
to Ernest Ansermet, with whom she swapped records and exchanged listening
experiences, participating vigorously in the commodity exchange characteristic of

Figure 5. continued

vernacular modernism. [63] Whenever she had liked any of the records in Ansermet's collection—including Gershwin's *Nashville Nightingale* in 1925—Ansermet quipped excitedly, "Oh Igor likes that record too. Take it. I want you to have it." "Igor, Igor, Igor came up all the time in our conversations," Ocampo remembered. [64]

Figure 5. continued

Ocampo invited Stravinsky and Soulima to stay with her during their visit, and did everything to make them feel "at home."[65] In this comfortable setting the composer let his guard down, and developed intimate friendships that lasted for the rest of his life (see Figure 5).[66] Ocampo introduced Stravinsky to the Mexican writer Alfonso Reyes, a friend of Salazar's and Bal y Gay's and frequent visitor to the Residencia de Estudiantes; the Argentine composer Juan José Castro; and the guitarist, singer, and composer of tango José Maria Aguilar, among other friends. Stravinsky also met many visiting friends from Chile; and some of the many Spanish intellectuals residing in the city that spring.[67] Ocampo arranged for Stravinsky to hear "Creole music" (*musique criolla*) organized by Mr. A. Rojas, "who is in contact with those people and already organized things of this kind for other celebrities passing through Buenos Aires."[68] And she helped Stravinsky buy a lovely Argentinian cowhide (*peau de vache*) that made Vera "ecstatic."[69] When he later asked her to give Vera another cowhide, which he had seen in her Parisian apartment, she replied that she thought it had gone missing in the war and "it's nothing at all to have perhaps lost all of that but I think about it with nostalgia, because a whole period of my life disappeared with those things. I attach myself to things only because they remind me of people and moments in my life. Things can be replaced, the rest can't be."[70] The emotions she invested in objects mattered more to Ocampo than their market value, and more perhaps than the pressing realities of the war. Imbuing her vast material wealth with affective memories allowed her, like other international aristocrats, to live out a kind of nostalgic capitalism, and to blur her financial privilege with the labor that enabled it.

Victoria Ocampo and her exclusive circle of friends knowingly imitated elite French modernists in constructing their vanguard intellectual identity. This is evident in a drawing by an unnamed guest at a party Ocampo hosted for Stravinsky at her ranch, La Martona. This drawing is titled *Project for "Liqueurs on the Grass in the manner of Manet,"* in a parody of his *Le Déjeuner sur l'herbe*, and hints at an affair (see Figure 6). The woman who drew it, "M.A. de C.C.," lies "hidden by the tree" and appears to be in intimate communication with a stick-figure Stravinsky. "I unfortunately have nothing to apologize for, I forget and my memories are erased is the silent response of a faithful woman," she utters. This woman does not appear to be Ocampo herself, who stands elsewhere. Stravinsky, seated on the other side of the tree, responds to the unidentified woman, "I forget but I don't forgive"—the stick figure, like the composer himself, mistrusting memories but not forgetting the feelings associated with them. The couple's elusive flirting perfectly encapsulates the secrecy and exclusivity of their social class. The group is contained in a space shaped like a luxury perfume bottle, one that seals them off hermetically from the world around them.

When he got home, Stravinsky memorialized the very same party in his photo album (Figure 7). Rather than depict the space of the party as closed and self-contained as the woman had, Stravinsky depicted it as open and fragmented. He pasted in a double-exposure photo that reveals the shadowy contours of an expensive car, as well as a nice profile shot of Victoria, and three photographs of a boisterous group of friends engaged in drunken merriment, with Stravinsky lying on the ground and playing the party clown, all of this under the label "Estancia

Figure 6. Drawing by a party guest at Victoria Ocampo's ranch, La Martona, spring 1936.

Martona, One of the most beautiful and richest in the province." Through this act of documentation, Stravinsky distances himself from his personal experience of the party, and situates himself both inside and outside its intimate circle—a movement that creates the tension and desire realized in his casual affair.

In Argentina, as in Spain and Russia, Stravinsky maintained his membership in his privileged aristocratic rank by stressing class over ethnic commonalities, and by consenting to the group's rules of exclusion and traditions of perceiving difference. He knew he did not belong by nationality to the Spanish-speaking world, a fact many cartoonists and reporters drove home by relentlessly mocking his physiognomy. But he felt confident about his class and racial associations, and soon began to speak regularly to the Spanish press about being distinct from the "folk" or "people"—an amorphous spontaneous collectivity that he observed only from the outside, and whose music he as an elite composer could not replicate but only use to construct something new.[71] He also developed a passionate love for capitalism—on his first trip to the United States he excitedly planned trips to the Chicago stockyards and the Ford plant in Detroit—and a hatred of Communism and materialism, the topic that got him in such hot water in Argentina.[72]

Years of being exposed to privately arranged performances of folkloric specta-cle in Spain, Argentina, and the other countries he visited led Stravinsky to develop

Figure 7. Social gathering at Victoria Ocampo's La Martona from
Stravinsky's photo album, Argentina, spring 1936.

distinct habits of racial spectatorship. His elitism took on racial overtones, as he increasingly kept people of color at a distance by projecting onto them less sophisticated listening practices and making them the object of his tourist gaze. "[Does] the effect of music [not] depend . . . upon the culture of the listener's ear?" he asked a reporter in Cleveland after returning from Argentina. "[Imagine a] room [with] an audience of four—a savage from darkest Africa, a laborer on the street, a doctor, a musician—and we play music for them, a good, sweet melody. Is it music to the savage? No. 'That is terrible,' he cries [since] for him music is boom! boom! boom! His ear is not cultured. To him it is abstract. So each listener calls that which is familiar to him, music."[73] He told another reporter in New York in May 1940, "Always I love to listen to the good swings [sic] orchestras, not only in this country but in Paris. Now it is to the Harlem I go. It is so sympathetic to watch the Negro boys and girls dancing and to watch them eating the long, what is it you call them, frankfurters, no—hot dogs—in the long roles [sic]."[74]

Wartime Shopping in Mexico

Stravinsky traveled to Mexico just months after Germany invaded France, Belgium, the Netherlands, and Luxembourg. When he arrived there, he encountered many of his aristocratic contacts from Barcelona and Buenos Aires, his cosmopolitanism collapsing into the local pleasure of reconnecting with familiar contexts and old friends. The Mexican president Lázaro Cárdenas had recognized the government of the Spanish Republic in exile and opened its arms to intellectuals, creating several institutions to support them, including La Casa de España in 1938 (which became El Colegio de México two years later). The Mexican writer Alfonso Reyes became its director, and Spanish exile Jesús Bal y Gay became his colleague in 1938, with Adolfo Salazar joining in 1939.[75] Carlos Chávez welcomed all of them into the musical community. Salazar and Bal y Gay reinvented the critical tradition around Stravinsky that they had both contributed to in Spain (Salazar much more so), helping out with newly established journals like *Nuestra Musica*, and writing reviews whenever Stravinsky came to town that invariably welcomed the composer as a conquering hero.

Reports of Stravinsky's trips to Mexico emphasize elaborate socializing, and his desire to entertain and be entertained at a time of war. Stravinsky and his old acquaintances all seemed delighted to see one another. A reporter from the *Revista de Revistas* described a scene in which Stravinsky, with his typical compulsive flair, ordered an elaborate breakfast for his Mexican friends, among them the composers Manuel Ponce, Carlo Chávez, and Eduardo Hernández Moncada. Salazar translated because Stravinsky spoke only French. "There was Salazar, standing at the car door, talking to a friend," the reporter observed. "Then suddenly Stravinsky emerged from his house running. And running right behind him, trying to catch every word, Salazar."[76] Alfonso Reyes wrote Ocampo of a wonderful evening with Stravinsky in Mexico in June 1940. "He was as charming as usual, and so enjoyed talking about theology. It is a delight to see him lose his temper over snobby reporters who ask him inane questions."[77]

One of the first items on the agenda when Stravinsky reunited with Salazar, Bal y Gay and his wife, Rosita Ascot—a pianist who had studied with Manuel de Falla and performed often at the Residencia—was for all of them to take a shopping trip to Taxco, where they posed for several photographs (Figures 8 and 9). These snapshots look quite different from the one Eisenstein and his friends posed for in 1931 (Figure 1). Stravinsky still wears a Parisian beret, as had Eisenstein and Urueta, but his clothes distinguish him more dramatically from the people milling about him. He is awkward and ill at ease in his surroundings rather than proud of them, as Eisenstein and his leftist friends had once been. In a second photo with Salazar, Rosita Ascot, and Vera, the group appears closed in on itself, laughing playfully at an inside joke or staring into Jesús Bal y Gay's camera and oblivious of the people around them. They revel in the amusement of spending an afternoon buying souvenirs, which they will transport home with the help of many local laborers. On a second outing to the Church of San Francisco Javier in Tepotzotlán—which Stravinsky later described to Robert Craft as "the most moving Christian building in the world"—Stravinsky solidified his Mexican tourist experience, as he had done in Spain in 1916 and 1921, with a selfless moment of intense Christian communion that erased ethnic, national, and class differences.[78]

During his many visits to Mexico from 1940 until the 1960s, Stravinsky became "inseparable" from Jesús Bal y Gay and Rosita. Bal y Gay remembers "infinite meals" together, attending all of Stravinsky's rehearsals, and excursions to tourist spots like the Basilica of our Lady of Guadeloupe, where Stravinsky shocked his Spanish Catholic friends with his curious religious practice of lighting a candle, then kneeling at the altar with his arms extended to make the sign of the cross, while still holding the candle in his right hand—their alienation countering the affinity for Spanish Catholicism Stravinsky had felt over twenty years earlier and rekindled in Mexico.[79] Stravinsky cherished the time alone with Bal y Gay and his wife, with whom he felt he could talk about Mexico (which he studied assiduously) and about his "picturesque" voyages to other countries. Stravinsky was also an extremely good listener, Bal y Gay later remembered, and patiently gave Bal y Gay extensive advice on his compositions.[80] Conversations with Stravinsky, Bal y Gay concluded, gave him the greatest comfort he knew in what he called his "unwanted and forced Mexican exile."[81]

Musical Souvenirs: The Divertimento in Mexico, 1941

The sonic consequences of Stravinsky's travels in the circuits of vernacular cosmopolitanism are evident in the recording he made in Mexico of his Divertimento. About twenty-two seconds into the second movement, "Danses suisses," a man disrupts the music by yelling loudly. It is not clear what he says or whether he is reacting to the music or to something else happening in the hall, but the timing of his protest (rehearsal number 40) suggests he is upset by the way in which the music is skipping from fragment to fragment. The Divertimento is a dance suite made up of sutured fragments of about fifteen piano works by Tchaikovsky and derived from the ballet *Le Baiser de la fée*, which Ida Rubinstein commissioned from Stravinsky in 1928.[82] Originally, Rubinstein's stage designer Alexandre Benois had suggested to Stravinsky the idea of composing a ballet based on Tchaikovsky's piano works, examples of which he sent for him to consider. Stravinsky had used about half of Benois's suggestions and other works to create a ballet in the tradition of Glazunov-Fokine's *Chopiniana*, which he at first called *Tchaikovskyana*. The connection to Tchaikovsky was obvious when the work was performed as a ballet, but the authorship became more ambiguous when Stravinsky created a suite from it for concert performance, and then arranged that suite for violin and piano.

Figure 8. Stravinsky in Taxco, Mexico, photo by Vera Stravinsky, summer 1940.

Although in their studies of the work Stravinsky's friends Robert Craft and Lawrence Morton immediately focused on identifying the fragments, the sutures between them are equally interesting in the context of vernacular cosmopolitanism. The "Danses suisses" (called "Une fête au village" in the original ballet) starts with an upbeat motive derived from the opening of Tchaikovsky's *Humoresque*, no. 1, op. 10, in D major. Three measures later it launches into two recognizable bars of the main theme of *Humoresque* itself, arranged for brass (Example 1). Stravinsky brazenly disrupts Tchaikovsky's original phrase structure of antecedent and consequent, however, by interrupting this main theme after two measures to return to his own opening motive, which is now reduced to one measure. He then switches back to the *Humoresque* theme, but disrupts it again two measures later, this time with new, distinctly Stravinskyian material that introduces an ironic-sounding A♯ in the horns. That A♯ sets up the next contrasting fragment, a modified version of the opening theme from Tchaikovsky's *Rêverie du soir*, no. 1, op. 19, in the strings at rehearsal number 39. This excerpt is in G minor, and in the original piece its effect is predicated on moving ambiguously to the subdominant only to return to the tonic in the consequent of the phrase that follows. But Stravinsky does not include the consequent of the original phrase; instead, he disrupts the original music with a jarring measure of 2/4 and a return to his opening motive. This leaves the ambiguity of a subdominant in G minor of the *Rêverie* to function like a foreign body in the D major of the already established *Humoresque*, especially because Stravinsky has also not changed the key signature, but let the original

Figure 9. Igor and Vera Stravinsky with Adolfo Salazar and Rosita Ascot,
Taxco, summer 1940.

G-minor excerpt appear in a D-major context. The affective switch between the two fragments is as striking as their harmonic and timbral difference. Only after the abrupt disruption of the opening motive does he offer, at rehearsal number 40, a consequent to the antecedent phrase from the *Rêverie du soir*—but one of his own making, based harmonically and stylistically on the original. This is the moment at which the man in Mexico City cried out—his protest ruining the second attempt to record this piece in Mexico and sonically disrupting Stravinsky's attempt at smooth technological domination of the global modern music scene.

The Frankensteinian sewing together of these musical "found objects" is formally reminiscent of the picture arrangements in Stravinsky's photo albums, except that here it is Tchaikovsky's music, rather than photographs, that have been pasted into an album/score. Perhaps not coincidentally, Stravinsky and Diaghilev had first hatched the idea of reviving Tchaikovsky's music at all—the ballet *Sleeping Beauty*—while on a tourist excursion to Seville in 1921. By cutting Tchaikovsky's compositions in pieces Stravinsky distances listeners from their original symbolic meaning and affect and transforms them into Russian souvenirs. Stravinsky had learned to separate music from emotions when he performed his own compositions on pianolas in the 1920s and noticed that "he was transmitting notes through the intervention of electricity that didn't correspond at all with his immediate feeling, because there was an intermediary." He liked this effect because, as he told Erik Satie, it "restored" rather than "reproduced" his oeuvres.[83] Adolfo Salazar recognized the nostalgic character of the souvenirs in Stravinsky's Divertimento when he heard it in Mexico City in 1940, and asked his readers to imagine Manuel de Falla writing such a Divertimento based on the multinational Madrilenian music of the zarazuela composer Federico Chueca.[84] Salazar also notes that the piece's subtitle, "Allegory," is an accurate reflection of the work.

The fragments of Tchaikovsky's music in the Divertimento function like Russian souvenirs—or the cowboy hats and berets in Figure 1—not only in their objectified arrangement, but in the way they evoke nostalgic memories. Stravinsky liked to tell people that the emotions in his music were in the music itself and not expressed by him. Using fragments of music by another composer made that assertion plausible.[85] The two Tchaikovsky fragments at the opening of "Danses suisses" express dramatically contrasting affects: the *Humoresque* is jolly, whereas the *Rêverie* is melancholic. Their affective content is felt immediately; they have what philosopher Walter Benjamin called "aura"—the quality of objects that carry the sentiments once invested in them, and that evoke involuntary memories. They achieve their impact precisely because of the way in which Stravinsky has cut and pasted them, forcing listeners to dwell in the moment by interrupting the music's development. This technique enables what Benjamin calls *Erlebnis* within an otherwise alienated modernity.[86] The auratic fragments in the Divertimento transform it into a souvenir shop—an aesthetic version of the marketplace of vernacular modernism.

Benjamin's notion of *Erlebnis* describes well the immediacy of experience Stravinsky hoped to create by performing this music himself. I want "music to be fresh and alive in the ears of the people," he had told a British reporter in 1934. "Music ought to be like an opened window that lets in clean air, perhaps cold air, to make the head spin. Music should be desire, not habit."[87] In an interview in Paris a year later, Stravinsky clarified that he didn't write music to please audiences, but that he did care deeply about how they received his work when he appeared before them onstage as a pianist or conductor. His goal was to connect with them honestly. "By making contact with the public, it is possible to influence one's own success, to influence it through the feeling one has that the proposed work is good and useful, and that the way it has been presented is void of affectation, artifice and complacency," he commented. "When I am able to share with listeners the faith that is in me, I feel joy in my success." This is why, Stravinsky explained, he had been performing his own music for the past fifteen years.[88]

But in spite of the unmediated performance, the message Stravinsky communicates in the Divertimento is veiled and indirect, the fragmentation having pushed the affects underground. No single affect is ever allowed to prevail, and most are dwarfed by the overwhelming effect of the work's jarringly disjunctive form. Stravinsky seems to want to keep the audience from knowing too much,

Example 1. Stravinsky, "Danses Suisses," second movement of Divertimento, rehearsal no. 38 to two measures after 40.

just as he remained mum on the intensity of feeling within his intimate circle of friends—any lavish display of emotion going against what he understood to be unbreakable rules of aristocratic public modesty and decorum. His fatherly

Example 1. Continued

protection of affect may also reflect his strong empathy for Tchaikovsky's maligned homosexuality—an empathy that led him as a young man to become the closest confidant of his beloved brother, Gury.[89]

Stravinsky's nostalgia for the emotional intensity of his intimate relationships in the past—his love for Tchaikovsky and Gury—leads in the Divertimento to occasional, unexpected sentimentality—an affect characteristic of the souvenir. This sentimentality may, in fact, have sometimes embarrassed Stravinsky,

Example 1. Continued

who admired Tchaikovsky for "restoring the melodic line" but thought his music could also "smell like oil from the fried food at a country fair"—the stench that reminded him of the lower class.[90] It also felt threatening to Lawrence Morton, who couldn't imagine that Stravinsky could really love Tchaikovsky "in spite of his unforgiveable flaws." Given the "sexual tragedy" of Tchaikovsky's life and

Example 1. Continued

the "vulgarity of his symphonic climaxes and boring sequences," Morton commented, *Le Baiser de la fée* must have been nothing more than an act of rigorous criticism on Stravinsky's part. [91] For very different reasons this sentimentality also bothered Richard Taruskin, who thought the Divertimento lacked irony and thus was not modern.[92] I would argue that the presence of sentimentality and of cutoff or contained emotions in the Divertimento does not disqualify the work as "modern," as Taruskin once claimed, but rather gives it pride of place in a history of modern music that takes into account the role of music as an exchange object between the local and global in vernacular cosmopolitanism.

Becoming an Angeleno

The knowledge of Stravinsky's Spanish-speaking networks and the perspective of vernacular cosmopolitanism broaden the lens for exploring his life in Los Angeles after 1941. This knowledge gives insight into the way he lived behind the styles of the works he created, and explain why he may not have always understood himself as an "exile" after he arrived in the United States in the fall of 1939. He felt at home there, speaking French, German, and Russian, following the French and Russian news, and gathering books for his polyglot library. As a vernacular cosmopolitan, Stravinsky had already engaged with the new technologies offered by the film industry in Los Angeles in the mid-1930s, before emigrating to the United States, and although he rejected a production system that he felt limited his creative freedom and felt enraged by Disney's *Fantasia*, he remained open to the technologies developed by the Los Angeles music and film industry through-out his life (see Figure 10).[93]

Stravinsky also moved to Los Angeles for the weather—an aspect of a compos-er's migration patterns that musicologists often mistakenly ignore—and because he on the whole loved the way of life in Southern California. "I'm finished with leaving for Europe," he wrote Victoria Ocampo in 1941. "And anyway, every-body is coming here, which is why you can't find an affordable place to live."[94] A year later he was "no longer homesick" and "perfectly content to make his home in Hollywood."[95] He "never wanted to return to Europe" he told a reporter in Montréal in 1945.[96] Pierre Schaeffer described him in 1946 as living apart from the world, enjoying a peaceful life of sun, friends, and music—an impression he illustrated in his article with personal photographs Stravinsky had given him.[97] In 1947 Stravinsky told Louise Weiss that he was living in Hollywood because of "the great climate, the peace and quiet to work, the easy way of life."[98] Other visitors noticed how much he liked to stay home tending to his beloved garden, playing Chinese checkers, doing Swedish and German gymnastics, and inviting friends for tea.[99] When Albert Goldberg asked composers in a survey in the *Los Angeles Times* in 1950 whether they agreed with an unnamed European composer who had recently stated that working in the United States was "a little below his proper level," Stravinsky gave an annoyed response. This was exactly the kind of argument the Soviets made against their emigrants, he wrote Goldberg, and that the history of art had proved wrong with the examples of Poussin, Handel, Gogol, Chopin, and Picasso. "I do not really think that this subject is really worthy of a column of your pen," he told him. Schoenberg and Mario Castelnuevo-Tedesco agreed that emigration to the United States in itself had not changed them.[100]

In Los Angeles, Stravinsky continued to collect omnivorously from cul-tures all over the world by going on outings and side trips with Vera and friends, traveling compulsively, and participating avidly in the burgeoning California tourist industry and marketing of nostalgia for the state's Hispanic past. He

Figure 10: George Balanchine, Stravinsky, Walt Disney, and an unidentified
assistant (behind the others) examining figures from *Fantasia*, Los Angeles, 1939.

recognized that in the 1940s Los Angeles was a city on the move—home to vibrant
jazz clubs on Central Avenue, an explosive Latin music scene, nascent Chicano
rock, a large European émigré community of musicians, composers, writers, and
artists, and established institutions of classical music. Stravinsky was divided by
race and class from some of these cultures but acutely aware of them all through
the circulation of goods (records, playbills, advertising). He also benefited from the
presence in Los Angeles of many former dancers from the Ballets Russes, including
his good friend Adolph Bolm, and from lavish, popular stagings of his ballets at the
Hollywood Bowl. When he was living in Los Angeles, Stravinsky did not always
look west toward the ocean and to the German émigrés in Santa Monica and
Pacific Palisades with whom musicologists always associate him, but rather south,
down across Central Avenue, through Tijuana to Mexico City, and to the Spanish-
speaking aristocratic culture with which he felt intimately familiar. Stravinsky's
sensitivity to this multiplicity of cultures led him to embrace his life in Los Angeles,
and to feel an affinity for what it meant to be an Angeleno in the 1940s. For the next
twenty-eight years, no matter where he traveled, how many borders he crossed,
and how many suitcases he packed and unpacked, he always came home—in the
end—to Los Angeles.

NOTES

This essay was inspired by the work of Ryan Dohoney, and profited immensely from critical exchanges with him, Paul De Angelis, Natalia Bieletto-Bueno, Jerome Camal, Tiffany Naiman, and Nina Eidsheim.

1. The trip was subsequently delayed and ran from 20 July to 5 August 1940.

2. See Carlos Chávez to Stravinsky, 23 and 27 February 1940; Alexis Kall (representing Stravinsky) to Chávez, 1 March; and Ricardo Ortega as manager of the Orquesta Sinfónica de México to Stravinsky, 5 April 1940, microfilm 129.1, 1466–75, Paul Sacher Stiftung (hereafter PSS).

3. Stravinsky to Ricardo Ortega, 23 April 1940, microfilm 129.1, 1475, PSS. In this letter, Stravinsky asked for changes to the program, which had included *Le Baiser de la fée* and *Le Chant du rossignol.* He thought either the *Petrushka* Suite or the Divertimento would be easier to prepare with the orchestra in such a short time.

4. See the contract between RCA Victor Mexicana, Ricardo Ortega, and Stravinsky dated 3 August 1940, microfilm 129.1, 1505–06, PSS.

5. Chávez offered Stravinsky $1,250 for the concert and $500 for the recording. Chávez to Stravinsky, 25 January 1941, microfilm 130.1, 446–47, PSS. See also Stravinsky's "agreement" in English, kept in the same microfilm, 454–55.

6. Stravinsky to Chávez, 28 January 1940, microfilm 130.1, 448, PSS; and further correspondence, 449–55.

7. Ricardo Ortega to Stravinsky, 11 and 13 July 1940; and Stravinsky to Ortega and Chávez, 13 July 1940, microfilm 129.1, 1493–94; 1499–1500, PSS. Official notes from the Mexican Department of Immigration and Adolfo de la Huerta are included in microfilm 129.1, 1499–1501, PSS.

8. See Vera's diary entry for 20 July 1940 in Robert Craft and Vera Stravinsky, *Stravinsky in Pictures and Documents* (New York: Simon and Schuster, 1978), 367 (hereafter *SPD*).

9. See Vera's diary entry, quoted in *SPD*, 368; and Stravinsky to Ortega, 4 July 1941, microfilm 130.1, 480 (in which he describes the border guard as "très méfiant"). The Immigration Act of 1924 put severe limitations on emigration to the United States from Eastern Europe. In that year the Border Patrol was established on the U.S.-Mexico border.

10. John P. Rhodes, "Prospect of Citizenship Charms Stravinsky as He Gets Ready for Cincinnati Concerts," *Cincinnati Enquirer*, 22 February 1940.

11. Stravinsky to Ricardo Ortega, 4 June 1941, microfilm 130.1, 469, PSS.

12. Adolfo de la Huerta, official note dated 1 July 1941, microfilm 130.1, 478, PSS.

13. Stravinsky to Ricardo Ortega, 4 July 1941, microfilm 130.1, 480, PSS.

14. When they were arranging Stravinsky's visas in 1940, Ricardo Ortega asked Stravinsky: "Could not you use your influence with your friends in Washington to speed this matter up?" See Ortega to Stravinsky, 13 July 1940, microfilm 129.1, 1499, PSS.

15. This fact puts into perspective Stravinsky's pampered complaints about the "inconvenience" of negotiating his entry into the U. S. at the Mexican border.

16. I am inspired in this project by Brigid Cohen's "Diasporic Dialogues in Mid-Century New York: Stefan Wolpe, George Russell, Hannah Arendt, and the Historiography of Displacement," *Journal of the Society for American Music* 6/2 (2012): 143–73.

17. Valérie Dufour wrote the first study of Stravinsky's network of French-speaking friends in Belgium, France, Russia, Italy, and Switzerland, thereby establishing a foundation for a transnational rather than national perspective on Stravinsky's music. See *Stravinsky et ses exégètes (1910–1940)* (Brussels: Editions de l'Université de Bruxelles, 2006). Musicologist Natalia Braginskaya is currently working on Stravinsky's transnational activities in multiple countries outside of Russia after 1910.

18. Adriana Cavarero, *Relating Narratives: Storytelling and Selfhood*, trans. from the Italian by Paul A. Kottman (New York: Routledge, 2000), 35–71.

19. Ibid., 19.

20. Stravinsky offered his most cogent critique of the label "modernist" in an interview with a reporter in Manchester in 1934, in which he stated that it was the generic nature of the label that bothered him most: "I do not think it just to give an age a label, and call it 'the age of steel' or 'the age of noise' for there are so many other manifestations of the age, at least equally as appropriate. If you are going to give it a handle, why not 'the age of social unrest' or something like that?" "Stravinsky and His Music: A Condemnation of the 'Watertight Compartment' Outlook. Decisions only Posterity Can Make," *Manchester Guardian*, 22 February 1934.

21. Homi K. Bhabha, "Unsatisfied: Notes on Vernacular Cosmopolitanism," in *Text and Nation: Cross-Disciplinary Essays on Cultural and National Identities*, ed. Laura García-Moreno and Peter C. Pfeiffer (Columbia, SC: Camden House, 1996), 193.

22. A. Joan Saab, "Modernist Networks: Taxco, 1931," *Modernism/Modernity* 18/2 (April 2011): 291. Stravinsky acknowledged Mexican fashion influence by later telling Robert Craft, "The Mexicans are the only men who know how to wear hats. Even Carlos Chávez's derby is just right." See Igor Stravinsky and Robert Craft, *Dialogues and a Diary* (New York: Doubleday & Co., 1963), 193.

23. Brent Hayes Edwards, *The Practice of Diaspora: Literature, Translation, and the Rise of Black Internationalism* (Cambridge, MA: Harvard University Press, 2003), 2: see 1–15.

24. I see the attempt to define cosmopolitanism as style as a fault of Rebecca L. Walkowitz's *Cosmpolitan Style: Modernism Beyond the Nation* (New York: Columbia University Press, 2006).

25. For a discussion of "critical cosmopolitanism," see ibid., 9.

26. See Yvan Nommick and Antonio Alvarez Cañibano, eds., *Los Ballets Russes de Diaghilev en España* (Granada: Archivo Manuel de Falla/INAEM, 2000).

27. Ortega y Gasset had announced the new intellectual generation or "generación del 14," in his speech "Vieja y nueva política"(Old and new politics) on 28 March 1914. This speech coincided with Manuel de Falla's and Joaquín Turina's return from Paris. See Consuelo Carredano, "Adolfo Salazar en España: Primeras incursiones en la crítica musical: *La Revista musical hispano-americana* (1914–1918)," *Anales del Instituto de investigaciones estéticas* 84 (2004): 119–144.

28. See Manuel de Falla, "El gran músico de nuestros tiempo: Igor Stravinsky," *La Tribuna*, 5 June 1916; and Adolfo Salazar, "Los Bailes Rusos: Disertaciones y Soliloquios, Igor Stravinsky," *Revista musical hispano-americana* 8/6 (June 1916): 7–14. The critics were not unanimous on *Petrushka*, however. Salazar's co-editor at the *Revista*, Rogelio Villar, wrote a scathing critique of it a few months later. On these harsh debates, see Carredano, "Adolfo Salazar en España," 141–43.

29. See Salazar to Stravinsky, 10 July, 4 and 20 August 1916, in Adolfo Salazar, *Epistolario 1912–1958*, ed. Consuelo Carredano (Madrid: Amigos de la Residencia de Estudiantes/Fundación Scherzo/INAEM, 2008), 19, 21–23.

30. The private performance of the *Rite* took place on 11 June 1916. Salazar already knew the *Three Japanese Lyrics*, the first two of which Manuel de Falla performed in a version for piano and voice with Madeleine Leymo in a concert of the Sociedad Nacional de Música on 13 December 1916. Salazar sent the program of this concert to Stravinsky. See Salazar to Stravinsky, 26 December 1926, *Epistolario*, 45.

31. Stravinsky, *Chroniques de ma vie* (Paris: Denoël, 1962), 72.

32. Ibid., 73–74.

33. Ibid., 79. Stravinsky uses the expression "casseroles automatiques" for "out-of-tune instruments."

34. On Stravinsky's activities and reception in Spain during these years, see Carol Hess, "Stravinsky in Spain, 1921–25," in *Manuel de Falla and Modernism in Spain, 1898–1936* (Chicago: Chicago University Press, 2002), 161–98.

35. See Adolfo Salazar, "Crónicas musicales: Ravel, Strawinsky y el perfil moderno: Varios conciertos," *El Sol*, 19 April 1921. For insight into the aesthetic of neoclassicism in Spain in this period, see Ruth Piquer Sanclemente, *Clasicismo moderno, neoclasicismo y retornos en el pensamiento musical español (1915–1939)* (Berlin: Editorial Doble J, 2010).

36. See Ortega y Gasset, "Incitaciones: Musicalia," *El Sol*, 24 March 1921. See also "Incitaciones: Apatía artística," *El Sol*, 18 October 1921.

37. See, for example, Adolfo Salazar, "La vida musical: Strawinsky, 'Pulcinella,' 'El Pájaro de Fuego,'" *El Sol*, 26 March 1924; and Hess, *Manuel de Falla and Modernism in Spain*, 180–86.

38. Adolfo Salazar, "Polchinela y Maese Pedro," *Revista de Occidente* 11 (May 1924): 229–37.

39. Oriol Martorell provides details and reviews of all the programs in "Stravinsky a Barcelona: Sis visites i dotze concerts," *d'arte* 8–9 (November 1983): 99–129.

40. Hess, "Stravinsky in Spain, 1921–25," 184. A *cobla* is a traditional ensemble of shawms, brass, flabiol, and tambor.

41. Jeroni de Moragas, "Stravinsky a l'Ateneu," *La Publicitat*, 20 March 1924; quoted in Oriol, "Stravinsky a Barcelona," 103–4.

42. Rafael Moragas, unpublished MS., Museu Nacional d'Art de Catalunya, quoted in Oriol Martorell, "Stravinsky a Barcelona," 124n31. See Stravinsky's and Falla's correspondence in *Stravinsky: Selected Correspondence*, ed. Robert Craft (New York: Alfred A. Knopf, 1984): 2:160–76.

43. These photo albums are kept at the PSS.

44. Stravinsky could become highly agitated if faced with the prospect of touring without Soulima or one of his intimate friends. He lashed out viciously at his son in spring 1939 when the latter refused to accompany him to Italy. On this story, see Tamara Levitz, *Modernist Mysteries: Perséphone* (New York: Oxford University Press, 2012), 355–56.

45. Stravinsky announced to a reporter in Chicago, in German, "I am Stravinsky" (*Ich bin Stravinsky*) in "Stravinsky, in German, Says He's French," *Chicago American*, 26 March 1935. Stravinsky said, "My music is 'global'—it belongs to the whole world," in "Sachlichkeit in der Musik: Eine Stunde mit Igor Stravinsky," *Prager Presse*, 23 February 1930. He told Edward Downes that his music was not "cosmopolitan because I do not like the word—but something which has grown out of the sum of European culture, especially the Latin culture," in "Igor Stravinsky: Plans and Views of a Tonal Giant Who Is Wintering in Cambridge," *Boston Evening Transcript*, 21 October 1939.

46. Stravinsky discusses Villa-Lobos in Jean-Louis Roux, "Igor Strawinsky," *Le Quartier Latin* (Montréal), 23 March 1945.

47. Stravinsky, quoted in "A Stravinsky no le gusta come tocan su música en 'Fantasia,'" *La Esfera* (Caracas), 9 April 1953.

48. *SPD*, 215. See also Craft's exposé on Dushkin and the published letters in "'Dear Samsky,'" in *Stravinsky: Selected Correspondence*, 2:293–311.

49. Samuel Dushkin to Stravinsky, 2 November 1931, microfilm 94.1, 263, PSS.

50. See "Stravinsky Is a Genius: Thrills in a Fine Hallé Program," *Manchester Evening Chronicle*, 23 February 1934; "Les Concerts: Igor Strawinsky Salle Rameau," *La Nouvelliste* (Lyon), 19 December 1934; and "Masterly Concert Puzzles L.A. Audience," *Illustrated Daily News* (Los Angeles), 1 March 1935.

51. The programs of all their concerts, as well as details about their tours, are kept in the PSS.

52. Jesús Bal y Gay, "La música en la Residencia," *Residencia*, commemorative issue published in Mexico (December 1963): 79; quoted in Margarita Sáenz de la Calzada, *La Residencia de Estudiantes: Los Residentes* (Madrid: Publicaciones de la Residencia de Estudiantes, 2011), 169.

53. On the cultural activities of the Residencia de Estudiantes, see Sáenz de la Calzada, *La Residencia de Estudiantes*, 105–26; and Isabel Pérez-Villanueva Tovar, *La Residencia de Estudiantes 1910–1936: Grupo Universitario y Residencia de Señoritas* (Madrid: Publicaciones de la Residencia de Estudiantes, 2011): 401–530.

54. This program is kept in microfilm 126.1, 862, PSS. The program notes quote extensively from Adolfo Salazar's writings.

55. Available on *Igor Stravinsky: Composer & Performer,* vol. 2, Andante (2003).

56. Stravinsky to Dushkin, 8 January 1936, microfilm 94.1, 617–18, PSS. Craft translates *morale* as "artistic" in *Stravinsky: Selected Correspondence*, 2:305.

57. Stravinsky to Dushkin, 24 October 1937, microfilm 94.1, 837-38, PSS. Craft translates the French incorrectly to imply this was good for Dushkin's career in *Stravinsky, Selected Correspondence*, 2:309.

58. Stravinsky wrote Ocampo shortly after his trip to Argentina that Germany was out of the question for performing *Perséphone* in light of the news and that Spain was as well because they were forbidding money from leaving the country. "Isn't it lovely!" (*C'est gai!*) he commented. See Stravinsky to Ocampo, 10 July 1936, microfilm 98.1, 689, PSS.

59. See Omar Corrado, "Stravinsky y la constelación ideológica argentina en 1936," *Latin American Music Review* 26/1 (Spring/Summer 2005): 88–101; and Levitz, *Modernist Mysteries: Perséphone*, 336–39.

60. See Omar Corrado, "Victoria Ocampo y la música: una experiencia social y estética de la modernidad," *Revista Musical Chilena* 61/208 (July–December 2007): 37–65.

61. Victoria Ocampo, *Autobiografía: IV Viraje* (Buenos Aires: Sur, 1982), 8.

62. Ocampo remembers this event nostalgically in a letter to Stravinsky dated 6 December 1949, microfilm 98.1, 862, PSS.

63. Ocampo met Ansermet in 1917, and got to know him after he became involved with the Orquesta de la Asociación del Profesorado Orquestal (A.P.O.) in 1924. See *Vies croisées de Victoria Ocampo et Ernest Ansermet: Correspondance 1924–1969*, ed. Jean-Jacques Langendorf (Paris: Buchet-Chastel, 2005).

64. Ocampo, *Autobiografía: IV Viraje*, 92.

65. Ocampo to Stravinsky, 24 December 1935, microfilm 98.1, 621, PSS. The letter is in French but Ocampo writes "at home" in English.

66. When Nicolas Nabokov wrote urging him to protest Ocampo's imprisonment in 1953, Stravinsky showed uncharacteristic concern, asking Nabokov to refrain from a public campaign that might harm more than help her. See the correspondence between Stravinsky, Louise Crane, Nicolas Nabokov, and the Congress for Cultural Freedom, microfilm 98.1, 881–89, PSS.

67. Stravinsky kept the cartes de visite of the many acquaintances he met in Buenos Aires, among them Armando Carvajal, director of the Conservatorio de Santiago de Chile. See microfilm 127.1, 1928–41, PSS.

68. Ocampo to Stravinsky, n.d., ca. March 1936, microfilm 98.1, 653–54, PSS.

69. Stravinsky to Ocampo, 10 July 1936, microfilm 98.1, 689, PSS.

70. Stravinsky asks for the cowhide in a letter to Ocampo dated 27 May 1941, microfilm 98.1, 782, PSS. Ocampo is quoted here from her letter of reply dated 12 November 1941, 784–90. She wrote again about the cowhide ca. 1948, 858.

71. See "Stravinsky Speaks to the Spanish-Speaking World," in this volume; also, see "Stravinsky compone al piano para sentir las notas en sus nervios," *El Universal* (Caracas), 9 April 1953.

72. See Charles Ludwig, "'I Love America,' Composer Declares," *Cincinnati Times-Star*, 4 March 1925. Stravinsky distinguished Marxist materialism from capitalism and treated the two as unrelated.

73. Stravinsky, *Cleveland News*, 22 February 1937; quoted in *SPD* without a proper source, 334. Stravinsky gives a similar argument in Wilhelm Gregor, "'Nicht jede music kann vom Publikum verstanden werden': Gespräch mit Igor Stravinsky," *Neues Politisches Volksblatt*, March 1933.

74. Elliott Arnold, "Called By Many the Biggest Man in Music, Igor Stravinsky Goes a Bit Ga-Ga on Swing," *New York World-Telegram*, May 1940 (kept in PSS, no exact date).

75. See Sáenz de la Calzada, *La Residencia de Estudiantes*, 251–302.

76. *Revista de Revistas* 31/1576 (4 August 1940).

77. Alfonso Reyes to Victoria Ocampo, 24 June 1940, in Alfonso Reyes and Victoria Ocampo, *Cartas Echadas: Correspondencia 1927–1959* (Medellín, Mexico: Universidad Autonoma Metropolitana, 1983), 37.

78. Stravinsky kept a blurry photograph of Mexican workers carrying large objects for him as he walks on a country road with an oversized basket. See photo labeled "50 STRAW 1345" "Mexico 1941," kept in an unnumbered binder in the PSS. Stravinsky displays the souvenirs he bought in 1941—a sombrero and blanket—in *Igor and Vera Stravinsky: A Photograph Album, 1921–1971*, ed. Robert Craft, Rita McCaffrey, and Vera Stravinsky (London: Thames and Hudson, 1982), photo 167. On his trip to Tepotzlán, see Stravinsky and Craft, *Dialogues and a Diary*, 163.

79. Jesús Bal y Gay and Rosita García Ascot, "Igor Strawinksy," in *Nuestros trabajos y nuestros días* (Madrid: Fundación Banco Exterior, 1990), 144.

80. Ibid., 140–41.

81. Ibid., 146–47.

82. Robert Craft included a list of the Tchaikovsky sources in Craft and Stravinksy, *Expositions and Developments* (Berkeley: University of California Press, 1959), app. C, 158; Lawrence Morton analyzed them in far greater detail in "Stravinsky and Tchaikovsky's 'Le Baisir de la fée.'" *The Musical Quarterly* 48/3 (July 1962): 313–26; and Richard Taruskin provided a detailed updated list in *Stravinsky and the Russian Traditions: A Biography of the Works through* Mavra (Berkeley: University of California, 1996), 2:1610–13. Stravinsky's recording of the Divertimento with the Orquesta was released as *Stravinsky & Prokofiev Conduct Their Works* (Woodstock, NY: Parnassus CD, PACD 96023, 2000).

83. Stravinsky, quoted in Florent Fels, "Un Entretien avec Igor Strawinsky à propos de l'enregistrement au phonographe de 'Petrouchka,'" *Les Nouvelles Littéraires*, 8 December 1928.

84. Adolfo Salazar, "La Vida Musical: Tchaikovsky y Stravinsky—'El Beso del Hada,'" *Excelsior* (Mexico City), 29 July 1940.

85. "The emotion is there all right," Stravinsky told Norman Cameron in 1934. "I myself feel it and express it, and for those who cannot or will not share it, I can only suggest that they consult a psychiatrist!" See Igor Stravinsky, "I—As I See Myself (In an interview with Norman Cameron)," *The Gramophone*, August 1934, 85–86.

86. See Miriam Bratu Hansen, "Benjamin's Aura," *Critical Inquiry* 34 (Winter 2008): 336–75.

87. "Stravinsky and His Music: A Condemnation of the 'Watertight Compartment' Outlook."

88. Stravinsky, quoted in Maurice Romain, "De Quoi le succès est-il fait?" *Excelsior*, 11 September 1935.

89. Perhaps for this reason Stravinsky's son Soulima felt people had not talked enough about the importance of the "tamed Romanticism" in the Divertimento. "I think that later we will discover the secret channels through which this work penetrated into contemporary thought," he wrote. See "Les Goûts d'Igor Strawinsky," *Spectateur* 2/81 (17 December 1946): 2, 6.

90. Stravinsky, quoted in Michel Georges-Michel, "Grands Européens en Amérique: Igor Strawinsky," *La Marche des temps*, 11 February 1945.

91. Morton, "Stravinsky and Tchaikovsky's 'Le Baisir de la fée,'" 314–15.

92. Taruskin, *Stravinsky and the Russian Traditions*, 2:1614.

93. Stravinsky created headlines in 1938 when he turned down a lucrative Hollywood contract because it gave the studios the right to make changes after he had submitted the score. See Darius Milhaud, "Le Respect de soi-même, de son art et le cinema: Une leçon morale d'Igor Strawinsky," *Figaro*, 19 January 1938.

94. Stravinsky to Ocampo, 10 April 1941, microfilm 98.1, 781, PSS.

95. "Igor Stravinsky: 'The Anthem Has a Fine Melody, but the Organization—Terrible,'" *San Francisco Chronicle*, 6 January 1942.

96. Marcel Valois, "Avec Igor Stravinsky," *Chronique musicale* (Montréal) (March 1945): 35.

97. Pierre Schaeffer, "Musique de Californie," *Opéra*, 2 January 1946.

98. Louise Weiss, "Musiciens en Californie: Igor Stravinski ne veut pas travailler pour Hollywood," no source, February 1946, copy kept in binders of photocopied interviews, PSS. A few years later, Stravinsky told another reporter that he left France because of the cold, and because of his fear of getting sick. He no longer had to bundle up in sweaters and furs in California. See O. B., "Der Einsiedler von Hollywood," *Der Abend*, 21 February 1949.

99. Charles Oulmont, "Strawinsky nous parle . . . ," *La Musique* (September 1946): n.p., copy kept in binders of photocopied interviews, PSS. Oulmont bases his commentary on conversations with Alexandre Tansman. See also Albert Goldberg's "The Sounding Board: Dynamic Stravinsky Active But Quiet Here," *Los Angeles Times*, 21 September 1947.

100. Albert Goldberg, "The Sounding Board: The Transplanted Composer," *Los Angeles Times*, 14 May 1950.

Stravinsky Speaks to the Spanish-Speaking World

INTRODUCTION BY LEONORA SAAVEDRA
INTERVIEWS TRANSLATED BY MARIEL FIORI
IN COLLABORATION WITH TAMARA LEVITZ
DOCUMENT NOTES BY TAMARA LEVITZ

The selection of interviews and profiles of Igor Stravinsky that follows, published for Spanish- and Catalan-speaking readers across and along two continents, is, naturally, but a small window into Stravinsky's relationship to Spain and Spanish-speaking America, and into the impact, both positive and negative, that his music and personality had on that vast part of the world.[1] Although Stravinsky must have understood some Spanish, he did not speak it; therefore, most of the interviews here were conducted in French and translated into Spanish or Catalan. Stravinsky gave virtually hundreds of interviews during his long career as a performing musician and conductor, but was also notoriously averse to them. The Spanish composer, critic, and musicologist Jesús Bal y Gay and his wife, the composer and pianist Rosa García Ascot, with whom Stravinsky socialized frequently in Mexico, recalled with delight in their memoirs that when a journalist came calling they often pronounced Stravinsky too sick to be interviewed. The composer would then call out from inside the apartment, "Rosita, je suis malade, malade, très malade" (Rosita, I am sick, sick, very sick), for greater effect.[2]

Despite this reticence, Stravinsky in these interviews is at times candid to the point of getting himself in trouble politically even without perhaps realizing it, as in his comment "I hate the poor." He contradicts his own previously expressed views as if he thought what happened in one country stayed in that country and transnational communication did not exist. Often, however, he sticks to well-known talking points, especially those previously formulated in his *Chroniques de ma vie* (*An Autobiography*) or *Poétique musicale*, which he delivers in sound bites carefully calculated to provoke: "There is no modernism in music." Then again, we also see him change his mind on such fundamental topics as, for example, the role of his religious beliefs in his creative process.

The interviews were written by intellectuals, writers, and reporters whom Stravinsky evidently delighted in provoking and even exploiting, but with whom he was not close, with the exception, perhaps, of Farran i Mayoral. His interview in Barcelona in 1928 has a more intimate tone, and took place at a bar that Stravinsky favored, the Petit Liceu. These press pieces present the public face that Stravinsky wanted to offer to the Spanish-speaking world. But we also know from his memoirs, and from his correspondence with his welcoming hosts, how much he enjoyed himself in those party-loving countries with which he felt he had so much in common. In his friends' private homes Stravinsky relaxed and joyously and endlessly talked, played, and listened to his and others' music, chain-smoking and drinking, and partying after a good meal. These moments form the background to the public persona we meet in the interviews.

Stravinsky gave the first interviews presented here (Madrid 1921 and 1924) in the crucial years of his *volte-face*, the years of *Les Noces*, *Mavra*, and his self-reinvention, when he was moving far away from his Russian works and the overt folklorism of Rimsky-Korsakov and closer to the internationalism of Tchaikovsky and Glinka. Stravinsky is explicit about this realignment and the accompanying emphasis on objectivism in his interview with André Révész in 1924. But Stravinsky's changing, even conflicting positions with respect to folk music, especially as these relate to audience expectations of Russianism in his music, strike one as already evident, in retrospect, when comparing his first Madrid interview from March 1921 with the article he wrote for the French newspaper *Comoedia* a couple of months later. In Madrid he praised the improvisational elements in flamenco dancing—which set the composer free, he claimed—and candidly expressed his delight in Andalusian music and folk music in general.[3] To be sure, Stravinsky carefully explained that he praised folk music not as a national tradition, but as a contemporaneous body of music that privileged the parameters with which he himself liked to work: rhythm and melody. Finally, despite his deliberate veiling of the folk sources he used in his compositions, while in Spain he plainly confessed to being a thief! Two months later, in Paris, lest the curiosity of the French audience—his regular audience—be piqued by folk music (again, as it was evident in his early compositions for the Ballets Russes), he denied the presence of improvisation in Andalusian song and dance, and wrong-headedly described it as practically a product of careful (objective) compositional work.

The absence of Manuel de Falla's name in the French and Spanish articles from 1921 is quite astonishing and equally telling. Stravinsky's first visit to Spain in 1916 had been with the Ballets Russes; when in March 1921 he was asked explicitly about a Spanish ballet by or in the style of the Ballets Russes, Stravinsky refused to mention the company's premiere in London in 1919 of Falla's *El Sombrero de tres picos*; moreover, he fled to Seville during its Madrid premiere a few days after the interview. When asked the same question a couple of months later in Paris, Stravinsky alluded exclusively to the *Cuadro Flamenco*, which the Ballets Russes had presented in Paris that month, and again did not mention Falla. Stravinsky was most probably being polite: as he told Falla personally, he did not like *El Sombrero de tres picos* on account of its clear basis in folk music. Knowing as well that there was some degree of national investment in the work, he passed on the opportunity to offer a public critique of it. In his Spanish interviews after 1924, Stravinsky made plenty clear which Falla he found praiseworthy, namely, the classicist Falla of *El Retablo de Maese Pedro* and the Harpsichord Concerto.[4] During the interview in Barcelona in 1936 Stravinsky spoke of Falla's return to the Spanish contrapuntalists of the Golden Age, finding there a parallel to his own return to Glinka and the Italians.

It would be wrong to assume that because the countries and continents involved here are unified by a common language they are also unified by a common culture and historical experience. In fact, the urban centers of Latin America were culturally closer to France than to Spain in the late nineteenth and early twentieth centuries. (Indeed, the term "Latin America" was first coined in those decades. It—as opposed to the idea of "Iberian America"—captures precisely the political move of France to the center of *latinité*—a *latinité* Stravinsky eventually subsumed into his vision of a Latin-Slav spiritual community.)[5] Thus Victoria Ocampo, Stravinsky's host in Buenos Aires, and the Chilean Eugenia Errázuriz, a generous patroness of Stravinsky, were members of the South American landed aristocracy, spoke French with their peers, and spent long sojourns in Paris.[6] Stravinsky—who was delighted with the presence of a "true king," Alfonso XIII of Spain, at a performance of *Petrushka* in Madrid on 18 April 1921—felt at ease among these "aristocrats of blood and art," and shared their love of France, as he affirmed many times in these interviews.

France was also a shared love with the Mexican writer and diplomat Alfonso Reyes, who in the 1920s attended the Ballets Russes rehearsals and Diaghilev's dinners, and met Stravinsky in Buenos Aires in 1936 and again in Mexico in the 1940s. Reyes's *Visión de Anáhuac (1519)*, written in Madrid in 1915 and published in French in 1927, was instrumental in introducing a vivid new vision of Mexico to French culture—and to Stravinsky himself.[7] Thus in his 1940 interviews the composer praised *Visión de Anáhuac (1519)* as the book that taught him the most about Mexico. And he saw in Reyes's style a parallel to his own aesthetic and compositional method, one that consisted of rearranging or ordering materials in such a way that they became intelligible, or, rather, eloquent, by virtue of their becoming a sum of parts (Richard Taruskin's *drobnost*).

Reyes and Stravinsky also shared a love of classicism and order, and the experience of exile caused by the simultaneous Russian and Mexican revolutions. Thus in his Mexican interviews, published after decades of (apparent) radical change and transformation for the composer, Stravinsky characterized revolutions as inimical to art. And earlier, in 1936 in Buenos Aires, he contested this notion of radical change by representing his own musical *parcours* as a constant, orderly, logical enlargement of the periphery of a circle drawn around a single point, no matter how fast the rotation around it might seem.

Along with millions of readers and listeners, a network of Spanish-speaking writers across the continents conducted a dialogue among themselves and, indirectly, with Stravinsky—their transnational conversations made possible by the proliferation of literary journals and the involuntary and voluntary displacements of intellectuals. For example, while acting as the Mexican ambassador to Argentina, Reyes met Victoria Ocampo, and witnessed her many efforts to support modern French music—from Debussy and Ravel through Les Six to Stravinsky. Indeed, in the 1920s Ocampo's personal patronage and relations among the wealthy *porteños* (residents of Buenos Aires) was crucial in making Stravinsky's music and ideas known in Argentina. Ernest Ansermet, whose appointment as conductor of Buenos Aires's Orquesta de la Asociación del Profesorado Orquestal she supported, conducted the first performances of Stravinsky's orchestral music in Argentina from 1924 to 1926 within a neoclassical and neo-Baroque context created by his performances of the works not only of Bach, Vivaldi, and Mozart, but also of Ravel, Casella, and Falla.[8] Even though shifts in gender, musical, and general politics often left Ocampo without control of the public performance spaces over which she had considerable influence, like the Teatro Colón, her efforts nevertheless enabled Ansermet to return again to Argentina to conduct Stravinsky's music in 1933. During this time, centrist, right- and left-wing political groups were very vocal in Argentina and controlled important publications in which they disseminated their views. Ocampo's support for the avant-garde contributed to the conflation of modernism with upper-class and intellectual snobbery in the minds of many. Undeterred in her support, Ocampo had the first volume of *Chroniques de ma vie* translated into Spanish and issued by her publishing house, Sur, in 1935, making Stravinsky's ideas accessible to much of the Spanish-speaking world.[9] When Stravinsky first visited Buenos Aires to conduct in 1936, Ocampo added the role of performer to those of publisher and patroness when she took on the title role of Persephone in the premiere of *Perséphone* at the Teatro Colón on 17 May. Stravinsky would call on her to perform this role again several times.[10]

Whatever unrest Stravinsky's earlier music may have caused in Buenos Aires in the early decades of the twentieth century when Ansermet first introduced it there, by 1936 the discomfort had subsided. Audiences were now well acquainted with his work; although his new, neoclassical music may have been puzzling, it was not controversial. His political views, however, were. Earlier that year, while visiting Barcelona in the midst of the Second Spanish Republic, Stravinsky had rehearsed a defense of the Catholic Church, which fiercely opposed the Republic. He had also condemned Communism (along with the bourgeoisie, naturally, aristocracy lover that he was!) shrouding his arguments in an aesthetic and spiritual opposition to the subjectivism and materialism of Surrealism. His own creative process was objective, he had claimed over and over again and, at least in 1928 and 1936, inspired by God (much later, in the 1949 interview with Santiago del Campo, for Chilean readers, he gave God a much less prominent role as co-creator). Moreover, although he was still friendly with the Surrealist sympathizer Picasso, his Christianity led him closer to another Spaniard, Manuel de Falla. A month later, in Buenos Aires, after speaking ill of Bolshevik music ("written with a doorman's taste in mind"), Soviet Russia, and Dmitry Shostakovich, Stravinsky once again praised Falla—this time because of the latter's refusal as a Christian to accept an honor bestowed upon him by the anti-clerical Spanish Republican government. Stravinsky pivoted from there into praising the Crusades and disparaging social revolutions, finally expressing his visceral disgust for the parliamentary system. Buenos Aires, however, was not Spain: the reaction of the political center and left was overwhelming, and an (unexpected?) controversy ensued, with critics from pro- and anti-fascist German and Italian émigré Argentine newspapers even adding their voices to the mix. Meanwhile, composers of different aesthetic credos discussed not the interview but the music, and its relevance for Argentine composition.[11]

Four years later, in Mexico, Stravinsky knew better. Perhaps he had gotten wind of the war between the Mexican government and the Catholic Church in the late 1920s, or perhaps he had learned that the Mexican government had officially opened Mexico's doors to Spanish Republican intellectuals, creating an intellectual home for them in the Casa de España, which Reyes himself directed after 1939. Or maybe Stravinsky did not know about any of this, and simply became aware of it when he met exiled Spaniards Adolfo Salazar—who had earlier accepted a position in the Spanish Republican government—and the Bal y Gays on his very first day in Mexico.[12] In any case, in his almost yearly visits to Mexico in the next dozen years, Stravinsky did not publicly talk about politics again. In 1946, he limited himself to launching yet another attack on Shostakovich just as his musical host, Carlos Chávez, was getting ready to conduct the composer's Symphony no. 7, whose score, signed by Shostakovich, he had received through the Soviet Embassy in 1943. The Bal y Gays and Salazar often accompanied Stravinsky in Mexico, since Chávez was busy with conducting engagements of his own. The manager of the Orquesta Sinfónica de México (OSM) nevertheless kept Chávez appraised of Stravinsky's needs (a doctor for Vera, for example) and predilections (a bottle of Saint-Emilion wine to refresh himself during a break in rehearsals). Chávez always went back to Mexico City in time to hear Stravinsky conduct and to fete him appropriately; and although Stravinsky most likely did not like Chávez's music (he politely claimed not to know it), he respected him as a conductor. Their thirty-year relationship developed during Stravinsky's many visits to Mexico, but above all during Chávez's even more numerous visits to the

United States. It is there that Stravinsky had occasion to call Chávez *mon frère cadet* (my little brother), and that an affectionate relationship grew between them, which we can only marginally glimpse in their business correspondence.[13]

As in Buenos Aires, the public in 1940s Mexico was well acquainted with Stravinsky's music, which Ansermet had conducted in Mexico City in the mid-1930s, Silvestre Revueltas had conducted between 1930 and 1935, and Chávez himself had performed throughout this period. Chávez, who was conductor and artistic director of OSM from its foundation in 1928 to 1948, programmed Stravinsky's music almost yearly after 1930 for an audience of wealthy people as bejeweled as the *porteños* (Friday evenings), regular folks (Sunday matinées), and in special performances for children and workers (who loved Stravinsky). OSM's Mexican premieres of Stravinsky's orchestral music in the early 1930s had been part of a profound controversy over the explosive arrival on the Mexican musical scene of Mexican and foreign modern music—an eruption caused by Chávez and his comrade-in-arms Revueltas. The ensuing public discussion of modern music and its relation to national music took place in the press—where critics praised the already internationally consecrated Stravinsky while lashing out against Chávez and Revueltas—as well as in public inquiries conducted by newspapers, conversations in theater hallways, and in Chávez's cleverly conducted surveys of Mexican audiences. By the 1940s, interviewers delighted in prompting Stravinsky to pronounce himself against modernism and nationalism ("not a profession for music"), without, however, expecting to stir the waters any more. The true political issue in the 1940s was Chávez's iron-handed control of Mexico's musical scene and the OSM—a control that repeatedly threatened to slip away from him. In 1946, Stravinsky stood behind Chávez and expanded upon the praise he had given six years earlier of the OSM and Chávez's firm directorship of it.

Most of the pieces first programmed by Chávez in the 1930s, with the exception of *Apollon musagète* and the Capriccio, were from Stravinsky's "Russian" period. Naturally, Stravinsky himself introduced works such as *Le Baiser de la fée* (The Fairy's Kiss), *Jeu de cartes*, Symphony in Three Movements, and his Symphony in C.[14] In his first concert in Mexico in 1940 he conducted *Le Baiser de la fée* within the context of Cherubini's *Anacreonte* Overture and Tchaikovsky's Symphony no. 2, making audible his classicism, the relation between his piece and Tchaikovsky's, and the general reinvention of his lineage. His concerts in Mexico were routinely reviewed in all the major and minor newspapers, by critics—including Salazar and Bal y Gay—whose reviews were often informed by their reading of Stravinsky's *Chroniques de ma vie* and the French edition of his *Poétique musicale*.[15] Salazar, in particular, had a conflicted relationship not with Stravinsky the man, but with his persona, in whose shadow Salazar's beloved teacher Manuel de Falla often labored. He also struggled with the music, about which he expressed skepticism as early as 1916.[16] Thus, his reviews of Stravinsky's concerts of 1940—especially the "Tchaikovsky concert," which he wrote entirely from a Spaniard's point of view—are indicative of his difficulty in conceptualizing Stravinsky as a model for Falla, who, naturally, had to remain the model for Spain.

Stravinsky was most certainly aware of the immediate effect of his presence on his Spanish-speaking audiences, since he himself performed, conducted, and spoke to and in the Spanish-speaking world. Was he ever cognizant of the short and long-range impact of his music there? Despite reports that he gladly examined, played, and commented upon his hosts' music when he felt at ease, he claimed not to know Latin American music, and to know very little about Spanish music as well. And yet his music became a fundamental part of local discussions on the nature of national music, in decades when this issue was of paramount importance. Indeed, if the Soviet Union had no use for Stravinsky's music, Spaniards and Latin Americans did; and Stravinsky's subsequent aesthetic changes became an important part of their continuing conversation on nationalism and modernism. This story, which we hardly glimpse in these interviews, has yet to be written.

La Voz (Madrid), 21 March 1921
A Conversation with Stravinsky
P. Victory

Igor Stravinsky conducts his *Petrushka* at the Real, marking the rhythm with his baton, with extraordinary energy, as if he were saying: "Here, my dear musicians, here, in this rhythm, is the foundation of future music . . . " and without a pause, with particular satisfaction, he makes the drum and the bass drum roll during the modulations [*mutaciones*].[17] People look at each other perplexed. A man exclaims, so that everyone can hear him: "I have the good taste not to like this music." Children are extraordinarily interested in the prolonged drum roll; and the female students from the Conservatorio[18] regret that the composer neither wears a wig, like Bach, nor is pockmarked like Beethoven. No wild head of hair for that matter. Could the great composer be a man like all others?

Stravinsky shakes hands and, as he eats his breakfast, smokes and talks nonstop.

"In 1916," he tells us, "touring Spain made a very deep impression on me.[19] I am in love with its popular music. The Gypsy dances! Have you seen more surprising and richer dances than these? And what about the king? Felipe IV by Velázquez, a pure son of the nation: he is a very interesting king, much more so than any other king.[20] The king of . . . for example."

Stravinsky cannot hide a smile at the thought of another king, whose name we won't say.

Stravinsky believes that music has been the victim of academic and philosophical preoccupation and that, because of this has little by little lost its purpose, which is, above all, to be an acoustic sensation.[21] Attempts have been made to express all sorts of feelings and philosophical theories in music, which has only resulted in the rhythm, little by little, losing its richness.

"The feelings in our soul!" he exclaims. "What does that mean? Doesn't every moment have a soul of its own? And is our soul not different in every moment? People have taken music as a medium and not as an end, and so we find that music has stagnated for centuries."[22]

We ask him about Russian musicians, and he responds, devastated:

"Pitiful! The influence of Berlin, my friend, of the academies and of the German tradition. Defend me, Spaniards, from the Germans, who do not understand, nor have ever understood music, even though, at first glance, Germany seems to be the land of the musicians. Pure philosophy, my friend, pure mathematics. They have no sense of music; it's just sheer musicality what they do, which is not the same. Beethoven! I am not saying that he wasn't a genius; but he did not make music; he felt great things in his soul, which he cloaked in notes that say nothing to the ear. All of Germany is Beethoven or Brahms, the last, chronologically, of his disciples. Wagner! He provided new elements to the orchestra; but with him, music did not advance even an inch. I sincerely believe that Wagner was everything he tried not to be; certainly he was neither a musician nor a philosopher. The general culture of the Germans is the cause of all this: their children know Greek too soon, they go into great depth, and then they don't have the strength to react against it, to contemplate nature impassively. Whereas, look at Mozart, he was a great musician, so simple, so musical; isn't it true that the ear rejoices when listening to his music? We can say the same thing about Schubert.

"My whole aspiration," he continues, "is to provide an acoustic sensation, seeking it wherever it is, and letting it come from wherever it comes. I run away from anything already made because it is conventional, academic;[23] the truth of art still lies within the people—and the truth of music particularly. Popular songs and dances are of such richness that they seduce me completely: wherever I encounter them, I make them my own and I write them into my works. What am I, a thief? Okay, I'm a thief. But all of these things, from the moment they impress themselves upon me, are mine and I see them my way, and I surround them with atmosphere as I see fit, and as exactly as possible. So I create the work, and in creating it, everything is mine and original!"

"Take note," he goes on, "that it is not a question of imbibing popular tradition, but of taking popular values as they are now; if we relied on tradition, if we were to drink from the fountains of Gregorian music, for example, we would do no more than create an academy like all the others, but without any freedom. We would create a new harmonic theory such as the one once sought by Scriabin, another unwitting victim of German influence.[24] Harmony is something absolutely conventional and arbitrary that with every moment manifests itself in different ways. Melody and rhythm are the foundation: the flageolet and the drum.[25] Do you understand? Harmony results from the melodic and rhythmic ambiance; it is constituted of those elements."

We ask him about the possibility of creating a Spanish dance show in the style of the Ballets Russes, and he doesn't let us finish the question.

"Without a doubt! I'm told that Spanish dance has a lot of individuality and is the opposite of ensemble dancing. But take note of the following observation, which I find extremely interesting: the Spanish dancer improvises most of the time, which gives the composer the right to improvise as well and put together the show as he sees fit. The dancer keeps the essential rhythm of the dance she is performing, and embellishes it in her own way with her movements. Magnificent! You have such an incredible wealth of rhythms and melodies, as do we, and as do the North Americans, who have it naturally thanks not to the English, but to the blacks."

We talk about orchestration, and Stravinsky says that he is amazed by all the richness that he has found in the piano. "For me, it was an 'enormous machine' that Chopin, more than anyone else, understood. Recently, at my home in Saint-Cloud,[26] I dedicated long months to studying its sounds, and I have found they are considerable and extremely varied. I have worked a lot and written some 'études' for pianola."

"For pianola?"

"Of course! For pianola, because the pianist only has ten fingers and a limited capacity for speed: it's a matter of not losing the simultaneity of many sounds, of different strings, nor sacrificing it to the limits of human capacity. I have written some études that have already made a big impression in London. I haven't been able to listen to them yet, but my friends wrote to me saying that they produce new and marvelous effects."[27]

Finally, Stravinsky expresses his belief that he has opened a new path for music.

"I don't know if I will manage to continue to perfect my theories, but others will do it."

Stravinsky is traveling to Seville to watch the processions of Holy Week, and he bids us good-bye, jovial and very likable, without long locks or strokes of genius: clean-shaven and with his hair cropped close.

Comoedia, 15 May 1921
Spaniards at the Ballets Russes
Igor Stravinsky

Spaniards at the Ballets Russes![28] Why? I am asked this question, and it's easy for me to respond that for a long time we have admired and studied Spain and those manifestations of its national life that are so original. It is therefore entirely natural that we seek to be inspired by it, and to take with us, so to speak, a piece of Spain. The main thing is to pick what can be transported. There are local wines that one must drink on site, and others that can make the trip.

There is more than mere curiosity in this. I perceive a deep affinity between Spanish popular music, especially Andalusian music, and Russian popular music, an affinity that stems, no doubt, from their common oriental origins.[29] Certain Andalusian songs remind me of melodies from our Russian provinces, awakening in me atavistic memories. Andalusians have nothing Latin about their music. They owe the sense of rhythm to their oriental heritage.

Rhythm is quite different from meter. In meter, four always equals four. Rhythm poses yet another question: which kind of number four is this—the one composed of three and one, or the one composed of two and two?

Another facet of this popular art is its extreme precision, down to seemingly accidental details: a quarter tone is always the same quarter tone, a rhythm that seems about to fall off actually does not, and is back on its feet in the very moment we thought it had vanished.

There is nothing in all of this of the passionate improvisation we ascribe to, for example, whirling dervishes. No improvisation: a very calculated, very meticulous art that is very logical in its own way, and coldly calculated. I would almost say a classical art, whose dogmas, though different from those of our schools, are no less rigorous. In a word: an art of composition.

ABC (Madrid), 25 March 1924
Igor Stravinsky and Modern Music
André Révész

What a pity that Fresno is not here with me![30] Stravinsky's characteristic profile, his aquiline nose, his big mouth, the monocle on his right eye, would lend themselves so well to a caricature. The famous composer is of medium height, really rather short for a Russian, very thin and slightly slouching. He greets us in the foyer of the Palace,[31] and guides us to an isolated and quiet corner, where we can't hear the rhythm of the *shimmy*.[32]

The Musicians He Prefers

"I see that you are in a hurry," we tell him, "so I will formulate my questions precisely. To start with: which modern musicians do you like?"[33]

"I will answer you with the same precision: very few. Manuel de Falla, an extremely worthy, cultivated, and sensitive musician. Then, my fellow countryman Prokofiev, whose exuberance is astonishing. Finally, two young Frenchmen, Poulenc and Auric, who composed dances performed by the Ballet Russes.[34]

"What about composers of previous generations?"

"In France: Bizet, Gounod, Chabrier, Debussy, and Delibes. I love *Carmen, Faust, Le Médecin malgré lui,* and *Philémon et Baucis.*[35] In Russia: Tchaikovsky."

"Even *1812*?"

"Not so much; *1812* is a little tacky and grandiloquent; *pompier* as the French say. However, *The Nutcracker, Eugene Onegin, The Queen of Spades,* and some sections of his symphonies are of incomparable rhythmic beauty. Have you noticed the very delicate and original orchestration in *The Nutcracker*? I think criticism has been unfair regarding Tchaikovsky; the admiration that persons of bad taste felt for him has greatly damaged his reputation among critics. Tchaikovsky is very easy, and for this reason he has been considered vulgar. In reality he is the most Russian of all the musicians from my country. I recognize the great merits of Musorgsky and Borodin—the only composers of 'The Five' who interest me—but at the moment I prefer Tchaikovsky. You don't need to have a full boyar beard or wear a long Eastern caftan to compose Russian music."

"Are you talking about Rimsky-Korsakov?"

"Him above all. He was my professor at the conservatory in Petrograd and I felt real admiration for him; but now I realize the artificial character of his 'Russianism' and his Orientalism."[36]

"It is said that your high praise of Tchaikovsky's music is, in fact, an indirect attack on Wagner."

"Let me be frank. I don't mean to deny that Wagner is a great musician, but I don't like his aesthetic. I like opera, but not musical drama. That is why I prefer *Tannhäuser* to *Lohengrin*, and *Lohengrin* to the *Ring* cycle. Weber's music suits my temperament better, although I recognize Wagner's superiority."

"And Verdi?"

"Verdi is immense; he has a brilliant imagination and he is even great at dramatic composition. But I stop liking him when he tries to be some sort of Italian Wagner. By my criteria, his best opera is *Rigoletto*."

How He Works

"Would you be so kind as to describe how you work?"

"With pleasure. I stick to the so-called work regimen;[37] that is to say, in order to economize my efforts, I complete the most difficult part of the composition in the morning; in the afternoon and the evening, I transcribe, copy, correct proofs, etc. I get up around 8 a.m. and do physical exercises. Then I work without interruption from 9 a.m. until 1 p.m. I live sometimes in Biarritz, sometimes in Paris: a simple life; I frequent society very little, and the outer monotony of my life is interrupted only when I travel."

"Do you have any time left for literature?"

"Very little. Besides, there are few writers who interest me. In France, I prefer the novelist Marcel Proust and the poet Jean Cocteau—Cocteau on account of his aesthetic theory and his admirable versification. Among the young Russian poets, I prefer Yesenin and Mayakovsky."[38]

His Self-Criticism

"You are considered an objective and anti-lyrical musician. Is this interpretation fair?"

"Let me tell you: I wouldn't want to be pigeonholed, nor carry a medal with the inscription 'I am an objective musician.' However, I am more objective than subjective, more constructive than lyrical. I present audiences with musical objects, musical facts;[39] I hide behind the work, to the point of retreating; the public comes in contact with those objects, with those facts, and they feel emotion, or they don't."

"How did you fight against the incomprehension of the critics?"

"Only through my works, never through polemics. What surprised me most about the unfavorable criticism was that it reproached my qualities and didn't notice my defects.[40] The critics didn't make a single effort to understand what was in my work, and instead, they criticized the absence of certain musical elements they were used to. That is to say, for many years the reviews of my work were negative. The critics didn't see that there was a new structure in my music, a new rhythm. Instead, they insisted on the lack of lyricism."

"Which of your works are you most fond of? *Petrushka*?"

"How do I answer that question? *The Rite of Spring*, *Petrushka*, and *Firebird* are already twelve, thirteen, and fourteen years old, respectively. So you can understand that for the time being they interest me less than other, more recent works, like the Concertino for String Quartet, which is very characteristic of my musical aesthetic, and like the *Pulcinella* Suite, taken from the ballet of the same name, written in 1920. The *Pulcinella* Suite is based on fragments of themes and melodies by Pergolesi, and aims to be a kind of Neapolitan *Petrushka*."[41]

"Have you also written operas?"

"Two: *The Nightingale*, in three short acts, taken from a short story by Andersen,[42] and *Mavra*, an opera buffa, from a short story by Pushkin, for whom I have a real veneration. *Mavra* is dedicated to the memory of Pushkin, Glinka, and Tchaikovsky. I have also written, together with the Swiss poet Ramuz, a "theatrical piece" titled *L'Histoire du soldat*, the theme of which I discovered in a Russian short story."

In Spain

"This is my third time in Spain. In 1916 I had the great honor of being welcomed by their majesties the King and Queen,[43] and of becoming acquainted with both the aristocracy of the blood and of art.[44] In 1921, I wanted to present my homage to the sovereigns by conducting *Petrushka* in the Teatro Real. I just came from Barcelona, where I conducted three concerts at the Liceu.[45] Three years ago, I spent Holy Week in Sevilla and I got to know admirable *saetas*.[46] To finish, please tell *ABC* that I have found uncommon comprehension and enthusiasm for modern music in the musicians of the Philarmonic. My impression of the Orchestra could not be better."

La Noche (Barcelona), 25 March 1925
Stravinsky, in Barcelona, Tells Us of His Travels in America
Rafael Moragas

Stravinsky, the musician who figures most prominently among innovators, is in Barcelona.[47] Barely arrived, this man of intense gaze and nervous, restless temperament has made his way to the Liceu.[48] He is surrounded by a group of admirers, Felipe Rodés, Pedro Soldevila, Luis Salgado, Mestres.[49] Igor Stravinsky talks and talks continually, and what he says has a powerful influence on those who listen to him. He talks about music, his travels, and his successes.

We will try to summarize what was said by this great musician, who speaks with such prodigious ease and has a just and precise phrase for everything.

"Since I left Europe, it has been nothing but satisfying for me," says the great composer. "In North America, the successes have been resounding."[50]

"Only artistic successes?" we ask.

"Artistic and also financial successes, since I earned a lot. I conducted my own works in Boston, Philadelphia, Chicago, Detroit, Cincinnati. I appeared as a concert pianist, that is, as the interpreter of my own works, and Mengelberg, Koussevitzky, and Reiner conducted my works.[51]

"You could not be more satisfied."

"I am extremely satisfied," he told us. "And now I hope to see confirmed in Barcelona—a city for which I retain such fond memories—the satisfaction I felt in America."

"Maestro, are you currently composing?"

"A sonata for piano, for solo piano. I am finishing it and I will probably introduce it in Paris next May. Now, I am going to Rome. I want to be in Italy. I adore *la latinidad*. As you well know. I work a lot and I want to introduce completely new programs in the coming year."

"Are you drawn to the piano?"

"As you cannot imagine. I am drawn to 'my piano.' And there must have been something about my way of playing on 'Steinway' pianos when I recorded my piano works on the gramophone—I'm one of those who when I'm not in Paris play only Steinways—that interested people."[52]

"Here, in Barcelona, your arrival is enthusiastically anticipated, my dear friend Stravinsky."

"I know, and above all I know that I am well loved here. I always want to come to Barcelona, I have my friends, my audience, and an impresario like Mestres who draws me here and understands me. It is a great thing for an artist to feel understood."

"We appreciate that, glory is so pleasing . . . "

"Yes, no doubt, but let me tell you, perhaps feeling glorified in an excessive manner is disturbing. Let me explain: recently, in Philadelphia, I was paid tribute, by whom, you may ask. . . ? Well, by two thousand old ladies!! Don't be scared. They made me sit on a throne and then they paraded by, one by one, kissing my hand. When the one they counted as number eight hundred! passed by, I could not stand it any longer. I excused myself as best I could and told them not to kiss my hand any more because otherwise, when I returned to Europe my hand would be worn out and I wouldn't be able to conduct concerts. And I had to say this through a loudspeaker so everyone could hear me."

Stravinsky laughs. Then he takes off his coat. He quickly arranges the music stands for the orchestra and tells the professors where they should situate themselves. The first rehearsal of his works is about to begin. The joyful sounds of *Petrushka* reach us.[53] And we marvel at the strong and free rhythm of this terrific Polish [*sic*] musician.

Veu de Catalunya, 25 March 1928
Conversation with Stravinsky

José Farran i Mayoral

This Is Not an Interview

No interviews now.[54] The strategic positions of interviewer and interviewee are not appropriate for the warm, trusting, and free conversation of friends: in the fraternal exchange of ideas, many things are simply taken for granted, understood; above all, one is allowed freedom of opinion about works and personalities, and a certain toying with paradoxes; the foundation of professionalism, of loyal and sincere admiration, remains unscathed. We say this because some quick, dazzling judgments of the Maestro, repeated without nuance or allusion to the understandings we have just described, literally reproduced, might seem compromising and would certainly distort his true and complete thought.[55]

Stravinsky is, no need to repeat it, a genius; his knowledge of culture as well is vast and well rooted; the penetration and agility of his thought causes wonder at each step; ideas spill richly and joyfully from his lips. He is an inexhaustible conversationalist. There are few like him who feel the sovereign joy of high conversation, which so pleases us and which we rarely find ways for satisfying among ourselves.

From the wealth of thoughts and opinions and observations that our memory retains from our conversation with Stravinsky, we are pleased to now excerpt for our readers some things that may interest them.

Stravinsky Religiosity

We meet again with the Maestro in a quiet room at the Ritz Hotel, shake his dear hand: and, while Igor Stravinsky poses for a portrait that his friend Callicó will make, the ideas immediately take flight.[56] The religiosity of the great musician is known; ladies, we discussed religion. He tells us about the spiritual and intellectual good attributed to Saint Thomas Aquinas. He talks about his friends Jean Cocteau and Jacques Maritain, the great French scholar, whom we know and love so well.[57] Stravinsky is now acutely interested in the great mystics: he speaks of St. John of the Cross, of St. Theresa.[58] Suddenly his large, strange eyes light up with greater enthusiasm and admiration: he has just mentioned St. Theresa of Child Jesus.[59] He complains that her message has been distorted, belittled, fireworks remade into sickly sweet chrome, whereas the girl saint is the most formidable example of heroic, strong will in our time. He names and comments on various saints—St. Jerome, for example—and religious philosophers—Solovyov, among others.[60] He talks at length of Ramon Llull.[61] The Maestro takes a lively interest in our great mystic, the great seat of intelligence and holiness.

Oedipus Rex

It is called *Oedipus*: Stravinsky's latest victory, the oratorio now famous everywhere.[62]

"See, see what I wanted to do," he says with that smile that glows with intelligence.

From the great number of explanations of techniques and ideologies we will extract, in the most straightforward possible manner, some essential points for our readers. Elsewhere, our "Music Page" has commented on the prodigious technique, the harmonic and polyphonic discipline that the Maestro has imposed on the strength of his brilliant conception.[63]

We thus insist above all on a point to which Stravinsky gives great importance: how to understand the relationship between word and music. It has now been three years since we spoke at length about an endeavor undertaken in his famous ballet *Les Noces*. His desire to purify music of every extramusical element is known. This leads him to want to cleanse words, too, of all extramusical elements. Some people object to this, and we speak with the Maestro about these experiments: "What necessity is there to use words in your music?" We think we have found a fitting explanation: the Maestro doesn't want to ignore the human voice as the wonderful instrument it is, and must necessarily use its articulated manifestation, speech. And it is not paradoxical, given his inclinations, to want to make use of it not as expression, but as pure music. In contrast to the traditional concept, which subjects music to psychological expressiveness or the dramatic meaning of the words, in *Oedipus*, the Maestro explains, word becomes pure matter to be manipulated musically, as marble or stone serve the work of sculpture. Thus in the ballet *Les Noces* there are different songs written in verse where the Russian words do not make logical sense, but are ordered instead according to their pure sonorous and rhythmic possibilities. *Oedipus* represents a step forward in this experiment; it is understood, the Maestro tells us, that no matter how much a musician reworks a living, present-day language, it contains for us many elements that evoke emotions and feelings that distract from its value as purely musical material. For this reason, a dead language was needed; Stravinsky thought of ancient Slavic, Greek, and Latin. Latin was the best, because it is a definitively fixed language: frozen we could say, and at the same time, more or less known by everyone, thanks to its diffusion by the Church; so that it does not confuse the ears as Slavic or Greek would.

So, the Latin version of *Oedipus Rex*, based on a libretto written by Jean Cocteau, provides an excellent text that can serve, as we would say in academic terms, as "material" suitable to receive the "form" of music.

It goes without saying that Stravinsky has taken into account Latin metrics and has made much of the musical values it establishes in syllables, short and long poetic feet, etc.

The choice of the fable of Oedipus also obeys the principle of distancing the audience, as much as possible, from any dramatic or extra-musical interest, offering a fable that is, as Stravinsky says, "archetypal."

It is precisely this concept of word-music-material that has distanced Stravinsky from song, the "*lied,*" which in younger years he had so gloriously cultivated.

And now some happy news: Stravinsky has already committed to presenting *Oedipus* to us next season.[64]

The Clarity of the *Rite*

Magnificent proof of this musical refinement: the *Rite*, without the ballet, gains rather than loses musically, since the listener is not distracted from the superb formal qualities of the piece.[65] Rhythmic and sonorous audacity: but the whole work has been given a wonderful backbone—we cannot find more just words to express its great architectural severity, and the great clarity of forms and lines, and the great clarity of conception, and all the conscious joy of "explaining it" to the listener. After the dress rehearsal, we ask Stravinsky:

"How do you 'explain' your work, Maestro?"

"To *explain*—that is the word!" he gives us the satisfaction of answering. He adds: "Isn't it true that [music] is clear and understandable? I am sure that your very intelligent public will understand it well. I think it is necessary to be hopeless at art and at music to find them obscure or confusing."

"We agree, Maestro."

The Classicism of *Petrushka*

The dress rehearsal for *Petrushka* is done.[66] How different the work seems when conducted by the Maestro! How wonderful and refined the forms that on other occasions go unnoticed. Not until now has that superb structure revealed itself in the perfection of its parts, the daintiness and grace of detail, the great harmonious beauty of the whole. Thinking about these things, we tell Stravinsky:

"If this work is not considered classic, I don't know what is meant by *classic*. Classic in the good sense, I mean to say."

"The word *classic,*" Stravinsky answered, "always has a good sense."

"Yes, for you and for me; but you know how often classicism is mistaken for just another formula, as academicism, servile imitation of antiquity, etc., etc."

"It's true," he answers with disdain, "but who is making these mistakes?"

Stravinsky and Modernity

"So, are you pleased to be a classic?"

"I feel honored by this adjective."

"Is it a pleasure as well to be called 'modern'"?[67]

"Ah, no! Not that!"

"This gives me great satisfaction, Maestro, because a few days ago I had to defend you against a dear friend of mine who, thinking he was praising you, applied the adjective 'modern' to you with all goodwill."

"Oh, how awful! See? All this about modern, avant-garde, everything that limits art to a fashion is insufferable; the era of 'isms,' of programs and manifestos, has surely passed. That was fifteen or twenty years ago; now that kind of thing is done in the provinces."

"That's right, Maestro, in art there is no ancient or modern; attributing any time to things of art is a deplorable mistake. We have to work in centuries, don't we?"

"In thousands of centuries," Stravinsky answers. "And because you see my aspirations so exactly, I will tell you something that happened to me in New York. One day, going back to the hotel, I find a long line of reporters from the big newspapers, asking for interviews. It being impossible to please them all one by one, I ask them to come into my room; there are not enough seats in the room so everyone sits on the floor, in a semicircle, with their notebooks and pencils in hand. And they ask me a collective question: What do you think about modern music? I am astonished: Sirs, I tell them, you are on the wrong floor, no doubt.

"The next day, the major New Yorker newspapers publish long and, needless to say, fantastical articles, with big capital letters: 'Stravinsky is not a modern musician,' and others of that nature."[68]

Apollon musagète

At the bar of the Petit Liceu, in a corner the Maestro likes, where three years ago, he is so kind to remember, we became good friends, Stravinsky talks about a piece he is working on that will have a very classic title: *Apollon musagète*. Apollo leads the Muses. A ballet: Apollo himself, crowned with laurels, will be the main character. The concept of the ballet is very simple and the dances something very traditional; it will use the *pas de deux*, for example, well known by the disciples of Pauleta Pàmies.[69] But Stravinsky can't touch anything without it being immediately transformed by the infusion of his creative originality. And the new ballet will be something both universal and highly personal, we are sure. However, the tradition is there. The scenery will have the classic forest, some temple or other, etc. Now, in the first scene, we witness—and this is unusual—the very birth of Apollo, or better put—look up your mythology or the Homeric Hymns so gloriously translated by Maragall—the delivery of Latona.[70] Nothing is lacking. A chorus of goddesses welcomes the Olympic child with joy, and in the second act he grants three of the muses—Calliope, Polyhymnia, and Terpsichore—the gifts they later grant to mankind. There's no lack of a timely apotheosis, either. Everything has a bit of a burlesque air, à la Lucian; everything takes place with great simplicity; the music itself, the Maestro tells us, is also a very simple thing of lines and combinations.

And now a detail rounds out the ensemble of our surprising new information: Stravinsky puts verses in the lips of his characters. Verses, you say? By whom? Oh, kind young men, crazy with modernity: verses by Boileau.

"A great poet, isn't he, Maestro? A great poet of the intelligentsia."

"That is very true: a great, wonderful poet."

Verses from which work? From the one cited so often by anarchists and all kinds of romantics: from *L'Art poétique*.

So now you know: Stravinsky the ultramodern, the ultra-Futurist, etc., etc.—so called by the many who don't understand him—will put onto the lips of his characters verses from the very same Nicolas Boileau-Despréaux.[71]

La Noche (Barcelona), 12 March 1936
Igor Stravinsky and Surrealism
Luis Góngora

Tonight at the Liceu Igor Stravinsky, the most important musician of our time, will conduct the first of the two concerts dedicated to his works during the Lent season, which begins today at our finest theater.[72]

Before the music of the Divertimento,[73] the Capriccio, the *Symphony of Psalms*, and *The Firebird* offers us an enthusiastic encounter tonight with the personality of this great composer, we wanted to be near to him so that not only his art, but also the entire aesthetic and ethics that have engendered it, might enrich our understanding of the vivid spiritual reality that is his.

In the foyer of the Ritz the famous composer welcomes us with open arms. After giving us some informative details that we requested regarding his "Concerto" for piano and orchestra,[74] the solo part of which will be performed this Sunday by his son, S. Soulima,[75] Stravinsky kindly agrees to answer some questions in which we attempt to determine his attitude toward important spiritual realities of our time.

When asked his opinion of Picasso's Surrealist tendencies and about Surrealism in general, Stravinsky says:[76]

"I am a very good friend of Picasso, and I admire all of his tendencies. He is always a great artist. Now, I haven't seen him in a while. We are both essentially solitary and we see each other only from time to time. Speaking for myself, I will say that in Paris, where I live, I go almost nowhere, not artist circles, or theaters, or concerts. I only go to the cinema.

"As for Surrealism, I confess that I haven't been able to penetrate completely its essence and principles. I can't agree with it because I don't work with subjective elements. My artistic purpose is to make an object, though of course I do so with the natural contribution of my own self.[77] I create the object because God makes me create it, as He created me. My art is the fruit of pure Christian dialectics. This is another reason why I can't accept Surrealism, or Communism either, even though I believe that in many respects they are right. It is the bourgeois who is not right. I am an Orthodox Christian, I sympathize with Catholicism and I recognize that in religious matters, those who are neutral—and there are many of them among the bourgeoisie, particularly in France—are more harmful than those who openly fight the Church as in Soviet Russia. Of course, I am in neither camp. Aesthetically, I cannot accept materialism either—championed by both the Surrealists and the Communists—because my religiosity makes me a dualist, and so I seek the beautiful fusion of materialism and spiritualism in everything."[78]

We ask him if he thinks the composer Schoenberg's investigations into atonality might be truly effective for musical composition:[79]

"Schoenberg is, in my opinion, more of a chemist of music than an artistic creator. His investigations are interesting, since they tend to widen the possibilities of auditory enjoyment, but both he and Hába, who discovered the quarter tone, base themselves[80] on quantitative rather than qualitative aspects of music. Their importance is evident, but limited, because after them there will be someone who will look for and find the eighth tone; but will he be able to make a true work of art with it?

"I admire Schoenberg and those who follow him, but I recognize that the chromatic scale upon which they base their compositions exists only scientifically, and, therefore, the dialectics derived from it are artificial."

Finally, Stravinsky talks about his works, particularly his last, the Concerto for Two Pianos, which he just performed with his son in Italy, to great success. And he tells us news of his upcoming trip to South America, where he will remain until June, and where the second volume of his work *Chroniques de ma vie*, translated into Spanish by Victoria Ocampo, is about to be released.[81]

Before saying good-bye, he offers high praise for the works of our Falla, with whom he is united by the same yearning for religiosity, despite their difference in religious dogma. He speaks particularly about *El Retablo de Maese Pedro* and the Concerto,[82] works in which, according to him, Falla comes close to the great Spanish counterpointists. Falla's music is now essentially Catholic, he asserts. Stravinsky also talks about Gustavo Pittaluga, who admirably conducted his "Concerto" in Madrid, with his son Soulima performing the solo part. He shows a vivid interest in this young composer, and for all the composers of the new Spanish school.[83] He also has words of praise for the pictorial talent of Salvador Dalí, whom he met in the train during his trip to Barcelona.

La Nación (Buenos Aires), 25 April 1936
Igor Stravinsky Talks About the Future Directions
of His Music and His Art

We find Igor Stravinsky onboard the *Cap Arcona*, surrounded by friends and photographers, who offer him a warm Argentine greeting.[84] The director of the Teatro Colón, Mr. Athos Palma, introduces us, and the great composer, cordial and kind, with the simplicity of a true artist, immediately recounts his excellent impressions of the voyage in flawless French, with a slight Slavic accent. "This is a trip I have been wanting to make for a long time," he tells us. "But an artist's career cannot always be coordinated with his personal desires. I meant to come here on numerous occasions. My work, at times, and other commitments too, kept those desires as mere plans. This time, the directorship of the Colón was able to iron out all the difficulties, and when Mr. Athos Palma recently met me in Paris, all the details were resolved, and here I am, ready to present some of my compositions to that theater's audiences.[85] I know of their sensitivity and intelligence in appreciating great musical works, and I have heard tell of the significance of the artistic movement in Buenos Aires on more than one occasion. In terms of myself, I have exact news about how my work has been received. My friend Ernest Ansermet has contributed, in great part, to that."[86]

The Future Direction of Music

Asked afterward about the future direction of music, he tells us: "It is very difficult to judge things that are constantly happening in front of our eyes and developing around us; we must have the necessary perspective of time in order to reach consequent conclusions and be able to judge. In my case, for example, I do what was done before, but in another way, and that is what makes it novel and contemporary. The problems may always be the same; the problem of creation, above all, is simply a question of finding the relationships that interest or suit each individual creator. It has been said that in the works I produce, I proceed in leaps, that my audience is disoriented because it cannot find what it expected in any one of them. The truth is nothing like that; I enlarge the borders of a starting point that I consider my point of departure, and the rotational movement produced around it is perfectly logical within the curve of its line. As exactly logical, I could say, as the movement of a wheel around its axis. The difference is that my 'tempo' is not the 'tempo' of those who use time to sleep through life. . . The movement of my work is fast. Many of my admirers are still stuck in *Petrushka*, they remain in the same place; whereas I enlarge my radius of action, and they don't follow me. Hence the frequent misunderstandings, which can generally be attributed to incomprehension or lack of preparation to fathom the meaning of my new ideas."

Contemporary Russian Music

We then talked about contemporary Russian music. "I know very little about the current music of my country," Stravinsky declares, "and I think deep down there isn't much there, or to put it better, nothing new. I think that, for the time being, a nation that has suffered such upset in its social structure cannot produce an interesting work of art. They are doing 'something else,' I know, but unfortunately this thing is not real art since it is simply used for propaganda. When Bolshevism broke out, everything that was produced was for the Left, and anything that the Left produced was good. It was really insignificant work, written with a doorman's taste in mind. Now, they're starting to compose for the Right, and the approach hasn't changed much. There is, however, a talented young composer, Dmitry Shostakovich. I know good compositions by him, as well as a *Lady Macbeth*—which is detestable in terms of its libretto, and backward in its musical spirit, resembling in its tendency something out of Musorgsky's era. This is what I can say about contemporary Russian music, which definitively confirms what I said before— that is, audiences in general are fifty years behind the truly original creator."

Emerging Compositions

Discussing the most important works to emerge in recent years, independently from his own, Igor Stravinsky says he knows very little about what is being produced these days. "My life is quite isolated. I work a lot, I compose, I write, I don't neglect the piano, because ever since I became convinced that most of those who perform my works don't know how to reproduce my way of thinking, I resolved that, while I can, I will perform my works myself, along with my son Soulima, who is a conscientious artist.[87] That is why I am not well informed about emerging compositions. I can say, however, that there are some composers I like a lot and others I don't care for at all. Among the young ones," he adds, "the name Conrad Beck attracted my attention at Baden-Baden not long ago—he is a Swiss musician of German culture—and among the Italians, I consider Rieti and Petracchi [*sic*] talented.[88] As to my personal preferences, quite honestly I am for Italianism, for Cimarosa, Rossini, Bellini, and Verdi, whom I adore.

"I also continue to have an enormous veneration for Debussy, with whom I had a deep friendship. However, it's very difficult to talk with precision today about the Impressionists who after all lay the groundwork for the vanguard movement that in its time we started: Picasso, Derain, Ravel, and others.[89] Then, to move on to other authors, I like Manuel de Falla a lot, even though he is not of my time. But I admire his profoundly religious spirit, and this pleases me, because with faith one can create great works. You probably know that when the Republic was established in Spain Falla was named honorary citizen of Granada and he, who considered a town that would burn down churches and convents to be sacrilegious, responded: 'I believe in Christ; therefore I do not accept such an award.'[90]

That's beautiful, isn't it? And I find it beautiful because materialism is something very distant from me. It is what forbade me from going back to my homeland. For men to give up their lives for a materialistic paradise I find degrading; whereas I can perfectly understand the ideal that inspires the spirit of the Crusades, for example. The oscillations of politics seem very alien to me. I am neither royalist nor republican. But I am anti-parliamentarian. That I can't stand, like a horse that can't put up with a camel."[91]

Chroniques de ma vie

We talked about his two-volume *Chroniques de ma vie,* which has been of such vivid interest to the musical world. "For the time being," he says, "I am not think-ing about publishing a new volume. It will come, probably, later. Here too, there has been a certain incomprehension as far as the public is concerned. I didn't want to present an anecdotal life story, the picturesque aspects of my behavior, or sentimental confidences, which do not interest anyone, after all. I only wanted to express what I think using simple, concise, and clear language—neither more nor less than I do musically—and not about doctrine, but about the practice of life from a creator's and a performer's perspective, because these are things I do myself. Here I lay out more broadly the reasons I decided to be the interpreter of my own works, after not having done so for a long time. That is why my trips have multiplied lately, and I always have the pleasure of confirming, by the way I am honored, that my purpose has been met. I have also begun explanatory confer-ences on my new works. That is what I did last year at the Université des Annales, in Paris, for the Concert for Two Pianos that I performed with my son Soulima.[92] Mr. Palma has invited me to repeat that conference at the Colón, which I will do with great pleasure." Finally, he concludes by saying: "Tomorrow I will begin rehearsals at the theatre, and please send my greetings to the great newspaper *La Nación*, the most important one in South America; the name was already familiar to me from having always seen it on the Avenue des Champs Elysées in Paris."

The Program He Will Perform at the Colón

The programs of Igor Stravinsky to be performed at the Colón have been defi-nitely set in the following manner: First concert, Tuesday the 28th, *Pulcinella* Suite; Concerto for Piano and Wind Instruments; and *Symphony of Psalms*. Second con-cert, May 2, *Feu d'artifice*; Capriccio for Piano and Orchestra; *Les Cinq Doigts*; and *The Rite of Spring*. First dance performance on May 6, *The Sorcerer's Apprentice* by Paul Dukas; *The Firebird;* and *Petrushka*. Second dance performance on May 9, *The Fairy's Kiss* and *Apollon musagète* (premiere). Third concert, May 10, Concerto for Piano and Wind Instruments and Capriccio for Piano and Orchestra; solo-ist Soulima Stravinsky. Fourth concert, May 14, premiere of *Perséphone* thanks to the collaboration of Mrs. Victoria Ocampo and Mr. Carlos Rodríguez. Third concert-conference, May 16, conference by Igor Stravinsky; premiere of Concerto for Two Pianos (Igor and Soulima Stravinsky); Serenade in A, Piano Sonata, Soulima Stravinsky; and second performance of Concerto for Two Pianos. Last concert, May 16, repetition of *Perséphone* with some of the previous works.

El Universal (Mexico City), 23 July 1940
Igor Stravinsky, the Eminent Composer and Conductor, Arrived in Mexico Yesterday and Will Conduct a Concert of the Orquesta Sinfónica de México

The distinguished Russian composer and conductor Igor Stravinsky is among us as of yesterday morning.[93] He came with his wife and is staying at the Hotel Reforma, where he met with a group of journalists who came to interview him last night.

Stravinsky had to leave Europe because of the war. Most recently he was in France. His sons remained there, but he knows nothing about them due to the lack of communications and the prevailing chaos in the territory conquered by Nazi forces.

We see in Stravinsky the terrible imprint he still carries from the European conflict. As he talks about the war, telling us that all his sympathies are with France, we see reflected in the face of this brilliant musician the dreadful situations he experienced.

"It is horrible!" he tells us.

But he didn't come here to talk about the conflict that has brought grief to so many nations, but to conduct a series of concerts with the orchestra of Maestro Carlos Chávez.[94]

In French—the language he prefers, though he is full of praise for Spanish—he tells us about his brief stay in the United States, where he gave a series of conferences at Harvard University about a variety of musical topics.[95]

He is accompanied by Carlos Chávez and Alfonso Reyes, two of his closest Mexican friends.[96] Everyone listens attentively to the voice of the Maestro, who talks tirelessly about the topic that brought him to Mexico: music.

"Mexico," says Stravinsky, "must be a musical country par excellence, since that was and is true of the Spaniards, from whom Mexicans descend. This is the first time I've come to Mexico, but I am certain that for me the trip will reveal many beautiful things. As soon as I finish my engagement with Maestro Chávez, I will go to the countryside to rest, to breathe in the sun, the air, to learn about the vernacular music of this very musical people."

Stravinsky will start rehearsals tomorrow with the orchestra of Carlos Chávez, because on Friday this week he will be performing before the Mexican public.

He is very thankful for all the kindness he has received and sends through *El Universal* his warmest greetings to the Mexican people, society, and those who love the art he so prominently represents.

El Nacional (Mexico City), 23 July 1940
An Hour with Stravinsky
Arqueles Vela

The intellectual figure of Igor Stravinsky is so strong that any physical effect vanishes with the power of his conversation.[97] We cannot see the man of daily life. His internal gesture imposes itself in such a way that we barely perceive any expression of emphasis to his words, words that encompass his feeling so purely. When his outward disposition surprises us, it is because it reveals the intimacy of an idea, an inner attitude. We ask him nothing. His passion for expressing what he thinks about music impels the conversation without any prior discussion—in a tonality so communicative, so much his own that we remain suspended, listening to him as if he had guessed what we wanted to know about his artistic life.

He begins by talking about his first contact with Mexican musical life, with his own musical life in Mexico: the rehearsals with the Orquesta Sinfónica that he will conduct, as a guest conductor, next Friday.

"It's a good orchestra . . . the musicians in it respond with enthusiasm, do a good job of interpreting what's called for. I don't say this to flatter, but it is a good orchestra. I work with pleasure, with . . . "

Now a question arises and Stravinsky is transported to France. "I remember it," he says, "the way we remember paradise. Not the paradise that's beyond life, but the paradise of our own life. The terrestrial paradise . . . "

The paradise where he so splendidly cut the fruit of art in order to share it with the uncertainty of creation—that's the important thing for Stravinsky, creation, the transformation of life into delectable material.

Someone asks another question: this time about modern music. And Stravinsky wonders aloud, partly to himself: "What does modern mean?"

And he answers: "All music has been modern, in all times. Schubert and Bach were modern, and all the musicians who were of their times. But the word *modern* has to mean 'classical' and 'neoclassical' as well or else it loses its meaning."

And he remembers how the critics appraise his work: "You are a neo-classical composer . . . Very well, if you believe that neoclassical means someone who creates by ordering material. Very well, I am neoclassical. If you think that label will do for me . . . Very well, thank you very much."

Then he talks about creative work, about considering life as the raw material of artistic creation, and says: "The important thing is to compose—in the most immediate sense of the word. Compose: put one thing after another, next to another; arrange things in such a way that they spark an interest in those things— for what they suggest in isolation and only say once ordered. The important thing is to present the material as it is, so it can say what it is. Nothing has told me more about Mexico than a book by Alfonso Reyes: *Anáhuac*.[98] More than from histories about Mexico, I learned what Mexico is by reading Alfonso Reyes, because he has taken the subject of his country and presented it so that it speaks for itself. Pure material has the most eloquence. The great artist does nothing but put it in order so that we can go deeper into it and understand it."

In the suspenseful pause, I make the following suggestion: "Excuse me if I insist that you talk about the Orquesta Sinfónica de México. That touches me more closely."

"No more than it touches me," Stravinsky answers quickly. "Mexico is a musical people. I believe there are musical races. And you are a musical race. And this is not just a phrase. The ancient Mexicans have left vestiges of their musical racialities.[99] And since the Spaniards are also a musical race, the musicalities of those two racial types have merged and produced your musical imperative. Because I feel that Mexico has a musical imperative."

And then—as if we didn't fully believe him—he resorts to an essay by Paul Valéry about the power of music. About its power to provoke a physiological potentiality in the body.[100]

"I have worked with the orchestra with great pleasure. It has made my glands work . . . It has inspired me . . . "

Suddenly, another question arises, about good music, and Stravinsky smiles for the first time and asks a question as well, emphatically: "What do we call good music?"

And he answers himself: "That which we must play. There is music we must play because it awakens vital sensations in us, and music that we must not play: that which is incapable of moving us, of extracting from within ourselves an inner energy that can increase the value of the material."

Remembering his last comment about critics, he quotes a letter of Schubert's, on the subject of the poetic and then he tells us:

"I did not mean any of those things that appear in the review. The poet is he: the critic.[101] I just tried to compose sonorous material. Music is made with sounds, like poetry is made with words, not with ideas . . . as Mallarmé said all so well."[102]

While I'm saying good-bye, already alone with Stravinsky's effusive handshake, I tell him: What beautiful things you have said about art!

"Beautiful because I have lived them," he answers. "Everything that is lived with passion is beautiful."

This is how Stravinsky has lived, to the depth of his material. That's why he is always so close to the popular. No great artist can distance himself from the popular, if he wants to convey the purest part of life.

Excélsior (Mexico), 25 July 1940
"Art Would Not Be Art Were It Not Done for the Glory of God," Stravinsky Says on Arriving in Mexico
Ana Salado Alvarez

Stravinsky, the most outstanding composer of our time, is in Mexico.[103] He has come here to conduct the Orquesta Sinfónica: Mexico City audiences will have the privilege of listening to one of the most outstanding musicians of our time as he conducts—one who, despite having revolutionized music, is loyal to musical tradition and a Bach disciple.

Though Russian by nationality, his facial features do not show the physiognomy of a man of his race. Of medium height, thin, with a pronounced nose, he dresses carelessly and has kind and elegant manners, like someone accustomed to constantly interacting with people and being in the public eye.[104]

The Maestro speaks a clean and correct French, and it is in this language that he prefers to express himself. He does so with clarity, and his ideas are of such depth that they reveal both the man of talent and the philosopher who sees everything from this perspective—especially when the topic is music.

Music was, of course, the topic of conversation when we entered the suite at the Reforma Hotel where he is staying. The Maestro was conferring with men greatly interested in the subject: Adolfo Salazar, Alfonso Reyes, Maestro Chávez, and Arqueles Vela.[105] They would not have wanted or intended to speak of anything else. The topic was mandatory and thus extremely interesting. The war was a variation on the theme.

Questions came from all of us there: Maestro, where were you when the war broke out? Will this worldwide commotion influence music? What effects will it have on the feelings of humanity? What will happen afterward?

"I left France on 16 September, a few days after war was declared. The French people are brave; they prepared for it with goodwill, even enthusiasm. They were doing their duty heroically. Still, there was sadness, alarm, uncertainty, maybe because of the sense of a coming catastrophe.

"But the French have a spiritual vitality unlike any other people on earth, and will not succumb. What will happen afterward? That is the tragic question. How will it affect humanity? Only God can know."

However, returning to the topic of music: Since we know the Maestro has come from the United States, he is interrupted with questions about musical trends in that country, about the American people's taste and capability for the art of music.

"There are truly great musicians, and of high quality. I have been teaching classes at the University of Cambridge[106] about the philosophy of music. I was asked to teach in French, and now the lectures are being translated into English so they can be published by the Harvard Press.[107] And there, in those classes, I had the opportunity to meet very serious musicians with the true qualities of composers and performers. There are peoples—races, I should say—that are naturally musical, and others that become musical by force of study. The latter can be compared to distilled water, which isn't as pleasant as natural water, but possesses the same essential qualities. Musically educated peoples are similar."

And how would you classify the Mexican people, Mr. Stravinsky?

"I would be surprised if the Mexican people were not musical. It has this inheritance by tradition. I had nothing less than proof of it today when I was rehearsing this afternoon with the orchestra. The Orquesta Sinfónica is a great orchestra, composed of magnificent musicians. Paul Valéry explained everything biologically; it was a curious obsession of his. He said that true writers or musicians or painters were those who made his glands work—the glands that awakened in him the feeling of enjoying these arts. And in the same way these Mexican musicians had the privilege of 'making my musical glands work.'"

We laughed at this amusing explanation from the great maestro, and asked him to tell us what modernism in music is.

"There is no modernism in music," he explains. "Music has been modernist in every age. Bach was a modernist in his time, and the modernist tendencies today or three centuries ago are the same, good or bad. If they are good, music is good, then and now; if they are bad, music is bad, then and now. In literature, in painting, in all the arts, there have always been certain rules to follow in order to produce a work of art, and good music is written or composed in these times just as it was in the past."

And addressing Mr. Alfonso Reyes, Stravinsky warned him that he had no intention to flatter him, but that Mr. Reyes's book, *La Vision de Anáhuac*, had given him a better knowledge of Mexico than any history he could have read, because the ideas in it were expressed with great harmony.

"That is the difficulty in any kind of art," Stravinsky continues. "To put ideas in the strictly required order, in the harmonious form that creates the whole in a composition. Without this perfect order, there is no art. And in literature, Alfonso Reyes possesses this sublime ease."

It was getting late, and we would have liked to continue talking with the Maestro, but time was running out for everyone. He stands up and says simply and naturally: "Art would not be art if it were not done for the glory of God. Even those who think they are creating it for other reasons and ideals glorify God with it, without meaning to."

And on the lips of this great man, these words resound richly and sweetly.

Russian by Origin, His Love Is France

Igor Stravinsky's presence in Mexico reminds us immediately of two names both familiar and beloved: Ana Pavlova, the eminent Russian and a singular character in the history of choreography, and the great pianist José Iturbi.[108] Through their days of glory, the biography of our guest the distinguished Maestro is linked to these two figures so loudly applauded here among us. We should also remember at this time the figure of the great Ansermet, whose performance as guest conductor of the Orquesta Sinfónica de México is one of those impossible to forget; and Ansermet, in fact, has been one of the most effective propagators of Stravinsky's work.[109]

Our educated audiences already know a lot about the illustrious author of *The Firebird* and *Petrushka*, thanks to the prolific work one afternoon of the Ukrainian Chorus, which found in the Plaza of "El Toreo" the perfect setting to delight us with the latter of these ballets;[110] they are also familiar with Stravinsky's autobiography, first published in Buenos Aires by Sur, with a beautiful prologue by Victoria Ocampo.

Buenos Aires had already had the privilege—after New York and before Mexico—of receiving a visit from the brilliant Russian musician, given that Ansermet had already conducted *The Firebird* in a memorable performance at the Teatro Colón in Buenos Aires in 1917.[111] For the Mexican people—who hold music as one of the purest sources of human freedom—Stravinsky's arrival will be a powerful stimulant, since his genius is in full maturity and—as he has expressed so well—he is not only continuing to create, but also to perform his own music.

Son of a remarkable singer at the St. Petersburg Imperial Opera, nephew of one of the most socially eminent in the Czarist Russia, disciple of Rimsky-Korsakov, great cultural traveler who has been able to enrich his culture with the most serious discipline, Stravinsky emphasizes here, while among us, his passionate love for France, his devotion to what he still considers his second homeland, as do other Russians of extraordinary quality both in science and art.

A Genius Who Is Able to Admire Others

Stravinsky—like all authentic geniuses—is one of the people most capable of admiring others, and enthusiastically burns magnificent myrrh in honor of others who have collaborated with him in brotherly artistic exploits.[112] What he says about Ansermet could not be more eloquent: "His reputation as a perfect performer of my works is already established, but what has surprised me most is that certain—apparently learned—people who have admired his performances of contemporary music have not paid enough attention to the way he interprets works from the past. Ansermet belongs to a category of orchestra conductors that confirm the conviction developing in me for a long time about the relationships between early and modern music."

Revista de Revistas, 4 August 1940
Stravinsky "The Yankee"!

Jorge Mendoza Carrasco

My first impression of the distinguished musician—personally, not artistically—was quite strange.[113] Tall, regular build, light eyes with a penetrating gaze and austere gestures, he seems terribly dry, maybe even despotic. A few minutes into the conversation with him one is convinced, however, that though he may well be the former, he is never the latter.

"If my life has any significance that merits writing articles about," he tells me, "its most important phases can be found in the pages of *Chroniques de ma vie*.[114] Not long ago," he adds, "I devoted my best efforts to becoming a pianist and a conductor. It's not up to me to say whether I have achieved my goal well, nor to talk about my own compositions."

Stravinsky recalls with a bit of irony that in Paris in 1913, when he premiered his work *The Rite of Spring*, the audience made it impossible to hear the last chords because of their whistling, screaming, and protests of all kinds. Only a year later—at the very beginning of the First World War—that same audience applauded wildly the same work by the Muscovite composer.[115]

"My aesthetic ideal is to have no imitators," he says.

"By a strange coincidence," Stravinsky adds, "I'm ending up in Mexico, where I was invited by Maestro Chávez to conduct the magnificent orchestra of Mexico in my first symphony, which will have its premiere at the end of the year with the Chicago Orchestra to celebrate its fiftieth anniversary."[116]

In fact, Igor Stravinsky had until then composed only "ballets."[117]

"How did you meet Pavlova?" the reporter asks.

IGOR STRAVINSKY, HUESPED ILUSTRE DE MEXICO.
Caricatura de FA-CHA.

Revista de Revistas

Figure 1. "Igor Stravinsky, Mexico's Illustrious Guest."
Cover of *Revista de Revistas*, 4 August 1940, caricature by Fa-cha.

The Russian takes a minute or two to answer: "Maybe she was attracted to my music, as I was attracted to her dancing. Two Russians who identify with each other is nothing strange.[118]

Speaking of his native country, the visiting musician compares his people with ours. "Also, I have found many affinities between the Russian people and the Mexican," he says.

Perhaps what best portrays Stravinsky's personality, apart from his music of course, are the anecdotes that abound in his life, spiced as they are with grace and wit.

It is said, for example, that a certain Italian association invited him to play their auditorium, advising him that the most important personalities of the musical world had performed there, although the society was so poor that they would never be able to pay what he might ask as honorarium. Stravinsky read the invitation and responded laconically by wire: "I hate the poor."

This brilliant Russian became a French citizen three years ago,[119] but now that the traditional land of freedom has fallen to Nazi cannons, Igor Stravinsky has the intention of becoming an American citizen.

Ultimas noticias (Mexico City), 25 July 1946
Stravinsky Says That the OSM Is Magnificent
Antonio Rodríguez

Those who know Stravinsky through his photos, or imagine him through the renown of his brilliant productions, will certainly not recognize him to see him as he is: a tiny body; "nonchalant" in dress; with a demanding look that hides behind a pair of half-chipped glasses; his absolute baldness covered with a small wool hat like a clown's, giving him the air of an eccentric tourist.[120]

Protective of his time, the author of *Petrushka* gives us only the few minutes it takes for the car to cover the distance between Bellas Artes and Prendes,[121] along with another few minutes, the following day, while he changes his rehearsal clothes for street clothes. Luckily, Stravinsky has the same prodigious capacity for synthesis in conversation that shows in his music, so that each of his answers contains the essence of an entire conversation.

Rule and Emotion

In a second he states, quickly but clearly, his criteria for so-called national music. He doesn't think that music should have that "profession," and cites, as examples, the cases of Copland, the American, and himself, Russian by origin, who do not produce national music.[122]

We talk about Béla Bartók and his theory about absorbing the national and expressing it by means of the personal language of each composer.[123] When we slip in the word "system," Stravinsky declares:

"I don't defend his system, or any system in music."

Looking for a connection, we allude to a phrase from Chávez: "The recipe, in art, is the barometer of mediocrity," except that, in lieu of barometer, we said the "rule."[124]

"I don't know if Chávez said that," replied Stravinsky. "As for me, I'm for the rule. The French painter Braque said one day, 'I love the rule that corrects emotion.'[125] I also think that the rule corrects emotion."

"Nonetheless, many say that emotion is everything in a piece of art, that intelligence, too much culture, 'cerebralism'—they say—kills inspiration.

"Emotion!" Stravinsky exclaims, raising his arms in the air. "We all have emotion. *Le bon Dieu*—the good Lord—gives it to everyone. But we need rules to make it into a work of art."

Once Rivera told us, on almost the same topic: "Can you imagine Leonardo da Vinci being ignorant?"[126]

Shostakovich: So Backward!

Stravinsky confesses that he doesn't know Latin American music; that among the Russians he is interested in Tchaikovsky and Glinka; that he barely respects some of the innovations of Musorgsky; and declares finally that he feels more Latinist or Latinizing than Slavic.

Naturally, we spoke to him about Shostakovich, the musician about whom Serge Koussevitzky had this to say: "He is the greatest master of musical opulence, the master of what he wants to do; he has an endless melodic inventiveness; his musical language is as rich as the world; and his emotion abundantly universal."[127]

Stravinsky declares sharply: "Shostakovich is not interesting. His symphonies are monsters that last one hour and make a lot of noise. I don't deny his talent. He has it, but he's stayed where music was forty years ago. He's a musician like Mahler, nothing more."

Moving from the artist to his concepts, we mentioned Shostakovich's viewpoint that "music is not only a combination of sounds, but an art capable of expressing the most diverse ideas and feelings."[128]

"Music expresses nothing," he replies energetically. "It is expressive in and of itself, but it does not express."

It can suggest, we suggest . . .

Everything he said in response to that can be summarized with these words:

"That is literature."

Throughout the conversation, he referred to his music as architectural construction: pure, free of anecdotes.

You try, then, to make—we were about to say, but he interrupted us, proclaiming: "I don't *try* to make. I *make!*" And he told us how Picasso answered those who called him a researcher: "I'm not a *searcher*, I'm a *finder!*" (Discoverer, let's say.)[129]

Mexico, the Symphony, and Carlos Chávez

And discussing the Symphony:

"It's a good orchestra. Its members are very enthusiastic. They never get tired. And you know, I am very demanding."

But you are a guest. Isn't this flattery?

"You are wrong. I am not a flatterer. Yes, it's a good orchestra. Many believe the only good orchestras are in the United States. Here's proof of the contrary. I am interested in the *mise au point*. That is to say, I am interested in perfect adjustment, in precision rather than range. This is something I achieve with the Orquesta de México. Chávez created a great musical instrument with the symphony. Someone who comes up with an orchestra like that can achieve many other important things. As a composer I don't know him deeply, but I know he is a good composer."

Period.

Pro Arte (Santiago de Chile), 2 June 1949
Stravinsky Judges Today's Musical Moment
Santiago del Campo

Hollywood, May 1949 (by airmail).[130] A voice may well become cosmopolitan over the phone, but Igor Stravinsky's Russian accent reached the height of Slavism when he told me in English, then French:

"Let's meet for tea at my home—1260 Wetherly Drive,[131] around the corner from Sunset Boulevard. To find your way, look for the café on the corner, A Bit of Sweden."

I don't know why it's been my lot to meet musicians in the middle of having tea or coffee. First, Gustav Mahler's widow. Then, Darius Milhaud. Now, Stravinsky. I can't complain. The tea hour brings on that feeling of literary circles, a kind of intimacy of the trenches. And, on another note, the Eastern magic of learning character through tea leaves contains more wisdom than the mental acrobatics of psychiatrists.

After crossing the paved jungle of Sunset Boulevard's hundreds of cars, hundreds of stores, hundreds of film agencies, the gimmick that's supposed to attract tourists to Ciro's,[132] the well-trained legs of Earl Carroll's girls,[133] the models of designer Don Loper,[134] Schwab's Restaurant[135] with its big tables filled with girls who are still waiting for something, and the endless parade of shop windows, gas stations, hotels I see the guiding sign: "A Bit of Sweden."

I turn onto a street that goes up the hill. The decor changes: instead of bright advertisements, the appealing green of lawns and gardens. There is something in the air that comes from the Mediterranean, as if the European sea had come to California for vacation.

The gates at 1260 Wetherly are open. They are short fences facing a garden that rises, among flowers and more flowers, particularly geraniums and roses. In the back, between the trees, the Pacific peeks out and hides, like a moon scattered and in pieces. The doors of the house open to a white, spacious, single-story house with a terrace on one side. An elderly maid—I'm reminded of Chile, maybe Providencia Street[136]—lets me into a long entrance hall, a mix of living room and library. I look at the paintings: several Picassos, five Dalís, two paintings by the lively Yves Tanguy,[137] sketches of scenery, a big painting by Theodore Stravinsky, son of Igor, who lives in Switzerland and is a stained-glass artist. There is order; none of that "craziness" that the public would applaud. A European would call it proper. A North American would call it "nice."

Madame Stravinsky comes in, tall, beautiful, sweet. She has such gentleness about her that even Dalí's raptures seem to render themselves romantic on the walls. I ask her about her sons: Soulima, the pianist, Theodore, the painter.[138] At the very moment she starts telling me that Soulima also lives in Hollywood, Stravinsky enters the scene.

I can't contain my astonishment. I imagined him very tall and thin, like that sketch by Cocteau where you see him bent like a Russian greyhound over Picasso's short pipe.[139] But he is short, incredibly short; nervous, active, tense, alert. It's impossible to judge his age by his strong, flexible and confident gesticulations. However, on June 17 he will be 67 years old. Below his scarce hair, Stravinsky's face is reflected in his large glasses—the woodpecker nose, the thick lips, the sharp ears. He bears an amazing resemblance to Mischa Auer, the Hollywood basso buffo.[140] And he is elegant, lordly, skillful at using a cigar box and his hands, for emphasis.

Within that second of first sight, similar to the second of death, I am excited to meet him, to be talking with him, to be participating in his home life. And rising within the excitement, contained, complete, synthesized, is all that this man represents for the history of contemporary music. And I see passing quickly before me his birth in Oranienbaum and the home of his father, who was a bass with the Imperial Opera. And the press clips from St. Petersburg that read, "The pianist boy Igor Fyodorovich Stravinsky showed great talent." And his encounter with Rimsky-Korsakov in Heidelberg. And his studies with Kalafati.[141] And then, the trajectory of his work: the premiere of his first symphony in St. Petersburg in 1908; the Debussyan style of *The Faun and the Shepherdess* in 1909. And the poem with Maximilian Steinberg, four days before Korsakov's death. And his encounter with Diaghilev, through the *Scherzo fantastique*, and the triumph of *The Firebird* ballet in Paris on 25 June 1910, date of the independence of modern music. And a year later, the success of *Petrushka*, the work that marks all of contemporary production with its polytonalist influence. And later, the public scandals of *The Rite of Spring*, and the Slavic accent of *Les Noces*, the burlesque irony of *L'Histoire du soldat*, and the use of jazz in *Ragtime*. And the last twenty-nine years, starting with *Pulcinella*, continuing with *Mavra*, *Apollon musagète*, *Oedipus Rex*, the *Symphony of Psalms*, *Perséphone*, *Jeu de cartes*, the Concerto in E-flat ("Dumbarton Oaks"), the *Berceuses du chat*, *Cinq Pièces faciles*, *Le Roi des étoiles*, Serenade in A, and culminating with the *Biblical Symphony*.[142] This whole ocean of musical life, tireless, throbbing, powerful, emerges in summary in the first look.

The taste of tea quiets the atmosphere, makes it more comfortable. Stravinsky talks about his life in California:

"In 1941, I came to Harvard to teach a course. The lectures of that season were published in a book, *Poétique musicale*. Since then, I haven't left North America. I don't know why people try to make me travel to Europe no matter what. It's the first thing they ask me: what am I going to do in Europe? I am doing well here, I'm happy. Apart from that, everyone is going to Europe right now. Let me work in peace. I have many things to do. Last year, I premiered a Mass, I have just finished the *Orpheus* ballet, and I am now preparing an opera with a libretto in English: *The Rake's Progress*. The poet William Auden has written an excellent text. It has three acts and nine scenes for a small orchestra, like *Così fan tutte*."

Without my asking, he gets excited talking about the musical quality obtained from chamber orchestras and few characters onstage:

"I was never able to understand Stokowski's obsession with using crowds of performers to play Bach and Mozart. It's a monstrosity. The only thing he succeeded in doing was moving the character of the music off-center and out of proportion. Bach's *Passions* were written for thirty people at most, including soloists, choir, and orchestra. I don't understand the reason to give them a superdose of vitamins. That's why I always prefer small, almost intimate spaces. People have talked to me about the Metropolitan Opera House several times. It terrifies me."

He smokes in between sips of tea. He moves, leans forward, switches from French to English. Madame Stravinsky watches him, pleasantly silent. To annoy him, I ask:

"Critics don't understand the religious tendencies in your music since your *Biblical Symphony* in 1940, and the complete departure from Russian-inspired themes."

He is visibly annoyed. He shakes his sharp face, he vibrates:

"That's like the critics, trying to find these little reasons to sink into what has become known as 'artistic feeling'! When they ask me if there's emotion in my music, I don't know what to answer. I don't know which emotion they are talking about. There are so many in this world. Of course there is emotion. I don't deny it. But in a work of art, emotion is implied. We always work with emotion. But the problem of art is a different one. It's what the Greeks called poetry: 'to know how to do.'[143] Music is a question of technique, of culture, of knowledge. It's an objective. It's as important as philosophy or mathematics. Emotion is for the audience. There's no reason to talk about it!"

"So your 'religious influence' . . . ?"

"Has never existed. I have written a Mass and a *Biblical Symphony*, like all composers who have used religious themes. Like Mozart, or Haydn, or Brahms. As a problem of form. As an incentive for musical development. I imagine that after listening to my ballet *Orpheus*, the critics won't think that I am looking for the path to hell…"

We talked about music in general. Here, in summary, are his words on a variety of topics:

"What is it they call classicism? We should talk in terms of periods: the classicism of the seventeenth century, of the eighteenth century, of the nineteenth century, and in sixty years, the classicism of the twentieth century. All great musicians become classic. Musicians of today, you ask? I don't know them much. Benjamin Britten, barely. Not Ives's music, either. Definitely, I do not like Messiaen. When it comes to current Russian musicians, it's better that we don't get into it—horrifying. The old Russians? Well, Rimsky-Korsakov was a great musician, a great teacher, but he was never a composer. He built his works like someone sculpting with marble. Musorgsky? A natural with lightning—uncultured musically, movingly so—great memory, sparks, but with a Franciscan poverty of technique."

I take advantage of his dive into this topic, his frank triple somersault of opinions and theories. I ask him to summarize his general ideas about music.

"Do you consider yourself a musical revolutionary?"

His answer is sharp, fast, incisive, without losing his elegance:

"Art is never revolutionary. Revolution implies a provisional chaos, and art is the opposite of chaos. The Middle Ages were correct in referring to art as craft. It was the Renaissance that invented the word *artist*. Why burden art with the resounding and ominous flavor of the term *revolution* . . . ? As to my personal preferences, I think the mere fact of creating is enough. If through a miracle—that fortunately will never happen—I was handed my work completed, before I had started creating it, I would feel deeply distressed. It's working that saves an artist, not the theories. Here's what Paul Valéry once said to me: 'I prefer work to recipes.'"

The afternoon has been whole, round as an apple. The trip from Hollywood to Los Angeles is so long that I move to make my good-byes. Stravinsky shows me around his house, the ocean view, the manuscripts of his new opera, the canvas chairs on the terrace, the flowers he likes best. And throughout our final handshake, he talks about Madame Errázuriz, "our best friend," "our unforgettable Chilean friend."[144] I promise to give her his regards when I return to Chile.

Back in the street, I steal a geranium.

NOTES

1. Tamara Levitz chose the interviews here from a selection Stravinsky himself kept that is today housed in his *Nachlaß* at the Paul Sacher Stiftung (hereafter PSS). She focused on the period from 1916 to 1949, and included Stravinsky's essay from the French newspaper *Comoedia* because it is one of few public statements he made about Spanish culture and music, and is thus of crucial importance in understanding his developing relationship to Spain in the early 1920s.

2. Jesús Bal y Gay and Rosita García Ascot, *Nuestros trabajos y nuestros días* (Madrid: Fundación Banco Exterior, 1990), 142.

3. Stravinsky's attentiveness to Spanish street music and soundscape is well documented. See, among many examples, Oriol Martorell, "Stravinsky a Barcelona: Sis visites i dotze concerts," *d'arte* 8–9 (November 1983): 103, 120; and Igor Stravinsky, *An Autobiography* (New York: W. W. Norton, 1936; repr. 1962), 62–64.

4. On Stravinsky's opinions on Manuel de Falla's *El Sombrero de tres picos* and *El Retablo de Maese Pedro* see his *Autobiography*, 133; and *Memories and Commentaries* (1960; repr., Berkeley: University of California Press, 1981), 81 (76 in 1960 ed.).

5. It is interesting, especially in the interviews of the 1920s, to see Stravinsky seeking to form spiritual and aesthetic alliances with countries on the European cultural periphery. In 1921 he even posits the existence of a Russian-Andalusian community that bypasses the Latin element in Spain. Later, he positions the entire Latin world against Germany.

6. Stravinsky received many presents from Eugenia Errázuriz after first meeting her in Madrid on 30 May 1916; he received a monthly subvention from her for a time, composed as a commission from her his Etude for pianola, dedicated his *Ragtime for Eleven Instruments* to her, and had an affair with her nephew's wife in London in 1921. See Vera Stravinsky and Robert Craft, *Stravinsky in Pictures and Documents* (New York: Simon and Schuster, 1978), 143, 618n231, hereafter *SPD*; and Stephen Walsh, *Stravinsky, A Creative Spring: Russia and France 1882–1934* (Berkeley: University of California Press, 1999), 266.

7. Anáhuac refers to the Mexican highlands, where the ancient Toltec and Mexican civilizations took root and Mexico City was founded in 1521. Alfonso Reyes offers a delightful account of a dress rehearsal he attended of *Les Noces* in "Improvisación," *Obras Completas* (Mexico: Fondo de Cultura Económica, 1956), 2:298–300. Picasso probably introduced Stravinsky to Reyes.

8. These programs were crucial for the aesthetic orientation of the Argentine composers who belonged to the Grupo Renovación, which included Juan Carlos Paz, Jacobo Fischer, Juan José Castro, Gilardo Gilardi, and José María Castro.

9. Igor Stravinsky, *Crónicas de mi vida*, trans. Guillermo de Torre (Buenos Aires: Sur, 1935).

10. Stravinsky also presented her with a manuscript copy of *Perséphone*. See Omar Corrado, "Victoria Ocampo y la música: Una experiencia social y estética de la modernidad," *Revista musical chilena* 61 (July–December 2007): 49.

11. See Omar Corrado, "Stravinsky y la constelación ideológica argentina en 1936," *Latin American Music Review* 26 (Spring–Summer 2005): 88–101.

12. Salazar and Stravinsky met in Spain in 1916. Stravinsky may have met Jesús Bal y Gay and Rosa García Ascot through Manuel de Falla or the Residencia de Estudiantes in Barcelona in the 1930s, but they became friends only in Mexico.

13. In contrast with Vera Stravinsky's unfortunate description of Chávez's last visit with Stravinsky in a diary entry of 31 January 1971 (cited in *SPD*, 498), Chávez wrote a very moving account of it in a letter to his closest friend, Aaron Copland, 21 November 1971, Fondo Carlos Chávez, Archivo General de la Nación, Mexico City.

14. Stravinsky also recorded with the OSM his Divertimento, which is a suite from *Le Baiser de la fée*. See the discussion of the Divertimento in "Igor the Angeleno," Tamara Levitz's essay in this volume.

15. Salazar reviewed Stravinsky's *Poétique musicale* in "Artes y letras: Igor Strawinsky, filósofo y poeta," *Novedades*, 16 February 1946. Carlos González Peña, noticing Stravinsky's reticence to be interviewed, published an avowedly fictive interview ("Una entrevista con Stravinsky," *El Universal*, 1 August 1940), in which the composer's answers were taken entirely from *Chroniques de ma vie*.

16. On Falla and Salazar see Consuelo Carredano, *Adolfo Salazar: De la España del resurgimiento musical al México de la modernidad postrevolucionaria* (Madrid: ICCMU, forthcoming). I am grateful to the author, who shared her ideas and prepublication materials with me. Salazar wrote numerous books on twentieth-century music, where he discussed Stravinsky's and Falla's music. For an interesting description of the relationship between Falla and Stravinsky see Gianfranco Vinay, "Falla et Stravinsky: Confrontation en deux volets," in *Manuel de Falla: Latinité et universalité: Actes du colloque international tenu en Sorbonne, 18–21 novembre 1996*, ed. Louis Jambou (Paris: Presses de l'Université de Paris-Sorbonne, 1999), 405–18.

17. Spanish title: "Los grandes compositores: Una conversación con Stravinsky—Sus propósitos—Los Bailes españoles—Música para pianola," *La Voz*, 21 March 1921. Stravinsky conducted *Petrushka* at the Teatro Real in Madrid on 19 March 1921. The expression "drum and the bass drum" (*el tambor y el bombo*) refers to instruments brought to Spain in the medieval period.

18. Real Conservatorio Superior de Música.

19. King Alfonso XIII invited Diaghilev and the Ballets Russes to stage shows in Madrid and San Sebastián from May to August 1916.

20. Stravinsky refers here to Diego Velázquez's famous portrait of Philip IV of Spain, kept in the Prado.

21. In Spanish, "sensación acústica."

22. Spanish critics were debating the role of feeling (*sentimiento*) in musical expression in this period.

23. "Huyo de todo lo hecho, proque es convencional, académico." Jacques Maritain was just popularizing the idea of "making" music with his *Art et scolastique* in 1921. Much later, in the 1930s, Stravinsky embraced the term *hecho* or "made" as central to his neo-Thomist aesthetics.

24. Pianist Alexander Brailowsky presented an all-Scriabin concert on the same day that Stravinsky conducted *Petrushka* in Madrid, leading some critics to compare the two composers. See Julio Gómez, "Tribunales de música: Scriabin en la Nacional y Stravinsky en el Teatro Real," *El Liberal*, 20 March 1921; and Carol Hess, *Manuel de Falla and Modernism in Spain, 1898–1936* (Chicago: University of Chicago Press, 2002), 169–70.

25. The flageolet and the drum (*el caramillo y el tambor*) are popular instruments in Spanish folk music.

26. Stravinsky lived for a time in 1920 with his family in Gabrielle Chanel's home in the Parisian suburb of Garches, which is close to Saint-Cloud.

27. Stravinsky's commentary on the pianola inspired further discussion in the Spanish press. See "Música para 'Pianola': Una curiosa innovación de Igor Strawinsky," *El Sol*, 22 March 1921.

28. French title: "Les Espagnols au Ballets russes," *Comoedia*, 15 May 1921. The Ballets Russes premiered Manuel de Falla's *Le Tricorne* (*El Sombrero de tres picos*) at the Alhambra Theater in London on 22 July 1919, and the *Cuadro flamenco*, starring María Albaicín (Pepita García Escudero), at the Théâtre de la Gaîté Lyrique in Paris on 17 May 1921. The Sevillian Félix Fernández García ("Félix el Loco") danced in rehearsals of *Le Tricorne*, which was staged with sets and costumes by Picasso. Images of María Dalbaicin (as she was known in France) and Igor Stravinsky in a "photograph taken in Seville" accompany this article.

29. Stravinsky tried to impress his French audiences and appeal to their taste for Orientalist music by drawing a connection between his own works and Andalusian music, the Romani origins of which were well known.

30. Spanish title: "Un gran compositor: Igor Strawinsky y la música moderna: Los músicos que prefiere—Cómo trabaja—Su autocrítica—En España," *ABC*, 25 March 1924. A. R., André Révész (1896–1970), was a Hungarian-born philosopher, intellectual, translator, political commentator, and journalist who lived in Spain for over thirty years, edited *El Sol*, published numerous books, and became an important international commentator in *ABC* (interviewing Albert Einstein when he visited Spain). Fernando Fresno (1881–1949) was one of the most prominent caricaturists in Spain in the first half of the twentieth century. He published caricatures in almost all of the Madrid press, including *ABC*.

31. Stravinsky stayed at the aristocratic Hotel Palace, today the Westin Palace Hotel.

32. Stravinsky traveled to Madrid to conduct the *Firebird* and *Pulcinella* suites with the Orquesta Filarmónica at the Teatro Real on 25 March 1924, in a concert that included Pérez Casas conducting Rimsky-Korsakov's *Scheherazade* and *Capriccio espagnol*, and Tcherepnin's Prelude to *The Distant Princess*. This was a charity event funded by the marquise of Salamanca. See "Un concierto de música rusa," *La Epoca*, 26 March 1924.

33. Révész's question may have been inspired by the fact that Manuel de Falla and Ravel were also in Madrid around this time. See V. Arregui, "Stravinsky, Ravel y Falla en Madrid," *El Debate*, 20 March 1924; and Carol Hess, *Manuel de Falla and Modernism in Spain, 1898–1936*, 187.

34. The Ballets Russes premiered Francis Poulenc's *Les Biches* on 6 January 1924 and Georges Auric's *Les Fâcheux* on 19 January 1924 at the Théâtre de Monte-Carlo.

35. Except for Bizet's *Carmen*, all these operas are by Charles Gounod.

36. Stravinsky's comments on Tchaikovsky and Rimsky-Korsakov angered Maurice Ravel, who responded to them in his own interview with André Révész a few weeks later. (See "El gran músico Mauricio Ravel habla de su arte," *ABC*, 1 May 1925.) "Stravinsky's fanaticism for Tchaikovsky is a paradox," Ravel comments. "The *Nutcracker* is a fine little work but less important, for example, than Delibes's *Coppélia* and *Sylvia*. Tchaikovsky is the least Russian of the Russians, and for that reason the one that can interest us least. Musorgsky is much superior to him. And concerning Rimsky-Korsakov, I think Stravinsky shows himself to be very ungrateful toward his teacher."

37. Stravinsky uses the expression "higiene del trabajo."

38. Sergey Yesenin and Vladimir Mayakovsky. Stravinsky had met Mayakovsky in Paris a few years previously. See Mayakovsky, "Parisian Sketches," in the section in this volume titled "Who Owns Mavra? A Transnational Dispute."

39. In Spanish, "objetos musicales, hechos musicales."

40. In the interview a handwritten image is inserted at this point of the opening bass line of *Firebird*: E♭–C–♭,–B♭,–A–C♮–D♭–E♭) with the Hungarian word *Tüzmadár* (Firebird) signed by Igor Stravinsky. Stravinsky clearly offered this autograph to Révész, who was Hungarian.

41. Stravinsky performed the *Pulcinella* Suite at the Liceu in Barcelona on 16 March, and at the Teatro Real in Madrid on 25 March 1924.

42. Hans Christian Andersen.

43. King Alfonso XIII and Queen Victoria Eugenie.

44. In Spanish, "aristocracia de la sangre y del arte."

45. Gran Teatre del Liceu. Stravinsky participated in concerts at the Liceu on 13, 16, and 19 March 1924, which included repertoire by Mozart, Wolf, Beethoven, Berlioz, Wagner, Brahms, and Korngold. On 13 March he conducted *Feu d'artifice* and *Le Chant du rossignol*, on 16 March he conducted *Song of the Volga Boatmen*, *Scherzo fantastique*, and *Pulcinella* Suite, and on 19 March *The Nightingale*, *Pastorale*, *Tilimbom*, and *The Faun and the Shepherdess* with the soprano Mercè Plantada.

46. Devotional songs sung during Holy Week in processions in Andalusia.

47. Spanish title: "Un gran compositor ruso: Stravinsky, en Barcelona, nos habla de sus viajes por América," *La Noche*, 25 March 1925. Rafael Moragas (1883–1966) was a Catalan music critic, intellectual, artistic director of the Gran Teatre del Liceu from 1912 to 1939 and a friend of Stravinsky's. He went into exile in Montpellier in 1939. See Luis Cabañas Guevara (pseud. Rafael

Moragas), *Cuarenta años de Barcelona (1890–1930)* (Barcelona: Ediciones Memphis, 1944); and Artur Bladé i Desumvila, *El senyor Moragas "Moraguetes"* (Barcelona: Editorial Pòrtic, 1970).

48. Juan Mestres Calvet organized a Stravinsky festival to take place at the Gran Teatre del Liceu on 28 March, 2 and 5 April 1925. Stravinsky conducted known works such as the *Pulcinella* Suite, as well as works not yet heard in Spain, including the suite from *L'Histoire du soldat*, the Octet, *Ragtime*, and the Concerto for Piano and Wind Instruments (in which he performed as a soloist and Pierre Monteux conducted). Frederic Longàs performed *Three Movements from Petrushka* for piano on the first concert and Mercè Plantada sang a selection of vocal works including *Three Japanese Lyrics* on the last one. See Martorell, "Stravinsky a Barcelona: Sis visites i dotze concerts," 104–7.

49. Felipe Rodés Baldrich (1878–1957) was a lawyer and politician who served as Minster of State Education and Fine Arts under King Alfonso XIII. Pedro Soldevila was a city councilor, Luis Salgado was a lawyer, and Juan Mestres Calvet was the impresario of the Gran Teatre del Liceu.

50. One of Picasso's well-known drawings of a frontal view of Stravinsky's face is inserted at this point in the interview. This drawing was frequently reprinted in Spanish articles on Stravinsky.

51. Stravinsky toured the United States for ten weeks from January to March 1925. He spent one month in New York City, where Serge Koussevitzky had conducted *The Rite of Spring* less than a week before he arrived, and where Willem Mengelberg conducted the New York Philharmonic in his Concerto for Piano and Wind Instruments. He then traveled by train to Cleveland, Philadelphia (where Fritz Reiner conducted his concerto), Chicago, Detroit, and Cincinnati (where Reiner again conducted his concerto).

52. Stravinsky recorded seven of his eight pieces from *Les Cinq Doigts* and *Valse pour les enfants* on a Steinway for Brunswick while in New York in March 1925.

53. Stravinsky conducted his *Petrushka* Suite on 5 April 1925 at the Liceu on a program that included his Symphony no. 1 and Concerto for Piano and Wind Instruments (in which he performed as the soloist).

54. Catalan title: "Conversant amb Strawinsky," *La Veu de Catalunya*, 25 March 1928. José Farran i Mayoral (1883–1955) was a humanist intellectual who translated Plato, Aristotle, and other authors into Catalan. A librarian, teacher, and critic, he published several books on critical and political subjects. See, for example, *Diàlegs crítics* (Barcelona: Societat Catalana d'Edicions, 1926).

55. José Farran i Mayoral first contacted Stravinsky after hearing him conduct *Feu d'artifice*, *Le Chant du rossignol*, and the suite from *Firebird* with the Orquestra Pau Casals at the Gran Teatre del Liceu in Barcelona on 13 March 1925. He had not yet met Stravinsky, but he wanted to express his admiration for the "clarity" and "perfection" of his music. "What fairy-tale music!" (*Quelle musique de fées!*) he exclaimed in a letter written in French. See José Farran i Mayoral to Stravinsky, 14 March 1925, microfilm 122.1, 710-13, PSS.

56. Stravinsky arrived in Barcelona to participate in two concerts of his music at the Liceu on 22 and 25 March 1928. He received 8,000 pesetas to conduct his Symphony no. 1, *The Rite of Spring*, and *Petrushka* Suite in the first concert, and *Feu d'artifice*, *Scherzo fantastique*, *The Rite of Spring*, and *Firebird* Suite in the second. See Stravinsky's contract with Juan Mestres Calvet and related materials, microfilm 123.1, 2264-89, PSS. Ferran Callicó was a Catalan graphic artist, painter, and writer. I believe it is his unsigned drawing of Stravinsky that is reprinted in Luis Gongora's "Igor Strawinsky y el surrealismo."

57. On Stravinsky's relationship to the neo-Thomist philosopher Jacques Maritain and the religious philosophy as expressed here see Tamara Levitz, *Modernist Mysteries:* Perséphone (New York: Oxford University Press, 2012), 117–81, 331–41.

58. San Juan de la Cruz and Santa Teresa de Avila are two of the greatest Spanish mystic writers.

59. In Spanish, Teresina del Niño Jesús.

60. Vladimir Solovyov, a Russian philosopher and theologian, was read and admired in Stravinsky's Russian émigré circle in Paris, especially by his friend Pyotr Suvchinsky.

61. Ramon Llull was a thirteenth-century Franciscan philosopher and logician from Majorca.

62. Excerpts from *Oedipus Rex* were performed in Barcelona on 13 March 1928 with soprano Pilar Ruff, pianist Pere Vallribera, and Sebastià Sánchez-Juan as the narrator. The composer

Joaquim Homs and artist Josep Franch-Clapers attended (for the notice, see microfilm 123.1, 2272, PSS). Farran i Mayoral wrote Stravinsky that "[the triumph of] *Oedipus* filled me with enthusiasm. I wanted to shake your dear hand." José Farran i Mayoral to Stravinsky, 7 September 1928 (date unclear), microfilm 123.1, 2291–92, PSS.

63. See Joan Llongueres, "Primer Festival Strawinsky al Liceu," *Veu de Catalunya*, 23 March 1928. Llongueres focuses primarily on *The Rite of Spring* in this article.

64. *Oedipus Rex* was not performed in Barcelona in 1929, and Stravinsky did not return there that year. *Oedipus* received its Spanish premiere with the Russian Opera Company in a program with Musorgsky's *Sorochinsky Fair* at the Liceu in Barcelona on 23 December 1933. On 16 November 1933, the Associació de Música 'Da Camera' also programmed an all-Stravinsky concert in which Samuel Dushkin performed the Violin Concerto in D, Soulima Stravinsky performed the Capriccio for Piano and Orchestra, and Stravinsky himself conducted his *Symphony of Psalms* (with the Orfeó Gracienc). This was Stravinsky's fourth visit to Barcelona, and his first since 1928.

65. The Spanish premiere of *The Rite of Spring* at the Liceu on 22 March (repeated on 25 March 1928) was a huge triumph for Stravinsky, although reviews were mixed. See Martorell, "Stravinsky a Barcelona: Sis visites i dotze concerts," 107–10.

66. Stravinsky conducted the *Petrushka* Suite at the Gran Teatre de Liceu on the day this interview appeared, 25 March 1928.

67. In articles he wrote for *La Veu de Catalunya*, Farran i Mayoral occasionally expressed his gratitude toward Stravinsky for having "purified" modern music and resisted its revolutionary strain. See, for example, José Farran i Mayoral, "Igor Strawinsky," *La Veu de Catalunya*, 22 March 1928.

68. Stravinsky complained for years about how U.S. journalists had misinterpreted his relationship to modernism after interviewing him upon his arrival in New York in 1925. For an example of the type of journalism Stravinsky regretted, see Henrietta Malkiel, "Modernists Have Ruined Modern Music, Stravinsky Says," *Musical America*, 10 January 1925.

69. Pauleta Pàmies i Serra (1850–1937) was a celebrated Catalan ballerina and dance teacher, and director of the Companyia de Dansa of the Gran Teatre del Liceu in Barcelona.

70. *Himnes Homèrics*, translated into verse by Joan Maragall with a literal translation by Pere Bosch-Gimpera (Barcelona: l'Avenç, 1913).

71. Nicolas Boileau-Despréaux (1636–1711) was a French poet who famously reformed French poetry in his *L'Art poétique* (1674), in which he established the rules for French verse. Stravinsky greatly valued this book. The muses in *Apollon* do not speak verses from *L'Art poétique*; rather, Stravinsky used a couplet from *L'Art poétique* as the epigraph for the "Variations de Calliope."

72. Spanish title: Luis Góngora, "Igor Strawinsky y el surrealismo: 'Mi arte define el gran músico—es hijo de la pura dialéctica cristiana', 'Schoenberg es un químico de la músico,'" *La Noche*, 12 March 1936. Juan Mestres Calvet planned a "Stravinsky Festival" made up of two concerts that took place at the Liceu on 12 and 15 March 1936 with the Orquestra de Gran Teatre del Liceu and Joan Balcells conducting the Orfeó Gracienc. Stravinsky's Divertimento was heard for the first time in Barcelona at the first concert, with the pieces Gongora mentions here in the order he lists them. The second concert on March 15 included Stravinsky's *Apollon musagète*, Concerto for Piano and Wind Instruments (with his son Soulima as soloist), *Symphony of Psalms*, and *The Firebird*. Stravinsky and Soulima received 7,500 pesetas for these concerts. See the contract between Juan Mestres Calvet and Stravinsky, microfilm 127.1, 1412, PSS. The program can be viewed on 1422–42.

73. From *The Fairy's Kiss*.

74. Concerto for Piano and Wind Instruments.

75. The "S." stands for Svetislav.

76. Although articles on Stravinsky in the Spanish press were often illustrated with Picasso's drawings of the composer, this particular interview is illustrated with what I believe to be Ferran Callicó's drawing of Stravinsky's face.

77. In Spanish, "mi propio yo." It is interesting to see Stravinsky discussing here how "his own I" or self contributes to his compositional process, especially in light of the critical tendency to identify his music of these years with objectivity and erasure of self.

78. Stravinsky's remarks on Communism and Christianity must have had particular relevance in Barcelona at this time due to the tremendous political turmoil caused by the national election of the Popular Front in February.

79. The Second Viennese School may have been on journalists' minds because of the imminent premiere of Alban Berg's Violin Concerto at the 14th International Society for Contemporary Music Festival in Barcelona on 19 April 1936. Critics in Barcelona had engaged with Schoenberg's music since before World War I, and in 1932 the composer lived there for several months at the invitation of his student Roberto Gerhard.

80. That is, their compositional technique. Stravinsky is referring here to Alois Hába.

81. Stravinsky's *Chroniques de ma vie* was published in Argentina by Sur, the publishing house that Victoria Ocampo owned. Although she wrote the prologue for the volume, the text itself was translated by Guillermo de Torre.

82. Concerto for Harpsichord, Flute, Oboe, Clarinet, Violin and Cello.

83. Gustavo Pittaluga González del Castillo (1906–1975) was a Spanish composer, conductor, and essayist and member of the Grupo de los Ocho (Group of Eight)—a group founded in the early 1930s on the model of Les Six in France and connected to the Residencia de Estudiantes in Madrid. Gustavo Pittaluga conducted Stravinsky's Concerto for Piano and Wind Instruments at the Auditorio de la Residencia de Estudiantes in Madrid on 25 May 1935. This concert included Francis Poulenc's Concerto for Two Pianos and Orchestra and Johann Sebastian Bach's Concerto for Four Pianos in A Minor. The soloists were Rosa García Ascot, Francis Poulenc, Soulima Stravinsky, and Leopoldo Querol.

84. Spanish title of this unsigned article: "Igor Strawinsky nos habla de las orientaciones futuras de la música y de su arte," *La Nación,* 25 April 1936. Stravinsky traveled to Argentina aboard the German luxury ocean liner *Cap Arcona.*

85. Athos Palma first approached Stravinsky about conducting his ballets at the Teatro Colón in a letter of 26 December 1935. The Cuban impresario Ernesto de Quesada and Victoria Ocampo facilitated the connection between the two men. Palma was most interested in the ballets, which were known in Buenos Aires, but he promised Stravinsky he would try to arrange concerts for Soulima in Argentina, and that he would tentatively stage *Perséphone* and *Oedipus Rex.* He also offered to pay for his and Soulima's voyage to Argentina (see Athos Palma to Stravinsky, 26 December 1935, microfilm 127.1, 1690, PSS). Palma and Stravinsky ironed out the details about the trip when they met in Paris in February 1936.

86. On Ernest Ansermet, see the introduction to these interviews.

87. This interview is illustrated with a professional photograph of Stravinsky and Soulima in formal concert attire, signed by both men with the dedication "For the *Nación* and the nation of Argentina."

88. Stravinsky is referring here to Vittorio Rieti (1898–1994), who composed *Barabau* for the Ballets Russes in 1925, and Goffredo Petrassi (1904–2003). Stravinsky had heard Conrad Beck's Serenade for Flute, Clarinet and Strings at the Internationales Zeitgenössisches Musikfest in Baden-Baden in April 1936, where he and Soulima had also performed the German premiere of his Concerto for Two Solo Pianos. On the role Nazi ideology played in the programming of this festival, see Joan Evans, "'International with National Emphasis': The Internationales Zeitgenössisches Musikfest in Baden-Baden, 1936–39," in *Music and Nazism*, eds. Michael H. Kater and Albrecht Riethmüller (Laaber: Laaber Verlag, 2003), 102–13.

89. Stravinsky appears here to be talking about the vanguard that formed around the premiere of Satie's *Parade* and his own *Mavra*, and in opposition to musical impressionism. Strangely, he associates this vanguard also with Ravel. See "Who Owns Mavra? A Transnational Dispute," in this volume.

90. Stravinsky has somewhat confused this story. Manuel de Falla did complain to the president of the Republic, Niceto Alcalá Zamora, about the looting of churches after King Alfonso XIII founded the Second Spanish Republic on 14 April 1931. He also refused the honorary citizenship of Seville with the famous words "If God is now officially denied all recognition, how could I, His poor creature, accept it?" But his relationship to the Spanish Right was more complex than

Stravinsky indicates. See Carol Hess, "Falla, the Spanish Civil War, and America," *Diagonal: Journal of the Center for Iberian and Latin American Music* (2011), available online at http://www.cilam.ucr.edu/diagonal/issues/2011/Hess.pdf.

91. Stravinsky's political remarks caused a public relations disaster in Argentina and Uruguay. Leftist critics condemned his commentary on the Soviet Union and Spain, whereas right-wing Christian journalists praised his orthodoxy. On this debate, see Levitz, *Modernist Mysteries: Perséphone*, 337–39; and Corrado, "Stravinsky y la constelación ideológica argentina en 1936," 88–101.

92. Stravinsky accompanied his performance with Soulima of his Concerto for Two Pianos at the Salle Gaveau in Paris on 21 November 1935 with a lecture presentation on the music, which was subsequently published as "Quelques confidences sur la musique," *Conferencia, Journal de l'Université des Annales* 29 (15 December 1935): 43–47; repr. in Eric White, *Stravinsky: The Composer and His Works*, 2nd ed. (Berkeley: University of California Press, 1979), 581–85. This concert was sponsored by the Université des Annales.

93. Spanish title of this unsigned article: "El eminente compositor y director Igor Stravinsky, que llegó ayer a México y que dirigerá un concierto de la Orquesta Sinfónica de México," *El Universal*, 23 July 1940. This title also serves as a caption above a photograph of Stravinsky reading contemplatively with his glasses in his hands.

94. Carlos Chávez invited Stravinsky to Mexico City to conduct the Orquesta Sinfónica de México in a series of concerts. On 26 and 28 July Stravinsky conducted Cherubini's *Anacreonte* Overture, Tchaikovsky's Symphony no. 2, his own Divertimento from *The Fairy's Kiss*, and the suite from *Petrushka*. On 2 August he conducted his *Apollon musagète*, Divertimento, *Jeu de cartes*, and *Firebird* Suite. He was paid $2,502.50 for these concerts.

95. At Harvard Stravinsky gave six lectures in French in the 1939–40 academic year as part of his appointment as the Charles Eliot Norton Professor. These lectures were published in French as *Poétique musicale* (Cambridge, MA: Harvard University Press, 1942), and translated into Spanish as *Poética musical* (Buenos Aires: Emecé, 1946). See Valérie Dufour's essay in this volume, "The *Poétique musicale*: A Counterpoint in Three Voices."

96. Alfonso Reyes (1889–1959) was a Mexican writer who served for varying terms as a diplomat in France, Spain, and Brazil from 1913 to 1938.

97. Spanish title: "Una hora con Stravinsky: El Gran Compositor se halla en esta Capital," *El Nacional*, 23 July 1940. Arqueles Vela (1899–1977) was a Mexican writer involved in Estridentismo—a Futurist-influenced avant-garde movement founded in 1921 that embraced the social concerns of the Mexican Revolution and was located in Xalapa. The title of this article appears under a large photograph of Stravinsky standing with Carlos Chávez and Vera Stravinsky with the caption: "A great composer has arrived. Igor Stravinsky, composer of *The Firebird* and *The Rite of Spring*, among other famous pieces, is in Mexico as of yesterday. Here we can see him with Maestro Chávez. Stravinsky will conduct the Orquesta Sinfónica de México as guest conductor."

98. Alfonso Reyes, *Visión de Anáhuac (1519)*, in *Obras Completas* (Mexico City: Letras Mexicanas, 1956), 13–34.

99. *Racialidad* is perhaps a translation of *racialité*, the quality of having a race. Until recently, the Spanish term *raza* had meant "people." It is unclear whether Stravinsky originally used the French "*race*," or whether he intended to say "race" or "racial type."

100. Stravinsky may have read Paul Valéry's "Première leçon du cours de poétique" (1937) while he was Valéry's neighbor in France in the late 1930s. This essay was later published in *Variétés V* (Paris: Gallimard, 1944), 295–322.

101. I could not find a source for this alleged quote.

102. When Degas complained to Mallarmé that he had many ideas and yet found it difficult to compose a sonnet, Mallarmé apparently replied, "But, Degas, it is not with ideas that we write verse. *It is with words*." Paul Valéry tells this story in "Poésie et pensée abstraite" (1939), also published in ibid., 158–59.

103. Spanish title: "El arte no sería arte si no se hicera por la gloria de Dios dice Strawinsky al llegar a México; No hay modernismo en la música, afirma el célebre maestro," *Excélsior*, 25

July 1940. The author of this article, Ana Salado Alvarez, was a prominent Mexican journalist and daughter of the writer, journalist, and diplomat Victoriano Salado Alvarez (1867–1931) from Teocaltiche. The article is illustrated with a photograph of Stravinsky standing with Vera and Carlos Chávez with the caption "Stravinsky in Mexico: Igor Stravinsky, who will soon conduct the symphony, in the company of his wife and Maestro Chávez, upon his arrival in Mexico." The photograph is from the same photo shoot, but taken at a different angle from the photograph used with Arqueles Vela's article, translated in this section.

104. Salado Alvarez may have been referring to the fact that he bundled up inordinately while in Mexico (according to existing photographs), for fear of catching a cold.

105. Salado Alvarez based this article on the same conversation with Stravinsky that Arqueles Vela used to write his article on the composer.

106. Stravinsky is referring to Harvard University in Cambridge, Massachusetts.

107. Harvard University Press published Stravinsky's *Poetics of Music* in French in 1942; it was translated into English by Arthur Knodel and Ingolf Dahl in 1947.

108. The Russian classical ballerina Ana Pavlova (1881–1931) first visited Mexico in 1919, and she had performed *La Fantasía mexicana*, inspiring some Mexican critics to believe she would elevate Mexican folk and popular dance forms to a universal art. She returned once again in 1925 to perform Petipa's classic *Don Quixote*. Her impact on Mexican literature and dance was tremendous. See Alberto Dallal, "Anna Pávlova en México," *Anales del Instituto de Investigaciones Estéticas* 15/60 (1989): 163–78. The Spanish pianist and conductor José Iturbi (1895–1980) performed and conducted in Mexico for the first time in 1933 on a hugely successful tour organized by the impresario Ernesto de Quesada.

109. Ernest Ansermet was the guest conductor of the Orquesta Sinfónica de México in October 1934, when he conducted Stravinsky's *Les Noces* and Concerto for Piano and Wind Instruments with Claudio Arrau as soloist. Although Carlos Chávez is not mentioned here, he performed Stravinsky's works regularly with the Orquesta Sinfónica, especially after he did the first all-Stravinsky program in 1930.

110. Salado Alvarez is referring to what later became known as the Toreo de Cuatro Caminos, a vast space on the limits of Mexico City where a bullfighting ring was established in 1894. Although the Ukranian National Chorus appears to have visited Mexico City in the 1920s, it remains unclear how they could have performed *Petrushka*, which has no vocal parts and was not part of their repertoire.

111. Ernest Ansermet conducted *The Firebird* when the Ballets Russes performed it at the Teatro Colón during their tour to Argentina in September 1917.

112. This is a reference to the Nativity.

113. Spanish title: "Strawinsky 'El Yanqui,'" *Revista de Revistas* 31/1576 (4 August 1940). The *Revista de Revistas* was an illustrated entertainment magazine that included many stories about Hollywood in the early 1940s. The article is accordingly richly illustrated. The first photograph shows a full-length view from the side of Stravinsky conducting with the caption: "The world-famous composer of *The Firebird* has conducted the Orquesta Sinfónica de México with resounding success, without any of the ridiculous poses favored by other conductors." The second photograph is explained fully by the caption: "Here, the brilliant Russian composer at the conductor's podium of our symphony orchestra; in the background, the audience that attended his first concert at the Teatro del Palacio de Bellas Artes (Photos by Julio León)." This issue also includes Guadalupe Segura's article on Stravinsky and Vera, "Strawinsky: En plena luna de miel." When Stravinsky returned to Mexico a year later, a picture of him and Vera graced the magazine's cover (*Revista de revistas* 32/1625, 20 July 1941). It is interesting that Jorge Mendoza Carrasco mockingly calls Stravinsky a "Yankee," given an article he would publish two years later on *pachucos*—a subculture in Los Angeles of Hispanic men who wore zoot suits. See Jorge Mendoza Carrasco, "Los Pachucos," *Excelsior*, 31 December 1942. This demonstrates how journalists in this time were negotiating the identities and class position of those who crossed borders or settled elsewhere.

114. Originally published in French in 1935, and translated into Spanish in 1936. Published in English as *An Autobiography*.

115. *The Rite of Spring* premiered as a ballet on 29 May 1913. It received its first concert performance in St. Petersburg under Serge Koussevitzky on 18 February 1914, and its second at the Casino de Paris under Pierre Monteux on 5 April 1914. Stravinsky refers here to the latter performance. Stravinsky was not from Moscow.

116. Stravinsky refers here to his Symphony in C, which was commissioned for the fiftieth anniversary of the Chicago Symphony Orchestra. He conducted the premiere with that orchestra on 7 November 1940, and also conducted the piece with the Orquesta Sinfónica de México in Mexico City on 18 and 20 July 1941.

117. This is an unusual comment, and entirely false.

118. Stravinsky may have hesitated because he did not have a close relationship with Anna Pavlova, who had refused to dance *The Firebird* in 1910 and had been replaced by Tamara Karsavina.

119. Stravinsky became a French citizen in 1934.

120. Spanish title: "Stravinsky dice que la OSM es magnífica: El Gran Creador, habla de la música, y de los músicos," *Ultimas Noticias*, 25 July 1946. This article is accompanied by a photograph in which Stravinsky is chatting with Antonio Rodríguez, and is dressed exactly as described here. The caption reads: "Stravinsky talking to Rodríguez about music and musicians is de rigueur."

121. Prendes was an expensive, well-known, and touristy restaurant founded in 1892 and located on the south corner of the Palacio de Bellas Artes, where Stravinsky was to conduct the Orquesta Sinfónica de México in two concerts that included the suite from *Petrushka*, Symphony in Three Movements, *Apollon musagète*, *Scènes de ballet*, *Scherzo à la russe*, and *Circus Polka*.

122. Stravinsky appears not to have known Copland's most recent works, including *Billy the Kid* (1939), *Fanfare for the Common Man* (1942), *Lincoln Portrait* (1942), and *Appalachian Spring* (1944).

123. Rodríguez may be referring to the essay "Hungarian Music," which had just appeared in Spanish translation in the first issue of the Mexican journal *Nuestra música* 1/1 (March 1946): 14–19. Bartók played an important role in debates about national identity in music in Mexico. See, for example, "Bartók en Mexico," *Heterofonía* 15/74–75 (July–December 1981): 20–26.

124. Rodríguez must have intended to replace the word *recipe* with *rule*. Chávez frequently commented that harmony and composition textbooks were recipes only mediocre composers used.

125. Georges Braque created a lithograph with the phrase "I love the rule that corrects emotion" "J'aime la règle qui corrige l'émotion."

126. Rodríguez is referring to the famous Mexican muralist Diego Rivera (1886–1957)

127. Serge Koussevitzky strongly supported Shostakovich in the 1942 season of the Boston Symphony Orchestra and especially in connection with the premiere in the United States that year of the Symphony no. 7. Koussevitzky's original defense of Shostakovich in English reads as follows: "He is the greatest master of musical wealth; he is the master of what he desires to do; he has melody without end; his language is as rich as the world; his emotion is absolutely universal," *Syracuse Herald-American*, 2 August 1942; abridged in the *New York Times*, 2 August 1942.

128. Shostakovich actually said: "I understood that music was not only a combination of sounds disposed in this or that order, but an art capable of expressing, by the proper means, the most diverse ideas or feelings." "Autobiographie," *La Revue musicale* 17/170 (December 1936): 432–33.

129. Picasso famously said: "In my opinion to search means nothing in painting. To find, is the thing." First cited in "Picasso Speaks: A Statement by the Artist," *The Arts* 7/5 (May 1923): 315.

130. Spanish title: "Stravinsky enjuicia el momento musical de hoy," *Pro Arte* 1/47 (2 June 1949). Santiago del Campo was a Chilean playwriter who cofounded the Teatro Experimental de la Universidad de Chile in 1941. He was known for plays such as *California* (1938) and *Morir con Catalina* (1948). Stravinsky first visited Chile in August 1960.

131. Stravinsky lived at 1260 North Wetherly Drive in Hollywood from 1940 to 1964.

132. The celebrity nightclub Ciro's opened on Sunset Boulevard in 1940.

133. Earl Carroll was a U.S. theatrical producer and director of Broadway musicals who opened a famous theater on Sunset Boulevard in 1938. A 20-foot neon image of one of his famous showgirls, Beryl Wallace, graced the building's façade and made it a landmark.

134. Don Loper was a Hollywood fashion designer who designed clothes for Joan Crawford, Marlene Dietrich, Ginger Rogers, and others.

135. The lunch counter at Schwab's Pharmacy was a meeting point for people from the film industry. It is featured in Billy Wilder's *Sunset Boulevard* (1950).

136. Avenida Providencia is one of the main boulevards in Santiago de Chile. Providencia is a green, upper-middle-class residential suburb in the city.

137. Yves Tanguy (1900–1955) was a French Surrealist painter. Stravinsky met the Catalan Surrealist Salvador Dalí in 1936 in Barcelona. See Luis Gongora's article, "Igor Stravinsky and Surrealism," in this section.

138. Soulima's and Théodore's mother, Yekaterina, died in 1939. Vera was their stepmother.

139. Del Campo is referring to Jean Cocteau's drawing of Stravinsky and Picasso bundled in coats from 1917; repr. in White, *Stravinsky: The Composer and His Works*, 96.

140. Misha Auer (1905–67) was a Russian-born U.S. actor who appeared most notably in the film *My Man Godfrey* (1936) and *You Can't Take It With You* (1938).

141. Stravinsky studied counterpoint with Vasily Kalafati (1869–1942) at the St. Petersburg Conservatory after 1902.

142. Del Campo may be referring to the Symphony in C or the *Symphony of Psalms*. Del Campo's title is rarely used.

143. The Greek *poiema* translates as "that which is made."

144. Eugenia Errázuriz (1860–1951) was a Chilean silver mine heiress and patron of the arts who supported Picasso and also Stravinsky after 1916. See Leonora Saavedra's introduction.

The *Poétique musicale:*
A Counterpoint in Three Voices

VALÉRIE DUFOUR
TRANSLATED BY BRIDGET BEHRMANN
AND TAMARA LEVITZ

Igor Stravinsky's *Poétique musicale* originated in a commission the composer received to give a series of lectures as Charles Eliot Norton Professor of Poetry at Harvard University in the academic year 1939–40 and was first published in its original French in 1942 by Harvard University Press. Stravinsky, Pyotr Suvchinsky, and Roland-Manuel collaborated in writing these lectures in Sancellemoz, France in May and June 1939; they remain today the keystone of the composer's thought and major point of reference for his artistic ideology. As this article will show, however, research into the genesis of the *Poétique* reveals something beyond the lectures' content—namely, Stravinsky's strategies of intellectual elaboration.

Historical Background

In order to write the *Poétique musicale*, Stravinsky called upon two collaborators with different cultural backgrounds—his fellow émigré and close collaborator Pyotr Suvchinsky and the French musicologist and teacher Roland Alexis Manuel Lévy, known as Roland-Manuel (1891–1966)—both of whom he paid for their work. Strangely, Stravinsky waited until the very last years of his life to admit grudgingly that he had been involved in this particular form of three-way "literary ghost-writing."[1] Despite Stravinsky's confession, Robert Craft, in his article on the genesis of the *Poétique musicale* from the early 1980s, radically and arbitrarily rejected the hypothesis that Suvchinsky had been involved in the project. His desire to leave Suvchinsky out of the story seems to have been motivated by personal resentment.[2]

 Introducing the work's new French edition in 2000, Myriam Soumagnac laid out the problem of the authorship of the *Poétique* without concealing her objective to pay "homage to the memory of Roland-Manuel."[3] She relied on Roland-Manuel's handwritten manuscripts, which her study shows correspond

• 225 •

Figure 1. Pyotr Suvchinsky with Igor Stravinsky, 1930s.

on the whole to the final draft of the text, excluding the fifth lesson, "The Avatars of Russian Music." Correspondence between Stravinsky, Suvchinsky, and Roland-Manuel confirms that Suvchinsky wrote the fifth lesson on his own.[4] Soumagnac also notes intuitively on the basis of this correspondence that Suvchinsky must have played a larger role in developing a general outline for the *Poétique* and super-vising the whole. But without conclusive evidence to prove this thesis, research stalled there.[5] Since that time, musicologists have felt obliged to admit the idea that Suvchinsky may have participated sporadically in the writing of the *Poétique*, though behind the scenes an unfortunately unverifiable rumor spread widely among Suvchinsky's entourage that he had played an essential role in it.[6]

The third volume of Viktor Varunts's edition of Stravinsky's correspondence in Russian includes letters that give evidence that Stravinsky originally planned to work with Suvchinsky alone.[7] For unknown reasons, Suvchinsky suggested to Stravinsky that he entrust part of the work to Roland-Manuel:

> Roland-Manuel leaves for Sancellemoz[8] Saturday morning and he will be at your place in the evening; it's better to strike the lectures while they're hot. . . . In a word, everything has worked out miraculously well. I am myself very happy primarily for you: you needed to be relieved of this burden, and favorable working conditions had to be created for you. Roland-Manuel will be able to help you more than I can in regard to all of this, owing to his knowledge of French and for a whole slew of other reasons. He has welcomed the proposal with enthusiasm, and from our discussion I understand that he would like to have 1,000 Francs right away, before he leaves;[9] . . . he will also bring all the necessary books. I sketched in broad strokes the outline and chapter headings for the lectures for him and he was quite pleased with them. I am happy for you and for Roland-Manuel. Of course I am not happy for me that a coincidence of circumstances doesn't allow me to be in his place.[10]

In 2003, Eric Humbertclaude showed me a previously unknown and unpublished manuscript in Suvchinsky's hand from the archive of Suzel Duval, one of Suvchinsky's close collaborators from the 1940s until his death. This document furnished the proof that he was the author of the general outline of the lectures, as well as a precise, paragraph by paragraph description of the content of each one.[11] When brought together with the sources discussed by Craft and Soumagnac, this manuscript solves the mystery of who wrote the Poétique: Suvchinsky conceived and generated the ideas, Stravinsky assimilated and briefly developed them, and Roland-Manuel unpacked them, gave them form, and amplified and completed them. In addition, the correspondence reveals that Roland-Manuel submitted his drafts for Suvchinsky's approval before bringing them to Stravinsky. For example, Suvchinsky wrote Stravinsky on 23 May 1939 that "Roland-Manuel showed me the text of the first lecture. It looks very good, but in my opinion, you offer too much material right off the bat; there are certain paragraphs I would transfer to the next lecture."[12] In a second letter to Stravinsky from 26 May 1939 Suvchinsky writes: "Don't you think that there is an element of discovery, a premonition of discovery, in the first lecture when you talk about the creative appetite? I spoke to Roland-Manuel about this and he will pass my thoughts on the matter along to you."[13] There are many other examples of Suvchinsky suggesting improvements to the text in the letters he wrote Stravinsky in May and June 1939.

Thus it is clear that in the genesis of Stravinsky's Poétique, a "triangular collaboration" took place, whose point of departure and return was Suvchinsky. The foundational document drawn up by Suvchinsky is the true keystone of the Poétique.

In the study that follows, I undertake an inventory of all the documents necessary to understanding the history of this process. This integral critical edition of the fundamental documents provides a strong basis for assessing how they are interrelated.

Inventory of Manuscripts Related to the Genesis of *Poétique musicale*

The manuscripts known to date and taken into account here to explain the genesis of the *Poétique musicale* include: 1) Suvchinsky's handwritten manuscript in French (with several annotations in Russian), consisting of an outline of the lectures in eight lessons;[14] 2) Stravinsky's handwritten manuscript in French and Russian, consisting of notes for the lectures in six lessons;[15] 3) Roland-Manuel's notebook and handwritten manuscripts in French consisting of rough drafts of the lectures;[16] 4) Suvchinsky's typed manuscript in Russian of the majority of the fifth lesson, "The Avatars of Russian Music";[17] and 5) Soulima Stravinsky's handwritten manuscript in French, consisting of a translation of Suvchinsky's Russian text for the fifth lesson, reworked by Roland-Manuel (Suvchinsky asked Soulima, Stravinsky's youngest son, to translate his Russian text for lesson 5).[18] The Paul Sacher Stiftung also owns two clean, typed copies of the entire work, both of which contain handwritten corrections by Stravinsky and Roland-Manuel.[19] The second typed version, which represents the final draft, includes a short summary of each paragraph in the margins, intended for the composer's use in oral presentation.[20] This version corresponds to the first edition of the complete text published in French by Harvard University Press in 1942.[21]

English Translation of a Diplomatic Edition of Suvchinsky's Manuscript

Suvchinsky's handwritten manuscript is four pages long and titled "Theses for an Explication of Music in the form of 8 Lessons."[22] It is written in French (with occasional phonetic spelling), in black ink, and includes scattered annotations in black pencil in Russian and sometimes French. The document was clearly written in two distinct phases, beginning with the neat and conscientiously articulated presentation, and followed by the annotations. A comparison with Stravinsky's handwritten document, which I will discuss later, suggests that the annotations were probably penciled in following a conversation with the composer.

Suvchinsky appended to his four-page manuscript a single page with writing on both sides in Russian.[23] On this extra sheet, he succinctly summarizes Clement of Alexandria's composite work, the *Stromata*, which is about the relationship between faith and knowledge.[24] Given that neither this material, nor the name of

Clement of Alexandria appears in the *Poétique musicale*, the connection between this appended page and the book is unclear. There is the material connection of the paper clip that connects this page to his general outline, but it provides little evidence that the two necessarily have anything to do with each other. Although I cannot reject out of hand the hypothesis that Suvchinsky or somebody else mistook the date of this two-page document and attached it erroneously here, I lean toward the idea that this loose page consists of a digression Suvchinsky originally planned in connection with what he once called—in reference to Stravinsky—the contradictory notion of "mystic rationalism."[25]

In the following English translation of the "diplomatic edition" of Suvchinsky's manuscript (as in those that follow) the translators and I attempt to indicate as much as is feasible of the state of the original manuscript. To do this, punctuation, underlining, and layout follow the original (with some allowances for North American conventions of style). Words in square brackets indicate Suvchinsky's annotations, added in black pencil to the original text, which is in black ink. An exception are words in *italics* in square brackets, which represent my own additional commentary. The translators have indicated in their own marked footnotes where misspellings and grammatical problems exist in the French.

I [*recto of first sheet*][1]

Theses for an Explication of Music
in the form of 8 lessons.
[*words added in pencil around this title in clockwise direction from left to right:* reactive;[II] Sauguet;[III] relationship]
1st Lesson. The Phenomenon of Music[IV]
What is not, to my mind, music.*[V] True musical experience. The notion of time and music. The "Khronos."[VI]

I. The handwritten Roman numeral "I" is on the top right-hand corner of this page.
II. Stravinsky seems to have dwelled on the word *reactive* when developing the lectures' introduction; he uses it several times in the section he wrote called "Getting Acquainted."
III. Suvchinsky wrote Stravinsky on 31 March 1939 that he had just seen Henri Sauguet's opera, *La Chartreuse de Parme*, and enjoyed it very much. Stravinsky replied a day later that he was glad to hear about Sauguet's success and that he had always liked his music and hoped to see *La Chartreuse* some day. See *SPRK*, 3:662–64. It seems, then, that the words written here in pencil were reminders.
IV. Misspelled as "Fenomêne" in the original French. —Trans.
V. Suvchinsky added a small "x)" here in order to indicate a footnote, which he included under the solid line at the bottom of this page. We have changed his x) to an asterisk for the sake of clarity.
VI. Suvchinsky originally wrote "Chronos" and then changed the "C" to a "K." —Trans.

II The sonorous instant. Musical duration; the flow of musical Time. The problem of "Lento" and "Scherzo." [(Coda)]

"The higher mathematics" of music. Musical speculation. The dialectic of the creative process in music. "Coincidentia oppositorum."[VII] The principle of contrast and similitude in musical creation. Meditation. Musical emotion. The limits of the art of music. The crisis of the unity of conscience and concepts.

2nd Lesson <u>The Musical work</u>. (Elements and morphology [Structure][VIII])

Melos, theme[IX] [melody difference 1) [illegible] or of melos[X]/motif]. Harmony, interval. [chord]. <u>Modes</u>. Polyphony, modulation, movement, meter, rhythm, Tempo, sonority; registers and timbres: phrase, word, spoken word,[XI] syllable, intonation. Developments. Form (the choral, fugue, sonata, symphony, poem, prelude, dance, cantata, opera.)[XII] Form. True and false duration.

[Схема[XIII] - форма[XIV] - System]

[(secular

sacred)[XV]]

---

*magic, the irrational, esoteric music[XVI]

II [*verso of first sheet*][XVII]

3rd Lesson <u>The musical métier</u>

The <u>Composition</u> of a musical work. Talent and musical talents, hearing. Composition, invention, imagination—"imaginative" and intellectual imagination,[XVIII] inspiration. The musical conception. The system. Musical writing—[the design or plan of a composition[XIX]]. Sound material. The assumptions and

---

VII. "A Coincidence of Opposites" is a Neoplatonic term originating with the fifteenth-century German philosopher Nicholas of Cusa.

VIII. The word "structure" is added in pencil above "morphology".

IX. Misspelled as "thême" in the original French. —Trans.

X. Misspelled as "melo" in the original French. —Trans.

XI. Suvchinsky distinguishes between the written word (*mot*) and spoken word (*parole*) in French, as Stravinsky will in his manuscript. —Trans.

XII. Some words in this list are capitalized unusually in the original, for example "La Forme" in contrast to "le poème" and "La cantate." —Trans.

XIII. Schema.

XIV. Form.

XV. The words "profane" and "sacre" are written on top of each other in the original. —Trans.

XVI. This is Suvchinsky's footnote to himself, originally marked with "x)," a commentary on the phrase above: "What is not, to my mind, music."

XVII. The handwritten Roman numeral "II" is on the top right-hand corner of this page.

XVIII. "'imaginative' and intellectual imagination" is our translation of Suvchinsky's somewhat awkward "l'imagination—'fantaisie' et intellectuelle" in French. —Trans.

XIX. Suvchinsky uses the French word "facture." —Trans. "Musical writing" is our translation of "L'ecriture musicale," which also translates as composition.

inertia of the creative process. The deliberate and the unexpected. [breathing strong and weak beats]. Culture and taste. The culture of taste. Order

"The kingdom of necessity and the kingdom of freedom."[xx]

4th Lesson. Musical Typology. [suppose distinction]

[I] Problem of style. Synoptic, synchronic, and parallel analyses. [of illustrative, associative purity[xxi]]. What we call "Classicism" [academicism[xxii]], "romanticism" and "modernism" in music. Music that "imposes itself" and music "that is subjected."[xxiii] Musical psychology. Parallelisms of the different arts.[xxiv] On banality[xxv] and platitudes. [II Sacred, profane]

[иллюстр[xxvi]] [+ *illegible Russian word*]

[V Чайковский[xxvii]]

[*two illegible Russian words*]

Independent[xxviii]

Conditional

[Haydn, Wagner]

[music кадре истории[xxix]]

Patrons[xxx]

Snobbery

public

[*Abbreviations of the words classicism, Romanticism, modernism, academicism, and history in Russian are added in the left-hand margin.*]

5th Lesson. Looking back through history

---

xx. Suvchinsky slightly misquotes the line "It is the ascent of man from the kingdom of necessity to the kingdom of freedom," from chapter 3 of Friedrich Engels's *Die Entwicklung des Sozialismus von der Utopie zur Wissenschaft* (*Socialism: Utopian and Scientific*) (1880). He draws a line from this quote to the Russian word added at the bottom of this page: иллюстр (abbreviation of illustration).

xxi. Misspelled as "purté" in the original French. —Trans.

xxii. Misspelled as "academisme" in the original French, an error repeated below. Suvchinsky writes this word in larger letters underlined heavily and draws a heavy arrow between it and "Classicism." —Trans.

xxiii. Suvchinsky was trying to build a parallel construction around "musique 'imposée' et musique 'soumise,'" but realized this did not work and changed "musique imposée" to "musique qui s'impose," which still does not work elegantly in French. He then circled this expression. Another rendering of it in English might be "music that 'subjects' and music that 'is subjected.'" —Trans.

xxiv. Suvchinsky heavily underlines this phrase.

xxv. Suvchinsky circles this word in the original.

xxvi. Abbreviation of иллюстрация (illustration).

xxvii. Tchaikovsky. (Suvchinsky perhaps thought of citing the Fifth Symphony as an example.)

xxviii. Misspelled as "Indépandant" in the original French. —Trans.

xxix. Framework of history.

xxx. Misspelled as "mècens" in the original French. —Trans.

Problem[XXXI] of the continuous and the discontinuous. "Revolutions" and evolution in the history of the arts. Causal relationships. The determinate and indeterminate. (Chance). The genesis and the phenomenon (the fact). Cycles. Progress. The arts and life.

Ideocracy. Main ideas. Patrons. <u>Snobbery</u> and scholasticism the bourgeois spirit.

III [*recto of second sheet*][XXXII]

   6–7th Lessons <u>Russian music</u>

   [citizen[XXXIII] of the world]

Folklore and musical culture. Plainchant. Kastalsky.[XXXIV] "Russia-Eurasia." "Italianisms," "Germanisms" and "Orientalisms" of Russian music. The fundamental elements of Russian historiography. The two Russias. The revolution and the Russian Reaction. The two "disorders."

Glinka, Tchaikovsky, Moussorgsky, R-Korsakoff. Scriabine. The new Soviet (Ukrainian, Georgian, Azerbaijani, Armenian, etc.) "folklorism" and downgrading of values [degradation[XXXV]].

8 Lessons <u>on Performance</u>

Nothingness and musical life. The music, the performers, the listeners. The public. Interpretation and performance. Music criticism; its aberrations and "classical" distractions. "Accessible" and "enigmatic" music. The true meaning of music. The "self," the "non-self"—and Being—creative monism. [Academicism]

III [*verso of second sheet*]
[illegible Russian words]

Словарь (Француз.)[XXXVI]	Stretto-Coda
Lesson	IV conf.
1 Симф. Брамса[XXXVII] —C minor	
4 Симф. Бетховена[XXXVIII] —B-flat Maj	

Commentary

Although Suvchinsky's manuscript is not dated, it is not difficult to approximate when it was written based on the chronology of the Harvard lectures. Stravinsky

---

XXXI. Misspelled as "problême" in the original French. —Trans.
XXXII. The handwritten number Roman numeral "III" is on the top right-hand corner of this page.
XXXIII. Misspelled as "citoien" in the original French. —Trans.
XXXIV. Alexander Kastalsky (1856–1926), Russian composer, choirmaster, and folklorist.
XXXV. Occasionally Suvchinsky writes a French word in the Cyrillic alphabet, as he does here with *dégradation*.
XXXVI. Dictionary (French).
XXXVII. 1st Symph. of Brahms.
XXXVIII. 4th Symph. of Beethoven.

received the commission from Harvard on 23 March 1939 and welcomed Suvchinsky alone at Sancellemoz a few days later; he cabled his acceptance to Harvard on 11 April.[26] Assuming Stravinsky asked Suvchinsky to create an outline for the lectures when he met him in Sancellemoz, I conclude that Suvchinsky's manuscript must date from around the middle of April 1939.[27]

How can we be sure that Stravinsky did not dictate this document to Suvchinsky? A number of clues lead us to reject this hypothesis, and to accord Suvchinsky full-fledged paternity for this manuscript in terms of both form and content. The first clue is that a manuscript in Stravinsky's hand already exists; the second is that this manuscript contains many ideas that Suvchinsky presented elsewhere in the fifteen years before he began working on the *Poétique*, and that are known to be his.[28] Many of these ideas found their way into the published version of the *Poétique* in almost identical wording. A comparison between Suvchinsky's manuscript and the published work reveals that Suvchinsky in his outline established the lectures' overall structure, creating the coherent foundation upon which they were built.

English Translation of the Diplomatic Edition of Stravinsky's Manuscript

The study of the genesis of the *Poétique musicale* becomes more complicated if we take into account the second source on our list above, Stravinsky's manuscript, which consists of nineteen pages of an outline with some text that closely matches Suvchinsky's manuscript in content.[29] These autograph pages are the only known physical evidence of Stravinsky's involvement in the writing of the lectures. Robert Craft transcribed and commented on them, and at the time assumed that they represented a significant point of departure for the writing of the *Poétique*.[30] The discovery of Suvchinsky's outline changes the status of this manuscript, which no longer appears as a starting point, but rather as nothing more than a copy of Suvchinsky's work. Given the many errors in Craft's transcription, the document is presented here in a new translation of the complete original French version.

[*on the verso of an envelope*]
and I am proud of it [*6 illegible Russian words*]

I am very happy to be giving my lectures at this university that etc. I want above all to thank the committee (или кто другой[xxxix]) for the initiative they showed in entrusting this lecture series to me.
Ladies and gentlemen, I will furthermore not hide my delight in being able to speak before you, above all [*sentence cut off here*]

---

xxxix. or somebody else.

[*folio 1*]^{XL}
2nd part of the 1st lesson
~~Polemic:~~ 1st lecture
I am obliged to polemicize <u>primo</u> because of the said reversal and displacement
of things in music and segundo for a reason that seems personal at first glance
~~but~~ and is in fact not.
It's that my musical biography and my work, by a twist of chance^{XLI} that I am
willing to consider a happy chance, had [*sic*] been given^{XLII} from the beginning of
my career the qualities of being "reactive." This [quality of being] "reactive,"^{XLIII}
entering [into contact] with ~~all the ideas and they~~ the musical reality that surrounds me, with the milieu of people and ideas, produced reactions as violent
as they were mismanaged. One would think they picked the wrong person. But,
grave matters that they are,

[*folio 2*]
these false reactions demonstrated the vice residing in all musical consciousness thanks
to which all ideas, theses, judgments and opinions concerning music as art and as one
of the principal faculties of the human mind were distorted.^{XLIV} We must not forget
that at the time when <u>Petrouchka</u>, <u>Le Sacre du Pr.</u>, and <u>Le Rossignol</u> appeared many
things changed. Things did not change on the level of aesthetics or ~~simply~~ mode of
expression (this change took place at a time before I began my activities). The change
of which I speak happened immediately in tandem with a ~~fundamental~~ general revision of the foundations and primary elements of musical art.

[*folio 3*]
This revision sketched out^{XLV} in the era I am speaking to you about continues its
uninterrupted development—something I ~~could~~ observe and that proves itself in the
chain of concrete facts and the events of musical life to which we are all witnesses.
  – I know very well that there is a point of view…. <u>revolution at the time of the</u>
    <u>"Sacre"</u> and assimilation of revolutionary conquests^{XLVI} now ——
  – this is false.^{XLVII}

XL. Numbering here matches Stravinsky's and the order of presentation in the file is preserved by
the Paul Sacher Stiftung.
XLI. Stravinsky conflates *caprice du destin* (twist of fate) and *hasard* (chance) in the expression "caprice
de hasard."
XLII. The grammatical error is present in the French: "C'est que ma biographie musicale et mon
oeuvre, . . . a reçu dès le début de ma carrière les qualités d'un 'réactif.'" —Trans.
XLIII. "réactif" in French. —Trans.
XLIV. *Faussés* misspelled as "fausé" in the original French. —Trans.
XLV. "Esquisse" in the original; Roland-Manuel corrects as "esquissée." —Trans.
XLVI. "conquêtes révolutionnaire" in the original. —Trans. Stravinsky brackets this sentence in the
left-hand margin.
XLVII. Stravinsky brackets this sentence with the next one in the left-hand margin.

— My course will be polemical—I am not afraid to admit it.[XLVIII] Not to defend myself, me, but to defend here verbally music and its principles just as I defend them through my musical compositions.[XLIX]

[*folio 4*]
— Now allow me to present to you the manner in which I will structure my course. It will be divided into eight lessons and I am keen that each have a title. I will name them right away
The 1st that I am in the process of conveying to you now is nothing more than a "getting acquainted."[L]
The 2nd
The 3rd etc….

— As you see, this "Explication" of music that I am tackling before you and with you, I hope, ~~that is to say with your interest for the material in question that I have the right to presume~~ will take the form of a system, a synthesis of perspectives beginning with an analysis of the phenomenon of music and finishing with the problem of the performance of

[*folio 5*]
music. ~~Don't think that~~ I warn you that I did not choose the most common method for this kind of undertaking ~~that is to say~~ which consists of developing a thesis departing from the general and leading to the particular (detail?) Quite the opposite. I will follow the method of "synchronization," that is to say I will speak simultaneously about the general and the detail[LI] always supporting one by the other. For it is necessary to realize that it is only by virtue of practical necessity that we are obliged to distinguish (to discern)[LII] things by placing them in purely conventional categories,[LIII]

[*folio 6*]
such as primary, secondary, principal—subordinate, etc[LIV]

XLVIII. Stravinsky originally wrote "pas peur de l'avouer" (not afraid to admit it) but Roland-Manuel added "Je n'ai" (I am) at the beginning of this sentence to make it more grammatically correct. —Trans.

XLIX. Stravinsky wrote "autant que je defends" but crossed out "defends" and replaced it with "le fais" to create the clause "autant que je le fais par mes compositions musicales." —Trans.

L. Stravinsky wrote "La 1ère qui vient de se passée," but somebody scribbled slightly illegible notes trying to figure out what he was saying. It appears he was trying to say that the first chapter was in the process of being written. —Trans.

LI. Stravinsky writes question marks over the original French for both "general" and "detail."

LII. Stravinsky circles this word and puts a question mark over it.

LIII. Misspelled as "cathegories" in the original French. —Trans.

LIV. Stravinsky puts an arrow between this line and the next.

(of Главный [principal] and of Второстепенный [secondary]).^{LV} The true hierarchy of phenomena and things and also of the relationships among things ~~is built and conceived totally differently~~ is incarnated, takes shape on an entirely different plane.^{LVI} And I harbor the hope and it is very desired by me that ~~this will be clear to you~~ clarification of this thesis will be one of the outcomes of my course.

[*unnumbered folio, recto*]

2nd lesson

a) the ph. of music   b) the musical work

   a) The phenomenon of music
What is not music: sound, noises, even birdsong. What is music is sounds organized as man's conscious action.^{LVII}
— I admit to not having much taste for problems of "origins" and prehistory. This excursion into the depths and darkness of the past that claims to have the qualities of a precise science and too often, alas, is nothing more than an interpretation of little-known facts, an interpretation that has its origins in clearly preconceived ideas and viewpoints. Example: I am a materialist, so long live Darwinism and consequently I seek the monkey in question before the man
— Formulate music's origins in magic, incantation, etc
[*in the margin, circled in red pencil and marked* "for me":] NB: talk about the fact in music. Не забыть коду 4-ой симф Чайковского^{LVIII}

[*verso*]
— Personally, I am beginning to interest myself in the phenomenon of music as it emanates from the whole man, that is to say a man armed with all the resources of our senses, psychic faculties and intellectual means.
— I declare above all that the phenomenon of music is a phenomenon of speculation (see my interview with Moreux).^{LIX} A speculation that is shaped by elements of sound and time.

LV. There is an "X" next to this sentence in the left-hand margin.
LVI. The sentence "is incarnated, takes shape on an entirely different plane" is written at the bottom of the page, and circled, with an arrow leading to it.
LVII. In the first typed transcription of this page (508, PSS), somebody had modified this by hand in French to read "What is not yet music: sound, noises, even birdsong. What becomes music. . ."
LVIII. Don't forget the coda of Tchaikovsky's 4th Symphony.
LIX. "Interview avec Serge Moreux de *L'Intransigeant* pour la radiodiffusion, Paris, 28 December 1938," in French, in Eric White, *Stravinsky: The Composer and His Works* (Berkeley: University of California Press, 1985), 585–87; typescripts in microfilm 118.1, 185–94, PSS.

– The Khronos.LX [Problem of movement and time. Совместное рассмотрение элементов муз(ыкального) времени и движения представляет собою вопрос о Lento и Presto в музыке]LXI
– The dialectic of the creative process in music. The principle of contrast and similitude in musical creation: my attitude regarding "variety" and "similitude" (polychromy, monochromy)
– Active and passive meditation in music (author-listener)LXII
– Musical emotion (interview)
– The limits of the art of music: pure music and descriptive music. I talk about works and I give examples in lesson 4)

[*unnumbered page, recto*]
2) b) The musical work
   (Elements—from which is made and morphology)
d) melos, melody, theme, motive + phrase, period, development = recapitulation. LXIII

—quote examples: Sonatas,
                          Cantata,
                                    etc.....
        don't forget Variations.
a) scaleLXIV
b) interval, chordLXV
e) harmony, polyphony
c) mode, tonalityLXVI
f) modulation
g) movement (or tempo), meter, rhythm
h) sonority: pitch, register, timbre
i) the instrument producing the sounds and the human voice

LX. Roland-Manuel spells this "Chronos" in the first typed transcription of this page (508, PSS).
LXI. Stravinsky adds this sentence in Russian by hand to the first typed transcription of this page. Translation: A simultaneous examination of musical time and movement represents the question of LENTO and PRESTO in music (508, PSS).
LXII. On the first typed transcription of this page, Roland-Manuel writes in French "speak about creative receptivity." At the bottom of this same page Stravinsky adds in French, "Meditate: to reflect profoundly on this or that" (509, PSS).
LXIII. Stravinsky's "+phrase, period, development=recapitulation" is an addendum tacked on at the bottom of the page, with an arrow indicating it belongs with point (d) here. The section from "—quote examples" to "Variations" is written on the verso of this unnumbered page as a continuation of the addendum.
LXIV. In French, "l'échelle sonore."
LXV. Roland-Manuel added "consonance-dissonance" by hand in French on the first typed transcription of this page (510, PSS).
LXVI. Roland-Manuel added "cadences" by hand in French on the first typed transcription of this page (510, PSS).

The human voice

The word and its syllable. Intonation (don't forget <u>accent,</u> that is to say strong beat, weak beat but not dynamic element).

j) Schema, form, system (coexistence of different forms in a mechanical or organic unity).

[*Roland-Manuel's two typescripts of the previous two unnumbered folios, starting with "2ⁿᵈ lesson," follow here*]

[*on the verso of an envelope*]

There are 2 attitudes of the musician toward speech[LXVII] put into music. One is that in which the musician finds in speech only sound material adequate to musical expression, the other is that in which the musician seeks to create the song out of it, plainchant,[LXVIII] music that was notated with neumes.[LXIX] The 1ˢᵗ case produces *Lieder* and *romances* as a type, the 2ⁿᵈ *chansons*. One is passive. ~~where the music is determined~~ The meaning of the music is determined by speech and speech's meaning in itself. The other is active; music monopolizes speech, which it uses solely as sound material without taking into account its meaning.

[*unnumbered page recto; blank verso*]

3) <u>The musical métier</u>

or rather <u>"On musical composition"</u>

The composition of a work: that is to say that the work is a <u>piece that is composed</u>.[LXX] <u>The composer</u> (reproach in the pejorative sense). See my interview, with Moreux (artist, artisan, etc.)

<u>Invention; imagination (Отсебятина),</u>[LXXI] <u>intellectual imagination</u>. (Я в процессе творчества и этот процесс в какой-то момент начинает идти по инерции.)[LXXII]

One can only speak of oneself. Сведя многочисл(енные) свидетельства в одно можно вывести некий закон творч(еского) процесса.[LXXIII]

LXVII. "la parole" in the original.

LXVIII. Misspelled as "plein-chant" in the original French here and below. —Trans.

LXIX. Neumes are an early form of musical notation. The original sentence ends with "cherche en" (seeks out of it). Stravinsky scribbles a possible continuation of the sentence sideways across the envelope. This text is hard to decipher and order. It reads "donne le chant, le plein-chant [*sic*] musique qui était note [*sic*] par les neumes. Le 1ᵉʳ cas donne les <u>Liders</u> [*sic*] des <u>romances</u> comme type. Le 2d les <u>chansons</u>."

LXX. The original French: "est une pièce qui se compose."

LXXI. what comes from oneself.

LXXII. I am in the process of creation and at some point this process begins to function through inertia.

LXXIII. Synthesizing numerous accounts into one makes it possible to deduce a certain law of the creative process. Stravinsky added this comment in the left-hand margin, circled it, and attached it to text with arrows.

The deliberate and the unexpected of the creative process. Я задумал что-то и в процессе работы пришел вдруг к неожиданному, что не надо путать с отсебятиной.[LXXIV]

Composition,[LXXV] the design or plan of a composition[LXXVI] (tight or flowing:[LXXVII] easy schemas of sequences, padding, Wagner, etc.)

Inspiration

Culture and taste. The culture of taste. One seeks good taste, imposes it upon oneself[LXXVIII] (breeding)[LXXIX] and upon others. It is culture and tradition.

— Order and disorder

    As <u>a rule</u>

    As <u>laws</u>   exterior order

                 interior order[LXXX]

— The kingdom of necessity and the kingdom of freedom. Диалектика такова: снобы думают, что искусство синоним своб(одного) творч(ества). Это неверно. Искусство тем свободнее чем оно ограниченнее и закономернее и каноничнее и догматичнее.[LXXXI]

[*Folio 1*]

4) <u>Musical typology (that we notice by looking back through history)</u> supposes a work of choosing that presumes a certain method of discernment. Choose, distinguish, compare, appreciate.

By doing synoptic, synchronic and parallel analyses, we arrive directly at the problem[LXXXII] of <u>style</u>, which is a thing difficult if not impossible to define, as well as at questions about the <u>history</u> of music. This brings us to the problem of the <u>continuous and the discontinuous</u>.

    <u>cycles</u>—period with a precise beginning and end

    <u>current</u>—it's the opposite, duration without limits, without end.[LXXXIII]

LXXIV. "I conceived something and in the process of working I arrived suddenly at the unexpected, which must not be confused with that which comes from oneself (imagination)."

LXXV. In French, "L'écriture" —Trans.

LXXVI. In French, "La Facture musicale" —Trans.

LXXVII. In Stravinsky's French, "serré ou de l'eau" —Trans.

LXXVIII. The original French grammar is doubtful here: "on le s'impose et on l'impose aux autres." This sentence is circled in the original. —Trans.

LXXIX. The word "l'élévage" (breeding) is added in brackets above "le s'impose."

LXXX. "Comme <u>règle</u>" and "<u>lois</u> ordre and exterior, interior" was added as an addendum at the bottom of the page and linked to the subheading "L'ordre et le désordre" by an arrow. The word "ordre" is circled.

LXXXI. The dialectic is as such: snobs think that art is synonymous with free creation. This is incorrect. The more limited, the more ruled by canonical and dogmatic laws, the more free art is.

LXXXII. Stravinsky originally wrote the grammatically incorrect "aux problème." —Trans.

LXXXIII. The two lines here about "cycles" and "current" are added as an addendum on the left margin of the page.

Revolutions and evolution in history. The determinate and the indeterminate. Chance (miracle) and Genesis (causal relationship):[LXXXIV] Haydn—Mozart—a shared genesis and yet each has his own miracle. A phenomenon that is simultaneously determined and indeterminate.[LXXXV] Before speaking about rather arbitrary classifications like, for ex., classicism and romanticism, I would like to set out the thesis to which all phenomenon of any art submits. This is the thesis of the subordinate and insubordinate[LXXXVI]— in Russian подчиняющийся и самочинный

Cite the Sophocles (from the interview).[LXXXVII]

[*Folio 2*]
— Insubordination asks of music things that are beyond its competence
— principle of illustration, imitation (leitmotif, abstract idea: theme of fate, of vengeance) etc. Example

negative: Wagner—Strauss (follower) Symph domestica[LXXXVIII]
positive: Beethoven Symph. pastorale[LXXXIX] | gesetzmässig[XC]
       Verdi   Storm — Rigoletto |

From this perspective resume the conversation on classicism and romanticism. For example a slow movement in Papa Haydn and in Chopin. And on the other hand, see the difference between two romantic [*sic*], that same Chopin and Weber. Discuss
— Schumann and Brahms.
On banality and platitude. Don't confuse specimens of this genre with diverse forms of lyric and even sentimental expression of yesteryear that have become anachronistic. Example of the music of Tchaikovsky, Gounod, etc.

[*Folio 3*][XCI]
— Now two words on the subject of "modernism" and "academicism"
— First of all what a failure of a word "modernism" is

LXXXIV. The words "miracle" and "rapport causal" (causal relationship) are written in brackets below "Le hasard" (chance) and "Genèse" (Genesis).

LXXXV. Stravinsky circles this sentence in the original.

LXXXVI. In French, "soumis" and "insoumis" —Trans.

LXXXVII. Stravinsky is referring to his discussion of Sophocles' *Antigone* in "Interview avec Serge Moreux de *L'Intransigeant* pour la radiodiffusion, Paris, 28 December 1938."

LXXXVIII. Strauss's *Sinfonica Domestica*.

LXXXIX. Beethoven's Symphony no. 6 in F Major, op. 68 (*Pastoral*).

XC. The word is in German in the original and would translate as "legitimate" here.

XCI. This page has a "4)" in the upper left-hand corner, and a "-3-" in the upper right-hand corner, the latter in Stravinsky's hand.

— The two "<u>academicisms</u>," I have nothing against good academicism, which—
 not laying claim to anything—cannot bother anybody, its (pedagogical?)
 role[XCII] consisting of doing service by preserving values etc.

— I am not modernist. People have always taken me for what I am not. I am not
 revolutionary. I am not conservative. (<u>Pulcinella</u>),[XCIII] I situate myself in the
 element of evolution.

[*Folio 4*][XCIV]
— Music in a historical framework. Of course music reflects all the historical
 conjuncture that surrounds it (the spirit of the historical period = example of
 the difference in spirit of eras like that of Bach—<u>Beethoven</u>—Chopin (try to
 find letters of the three).

The Patron	Obviously I cannot give a music history class and
The public	illustrate for you with anecdotes all the situations[XCV]
Snobbery	in which different authors found themselves but
The bourgeois spirit.	allow [me] to broach a few questions I consider
	interesting and topical.[XCVI]

— Beethoven hates Napoleon, resembles him a lot. —Napoleon had never heard
 of him.

[*Unnumbered folio, recto*]
5) <u>Russian music</u>
Почему я вдруг заговорил именно о русск муз(ыке) Не потому что
я русский или что я ее особ(енно) ценю по сравнению с другими
музыками. Так же не думайте что я враждебен к проявлению
национ (ального) . . . начала разумеется поскольку такое проявление
бессознательно.[XCVII]
I do not claim to be a citizen of the world as the nineteenth-century Russian
revo- lutionaries liked to say.

XCII. Stravinsky added the word "pédagogique" (pedagogic) with a question mark and opening but
not closing bracket underneath the word "rôle" and then circled both words together.
XCIII. Stravinsky omits punctuation here. The title *Pulcinella* is written in brackets under the word
"conservateur" (conservative) and both are circled together.
XCIV. Stravinsky numbers this page "-4" in the upper right-hand corner.
XCV. Misspelled as "cituations" in the original French. —Trans.
XCVI. Stravinsky wrote the text on the right-hand side of the page and than drew an arrow from it
to the bracketed list on the left-hand side (starting with "The Patron"), to indicate it should follow.
This list on the left-hand side consists of the questions he has just described as "interesting and
topical."
XCVII. Why have I suddenly started talking about Russian music, not because I am Russian or
because I particularly value it in relation to other music. Similarly, do not think I am hostile to
the appearance of a national beginning, that goes without saying insofar as such an appearance is
unconscious.

Folklore and musical culture. Plainchant, sacred and profane music. Italianisms, Germanisms and the Orientalisms of nineteenth-century Russian music. The complexity of Russian culture. The two Russias (the revolution and Russian conservatism—the two disorders). <u>Glinka, Tchaikovsky</u>.

[*Unnumbered folio, verso*]
order, <u>Scriabine</u>, disorder (religious, political, ideological, psychological and musical), Mousorgski[XCVIII]—between the two.
The new Soviet, Ukrainian, Georgian, Armenian, Azerbaijani etc. folklorism and the <u>degradation of values</u>.

[*Unnumbered folio, recto*]
6) <u>On performance</u>[XCIX]
  1) music is <u>written</u> and 2) <u>performed</u>[C]

Simultaneous[CI] <u>nothingness and reality</u> of a musical work. Music exists as long as it sounds. Exists again as long as it reverberates.[CII] Between these two moments, music does not exist (a painting or a sculpture exists)
Interpretation—performance
Performers, listeners and the public. Presence and absence in the face of music: the public's activity and passivity in the face of music.
The problem of music criticism its aberrations[CIII] and classical distractions (Klassische Kritiken—anfragen Strecker).[CIV]
And now it's the <u>epilogue</u>.[CV]

[*verso*]
— The true meaning of music. Like all of man's creative faculties it is a search for unity, communion, union with one's neighbor and with Being (бытие). creative Monism.
[*Roland-Manuel's typescript of the recto and verso of this page on performance follows here.*]

XCVIII. Alexander Scriabin and Modest Musorgsky.
XCIX. "De l'exécution" in original French. —Trans.
C. This line appears in the left-hand margin.
CI. Stravinsky first writes "au meme [*sic*] temps" (at the same time) and then crosses that out and writes "simultanés" (simultaneous).
CII. The wordplay here of "existe—réexiste/sonne—resonne" (exist—reexist/sound—resound) is lost in a proper English translation. —Trans.
CIII. Misspelled as "abbérations" in the original French. —Trans.
CIV. "Classic criticisms—inquire Strecker." Willi Strecker (1884–1951) was Stravinsky's publisher and director of the Schott publishing house. In the typescript of this page, Roland-Manuel changes this line to "Classical criticisms to ask Strecker about" ("Klassische Kritiken à demander à Strecker"). An unidentified journal article titled "Klassische Kritiken" and consisting of critical responses to Wagner and Beethoven, is on microfilm 117.1, 493, PSS.
CV. Misspelled as "épylogue" in the original French. —Trans.

Craft states that none of Stravinsky's 1500-word manuscript was used in the published *Poétique musicale*.[31] This assertion is inaccurate. In fact, Stravinsky's manuscript consists of 1) six pages of material that served as the basis for two substantial sections of the first chapter, "Getting Acquainted"; and 2) a twelve-page revised version of Suvchinsky's outline with adjustments and elaborations. Roland-Manuel reviewed and corrected Stravinsky's French in his typed transcription of the first six pages of this manuscript and then used this to write "Getting Acquainted."[32] As Suvchinsky's outline does not include the idea of an introduction, this part of the manuscript must have been Stravinsky's idea. But after having prepared the first six pages as a draft of an introduction, Stravinsky then relied entirely on Suvchinsky's work. At the outset of his notes, Stravinsky announces eight lessons, establishing a direct link with Suvchinsky's outline in eight parts. But he tacitly retracts the number eight in the pages that follow and in the end presents a sketch of the work structured in six lessons. The reason for this change can be clarified in a letter from Stravinsky to Edward Forbes, chairman of the Harvard committee, dated 3 June 1939, in which Stravinsky insists on limiting the number of conferences—initially eight—to six due to a question of time management: he was planning a series of concerts in America for the end of the season.[33]

Comparison of the Three Versions of the General Outline

A comparison between Suvchinsky's and Stravinsky's outlines and the chapter outline of Harvard University Press's first published edition (1942) of the *Poétique musicale* in French clearly demonstrates that Suvchinsky's outline must have come first and that the definitive version of the work remained relatively close to Suvchinsky's initial conception. This conclusion counters that of Robert Craft, who argued that "Suvchinsky's roles were that of adviser on the state of music in the USSR and that of translator of the Russian words and phrases in Stravinsky's notes."[34] The chart below shows how the book developed from Suvchinsky's original outline through Stravinsky's to the final product. Stravinsky incorporated Suvchinsky's original stand-alone lesson on "The Work of Music" into the first lesson, which Roland-Manuel ultimately titled "On the Phenomenon of Music." Roland-Manuel or somebody else also replaced "Musical Métier" with "Composition of Music" for lesson 3. Stravinsky combined two chapters that were initially separate, "Musical Typology" and "Looking Back through History," to create chapter 4. Finally, the two chapters devoted to Russian music became just one.

SUVCHINSKY'S MANUSCRIPT (3 SHEETS)	STRAVINSKY'S MANUSCRIPT (19 SHEETS)	FIRST EDITION HARVARD 1942 (IN FRENCH)
Thesis for an Explication of Music in the Form of 8 Lessons	[untitled]	Poetics of Music in the Form of Six Lessons
	I. Getting Acquainted	I. Getting Acquainted
I. The Phenomenon of Music	II. a. The Phenomenon of Music	II. On the Phenomenon of Music
II. The Musical Work	II. b. The Musical Work	
III. The Musical Métier	III. The Musical Métier or, rather, On Musical Composition	III. On Musical Composition
IV. Musical Typology V. Looking Back through History	IV. Musical Typology (that we notice by looking back through history)	IV. Musical Typology
VI. and VII. Russian Music	V. Russian Music	V. The Avatars of Russian Music
VIII. On Performance	VI. On Performance	VI. On Performance
	Epilogue	Epilogue

A comparative analysis of Suvchinsky's and Stravinsky's manuscripts shows that Stravinsky integrated almost all of Suvchinsky's outline into his own and then made additions to it.[35] Stravinsky commented upon his intent to give a "polemical" course and his claimed quality of being "reactive" (as opposed to revolutionary). He insisted on the terms "academicism" and "modernism"; on the opposition between sacred and profane; and on the examples of Haydn and Wagner. And he expressed a desire to incorporate into his work the notions of patronage, the public, snobbery, and the bourgeois spirit. Finally, Stravinsky provided commentary in his notes on the ideas Suvchinsky suggested, formulating a few snippets of text in the first person. Some of Stravinsky's words made their way into the published edition; clearly, Stravinsky's notes constituted the point of departure for his work with Roland-Manuel.

The chart above demonstrates that there were at least two significant stages in the genesis of the *Poétique musicale*: the written transfer of ideas from Suvchinsky to Stravinsky, and the written transfer of ideas from Stravinsky to Roland-Manuel. This is not to mention the possible verbal exchanges among the three collaborators for which there is no historical record, although the manuscripts give certain clues.

From Suvchinsky to Stravinsky

Comparing these two texts, and studying the passage from one to the other, places this enterprise squarely in the domain of intertextuality or, more precisely, in one of its branches: transtextuality. In theory, text B results from text A through an operation of transformation. Thus when confronted with a "hypotext" and a "hypertext," to use Gérard Genette's terminology, it is possible to observe the nature of the variants that lead from one to the other.[36] In the case of the *Poétique musicale*, imitation forms the basis for the transformation: Stravinsky first copied Suvchinsky's outline in its entirety, reorganizing and fleshing it out somewhat. Then he replaced certain terms, and rephrased, added to, modified, and expanded the text. At the same time he reduced the number of lessons to five, adding an introductory lesson to make six in all—and explained ideas that Suvchinsky had touched on only briefly. Here are four examples of the types of "transfers" that took place between Suvchinsky's outline (hypotext) and Stravinsky's (hypertext):

HYPOTEXT (SUVCHINSKY)	HYPERTEXT (STRAVINSKY)

1) Development
[Selection from the second lesson: The Phenomenon of Music]

True musical experience. . . . Musical speculation.	What is music is sounds organized as man's conscious action. . . . Personally, I am beginning to interest myself in the phenomenon of music as it emanates from the whole man, that is to say a man armed with all the resources of our senses, psychic faculties and intellectual means. I declare above all that the phenomenon of music is a phenomenon of speculation . . . A speculation formed that is shaped by the elements of sound and time.

2) Clarification and Deletion
[Selection from the second lesson: The Phenomenon of Music]

The limits of the art of music.	The limits of the art of music: pure music and descriptive music.
The crisis of the unity of conscience and concepts.	[idea abandoned by Stravinsky]

[Selection from the third lesson: The Musical Métier]

Order.	Order and disorder. As a <u>rule</u>/As <u>laws</u>—exterior order/interior order.

3) Extrapolation
[Selection from the fifth lesson: Russian Music]

The two Russias. The revolution and the Russian Reaction. The two "disorders."	The two Russias (the revolution and Russian conservatism—the two disorders). Glinka, Tchaikovsky, order; Scriabin, disorder (religious, political, ideological, psychological and musical). Mussorgsky—between the two.

4) Simplification
[Selection from On Performance]

The true meaning of music. The "self," the "non-self"—and Being—creative monism.	The true meaning of music. Like all of man's creative faculties it is a search for unity, communion, union with one's neighbor and with Being (бытие). creative Monism.

It is difficult not to make an analogy here between the manner in which Stravinsky appropriates Suvchinsky's concepts and his working method as a composer who reinvents music of the past. In the case of the *Poétique musicale*, however, the lender is listening to the borrower: Suvchinsky presented his theses to Stravinsky, who—while assimilating the theses and transcribing the concepts—brought them in line with his own point of view and then gave them back to his friend. Suvchinsky's hasty pencil annotations give evidence of the dialogue between the two men, and clearly represent clarifications requested by the composer. Stravinsky thus emerges as the authority in this text, becoming the author of something that at first did not belong to him. This is precisely what constitutes the hypertextual relationship here.

Is this a case of Stravinsky borrowing, adapting, reorganizing, or perhaps even usurping Suvchinsky's text? I would argue that the ontological foundations of this "transtextual transfer" are based on Suvchinsky's having suggested a series of points of view to Stravinsky for him to defend. The concepts Suvchinsky laid out in his outline are for the most part consistent with convictions he expressed in numerous articles published over the previous twenty years. Through the *Poétique*, he entrusted these ideas to Stravinsky, making sure they would suit him. Suvchinsky custom-tailored these ideas for Stravinsky by combining them with certain ideas more specific to the composer: critics, order, the opposition between interpreter and performer, ideas of academicism and modernism. For his part, Stravinsky uses the planned terms without hesitating to move slightly beyond his partner's rudimentary ideas (for example, when he extrapolates). The more I examine the situation, the more this seems to be a two-way exchange. The dialogue reflected in these manuscripts grows out of Suvchinsky's sense of collaboration, trust, and generosity with Stravinsky, who—strengthened by his friend's theses—offered the world his most important testimony on his concept of the art of music. The two-headed origin of the *Poétique musicale* explains its occasionally heterogeneous nature.

Roland-Manuel's Manuscripts

The archives of Roland-Manuel, in the possession of his son, Claude Roland-Manuel, contain a file important to the *Poétique*'s production. In 2000, when Myriam Soumagnac's new edition of the *Poétique musicale* was published, this file had been given to the Paul Sacher Foundation and become part of its Stravinsky collection. It contains Roland-Manuel's small notebook and drafts of the lessons.[37] Roland-Manuel used only the notebook's first six pages: the first three dated from November 1938 and the last three from February 1939. Soumagnac reproduced these six pages in the appendix of her edition, even though they relate somewhat problematically to the *Poétique*.[38] First, the notebook entries are explicitly dated from November 1938 and February 1939, before Stravinsky received the commission from Harvard to give the Norton lectures (which happened in March 1939), and before Stravinsky contacted Roland-Manuel about the *Poétique* that April. Second, Soumagnac incorrectly labels this document a "Conversation Book with Stravinsky," thereby implying that it contains the transcription of a continuous dialogue with the composer in preparation for the *Poétique*.[39] But the notebook obviously contains nothing more than notes Roland-Manuel took very carefully after a (likely unexpected) encounter with Stravinsky, probably in order not to forget several striking things he said. It is comparable in historic value to Stravinsky's published interviews in how it transmits ideas articulated by Stravinsky on the nature of musical expression, silence, his attachment to France, and other topics. But it played no part in the *Poétique*'s development, and definitely did not contribute to its genesis.

The various manuscripts in Roland-Manuel's hand that are of use in examining the origins of the *Poétique* are kept in a large file subdivided into six sub-folders corresponding to the six lessons, with the addition of a seventh sub-folder titled "Miscellany." Although the sheets are not numbered in continuous fashion, the whole folder adds up to nearly two hundred pages, several samples of which will be described below. Filing the sheets by lesson was not an ideal strategy on the part of whoever did it, because in the final stages of work, numerous passages were shuffled among the *Poétique*'s chapters. A deep familiarity with the materials is required to perceive what they can reveal about Stravinsky's and Roland-Manuel's exchanges at Sancellemoz in the spring of 1939. Thorough study reveals that there are two types of notes, which I designate here with the labels "note-taking" and "written-up notes."

Note-taking. Some pages of Roland-Manuel's notes display very rapid writing, rather disorganized subject matter, and unfinished words and sentences. Their general graphical presentation—for example, margins listing toward the right— makes it plain that Roland-Manuel was hastily taking notes. These sheets are nearly always crossed out with a large red diagonal line, perhaps indicating that Roland-Manuel used the ideas and content contained within them. At other times, he circled in red the parts he did not use.

[Roland-Manuel rough draft, folio no. 2, last paragraph]

You cannot[CVI] consciously[CVII] embrace

the creative phenomenon without

considering it in a certain form.

It's the process of logos.

don't consider it outside of a form

that manifests existence.

I expect the word dogma

to make you realize

That's why it in no way usurps its function

~~It's him that~~
~~will~~ [illegible]
follows
from the formalizing
process, not[CVIII]

establishes the principle

natural defense
mechanism[CIX]

Only Stravinsky and Roland-Manuel would be able to decode the chain of thought necessary to understand these notes. Without the context of their oral conversations, the notes remain partially incomprehensible. These are indeed "notes on conversations," the immediacy of which reveals that Roland-Manuel probably took them as mnemonic aids while listening to Stravinsky speak. The composer's presence is evident in the use of the first-person singular ("I expect"), which Roland-Manuel seems to transcribe directly, in a moment of enthusiasm, as if taking the words right out of Stravinsky's mouth. Roland-Manuel's process becomes quite evident when one compares the first person he used in his note-taking drafts with the impersonal tone of his finalized notes:[40]

ROLAND-MANUEL'S NOTE-TAKING	TEXT WRITTEN BY ROLAND-MANUEL
Distinction between natural and artificial benefits. I know it is not art that is sent to us from heaven through a bird's song, and I know there is art even in the simplest modulation.	For it is not art that falls from the heavens through a bird's song; rather, the simplest modulation, correctly executed, is already incontestably art.

CVI. Misspelled as "vous ne pouv" in the original French. —Trans.

CVII. Misspelled as "consciesment" in the original French. —Trans.

CVIII. Roland-Manuel appears to write the grammatically incorrect clause "découle du processus formalisantes pas." —Trans.

CIX. The boxed notes correspond to circled additions in the right margin in the original. The text given here takes up the bottom half of a full page of notes.

Some of Roland-Manuel's "note-taking" drafts are clearer than others, as in the example below. And yet even such a page as this one can hardly be considered a composed text; rather it remains an example of written-down speech, as is clear by the large number of truncated words, unintended repetitions, and errors in syntax and spelling it contains. Under any other writing conditions, Roland-Manuel would have had time to finish his words and correct the punctuation:

> But having arrived at this point it is no less necessary to obey not new idols but the eternal necessity to found ~~our~~ solidly our music and to ~~reco~~ yield to the need to ~~fix poles~~ recognize the existence of to recognize poles of attraction. Tonality is only one way of orienting music, the function of tonality seems to us subordinate to the function of attraction of the poles[cx]

> all music being made up of a series of surges and rests supposes an orientation toward a definite pole. in every specific case, this true for Gregorian cantilena as[cxi] for the music of Mozart—of Brahms or of Debussy. ~~There is~~ To this general law of attraction the traditional tonal system brings nothing more than a provisory solution <u>because there is no absolute value</u>.

This type of note-taking conjures up the image of someone rapidly transcribing a lecture given by Stravinsky. Indeed, in certain cases, it seems the composer's ideas were very definite before being passed along to Roland-Manuel. This was under no circumstances a meandering discussion, but rather a dictation of ideas Stravinsky wished to see included in the lessons.

Written-up Notes. Roland-Manuel's files also contain manuscript pages that are much more finalized. The handwriting of these pages is much more careful, their sentences complete; the organized whole makes sense and there are few grammatical or spelling errors. For his written-up notes, Roland-Manuel used different paper—larger, faintly lined sheets that he folded, or more often cut in two, to create pages similar in size to the ones he used for note-taking. The presence of these two paper types reveals what we already know, namely that there were two stages in his process, corresponding to Roland-Manuel's two trips to Sancellemoz: the first, in which Roland-Manuel wrote down what Stravinsky said; and the second, in which he read to Stravinsky the written-up drafts of their conversation, noting on them any additional observations from the composer (as is suggested by the numerous cross-outs and rephrasings they contain). This two-fold process

---

cx. Several spelling errors are present in the original French: "la fonction de la tonalité nous apparaît come [*sic*] subordonee [*sic*] à la fonction attractive des pôle [*sic*]." —Trans.
cxi. *Comme* misspelled as "comm" in the original French. —Trans.

allows readers to distinguish clearly between what Stravinsky originally said and what Roland-Manuel added later, as well as to realize how truly involved Roland-Manuel was in the project.

Despite the many modifications and annotations they contain, Roland-Manuel's written-up notes strongly resemble the final published version of the *Poétique musicale*. Except for minor changes in vocabulary and turns of phrase, the only larger differences are that several paragraphs have been shifted within or among lessons, and that ideas have been added. Roland-Manuel also took notes on the fly on the back of some of these pages, writing all over the place, cutting off sentences, and creating a chaotic order of thoughts as he tried to write down at the last minute what Stravinsky probably asked him to add.[41]

Roland-Manuel's written-up notes also contain certain sections in which he was clearly trying to put into prose what Stravinsky had listed in his original outline for the project. Here Roland-Manuel acted more as a transcriber than collaborator; even though the notes are in his hand, the content belongs to Stravinsky, as is evident in the following example:

[but I must warn you that this material is a bit serious
or don't be afraid of the specific gravity this material entails and requires][CXII]
Lesson III
The musical métier
[I feel all the responsibility]
. . .
I find myself in the process of creation and this process at some point is driven by inertia. . . .
The deliberate and the unexpected in the creative process: I have an idea and in the process of working I arrived at something unexpected (which is not to be confused with fantasy).
. . . The kingdom of necessity and the kingdom of liberty. The dialectic is the following. Everyone thinks art is synonymous with free creation, which is not quite right. Art is all the more free the more it is limited in the canonic and dogmatic legal order.[CXIII]

These notes give a fairly obvious impression of how Roland-Manuel and Stravinsky communicated: Stravinsky probably relied on his outline, developing ideas out loud from it for Roland-Manuel as they spoke. Stravinsky may have drafted another written document to help him gather his thoughts before meeting with Roland-Manuel, but there is no evidence to suggest this thesis and it offers

---

CXII. Bracketed notes in this example indicate words Roland-Manuel added later, in a second phase of writing.
CXIII. Stravinsky had originally written down these ideas in part in Russian in his outline.

no new perspective on their basic process. Roland-Manuel's written-up notes also give a clear impression of how Stravinsky positioned himself in the conversation. When Roland-Manuel writes down a sentence like "But I must warn you that this material is a bit serious or don't be afraid of the specific gravity this material entails and requires," he is already facing a man who has taken on the role of a lecturer. This proves yet again that it was Stravinsky who controlled the broad outlines of his lectures, even before he transmitted them to Roland-Manuel.

Commentary

Roland-Manuel's extended drafts and notes on the *Poétique musicale* reveals less his intervention in the project than the primacy of Stravinsky's spoken word; they give evidence of the composer's true contribution to the book he authored, in addition to the nineteen pages of outline he completed in written form. It becomes clear that Roland-Manuel's contribution is much less important than Myriam Soumagnac made it out to be, and that to say he "wrote" the *Poétique* is incorrect.[42] It is more precise to say that he took note of Stravinsky's ideas and gave them literary form. If Roland-Manuel also sometimes brought in philosophical, historical, and literary examples, perhaps most notably in reference to Aristotle and Jean Mounet-Sully, it was with the goal of improving the text's structure and readability, rather than because he wanted to express his own convictions, equivalent to those of Suvchinsky and Stravinsky, concerning the making, the *poiesis* of music. Roland-Manuel worked essentially at the level of form. He was an impressive editor who effaced himself in the service of conveying Stravinsky's speech as truthfully as possible and in its most direct, rough, and unadorned state. His greatest contribution to these lectures was to have formulated Stravinsky's concepts so faithfully, without unduly infusing the text with his own convictions.

The term "ghostwriter," which commentators use and abuse in referring to Stravinsky's *Poétique musicale*, implies a certain fraudulence. The imposter, in this case Stravinsky, whose signature shines on the cover of a book, is immediately tacitly accused of usurping, lacking talent, and of incompetence and hypocrisy. In the present case, as I have hoped to demonstrate in this essay, the truth lies elsewhere. The process can be summarized as follows: the *Poétique*'s first collaborator—Pyotr Suvchinsky—gave the text its structure, and inspired the ideas of its "sponsor"—Igor Stravinsky. He probably discussed his outline with Stravinsky, leading the latter to draft his own outline, in which Stravinsky developed Suvchinsky's ideas and transmitted them to an editor, a secretary—Roland-Manuel—who offered his informed opinions while putting the manuscript into shape. As I mentioned earlier, Roland-Manuel then presented the lessons to Suvchinsky, who made potential modifications before the final text was sent back to Stravinsky. In conclusion, I argue that although Suvchinsky dominated the entire working process and was responsible for the *Poétique*'s structure and fundamental ideas, the final work expresses Stravinsky's wishes, and can be considered a fully authoritative work of the composer.

NOTES

An extended version of this article was previously published in French as *"Poétique musicale:* Miroir des échanges dialectiques—genèse du texte et emprunts conceptuels," in Valérie Dufour, *Stravinski et ses exégètes (1910–1940)* (Brussels: Editions de l'Université de Bruxelles, 2006), 213–44.

1. Igor Stravinsky and Robert Craft, *Themes and Conclusions* (London: Faber & Faber, 1971), 49.

2. Robert Craft, "Roland-Manuel and the *Poetics of Music," Perspectives of New Music* 21/1–2 (Autumn 1982–Summer 1983): 487–505; repr. as "Roland-Manuel and *La Poétique musicale,"* in *Stravinsky: Selected Correspondence,* ed. Robert Craft (London: Faber & Faber, 1984), 2:503–17. In this essay citations are from the former source. Suvchinsky gives a sense of the real divergence of his and Craft's views on Stravinsky, in "(Notice autobiographique inédite écrite en 1982)," in *(Re)Lire Souvtchinski: Textes choisis par Eric Humbertclaude* (Paris: Efflorescence, 1990), 8.

3. Myriam Soumagnac, foreword to Igor Stravinsky, *Poétique musicale,* ed. Myriam Soumagnac (Paris: Flammarion, 2000), 9.

4. Soumagnac, preface in ibid., 38–39. Suvchinsky explained to Stravinsky in a letter dated 23 May 1939: "I am sending you the text of the fifth part rather than the materials. I decided to articulate and elaborate them to make things easier for you." Suvchinsky to Stravinsky, 23 May 1939, in *I. F. Stravinskiy: Perepiska s russkimi korrespondentami. Materialï k biografii,* ed. Viktor Varunts (Moscow: Kompozitor, 2003), 3:676–77 (hereafter *SPRK*).

5. See especially Felix Meyer's summary in *Settling New Scores: Music Manuscripts from the Paul Sacher Foundation* (Mainz: Schott, 1998), 134n67. See also Heinz Werner Zimmermann, "Igor Strawinsky— Verfasser seiner *Musikalischen Poetik?* Zur Entstehung seiner Schriften," *Neue Zeitschrift für Musik* 1467–68 (1985): 17–25.

6. In the biographical note he wrote about Suvchinsky as a foreword to his composition *Sonate Souvtchinsky* (Paris: Salabert Editions, 1986), composer Gérard Masson assumes a collaboration: "It was in Berlin, 1922," he writes, "that the indestructible friendship between Stravinsky and Suvchinsky formed, a friendship that would lead in 1952 to Suvchinsky collaborating, on the composer's request, on the *Poetics of Music."* (Masson mistakes the date of the collaboration, which took place in 1939 and not in 1952, when the second French edition appeared.) In his article "Souvenirs d'un ami en commun: Pierre Souvtchinski," Claude Helffer briefly evokes Suvchinsky's journey to Sancellemoz to "write" the *Poétique* "with" Stravinsky, in *Musiques, Signes, Images: Liber amicorum François Lesure,* ed. Joël-Marie Fauquet (Geneva: Minkoff, 1988), 159–61.

7. See *SPRK,* vol. 3; and Alla Bretanitskaya, ed., *Pyotr Suvchinskiy i ego vremya* (Moscow: Izdatel' skoye ob'yedineniye, 1999).

8. Sancellemoz, a village in the Haute-Savoie region of France, was Stravinsky's place of retreat in 1938 and 1939.

9. Suvchinsky discusses the matter of payment in a letter to Stravinsky a few days later: "Roland-Manuel said, as was agreed upon, that you can give a total of 10,000 francs for all the preparatory work concerning the writing of the lectures, including traveling expenses, coming to Sancellemoz, the purchase of books, etc. After tallying up the expenses, there will be an amount left over that will be for the participants and that will be divided among them according to the amount of work each person does. You will see for yourself in a few days of collaborative work if Roland-Manuel is indeed a suitable fit or not. This circumstance will determine whether I participate or not in the project in the future. I personally think that Roland-Manuel will now definitely be able to manage on his own, and that is why I leave it entirely to you and him to decide if there will still be something or nothing for me beyond the 1,000 francs." Suvchinsky to Stravinsky, 29 April 1939, *SPRK,* 3:673.

10. Suvchinsky to Stravinsky, 26 April 1939, *SPRK,* 3:671.

11. Eric Humbertclaude provided me with a copy of this document, for which I am deeply grateful.

12. *SPRK,* 3:676–77.

13. Ibid., 3:680–81.

14. This manuscript is in the Collection Suzel Duval and is the property of Eric Humbertclaude. I published a facsimile of it in ibid., 387–90.

15. This manuscript is kept in microfilm 117.1, 497–507, Paul Sacher Stiftung (hereafter PSS). Craft provides an incomplete and very faulty English translation of this document in "Roland-Manuel and the *Poetics of Music*," 496–501.

16. These are kept in microfilm 257.1, "Dossier Roland-Manuel," 29–189, PSS. Myriam Soumagnac uses and discusses these documents in Stravinsky, *Poétique musicale*.

17. This manuscript is kept in the "Dossier Souvtchinsky," not on microfilm, PSS. Svetlana Savenko presented this document in "'Chudo Stravinskogo' dlitsya mnogiye desyatiletiya: Iz perepiski P. P. Suvchinskogo i I. F. Stravinskogo" (Stravinsky's wonder lasts many decades: P. P. Suvchinsky and I. F. Stravinsky's *Poetics of Music*) in Bretanitskaya, *Pyotr Suvchinskiy i ego vremya*, 259–72. Savenko does not mention that this text is the oldest version of the fifth lesson, which was subsequently largely reworked. The value of this original text comes from its status as the only surviving document in Russian linked to the production of the lectures.

18. The composer's youngest son, Soulima Stravinsky (1910–1998) was close to Suvchinsky during his father's stay at Sancellemoz. The subject of Soulima's mental state dominates the letters exchanged between Suvchinsky and Stravinsky in spring 1939. Suvchinsky discussed with Stravinsky the possibility of Soulima translating his Russian text in a letter dated 23 May 1939, *SPRK*, 3:676–78.

19. These are kept in microfilm 117.1, PSS.

20. An English summary of each lesson was also planned for those who attended the lecture and published by Alexis Kall in "Stravinsky in the Chair of Poetry," *The Musical Quarterly* 26/3 (1940): 283–96.

21. Igor Stravinsky, *Poétique musicale sous forme de six leçons* (Cambridge, MA: Harvard University Press, 1942). For an inventory of later editions of the *Poetics of Music*, see Soumagnac's preface to the *Poétique musicale*, 21–24. Concerning the text's reception, see Gianfranco Vinay, "'Pour' et 'contre' Stravinski: La réception de la *Poétique musicale* en France et en Allemagne après la deuxième guerre mondiale," in *La Musique depuis 1945: Matériaux, esthétique et perception*, ed. Hugues Dufourt and Joël-Marie Fauquet (Sprimont: Mardaga, 1996), 195–210.

22. This section is based on my article "La *Poétique musicale* de Stravinsky: Un manuscrit inédit de Souvtchinsky," *Revue de musicologie* 89/2 (2003): 373–92.

23. This document is reproduced in Dufour, "La *Poétique musicale* de Stravinsky: Un manuscrit inédit de Souvtchinsky," 391–92.

24. On this topic, see Alain Le Boulluec's summary of Clement of Alexandria in *Histoire du christianisme*, ed. Luce Pietri (Paris: Desclée, 2000), 1:536–39.

25. Pyotr Suvchinsky, "Igor Strawinsky," *Contrepoints* 2 (February 1946): 20–21.

26. See Myriam Soumagnac's introduction in Stravinsky, *Poétique musicale*, 19; and Christian Goubault, *Igor Stravinsky* (Paris, Champion, 1991), 88.

27. See Suvchinsky to Stravinsky, 26 April 1939, *SPRK*, 3:671.

28. See Dufour, *Stravinski et ses exégètes*.

29. This document is kept in microfilm 117.1, PSS, and includes a note on reverse of an envelope (497); folios 1–6 (498–503); 2 unnumbered folios (504–7); Roland-Manuel's typescript of pages 504–7 (508–10); second typescript of pages 504–7 (511–13); envelope (514–15); unnumbered folio (516); 4 numbered folios (517–20); 2 unnumbered folios (521–24); and a typed transcription of pages 523–24 (525). Somebody, probably Roland-Manuel, regularly transcribed some of Stravinsky's words in more legible writing above his original text in the manuscript pages included here.

30. Craft, "Roland-Manuel and the *Poetics of Music*," 496–501.

31. Ibid., 487.

32. In Soumagnac's edition of the *Poétique* in French, the two sections in question appear on pages 67–68 ("So I am obliged to be polemical" to "A revolution whose conquests are said to be in the process of assimilation today") and on pages 74–75 ("As you see, this *explanation*" to "one of the results of my course, a result I greatly desire"). In Stravinsky's manuscript these two sections are connected by two small paragraphs, also used by Roland-Manuel, found on page 72 ("Therefore, I

am going to be polemical" to ". . . each of which I want to have a separate title"). For the English version of these passages see Igor Stravinsky, *Poetics of Music in the Form of Six Lessons*, trans. Arthur Knodel and Ingolf Dahl (Cambridge, MA: Harvard University Press, 1947), 8–9, 18–19, 15.

33. See Stravinsky to Edward Forbes, *ex officio* chairman of the committee for the Charles Eliot Norton Chair of Poetry, 3 June 1939, summarized in Craft, "Roland-Manuel and the *Poetics of Music*," 493.

34. See Craft, "Roland-Manuel and the *Poetics of Music*," 489.

35. The two friends must have talked, since in almost every case Stravinsky's additions are identical to the notes Suvchinsky added in pencil to his own outline.

36. Gérard Genette, *Palimpsestes: La littérature au second degré* (1982; repr., Paris: Seuil, 1992), 16. A portion of the following analysis was previously published in Valérie Dufour, "Strawinsky vers Souvtchinsky: Thèmes et variations sur la *Poétique musicale*," *Mitteilungen der Paul Sacher Stiftung* 17 (March 2004): 17–23.

37. These are kept in microfilm 257.1, "Dossier Roland-Manuel," PSS.

38. Soumagnac, "Annexe I," in Stravinsky, *Poétique musicale*, 159–62. This appendix contains an error in the pages' order, with the three pages dated November 1938 placed after those dated February 1939.

39. Soumagnac labels them *Cahier de conversations avec Stravinsky* in Stravinsky, *Poétique musicale*, app. 1. In the PSS, the notebook is simply labeled *Notizbuch*.

40. Stravinsky may be referring to the legend about Pope St. Gregory's invention of Gregorian chant here. See Stravinsky, *Poétique musicale*, 78; Ingolf Dahl and Arthur Knodel translated this passage as "For it is not art that rains down upon us in the song of a bird; but the simplest modulation correctly executed is already art, without any possible doubt." See *Poetics of Music*, 24.

41. For example, on the back of a page numbered 23 in folder 1, Roland-Manuel writes considerations linked to the word *cacophony*, a word present in the text on the page's front.

42. Soumagnac's comments in her introduction are handicapped by her unwavering belief that Roland-Manuel was Stravinsky's ghostwriter. She erroneously assumes, for example, that Roland-Manuel introduced Jacques Maritain's ideas into the text, when it is clear Stravinsky had known these texts since the early 1920s.

Stravinsky: The View from Russia

SVETLANA SAVENKO
TRANSLATED BY PHILIPP PENKA

In recent years Stravinsky has experienced something of a renaissance in Russia. Performances abound, scholarship is flourishing, and recently Natalia Braginskaya and Valérie Dufour formed the "Stravinsky Between East and West" study group of the International Musicological Society to broaden the dialogue. Such moments of expansive intellectual growth offer excellent opportunities for reflecting on the composer's lasting influence in his homeland, and on questions most pertinent to Russian scholars. How did Stravinsky shape compositional trends in Russia in the twentieth century? And in what way did he remain intellectually and musically rooted in Russian traditions? By briefly examining Stravinsky's reception in Russia, use of folklore, and aesthetic affinity with the Acmeist poets of St. Petersburg, I hope to show that he maintained a steadfast tie with his homeland throughout his life—a tie that explains the importance he continues to hold there today.

Stravinsky's Reception in Russia

Stravinsky's career began rather innocuously in Russia, as an "imitator" and devoted student of Nikolay Rimsky-Korsakov, and "fourth-generation Belyayevets."[1] His debut compositions, the Symphony in E-flat and *The Faun and the Shepherdess*, fit well within the concert repertoire of the time and within Russian concert traditions in general.[2] Yet, not entirely without reason, most critics found Stravinsky's devotion to his "elders" excessive. "The stylization, and his fear of moving away from the manner of his teacher, are apparent . . . he failed to go beyond slavish imitation," an anonymous reviewer commented after the Court Orchestra's premiere of the two works in 1908.[3] At the same concert, the influential critic Vyacheslav Karatygin applauded the "excellent technique and good knowledge of the orchestra," but singled out as the "main fault of the entire suite [*The Faun and the Shepherdess*] its lack of style."[4] This judgment is rather tantalizing in light of the composer's future development. Karatygin seems to assume that Stravinsky will follow the dignified, if entirely routine path of becoming a successor to the traditions of the Russian national school. Clearly he expected no more from him.

Stravinsky's life, and his career in Russia, changed dramatically after the Ballets Russes' spectacular premiere of *Firebird* in Paris on 25 June 1910. He had performed sections of the work on the piano at the offices of the journal *Apollon* in St. Petersburg on 10 April 1910, but Russian audiences received their first impression of its orchestral sound when Alexander Siloti conducted what is known as its first suite—a truncated version of the ballet—in St. Petersburg on 23 October 1910.[5] Stravinsky's newfound success in France did not mean that his music was universally acknowledged in Russia, however. Ever since the premiere of the *Scherzo fantastique* and *Feu d'artifice* in 1909, Russian critics had admired Stravinsky's richness of orchestral color, luxurious harmonies, and brilliant orchestral arrangements, yet they considered his talent to be one-sided and refused to admit his gift for melody and ability to invent striking thematic material. Everyone from superficial newspaper critics to sophisticated musicians who were positively predisposed toward Stravinsky's music expressed such concerns. "Even though this music is somewhat superficial in spite of all its brilliance," Karatygin wrote after hearing Siloti's performance of the truncated *Firebird* Suite in 1910, "would you not put it the other way around after listening to *Firebird*: that this music is brilliant despite a certain superficiality?[6] "What abundance of invention, what intelligence, temperament, talent, what a wonderful and rare work!" the symphonist Nikolay Myaskovsky wrote a year later about studying a score of the piano reduction of the full ballet. But no sooner had he uttered these words than he followed them with "it lacks originality . . . . the very essence of its musical material is not yet marked by a vividly expressed individuality."[7] Prokofiev reacted similary when he heard *Firebird* and *Petrushka* in London in 1914: "How dazzling the colors in the orchestra are, and how ingenious all those flourishes and grimaces; what a sincere ingenuity and how lively it all comes across! But I did not give in to the charm of the music for one minute. And what music! Nothing but rot. But it is so interesting that I will no doubt go again."[8]

In spite of reservations, there were signs that the tone of Russian criticism was changing in the years before the revolution, along with Stravinsky's music. "There is a new phenomenon—Stravinsky," Vladimir Derzhanovsky declared after the first all-Stravinsky concert in Russia, organized by the journal *Muzïka* in Moscow, 22 August 1912.[9] But Stravinsky's career in Russia also started to face tremendous difficulties. If no performances of his ballets took place before the revolution, few followed directly afterward. Listeners could not always acquaint themselves with Stravinsky's instrumental works either, and when they did, it was often years after the premieres had taken place in Western Europe. As a consequence, musical modernism—defined as it was in Europe in part by Stravinsky's successes in these years—unfolded somewhat differently in Russia than it did elsewhere.

The story of the *The Rite of Spring*'s reception in Russia is a case in point. Although as a ballet it was performed in the Soviet Union for the first time in 1965, as an orchestral piece the work had found its way into Russian concert halls much earlier. The reception of the music was not continually positive, however. When Serge Koussevitzky conducted the *Rite* for the first time on 5 February 1914 in Moscow, responses were muted. Vyacheslav Karatygin found its "polytonal chords" and other harmonic peculiarities of the score interesting, but also noted that it contained "certain unpleasant traits"—above all, monotony: "It seems to me that its historical, symptomatic significance nevertheless exceeds its artistic significance."[10] Prokofiev's response was equally ambivalent: "I listened to *The Rite of Spring* and listened with heightened attention. In any case, this work is lively and almost captivating. I was simply delighted by the 'Dance of the Earth.' But it is so shrill, and in some other, quieter places the music is so hopelessly false that you have to wonder if the talented and imaginative Stravinsky somehow has a screw loose. There were many listeners who applauded hard, but the majority was either at a loss or exchanged triumphantly derisive glances, as if saying, now this is the kind of filth the Futurists write."[11]

But reactions were dramatically different when Fritz Stiedry conducted the *Rite* to sold-out audiences in Leningrad and Moscow in 1926.[12] This time, *The Rite of Spring* met with exceptional success. Judging from the reviews, Stiedry and both Russian orchestras managed to convey the music to listeners in all its brilliance. "After the *Rite* the audience greeted Stiedry with unanimous ovations that were entirely deserved," Boris Asafyev wrote of the performance in Leningrad. "*The Rite of Spring* is now treated as a simple lapidary work created in a single sweep."[13] The Moscow critic Anton Uglov echoed his response: "The Viennese conductor Fritz Stiedry quickly and skillfully 'organized' the concert. And the delivery was wonderfully successful. . . . This work has not lost its rich relevance and contemporariness, and and must under no circumstances fade into the background."[14]

The impact of Stiedry's *Rite* was tremendous. Further performances followed, and a scholarly tradition around Stravinsky began to take shape.[15] All of this gave evidence of openness toward Stravinsky's works in the Soviet Union in these years. Vsevolod Meyerhold premiered *The Nightingale* at the Mariinsky Theatre on 30 May 1918; Leonid Leontiev modified Fokine's choreography for a performance of *Petrushka* in Petrograd in 1920; and famous tenor Ivan Yershov and pianist Mikhail Druskin—a future scholar of Stravinsky's work—performed a piano-vocal reduction of *Renard* in 1926.[16] One of the most talented Russian ballet masters, Fyodor Lopukhov, whose aesthetic explorations resonated with the pioneering work of another student who later attended the Petrograd Theatre School, George Balanchine, staged *Firebird* in October 1921, *Pulcinella* in May 1926, and *Renard* in January 1927.[17] Anatoly Lunacharsky of the Ministry of Education sent Stravinsky an official invitation to conduct in Leningrad 1925, but he declined.[18] Concerts continued, nonetheless. Mikhail Klimov conducted *Les Noces* with Maria Yudina, Dmitry Shostakovich, Alla Maslakovetz, and Isai Renzin on piano on 12 December 1926, and premiered a concert performance of *Oedipus Rex* in April 1928. At this time, Boris Asafyev also published his important monograph *Kniga o Stravinskom* (*A Book About Stravinsky*).[19] Concert programmers and public alike also showed interest in Stravinksy's neoclassical works: *L'Histoire du soldat*, a concert version of *Apollon musagète*, the Concerto for Piano and Wind Instruments, the *Symphonies d'instruments à vent*, the Octet, Piano Sonata, Serenade in A, and *Ragtime* were all performed in the Soviet Union in this period, among other compositions.

Stravinsky's works, and primarily the *Rite,* touched the hearts and minds of many young Russian composers and musicians. "Did I already write you about Stravinsky's *Spring?*" the twenty-three-year-old composer Vissarion Shebalin wrote his wife, Alissa, while still a student at the Moscow Conservatory in 1926. "It was performed here twice—it captivated me utterly from start to finish and made me think about a lot of things."[20] "Prokofiev's *Scythian* Suite, Stravinsky's *Rite of Spring*, and [Rimsky-Korsakov's] *Kitezh* left the strongest and most lasting impression on me. *Spring* captivated me in particular, with its vivid rhythms and the wittiness and brilliance of its presentation," he wrote his former teacher Mikhail Nevitov a few months later.[21] "After listening to [Stravinsky's Three Pieces for String Quartet], I realized for the first time in my life that music can provoke uncontrollable laughter: it was so funny and amusing that the entire audience roared with laughter."[22] Composer Gavriil Popov, who also played piano in performances of *Les Noces*, wrote in his diary in 1930: "I am reading the score of Stravinsky's *Rite of Spring*. Aside from its usefulness (technical), I am experiencing an enormous amount of pleasure that borders on sensations of happiness. Hearing and experiencing Stravinsky's high mastery and subtlest musical intuition, I am somehow comforted and am trying to learn even the tiniest bit from the artistic treasures of this musical giant."[23] Composer Aleksey Zhivotov also let echoes of *L'Histoire du soldat* and *Petrushka* surface in his aphoristic cycle *Fragments for Nonet* (1929), and Vladimir Deshevov based "Barakholka," the first scene of his 1930 opera *Ice and Steel*, on the model of crowd scenes in *Petrushka*.

One of the most important young composers to witness the impact of Stravinsky's music in these years was Dmitry Shostakovich, who attended Stiedry's performance of the *Rite* at age nineteen. "Saw the conductor Fritz Stiedry yesterday," he wrote his friend, eighteen-year-old Lev Oborin, who would go on to become a famous pianist. "Mozart's overture from *The Magic Flute*, Tchaikovsky's Serenade [for Strings], Stravinsky's *Rite of Spring*. . . . [The latter work] is an astonishing piece. I have never heard such orchestral brilliance. A hell of a sound. The music itself is a bit rough, but as captivating as can be. The most striking thing, of course, is its sound. Stiedry is a fantastic conductor. Wonderful technique, excellent taste, temperament and all other resources needed to provide pleasure to the audience.

Spring was extremely successful. A very pleasing fact. The listeners are starting to like contemporary music."[24]

Shostakovich soon developed an equally intense interest in Stravinsky's neoclassical works, and especially those performed in Leningrad in these years, including *L'Histoire du soldat* and *Oedipus Rex*. He considered Stravinsky—with Tchaikovsky—to be one of the greatest Russian composers; all others, including Sergey Prokofiev, lagged far behind.[25] Shostakovich also arranged the *Symphony of Psalms*, which could not be heard in Russia at the time, for piano four hands and regularly played it with students in his composition class.[26] This piece had an obvious impact on Shostakovich's own work in the second half of the 1930s, because without Stravinsky's influence, how can one explain the neo-Baroque style of Shostakovich's Symphonies no. 5 and 6; Piano Quintet in G Minor, op. 57; or Piano Trio no. 2 in E Minor, op. 67? In spite of these connections, Shostakovich's neoclassicism remained entirely his own.

This era of hopeful, fruitful exchange came to an abrupt end with Stalin's consolidation and exploitation of power during the 1930s and '40s.[27] Starting in the 1930s, there was a sharp drop-off in Stravinsky performances in the Soviet Union. In 1933, Arnold Alshvang published a devastating critique, and in 1948 the Central Committee of the All-Union Communist Party of the Bolsheviks forbade his works entirely.[28] In that year this committee, following on Andrey Zhdanov's remarks at the Musicians' Conference a month earlier, issued the infamous resolution "On the Opera *Velikaia Druzhba* by Vano Muradeli," in which it condemned "formalism in Soviet music." Tikhon Khrennikov described Stravinsky's works, and above all *The Rite of Spring*, as "obvious manifestations of decadence in music." In the *Rite*, Khrennikov continued, "ancient folksongs are hideously distorted, exaggerated, and presented as though in a carnival mirror."[29] Asafyev had a statement read in which he renounced his previous interest in Stravinsky at the first All-Union Congress of Soviet Composers in February of that year, and when the Moscow Academy of Science began publishing Asafyev's selected works in five volumes a few years later, Dmitry Kabalevsky wrote a critical note to explain why they omitted Asafyev's monograph on Stravinsky.[30] In spite of these measures composers continued to listen to Stravinsky in the privacy of their homes and through foreign broadcasts.[31]

Stravinsky's music began to return to Soviet concert halls only in the late 1950s, in part because of Leonard Bernstein's sensational guest performances with the New York Philharmonic Orchestra. Bernstein conducted *The Rite of Spring*, Concerto for Piano and Wind Instruments (with soloist Seymour Lipkin), and other works in concerts in Moscow and Leningrad in August and September 1959. Stravinsky quickly found new advocates in the Soviet Union, among them pianist Maria Yudina (an old-time supporter), conductors Gennady Rozhdestvensky and Igor Blazhkov, and, later, the pianist Aleksey Lubimov. Stravinsky's music returned more emphatically after the eighty-year-old composer's memorable and enormously significant visit to his homeland in October 1962. Composer Karen Khachaturian remembers Stravinsky describing the trip to young musicians during a meeting at the Leningrad Philharmonic as a kind of cultural mission. "This is not any kind of nostalgia, that is to say, gushiness," he recorded Stravinsky as saying. "I decided to come here because it seemed to me that my trip would help your musical work. . . . After all, in the first half of the century, Russian art burst out to the [artistic] forefront. . . . My arrival is supposed to help musicians get past this impasse with greater determination. . . . In that I see my mission and my duty."[32]

The surge of renewed interest in Stravinsky's work in the early 1960s coincided with a "new folkloric wave" beginning to take shape in Soviet music—the belated heir to the neo-folklorism of the early twentieth century. Compositions in this style refracted folkloric idioms in innovative ways, at times even approaching the musical language of the avant-garde—that is, more or less as Stravinsky had done in his earlier Russian works. Folklore, especially archaic folklore, became a symbol of renewal. Rodion Shchedrin appeared as Stravinsky's obvious successor in this respect, his 1963 Concerto for Orchestra no. 1 (*Naughty Limericks*) emblematic of the new folkloric wave. But Edison Denisov, a leader of the Soviet avant-garde in the 1960s, is just as obvious a successor. His chamber cantata *Lamentations*, composed to the lyrics of actual funeral laments from the Russian North (1966) is, consciously or not, clearly based on *Les Noces*. Both the texts and the instrumentation belie this influence. Denisov's melodies are not archaic little *popevkas*, however, but rather twelve-tone thematic complexes organized according to the serial method.[33] Here and there reminiscences of *Les Noces* still shine through, however, for example in the "sobbing" grace notes in the vocal part, which bring to mind Stravinsky's Bride.

Stravinsky's music gradually returned to Russia in the 1960s, and started to have significant influence again, not only in the works of the new folkloric wave but in other areas as well. Alfred Schnittke's and others' polystylistics originated in the neoclassical works of the master; others first heard about the serial method through Stravinsky, who had defended it passionately during his above-mentioned meeting with young composers in Leningrad in 1962. Alexander Vustin's *The Word* for chamber orchestra (1975) echoes the archaic melodies and the timbral hues of the *Symphonies d' instruments à vent*. Leonid Desyatnikov's song cycle *Russian Seasons* (2000) alludes to the *Four Seasons* of Antonio Vivaldi and Diaghilev's famous Parisian *saisons* and shows the distinct influence of *Les Noces*. Such traces of Stravinsky's influence have remained in Russian music to the present day.

The New Russian Style

The folkloric basis of Stravinsky's works from *Firebird* to *Les Noces* was evident both to its first listeners and first reviewers. Eventually, folklore came to be viewed as the source of Stravinsky's innovation and as the most important component of his style as a whole, a view that has become firmly established, especially in the composer's homeland. That Stravinsky was above all a Russian composer always sounded like a truism to his compatriots, although it did not imply a lack of scholarly interest in the question.[34] Beyond Russia, the situation was somewhat different: to prove this thesis to the Western musical establishment, Richard Taruskin needed to write an enormous book.[35]

However, even in Stravinsky's homeland the question was not resolved without debate. This had to do with the nature of Stravinsky's borrowings. In Stravinsky's youth, composers routinely used folklore that had been published in numerous collections, many of which Stravinsky later spoke about, including the collections of Pyotr Tchaikovsky, Anatoly Lyadov, and Nikolay Rimsky-Korsakov. He showed particular interest in publications of the Music Ethnography Commission, and particularly the collection of Yevgeniya Linyova, who used a phonograph for her documentation.[36] "Don't take others, which aren't recorded by phonographs," Stravinsky wrote his mother in reference to Linyova's collections in 1916, confirming a belief shared by many leading researchers in his time in authentic, unedited folklore.[37] This same interest led Stravinsky to copy from his friends the urban "street" themes of *Petrushka*,[38] and the "factory" melody of *Les Noces* (which is really an old peasant song).

Stravinsky's more or less direct quotations of authentic material rather quickly gave way to compositional elaboration, leading to the crystallization of his characteristic melodic forms. The distinct line between citation and non-citation disappeared. This was just as new for Russian music as Stravinsky's unusual, "deforming" approach to working with folklore, which included varying accents and motives, and dissonant "shading" (a famous example being the melody "Oh you, front porch, my front porch" (*Akh vï, seni moi, seni*) in *Petrushka*, which is doubled at the tritone). The "false" consonances of *The Rite of Spring* are the result of the superimposition of nonharmonic countermelodies onto the basic melody, a characteristic device of Russian folk polyphony.

Stravinsky's new Russian style, clearly indicated in *Petrushka* and developed in the following works, was sharply rejected by many. Andrey Rimsky-Korsakov and other members of his father's circle, did not accept it. Andrey called *Petrushka* "a mixture of Russian homebrew" (the "folk scenes") with French perfume ("the puppet comedy").[39] In *The Rite of Spring* he claimed only to hear "pathetic hints of a melodic pattern"—apparently in place of the national themes he had expected.[40] The composer Nikolay Myaskovsky, in contrast, considered *Petrushka* an absolute masterpiece precisely on account of its Russianness and viewed the ballet's author as an authentic successor to his teacher, the senior Rimsky-Korsakov. The sharpness of these polemics was compounded by the efforts on the part of many Russian composers at this time toward creating a new national music. Alexander Kastalsky, for instance, the master of Russian Church music and an expert in folklore, had begun working on the cycle *Scenes from Peasant Merrymaking in Rus*, which was to include, among other things, a representation of a Russian folk wedding. Curiously, Stravinsky's name surfaced in discussions about the cycle (in the context of its suitability for publication) between Kastalsky and Sergey Rachmaninoff. "I came to convince you to undertake this work," Rachmaninoff said to Kastalsky, "After all, anyone would give you as much as you want to give it up. Take Stravinsky – this is simply a treasure trove for him! He'll give you 100,000 for it!"[41] Indeed, Stravinsky was planning *Les Noces* at the same time, which Rachmaninoff could not have known, of course. But Kastalsky's taste was completely different than Stravinsky's: he created ethnographic restorations based on precise adaptations of folkloric material, and did not entirely accept Stravinsky's new Russian style.[42]

Boris Asafyev explained Stravinsky's relationship to folklore for Soviet readers in his monograph of 1928: "Stravinsky adopted Russian folk art not as a deft stylist capable of hiding citations, and not as a populist ethnographer unable to assimilate the material and transform it on an artistic level, but as a master of his native language. In this regard Stravinsky became the Pushkin of Russian music."[43] The comparison with Pushkin, the great poet and pioneer of the modern Russian language, becomes particularly significant when one considers that it is still impossible to tell which songs from Pyotr Kireyevsky's collection (from which Stravinsky extracted the texts for *Les Noces*) were written by Pushkin as imitations of folksongs, and which are authentic folksongs. In the same way, it has proven impossible to identify all the sources in the *Rite* and *Les Noces*. It is no coincidence that Stravinsky gradually forgot about these citations, and in his conversations with Robert Craft the only quotations he referred to were the introductory melody of *The Rite of Spring* and a single song in *Les Noces*. Stravinsky, "the master of folk speech," had "appropriated" the other cited material, apparently by virtue of its indistinguishability from his own. The composer "had the right"—so to speak—to forget.

Yet with time, the question of folkloric borrowings in Stravinsky's work became crucial and even acquired a famous urgency—though one must agree with Richard Taruskin that "an exhaustive accounting of Stravinsky's musical sources will never be made."[44] The interest in this subject in Russia stems partly from the unfortunate situation that the live sound environment in which the composer matured has disappeared almost entirely: folk music has turned from a natural and in many ways unconscious premise for musical composition into something almost equally exotic for foreigners and Russians alike.[45] As a consequence, certain sources in Stravinsky's music are a true mystery. Thus, page 35 of the sketchbook for *The Rite of Spring* contains a major-third theme in a whole-tone scale, meant for the finale of the ballet's first part—"Dance of the Earth"—where it is used in a somewhat altered version. The whole-tone scale is in fact encountered in Russian archaic folklore of the southern provinces (Kurskaya, Belgorodskaya) as well as in the Lithuanian Sutartinės, most often in the form of the Lydian tetrachord.

But Russian folklorists discovered and described this type of scale only during expeditions in the 1950s, and it was not recorded earlier. Thus Stravinsky could not have taken this theme from any of the print sources he consulted.[46]

Another detailed example can be found in *Les Noces*, in the two-part episode of the second scene, rehearsal number 50, "Boslovite, otech s materyu," which mimics Russian Church psalmody. Its high-voice part is an adapted citation from the Octoechos, a collection of liturgical hymns of the Russian Orthodox Church. The two-part structure itself is rather reminiscent of so-called line singing (*strochnoye peniye*) which was used in the Russian Church in the sixteenth and seventeenth centuries and later fell out of use. Line singing was characterized by the free use of pure fourths, fifths, and dissonances (compare the parallel major seconds in the passage of *Les Noces* mentioned above). Certain attributes of line singing are close to folkloric heterophony, but these practices remained obscure until the decodings and publications of more recent times.[47] Stravinsky could not have heard anything like this in the church services of his time. If both of these examples are the result of brilliant intuition, then perhaps that intuition could have worked in other cases? Clearly we must listen closely to the composer's words: "If any of these pieces sounds like aboriginal folk music, it may be because my powers of fabrication were able to tap some unconscious 'folk memory.'"[48] Either way, an element of mystery remains.

But it is also important to approach the problem of citations from a wider perspective. Stravinsky's pioneering work in the interpretation of folklore was not just based on folklore. Many of Stravinsky's neo-folkloric innovations resonate not only with folkloric sources but also with the new music of his time, including that of Claude Debussy. Not without reason, Stravinsky said that *The Rite of Spring* was indebted to Debussy more than to any other composer. He was referring not only to details such as the solo opening of the *Rite*, which reminded contemporary listeners of the beginning of *Prélude à l'après-midi d'un faune*, but also about deeper elements, in which "Debussyisms" naturally resonated with "folklorisms." Stravinsky favored parallel chords, for example, which accompany melodic lines of a folkloric nature (whether authentic or not is irrelevant in this case). Examples of this can be found in the most vivid moments of Stravinsky's neo-folkloric works: "Russkaya" in *Petrushka*, and in the motive of the four French horns from the "Spring Rounds," as well as the motives from the "Rituals of the Rival Tribes," "Dance of the Earth," and "Mystic Circles of the Young Girls" in the *Rite*.[49] It is doubtful that the recurring chord parallelism in *Les Noces* was directly copied from any particular source. Most likely it represents an amalgamation of sources.[50] Stravinsky's ear did not need to differentiate between folkloric and non-folkloric material. On the contrary, it became the composer's artistic goal, likely on a subconscious level, to combine and reconcile these various influences. In this way, refined "modernist" harmonies confronted the "accordeonic" excesses of the Russian city.

Such a synthesis was not entirely new to Russian music. Folk and Western art music had interacted since Glinka's time, yet without becoming reconciled. "Avant-garde" composers had focused primarily on harmonic innovation in the nineteenth century. Famously remote from folk sources, they rarely if ever used folkloric or folk-like material by itself in their operas and symphonies. Even in a work such as Rimsky-Korsakov's *Snegurochka*, which is almost entirely submerged in the elements of folk culture, the most significant moments in the part of the heroine are excluded from this folkloric sphere as a sign of her romantic detachment from the world of ordinary people.

Such well-known facts must be kept in mind to grasp fully Stravinsky's role in the creation of the New Russian Style. In his first two ballets, *The Firebird* and *Petrushka*, folklore still retains its traditional role. *The Rite of Spring*, however, was a decisive turning point. Here folkloric material in the broad sense of the term became, first, absolute in its significance, and second, aligned with the avant-garde and transformed into a key source for it. The famous scandal during the Paris premiere of *The Rite of Spring* presaged its future role as the beacon of a new music. At the same time, it was the recognition of the universal significance of Russian folklore.

A Poetics of Music

Despite Stravinsky's "proteism" and the wide variety of musical sources he used, the individuality of his style on a fundamental aural level remains indisputable. It is enough to hear two or three measures of any of his works to be convinced of this. His musical language is stable on the one hand and breathtakingly intertextual on the other. It seems as though Stravinsky's work absorbed the entire twentieth century. His music can be exalted and farcical, erudite and childishly naïve, frenetic and pagan or humbly restrained. It is as though Stravinsky was entranced by the rich multiplicity of life and art, and his music is just as entrancing.

But though his musical idiom, the fabric of his style, is important, it is clearly not all-encompassing in determining the music's meaning. Stylistic definitions of Stravinsky's music are famously too narrow anyway, especially because the music was so often associated with the other arts, and so inspired many hybrid analogies. Some believed Stravinsky's music resembled fauvist paintings, for example, because of the unique saturation and brightness of its "color scheme." Others explained his music's similarity with Cubism through its temporal shifts and irregular accent patterns, which were seen as analogous to spatial deformations. Both analogies were made early on. In the late twentieth century, Stravinsky's music was likened to art nouveau, because of the way it equalizes relief and background. But such stylistic terms are nothing more than metaphors or comparisons. They are inevitably tentative, because irregularity of accent and deformation of space, or the emancipation of tone quality in music and of color in painting, are very different phenomena. Nonetheless, such parallels serve to give us a sense of certain general patterns, on the basis of which we can construct ideas about concrete historical types of culture.

I would like to suggest a more useful way of viewing Stravinsky's music, based on the opposition of *symbol* and *thing*. In the most general sense, the symbolic type of art presupposes the existence of a kind of hidden reality to which the work of art refers. Of course, art as a general human endeavor can justifiably be treated as having symbolic character. As Ernst Cassirer argued in his *Philosophy of Symbolic Forms*, "All culture is manifested in the creation of specific image-worlds, of specific symbolic forms."[51] The creation of symbolic forms is based on the principle of the "representation of one content in and through another."[52] In essence, Cassirer's theory represents a theoretical abstraction and universalization of the creative practices of Symbolism, an influential movement around the turn of the twentieth century. I am referring to symbolism in this historical sense when I set up the antithesis of thing and symbol. In contrast to the universal interpretation of the symbol that Cassirer suggests—of the sign as such—historical Symbolism elaborates a more specific understanding. Created by an act of extrasensory intuition, the symbol, as a mediating link between the transcendental world and the visible world, forms a broad spectrum of oscillating meanings. In this context, lexical units—words, sound, and color—acquire a particularly suggestive quality, an internal intensity that is only effective, however, within a given cultural tradition, an intensity engendered by that tradition through a system of conventions.

By contrast, "thing-like" art represents an attempt to flee the captivity of "distant meanings" with their characteristic ambiguity. It concentrates on the very fabric of art—the word as such, sound as such, and color as such. In fact, "thingliness" arose historically as a reaction to Symbolism, uniting such divergent trends in literature and painting as Cubism, Acmeism, and Constructivism. No special term exists with respect to music to indicate its "thingliness" (the term Constructivism is sometimes used in the musical world; German *Neue Sachlichkeit*, by contrast, appeared later and is of a more local nature). We will therefore use a word from the Russian poetical lexicon: Acmeism, choosing this in particular because its etymological meaning is broad.

The Greek word *acme* denotes a zenith or peak; Acmeism was a Russian poetic school that emerged around 1910 and included Osip Mandelshtam, Nikolay Gumilyov, Sergey Gorodetsky, Anna Akhmatova, Georgy Ivanov, and others.[53] Stravinsky shared with these poets not a style, but rather the same St. Petersburg cultural background, which meant immeasurably more to Stravinsky than is commonly assumed. Walter Nouvel, the ghostwriter of Stravinsky's *Autobiography*, became the connecting link between Stravinsky and the composer's "past that might have been"—after all, Stravinsky was not close to the newer poets and artists when he lived in St. Petersburg.

Stravinsky's approach to sound material was marked by an Acmeistic sense of "thingliness," which he retained throughout his life just as he did his native musical lexicon. For him, music was essentially plastic and material. This attitude can be seen in his work as a whole and in its details; for example, in the way he combined specific—"correct," as he put it—chords and sets of instruments in almost every new work as if they were intended to be there from the start. One sees it as well in his wonderful dream about an interval that at first he simply couldn't get right: "I dreamed about this interval. It had become an elastic substance stretching exactly between the two notes I had composed, but underneath these notes at either end was an egg, a large testicular egg. The eggs were gelatinous to the touch (I touched them). . . . I woke up knowing that my interval was right."[54]

The Acmeist poets' return to the objectivity of the material world, the precise meaning of the poetic word, and to the spontaneity of "natural" expression is typologically related to Stravinsky's artistic breakthrough in *The Rite of Spring*. The ponderous and supple "Augurs of Spring" chord is a "sound as such"[55] that reveals itself in all its acoustic force and implies no hidden reality; this "self-sufficient" sound is similar to the "self-sufficient word" of Futurism—another movement I consider Acmeistic in the broadest sense. In parallel, Osip Mandelshtam wrote in 1913, "To exist is the artist's greatest pride. He desires no other paradise than existence, and when people talk to him about reality he only smiles bitterly, for he knows the infinitely more convincing reality of art. . . . The modest appearance of a work of art frequently misleads us concerning the monstrously condensed reality that it possesses. In poetry this reality is the word as such."[56]

During his neoclassical period, Stravinsky reevaluated the idea of Acmeistic "thingliness." He did not want to invent, but to build on a firm foundation of archetypal forms and genres. In a programmatic article, he called his Octet a "musical object" and said of *Perséphone* that "there is nothing to discuss and nothing to critique here . . . . a nose was not created, it just exists. The same goes for my art."[57] At the very same time, Daniil Kharms, a poet unknown to Stravinsky but living in his hometown, wrote the following words: "These are no longer just words and thoughts printed on paper. They are a thing, just as real as the crystal ink bottle standing on the table in front of me. . . . It seems as though one could pick up from the page these poems that have become things and throw them at the window, and the window would break. That's what poetry can do!"[58] This attitude was crystalized in Stravinsky's *Autobiography*, which shows marked affinities with the writings of Mikhail Kuzmin. Its francophile spirit (it was written for French readers) would have pleased Kuzmin, as would its anti-Wagnerian attitude, especially given the adoration of Wagner in Symbolist and *Mir iskusstva* circles. But it is the affinity of their ideas that is most striking. Stravinsky uses the Nietzschean categories of Apollonian and Dionysian—which can be traced back to the work of Vyacheslav Ivanov and Mikhail Kuzmin.[59] He also echoes Kuzmin's notion of "beautiful clarity," written in 1910: "Be logical . . . be skillful architects . . . be economical and sparing in your words, precise and authentic."[60] Both see the artwork as a self-sufficient reality. "People always want to find in music something it is not," Stravinsky writes. "The main thing for them is to know what the piece expresses, and what the author had in mind when he composed it. They never seem to understand that music is a thing in itself apart from anything that it may suggest to them."[61] In comparison, Kuzmin writes, "The work of art cannot be grasped based on its fruits, because it is itself already a fruit. . . . There still seem to be those who approach a work of art with demands of a social, moral, and political character."[62] Even Stravinsky's opinion that music is "powerless to express anything whatsoever—a feeling, attitude, psychological state, natural phenomenon, etc.," which greatly astounded the readers of *Autobiography*, is echoed in an aphorism by Kuzmin: "The best test of talent is to write about nothing." And finally, Stravinsky's crowning thought in a lengthy passage about "ideas" and "sound content" in Beethoven's music—"How immaterial it is whether the Third Symphony was inspired by the figure of the Republican Bonaparte or the Emperor Napoleon!"—could almost be a quote from Kuzmin: "Auber's opera *The Mute Girl of Portici* inspired the masses to revolt, but it still remains an ordinary comic opera, neither bad nor good, just like the majority of this composer's works."[63] Of course, similar thoughts were in the air and by the 1930s had become commonplace. But considered as a whole, they suggest not only a certain cohesiveness in the relationship between Stravinsky and the Acmeists, but a powerful typology of creativity.

The historical significance of Stravinsky's neoclassicism, so apparent today, was not immediately understood. Equally unclear was the composer's role in the evolution of Russian music, onto which Stravinsky grafted European forms, just as Pushkin had deliberately grafted borrowed story lines and genres onto the tree of Russian literature. One way or another, by the end of the century it became clear that Stravinsky's evolution could serve as an ideal model for the history of Russian music in the twentieth century. As one of the most astute connoisseurs of Stravinsky's work, Pyotr Suvchinsky said to Stravinsky in 1962, "It is now more important and more interesting to talk about the all-encompassing unity of your work. . . . The internal most essential *ritus* of all of your music is one and the same. . . . [This music] is ritual by its very nature. . . . Rituality is the combination of order and confession.[64] But there is another word for it in Russian: celebration. The highest and rarest form of confession is the celebratory sensation and realization of the lawfulness of life and being."[65]

NOTES

Many parts of this essay owe a significant debt to Tamara Levitz, who contributed especially to the first part in order to clarify for a Western audience aspects of Stravinsky's reception in the U.S.S.R. that might be taken for granted by a Russian reader. In more ways than one this essay is as much of a collaboration as it is a work of my own.

1. Richard Taruskin, *Stravinsky and the Russian Traditions* (Berkeley: University of California Press, 1996), 1:163. Taruskin coined the term "fourth-generation Belyayevets" to describe composers trained in the tradition and receiving the privileged patronage of the "Belyayev circle"—a society of Russian musicians named after the timber merchant and music patron Mitrofan Belyayev, and active in St. Petersburg from 1885 to 1908. This group included composers Alexander Glazunov, Anatoly Lyadov, and Rimsky-Korsakov, and initially had close ties to Tchaikovsky.

2. On this topic, see also Svetlana Savenko, "Stravinskiy in ruska glasba 20. stoletja," *Muzikološki zbornik* 43/2 (2007): 93–98; and Anatoliy Kuznetsov, "Muzika Stravinskogo na kontsertnoy estrade Rossii," *Muzïkal'naya akademiya* 4 (1992): 119–27.

3. "Kontsert 'Muzïkal'nïkh novostey,'" *Sankt-Peterburgskiye vedomosti*, 24 January 1908; in *Igor' Stravinskiy: Perepiska s russkimi korrespondentami. Materialï k biografii*, ed. Viktor Varunts (Moscow: Kompozitor, 1998), 1:443. (Hereafter *SPRK.*)

4. Karatygin and other critics reacted more positively to Stravinsky's symphony. See Vyacheslav Karatïgin, "Pridvornïy orkestr: 21-e orkestrovoye sobraniye 'Muzïkal'nykh novostey'," *Stolichnaya pochta*, 25 January 1908; in *SPRK*, 1:444. See Taruskin, *Stravinsky and the Russian Traditions*, 1:222–26.

5. See Taruskin, *Stravinsky and the Russian Traditions*, 1:641–42.

6. Vyacheslav Karatïgin, "Po kontsertam," *Otkliki khudozhestvennoy zhizni* 4 (25 November 1910): column 158; in *SPRK*, 1:460.

7. Nikolay Myaskovskiy, "Ig. Stravinskiy, '*Zhar-ptitsa,*' *skazka-balet dlya fortepiano v dve ruki*," ed. Pyotr Yurgenson,"*Muzïka* 45 (1911): 970–72; quoted in Nikolay Myaskovskiy, *Sobraniye materialov v dvukh tomakh* (Moscow: Sovetskiy kompozitor, 1960), 2:26.

8. Prokofiev to Nikolay Myaskovsky, 25 June 1914, in *S. S. Prokof'yev i N. Ya Myaskovskiy: Perepiska*, ed. Miral'da Kozlova and Nina Yatsenko (Moscow: Sovetskiy kompozitor, 1977), 116–17.

9. Florestan [Vladimir Derzhanovskiy], "Igor' Stravinskiy," *Utro Rossii*, 22 August 1912. The concert included Stravinsky's Symphony in E-flat and the first *Firebird* Suite. See Taruskin, *Stravinsky and the Russian Traditions*, 1:227–33.

10. Vyacheslav Karatïgin, "Vesna svyashchennaya," *Rech'*, 16 February 1914; in *SPRK*, 2: 591.

11. Entry from 12 February 1914, St. Petersburg, in Sergey Prokof'yev, *Dnevnik: Chast' pervaya 1907–1918* (Paris: sprkfv, 2002), 413. Prokofiev radically revised his opinion about the *Rite* in 1921; see entry for 23 May 1921, in ibid., 160–61.

12. The concerts took place on 17 and 20 March in Leningrad and on 28 March and 11 April in Moscow. Stiedry began to perform regularly in the Soviet Union after this time, and immigrated there in 1933. He directed the Leningrad Philharmonic Orchestra from 1933 to 1937.

13. Igor' Glebov, [Boris Asaf'yev], "Vesna svyashchennaya," *Krasnaya gazeta (vecherniy vïpusk)*, 20 March 1926; in *SPRK*, 3:753.

14. Anton Uglov [Dmitriy Kashintsev], "*Vesna* Stravinskogo u Stidri," *Izvestiya*, 31 March 1926; in *SPRK*, 3:754.

15. Oskar Fried performed the *Rite* in 1927 and 1928 in Moscow; Ernest Ansermet performed it twice in 1928 and once in 1929 in Leningrad; and pianist Alexander Kamensky gave a concert performance of his own arrangement of it in 1928.

16. Mikhail Druskin provided commentary on Stravinsky's piano music in *Novaya fortepiannaya muzika* (Leningrad: Triton, 1928) and a monograph on Stravinsky decades later. See *Igor' Stravinskiy* (Moscow: Sovetskiy kompozitor, 1974); translated into English by Martin Cooper as *Stravinsky: His Life, Works, and Views* (Cambridge: Cambridge University Press, 1983).

17. Stravinsky commented on these performances in his *Autobiography* (New York: W. W. Norton, 1936; repr. 1962), 141. He noted that "a clumsy attempt to stage *Renard* was a failure," and that few of his stage works were done in the Soviet Union outside of *Petrushka*. He concluded that "a change in regime cannot change the truth of the old adage that no man is a prophet in his own country." On Stravinsky's reception in this period, see Boris Schwarz, "Stravinsky in Soviet Russian Criticism," *The Musical Quarterly* 48/3, *Special Issue for Igor Stravinsky on His 80th Anniversary* (July 1962): 340–45.

18. See *SPRK*, 3:145, 149. See also Robert Craft and Igor Stravinsky, *Expositions and Developments* (Berkeley: University of California Press, 1959), 50. The Politburo allowed Prokofiev and Stravinsky to visit the USSR on 21 July 1925. For more details on the politics of this period, see Marina Frolova-Walker and Jonathan Walker, *Music and Soviet Power, 1917–1932* (Woodbridge, Suffolk: Boydell Press, 2012).

19. Boris Asaf'yev, *Kniga o Stravinskom* (Leningrad: Triton, 1929; Leningrad: Muzïka, 1977); translated into English by Robert French, with a preface by Robert Craft as *A Book about Stravinsky* (Ann Arbor: UMI Research Press, 1982).

20. Vissarion Shebalin to Alissa Shebalin, 15 April 1926, in *Zhizn' i tvorchestvo*, ed. Viktoriya Razheva (Moscow: Molodaya gvardiya, 2003), 163.

21. Vissarion Shebalin to M. I. Nevitov, 8 July 1926, in ibid., 166.

22. Vissarion Shebalin, fragment from his memoirs, in ibid., 157.

23. Gavriyil Popov, *Iz literaturnogo naslediya*, ed. Zarui Apetovna Apetyan (Moscow: Sovetskiy kompozitor, 1986), 238.

24. Dmitry Shostakovich to Lev Oborin, 18 March 1926, in *Vstrechi s proshlïm*, *vïpusk* 5 (Moscow: Sovetskaya Rossiya, 1984), 256.

25. Dmitriy Shostakovich "Anketa po psikhologii tvorcheskogo protsessa, sostavlena 2–10 sentyabrya 1927 g," in *Dmitriy Shostakovich v pis'makh i dokumentakh*, ed. Irina Bobïkina (Moscow: RIF "Antikva," 2000), 475.

26. Shostakovich became a professor at the Leningrad Conservatory in 1937. Igor Markevich conducted the Russian premiere of the *Symphony of Psalms* in Moscow on 25 May 1962.

27. Although scholars now know much about music in the Soviet Union in this period, they have yet to explore the specific details of Stravinsky's reception there, and the topic remains a lacuna in Stravinsky research. Within the context of this brief overview, I can only note the musicological gap, and point toward signs on the horizon that it will be filled. For more insight into the period, see these sources recommended by Tamara Levitz: Neil Edmund, *The Soviet Proletarian Music Movement* (Bern: Peter Lang, 2006); Marina Frolova-Walker, *Russian Music and Nationalism: From Glinka to Stalin* (New Haven: Yale University Press, 2007); Simo Mikkonen, *Music and Power in the Soviet 1930s: A History of Composers' Bureaucracy* (New York: Edwin Mellon, 2009); Simon Morrison, *The People's Artist: Prokofiev's Soviet Years* (Oxford: Oxford University Press, 2009); Amy Nelson, *Music for the Revolution: Musicians and Power in Early Soviet Russia* (Philadelphia: Pennsylvania State University Press 2004); Svetlana Savenko, "Die Rezeption emigrierter Komponisten in der UdSSR," in *Musik zwischen Emigration und Stalinismus: Russische Komponisten in den 1930er und 1940er Jahren*, ed. Friedrich Geiger and Eckhard John (Stuttgart: Metzger, 2004), 158–67; and Kiril Tomoff, *Creative Union: The Professional Organization of Soviet Composers, 1939–1953* (Ithaca, NY: Cornell University Press, 2006).

28. Arnol'd Al'shvang, "Ideynïy put' Stravinskogo," *Sovetskaya muzïka* 5 (1933): 90–100, reprinted in Al'shvang's *Izbrannïye stat'i* (Moscow: Sovetskiy kompozitor, 1959), and in *SPRK*, 3:834–49. *Petrushka* survived the longest in this environment and was performed by the Leningrad Philharmonic Orchestra under Yevgeny Mravinsky in 1946. See also Schwarz, "Stravinsky in Soviet Russian Criticism," 346–48.

29. Tikhon Khrennikov, "Za tvorchestvo, dostoynoye sovetskogo naroda," *Sovetskaya muzïka* 1 (January–February 1948): 58–59.

30. See Kabalevsky's introduction to *Akademik B. V. Asaf'yev: Izbrannïye trudï* (Moscow: Izdatel'stvo Akademii nauk SSSR, 1952), 1:15. This introduction also contains the note Asafyev had requested to be read at the first All-Union Congress of Soviet Composers in February 1948.

31. Kiril Tomoff makes this very important point in *Creative Union: The Professional Organization of Soviet Composers, 1939–1953*, 210.

32. Karen Khachaturyan, "Ya bïl rozhdyon dlya muzïki," *Muzïkal'naya akademiya* 4 (1992): 222.

33. *Popevka* are distinctive melodic phrases or formulas used in early Russian church singing and serving as building blocks for the melodies of Znamenny chant. They are also the foundation of Russian folklore.

34. See Asafy'ev, *Kniga o Stravinskom*; R. I. Birkan, "Fol'klornïye istochniki i stilevïye chertï muzïkal'no-stsenicheskikh proizvedenii I. F. Stravinskogo kontsa 1910—nachala 1920-kh godov" (PhD diss., Leningrad State University, 1971); Grigoriy Golovinskiy, *Kompozitor i fol'klor* (Moscow: Muzïka, 1981); Yuriy Paisov, "Russkiy fol'klor v vokal'no-khorovom tvorchestve Stravinskogo," in *I. F. Stravinskiy: Stat'i vospominaniya*, ed. Galina Alfeyevskaya and Irina Vershinina (Moscow: Sovetskiy kompozitor, 1985); Dmitriy Pokrovskiy, "Strukturnaya stilizatsiiya v 'Svadebke' Stravinskogo," in Viktor Varunts, *I. F. Stravinskiy: Sbornik statey* (Moscow: Moscow Conservatory, 1997); Svetlana Savenko, *Mir Stravinskogo* (Moscow: Kompozitor, 2001).

35. Taruskin, *Stravinsky and the Russian Traditions*, 2 vols.

36. Yevgeniya Linyova, *Velikorusskiye pesni v narodnoy garmonizatsii: Zapisanï E. Linevoy* (St. Petersburg: Imp. Akademiya nauk, 1904–9), 2 vols.

37. Stravinsky to his mother, 10/23 February 1916, in *SPRK*, 2:360.

38. Stravinsky asked Andrey Rimsky-Korsakov to send him the melodies of two highly popular art songs; see his letter from 3/16 December 1910 in *SPRK*, 1:250–51.

39. Andrey Rimskiy-Korsakov, "7-y simfonicheskiy kontsert S. Kusevitskogo," *Russkaya molva* 45 (25 January/7 February 1913).

40. Andrey Rimskiy-Korsakov "Russkiye opernïye i baletnïye spektakli v Parizhe," *Russkaya molva*, 27 June 1913; Taruskin, *Stravinsky and the Russian Traditions*, 2:1014–15. On *Petrushka*'s and the *Rite*'s reception in Russia, see Taruskin, 1:759-70, 1006-31.

41. Cited in Svetlana Zvereva, *Aleksandr Kastal'skiy* (Moscow: Vuzovskaya kniga, 1999), 146–47.

42. "Stravinsky's *Les Noces* contains a few interesting attempts to approach the folk manner of choral song. But he makes excessive and unnecessary use of dissonance, apparently wishing to reproduce the singing of a wild and drunken crowd in the countryside (as though debauchery and cacophony make the wedding ceremony interesting)." Aleksandr Kastal'skiy, "Iz zapisok," in *I. F. Stravinskiy: Stat' i materiali*, compiled by L. S. D'yachkova, ed. Boris Yarustovskiy (Moscow: Sovetskiy kompozitor, 1973), 208.

43. Asaf'yev, *Kniga o Stravinskom*, 20.

44. Taruskin, *Stravinsky and the Russian Traditions*, 1: 893.

45. See Stravinsky's recollections about the sounds of old Petersburg in Igor Stravinsky and Robert Craft, *Memories and Commentaries* (London: Faber & Faber, 2002), 20–21.

46. Taruskin suggests that he used Anna Rudneva, *Narodnïye pesni Kurskoy oblasti*, but that collection appeared in 1957 (*Stravinsky and the Russian Traditions*, 1:923–24).

47. Nikolay Uspenskiy, *Obraztsï drevnerusskogo pevcheskogo iskusstva* (Leningrad: Muzïka, 1968).

48. Igor Stravinsky and Robert Craft, *Memories and Commentaries* (Berkeley: University of California Press, 1959), 98.

49. Even earlier this device is found in the finale of *Firebird*.

50. Taruskin connects the origin of parallel triads in *Les Noces* with the publication of examples of Georgian liturgical song in *Stravinsky and the Russian Traditions*, 2:1414.

51. Ernst Cassirer, *Philosophie der symbolischen Formen* (Darmstadt: Wissenschaftliche Buchgesellschaft, 1964): 1: 51.

52. Ibid., 41.

53. I want to emphasize that I am not interested here in making specific parallels between Stravinsky and the Acmeists but rather with understanding a certain typology.

54. Robert Craft and Igor Stravinsky, *Conversations with Stravinsky* (New York: Doubleday, 1959), 14.

55. Aleksey Kruchenykh and Velimir Khlebnikov speak of "the word as such" in their Futurist manifesto of 1913.

56. Osip Mandelshtam, *Slovo i kul'tura* (Moscow: Sovetskiy pisatel', 1987), 168.

57. Stravinsky, quoted in Paul Sacher, "Igor Strawinsky zum Gedächtnis [1971]," in *Reden und Aufsätze* (Zurich: Atlantis, 1986), 105.

58. Daniil Kharms to K. V. Pugacheva, 16 October 1933, in *Novïy mir* 4 (1988): 137; repr. in *Polyot v nebesa*, ed. A. Aleksandrov (Leningrad: Sovetskiy pisatel', 1991), 483–84.

59. Nouvel was a regular visitor to the gatherings at the home of Vyacheslav Ivanov.

60. Mikhail Kuzmin, "O prekrasnoy yasnosti: Zametki o proze," *Apollon* 4 (January 1910): 10.

61. Stravinsky, *An Autobigraphy,* 162–63.

62. Mikhail Kuzmin, "Zametki o literature [1914]," in *Stikhi i proza* (Moscow: Sovremennik, 1989), 385–86.

63. Ibid. Compare Stravinsky, *An Autobiography*, 53.

64. Suvchinsky included the French words, *ordre* and *célébration* in brackets here next to the Russian words for "order" and "confession." He conflates confession with celebration in French.

65. Pyotr Suvchinsky to Stravinsky, 9 April 1962, microfilm 277.1, Paul Sacher Stiftung.

Stravinsky's Cold War: Letters About the Composer's Return to Russia, 1960–1963

LETTERS TRANSLATED BY PHILIPP PENKA
WITH ALEXANDRA GRABARCHUK
INTRODUCTION, COMMENTARY, AND NOTES
BY TAMARA LEVITZ

In memory of Viktor Varunts (1945–2003)

In fall 1962, Igor Stravinsky returned to Russia for the first time in forty-eight years. He had left in 1914, not knowing at the time, of course, how long the separation would last. When Lenin revoked citizenship for expatriates in 1921, Stravinsky had become stateless and could remain in Europe only with a Nansen passport, which he kept until he acquired French citizenship in 1934.[1] Many observers underplayed his refugee status, and operated under the false assumption that Stravinsky had "slipped" into becoming an émigré, rather than being forced into exile. But he was in fact stateless, and in a far more unsettled situation than is commonly assumed.

During his early years of exile, Stravinsky mostly kept a public silence about his homeland, sharing his feelings only with intimate friends. He developed a deep mistrust of reporters and critics, and evaded their questions about the Soviet Union, especially as the situation in his homeland worsened.[2] "I used to say I was a 'Westerner,'" he ventured to tell a Viennese reporter in 1926. "This should not be misinterpreted. I have been living for sixteen years away from Russia, mostly in Paris and Nice. For that reason alone I don't have much insight into the political situation in Russia and thus can't be for or against the Soviets. Thankfully I am not a politician but solely and exclusively a musician. And indeed as a musician Western culture means a tremendous amount to me."[3] In spite of such public statements and of his difficult relationships with Russian émigré circles, Stravinsky avidly read émigré and Soviet newspapers and books, nurtured deep friendships with select émigré friends, and after 1926, reconnected in a profound way with his religion, Russian Orthodoxy. He also never gave up Russian traditions and customs. The tense demands of his exile led him to separate dramatically the public and private spheres of his life; by the early 1930s the two had become irreconcilable.

• 273 •

Stravinsky's public silence on his private attachment to Russia led him to feel an affinity for two fellow Russian émigrés who felt a similar need to keep secrets: Arthur Lourié and Pyotr Suvchinsky. Stravinsky first met Suvchinsky in 1922, and became his close friend in the 1930s.[4] Suvchinsky was descended from Polish nobility and had spent his childhood and youth at the family estate south of Poltava in Ukraine. He actively promoted modern music before leaving Russia by publishing the St. Petersburg almanac *Muzikal'nïy sovremennik* with Andrey Rimsky-Korsakov in 1914–15; in 1917 he cofounded the Russian journal *Melos*. In the 1920s, Suvchinsky became deeply involved in the leadership of the Eurasianist movement in exile.[5] Stravinsky left no evidence that he was at all aware of his friend's covert political activities; he cherished Suvchinsky as an intellectual partner, musician, fellow émigré, and sympathetic listener. In 1939 they collaborated on Stravinsky's *Poétique musicale*.[6]

Stravinsky became increasingly hostile toward the Soviet Union, and Communism, as Stalin consolidated his power in the 1930s. He relied on Suvchinsky to keep him informed, and trusted him so deeply on the subject of the Soviet Union that he even allowed him to write about it in the fifth chapter of his own *Poétique musicale*. Stravinsky and Suvchinsky also discussed Dmitry Shostakovich, whose *Lady Macbeth of the Mtsensk District* Stravinsky heard Artur Rodzinski conduct in New York on 4 February 1935. Stravinsky described *Lady Macbeth* to Ernest Ansermet immediately after the performance as "a work of lamentable provincialism, in which the music plays the miserable role of illustrating in a very embarrassing realist style. . . . [Shostakovich] has profoundly disappointed me both in his mentality and musical value. . . . *Lady Macbeth* is not the work of a musician but it is surely the product of the total indifference for music in the land of the Soviets. What a relief I am not going there!"[7] When Suvchinsky sent Stravinsky the devastating anonymous article from *Pravda* denouncing Shostakovich's *Lady Macbeth* about a year later, Stravinsky ignored its political implications and used it instead to confirm his own fixed aesthetic judgment. He underlined sentences and made notes in the margins, and in one spot explicitly called Shostakovich's opera "rubbish."[8] Interpreting Shostakovich as a representative rather than a victim of Stalin's Soviet Union, Stravinsky made a point of emphasizing again how much he detested Shostakovich's opera in an interview he gave in Argentina a few months later.[9]

Stravinsky's public political persona and relationship to Suvchinsky and Shostakovich changed when he immigrated to the United States in 1939. Separated from friends and family, and immersed in new relationships, he began to promote himself in the U.S. press as an American patriot and foe of the Nazis and Soviet Union.[10] In December 1940 he told a reporter in Minneapolis that "America has always been good to me, so why shouldn't I [become a citizen]? I like the free American spirit, and it fits my own temperament."[11] Soon, he was commenting that Shostakovich "is a very clever young man, but I have not heard his later symphonies, the fifth and the sixth."[12] And very quickly, he accompanied his newfound

U.S. patriotism with a critique of the Soviet Union: "Russian music is still in a state of transition," he told a reporter in Rochester in February 1945. "Music reaches its highest development in times of peace rather than in periods of upheaval."[13] "The Russians have not yet ended their revolution," he elaborated to Jean-Louis Roux in Montréal a month later. "They have too much work to do in the political domain before they can really concern themselves with art. They don't have time at the moment."[14] By 1946, he had crystalized these thoughts into a convincing political sound bite: "Art cannot flourish under dictatorships. No artist can develop when creating according to prescription rather than through freedom of choice."[15]

When the war ended, Stravinsky, at age sixty-three, emerged on the international contemporary music scene as both the "elder statesman" of modern music and catalyst for its deepest controversies. In the period of relatively open dialogue over the future of music immediately after the war, young composers began to map ideological categories onto stylistic ones, and to define Stravinsky's usefulness to their political agendas based on their allegiance to either his early Russian or neoclassical works. Old European debates over the value of his compositional style—painfully fought out in France at the premiere of his Concerto in E-flat (*Dumbarton Oaks*) in 1938—came back to haunt Stravinsky in 1945 when Manuel Rosenthal and the Orchestre national de France staged a "homecoming" for him in Paris in a January to July series of seven concerts of his music.[16] Rosenthal's series included Stravinsky's popular Russian favorites, the *Rite* and *Petrushka*; neoclassical standards like the Concerto for Piano and Wind Instruments; rarely performed works like *Mavra* and *Perséphone*; and a new work Stravinsky had composed during the war: *Four Norwegian Moods*. Just before the festivities really began to unfold, however, representatives of the older generation, including Georges Auric and Francis Poulenc, had responded effusively to Roger Désormière's performance of Stravinsky's *Danses concertantes* (1940–42) at a concert of the Société privée de musique de chambre on 27 February 1945. The older generation's smug mutual support of one another and of this work irked Olivier Messiaen's students, who expressed their dissatisfaction at a protest during a performance of Stravinsky's *Four Norwegian Moods* at Rosenthal's festival on 15 March.[17] Serge Nigg and other students found Stravinsky's neoclassicism retrospective, though they did not oppose it in principle. They were more concerned about whether Stravinsky represented the right direction for French composers in a time of great uncertainty. It did not help that their elders immediately scolded them for their insolence. By the end of the debates, the Polish-born French composer René Leibowitz had entered the fray, rejecting Stravinsky's neoclassicism in favor of Schoenberg's serialism. The stage was set for a Cold War musical battle of epic proportions.

As always, Stravinsky experienced the conflict indirectly, from a distance, through old friends. Suvchinsky defended his honor by exploring his unique Russian typology in a long article in *Contrepoints*, which another old friend, André Schaeffner, sent on to the composer.[18] "Friends in New York told me you think the attacks to which you were subject in Paris originated with the Soviets," Schaeffner commented in the accompanying letter, "You know that I was never Communist, and never a supporter of any totalitarian regime. But I can assure you that to the best of my knowledge there has not been an unfavorable review of you in any of the Communist or communizing [*communisants*] newspapers, on the contrary. You have friends among the Communists: Désormière, Auric (!) etc." It was the White Russians and Germanophiles who disliked Stravinsky, he explained. "And as for Messiaen, he is a Catholic, a poor dupe of the fuss they are making around him who doesn't dare to speak out—either for or against you." Stravinsky responded that he never thought the attacks were Soviet, and that Schaeffner must have been misinformed. "It's interesting to hear about the White Russians' attitude toward me. Do those anachronistic groups still exist after the liberation? How funny."[19] He thanked him for Suvchinsky's brilliant article.

Stravinsky became personally embroiled in a major public Cold War dispute a few years later, when the Cominform organized a Cultural and Scientific Conference for World Peace at the Waldorf-Astoria in New York City, 25–27 March 1949, just ten months after the Prague Manifesto.[20] Stravinsky had heard Shostakovich was invited but doubted he would be permitted to come. "The Soviets want to control everything," he told a reporter on 3 March. "They will enslave everybody to get control—I do not think he will come to this country as announced."[21] Two weeks later, Olin Downes, music critic of the *New York Times*, asked Stravinsky to sign his name to a telegram welcoming Shostakovich to the United States.[22] Having recently become aware of the dangers of getting involved in Cold War conflict when Hanns Eisler's supporters had used his co-sponsorship of an Eisler concert in Los Angeles to political ends without his permission, Stravinsky was hesitant.[23] He responded that he would not be able "to join welcomers of Soviet artists coming to this country. But all of my ethical and aesthetic convictions oppose such gesture [*sic*]." He then dutifully informed his new best friend, Robert Craft, of his actions.[24]

In the end Shostakovich and six other guests from the Soviet Union attended, as well as Leonard Bernstein, Marc Blitzstein, Aaron Copland, Paul Robeson, and other U.S. musicians.[25] At the Fine Arts Panel with Copland and Shostakovich that Olin Downes chaired on 27 March, Shostakovich "gazed intently at the audience" while Paul Mann read his 5,200-word speech in English, according to reporter Herbert Kupferberg.[26] "His beginnings were promising," Irving Kolodin quoted Shostakovich as saying about Stravinsky in the *New York Sun*, "but having broken with the traditions of the Russian national school of music, having betrayed his native land and severed himself from his people, Stravinsky joined the camp of reactionary modernistic musicians." A "moral barrenness reveals itself in his openly nihilistic writings," Shostakovich's speech continued, "Stravinsky has no fear of that gaping abyss which separates him from the spiritual life of the people."[27] After the talk was over, Stravinsky's friend Nicolas Nabokov asked Shostakovich whether he agreed with an anonymous article in *Pravda* that denounced Stravinsky, Hindemith, and Schoenberg. According to press reports, Shostakovich agreed immediately to the first two names, but hesitated on Schoenberg. Finally, when pressed, he uttered the words "And Schoenberg too."[28] That night Shostakovich performed a piano reduction of the second movement of his Fifth Symphony to a tremendous crowd at Madison Square Garden.

Stravinsky's name and musical brand became inextricably linked with the Cold War when Nicolas Nabokov highlighted both in L'Oeuvre du XXe siècle—a festival sponsored by the Congress for Cultural Freedom and held in Paris in May 1952. Stravinsky and Nabokov had met in the 1920s, but became close around the time of this festival; Nabokov served as an important entrepreneur for Stravinsky's music in the last decades of his life.[29] As secretary-general of the Congress, Nabokov designed the festival to solidify the organization's anti-Soviet agenda and role as a "defender of freedom." In the accompanying brochure, he condemned injustices in the Soviet Union by speaking of the continued ban there on Shostakovich's *Lady Macbeth*.[30] Stravinsky fit his agenda both as a friend and a victim of Soviet attack: Stravinsky's Russian and neoclassical works became centerpieces of the festival. Audiences heard classics like *The Firebird* and *The Rite of Spring* (performed by the Boston Symphony Orchestra—shipped to Paris on the CIA's tab expressly for that purpose),[31] as well as *Orpheus*, *Oedipus Rex*, and central neoclassical works such as the Symphony in C. The festival had a highly controversial reception in France.

Stravinsky did not comment publicly on the political implications of this event, but rather used it as an opportunity to enjoy his first trip to Paris in fourteen years. He dined, visited museums, saw old friends like André Schaeffner and Charles-Albert Cingria, and collaborated with Jean Cocteau on a new staging of *Oedipus Rex*. Although in the know about Nicolas Nabokov's staunch anti-Soviet agenda, he acted ignorant of it, just as he had with Suvchinsky's Eurasianist activities decades earlier. Two other dramatic changes in his life also shaped this trip: he had heard and fallen in love with the music of Webern, and he had become more deeply attached to Robert Craft, who traveled with him and Vera.[32] He was also in the midst of composing what historians consider one of his first important attempts at serialism in the "Ricercar II" of the Cantata—a work that at the age of seventy would allow him to capture the Cold War spotlight by joining in his own person the styles that haunted it ideologically: the folk exoticism of *Firebird* and *Rite*, neoclassicism, and serialism. For whatever reason, however, Stravinsky did not see Suvchinsky in Paris.[33]

Stravinsky's role in the Cold War musical face-off shifted yet again when Nikita Khrushchev became Soviet premier in March 1958, and the Communist Party resolved on 28 May to acknowledge the unfairness of previous judgments about leading composers, paving the way for their rehabilitation.[34] The Thaw had begun, but progress was slow and unsure. Leonard Bernstein's tour of the Soviet Union with the New York Philharmonic in August and September 1959 opened up new possibilities for Stravinsky's reception in his homeland. Bernstein performed Stravinsky's *Firebird* Suite, Concerto for Piano and Wind Instruments (with Seymour Lipkin as soloist), and *The Rite of Spring*, setting the tone for the repertoire favored there for years to come. But musicologist Boris Schwarz warned U.S. audiences that appearances were deceptive: textbooks in the Soviet Union were still not discussing Stravinsky's works after 1930, he claimed, and the composer's serialist turn, support of Webern, and public rejection of the Soviet Union were still causing considerable controversy there.[35]

The selection of correspondence between Stravinsky, Suvchinsky, and Maria Yudina included here documents Stravinsky's first tentative contact with Soviet colleagues during the Thaw, and his personal response to the invitation to visit the Soviet Union on the occasion of his eightieth birthday in 1962.[36] Just as Suvchinsky had served as Stravinsky's messenger when contact with the Soviet Union broke down dramatically in the 1930s, he returned now to become the mediator in establishing that contact anew. Stravinsky rekindled a deep friendship with Suvchinsky precisely in these years. But Stravinsky's affections were divided. His friendship with Suvchinsky existed as if in a parallel universe to the one he shared with Craft, and as a consequence, the stories the two men told about him did not always correspond. Whereas Robert Craft carefully documented Stravinsky's trip to the Soviet Union in the CIA-funded British journal *Encounter* and in the diaries he published upon his return, Suvchinsky's perspective is less well known.[37] The historical tension between Suvchinsky and Craft culminated in disputes over Stravinsky's archive after he died.[38]

Suvchinsky provided the connection to Maria Yudina, a brilliant pianist who had studied at the St. Petersburg Conservatory in 1921, taught at the same institution until 1930, and then at the Moscow Conservatory from 1936 to 1951, and at the Gnesin Institute from 1944 to 1960. Stalin had famously spared Yudina despite her outspoken opinions on religion and politics (she was a Jewish convert to Russian Orthodoxy),[39] because he felt emotionally moved by her playing. She had performed *Les Noces* with Shostakovich in 1926, and, as Peter Schmelz has noted, "served as a crucial bridge across the chasm of the Stalinist 1930s and 1940s, the 'forgotten years' that haunted" most young composers during the post-Stalin Thaw.[40]

Yudina's first letter to Suvchinsky dates from 16 September 1959, just weeks after Leonard Bernstein's visit to the Soviet Union and at a time when she was beginning to make emboldened choices as a performer of avant-garde music and supporter of the composer Andrey Volkonsky within Soviet professional circles.[41] In this and other initial letters to Suvchinsky, Yudina requests scores not available in the Soviet Union, and plans a proposed visit to France organized by André Jolivet for winter or spring 1961, which never materialized.[42] Although she shows interest in Stockhausen, Boulez, and others, she describes Stravinsky as towering above everybody else, his superiority assured by the fact that he dedicated his scores to God.[43] Through Suvchinsky, Yudina came into contact with Stravinsky himself, and began sending him rhapsodic letters of praise and gifts of rare books. Her correspondence with Stravinsky began at the very time—1960—when she lost her job at the Gnesin Institute and was deprived of the possibility to teach. Stravinsky seemed largely unaware of the difficulties and complexity of her situation and the courage she displayed in disseminating his music. He usually responded to her missives with brief, polite thank-you notes, in which, most importantly, he showed interest in her and asked her to write.

This correspondence between Stravinsky, Suvchinsky, and Yudina brings together the strands of their Cold War story: Stravinsky returns home after almost half a century, accompanied on his journey emotionally by Pyotr Suvchinsky and physically by Robert Craft. As the people around him plan political spectacle, Stravinsky worries about music, books, illnesses, and himself, separating the public and private as he always had. He is aware of the political consequences of his actions and of his role as a pawn in a Cold War conflict, but keeps that knowledge at a distance, not allowing public obligation to determine fully the life choices he makes. He enjoys socializing and good conversation with acquaintances whose politics he detests. He slips damaging comments to the press, covering up for his indiscretions with lies afterward, as he had always done. And his attention focuses on Dmitry Shostakovich—the composer who had served as his greatest Soviet rival for over a quarter of a century. Stravinsky is celebrated in Russia as a twentieth-century icon—his fame far outweighing the importance of his musical compositions for most people, as Arthur Berger recognized at the time.[44] But he is also ill and fragile, possibly abusing alcohol, and focused on his own comfort and musical pleasure. Fussy and obstinate, he trusts his closest and most intimate confidants, Robert Craft and Vera, but also Pyotr Suvchinsky, to serve as his human shields against a potentially hostile Cold War world.[45]

1. Pyotr Suvchinsky to Igor Stravinsky

Paris
22 April 1960

My dearly beloved Igor Fyodorovich!

I just received 28 (!) scores, which I will start sending to Yudina. How can I thank you?!

Recently I had an endless conversation with L. Morton.[46] What a wonderful, calm person he is! He suffered from some strange illness all this time; now he is feeling better.

I told him what I always think and say: *the miracle of Stravinsky* happened in Russia.[47] After all, miracles are always "instantaneous," they are localized in time and space. That is their "specificity." Remember all the miracles in the Gospels, remember Gogol: "*Suddenly* in all directions even the ends of the earth had become visible."[48] A brilliant expression.

And then he who has "seen the light" begins a new life and if he was worthy of the miracle that happened to him (and in him), then this miracle will last his entire life. Of course, the "miracle of Stravinsky" continues to take place right in front of everyone's eyes for many decades, but the *moment* of the miracle is connected with Russia and with your youth.

Don't think that I am russophiling. I never told you about it, but I didn't like my childhood and youth; I felt like protesting against almost everything. My relationship with my parents and with our "bourgeois" life were and remain a burdensome memory for me. But nevertheless, a feeling for *language* and some fundamental past have stayed with me forever; I gave birth to myself once more (we are our own parents). I'm writing all this because I was very pleased to learn that Morton is planning to go to Russia.[49] Perhaps M. V. Yudina's appearance is providential.

So let me thank you once more for being so sympathetic and attentive to her. I received an Easter letter from her that touched me very much.

I embrace you warmly.

Yours truly
P. Suvchinsky

2. Igor Stravinsky to Pyotr Suvchinsky

Hollywood
7 May 1960

Dear Pyotr Petrovich, please send this carte-de-visite of mine to M. V. Yudina with my greetings and thanks.[50]

After you read her letter,[51] please send it back to me (you may use regular mail). I embrace you and Marianna.[52]

Your I. Stravinsky

In the months following this initial contact, Stravinsky continued to critique the Soviet Union in the U.S. press, frustrating Yudina and other colleagues in Russia who were trying to fight for his rehabilitation there. In December 1960 Stravinsky gave an interview to the Washington Post *in which he commented: "They're bad. Poor Shostakovich, the most talented, is just trembling all his life. Russia is a very conservative and old country for music. It was new just before the Soviets. Under Lenin they invited me. I couldn't go. Stalin never invited me."[53] A few weeks later he wrote Yudina that he was pleased to see that her concert programs included works of his that the Soviets had recently branded as decadent. "I should so much like to get to you this year," he wrote her, "but it won't happen: too many commitments that I can't fulfill."*[54] *After his negative remarks were reported in* Sovetskaya kul'tura *in February 1961, Yudina wrote Suvchinsky urging him to tell Stravinsky to stop speaking out. "If I. F. in fact said something [negative about the Soviet Union]—then why, why?! People have slowly started writing to him and expressing their kind feelings,* admiration, respect, reverence. . . . *I don't speak about myself, but my aim was to orient him toward us, to our quest, our difficulties, our aspiration toward Love between people, toward the best that we have and is in us. . . .* the goal is to bring him closer, to bring our genius closer to us, his kin.*"*[55]

    Stravinsky's feelings about traveling to the Soviet Union shifted after he met Tikhon Khrennikov in Los Angeles in June 1962. A highly decorated Soviet composer and secretary of the powerful Union of Soviet Composers, Khrennikov had once denounced Stravinsky, decades earlier, at the height of Stalin's purges.[56] *But times had changed, and Khrennikov had arrived in the United States in a far different mood to attend the first International Los Angeles Music Festival, which took place at Royce Hall on the campus of UCLA, 1–11 June 1961. The festival included eight concerts, as well as an International Composers' Conference moderated by Roy Harris in Schoenberg Hall and involving Werner Egk, Lukas Foss, Blas Galindo, Iain Hamilton, Walter Piston, John Vincent, Darius Milhaud, Stravinsky, Khrennikov, and the second invited Soviet guest, Azerbaijani composer Kara Karayev, among others.*[57] *Schoenberg's* Die glückliche Hand *and Stravinsky conducting his Violin Concerto and* Symphony of Psalms *were highlights of the festival, as was a "Soviet Night" introduced by Lukas Foss on 11 June, which included the Suite from Karayev's ballet* Paths of Thunder *and Khrennikov's Symphony no. 2 and Violin Concerto, with Igor Bezrodny as soloist. The music did not go over well—Craft remembers Stravinsky squirming, fidgeting, and groaning throughout and leaving before intermission.*[58] *Critic Albert Goldberg called Karayev's Suite "the kind of commercial music dished up in this country for Las Vegas, extravaganza and Hollywood B-movies—pseudo-Spanish, pseudo-jazz and pseudo everything else."*[59] *Afterward Khrennikov caught Stravinsky in the green room at UCLA and invited him to the Soviet Union.*[60] *Although Khrennikov later remembered the invitation as spontaneous, it remains unclear whether it was.*[61] *When Khrennikov, upon meeting Stravinsky directly, questioned him about his bad-mouthing of the Soviet Union, the composer responded brazenly, "I've never said anything bad either about Soviet music or about Soviet musicians. All these opinions were imputed to me in the interview by unscrupulous journalists."*[62]

3. Igor Stravinsky to Pyotr Suvchinsky

Hollywood
12 June 1961

Dearest Pyotr Petrovich!

    Your package with Balmont pleased me very much, as did your letter (5 June). Of course, this is a bibliographic rarity and I will have to thank Yudina and Balmont's daughter[63] (what is her address?), but now I am insanely busy . . . .

Our international festival here lasted for about a week. I conducted my Violin Concerto and *Symphony of Psalms*. Yesterday the festival ended with a concert of Soviet music with a (wonderful) Soviet violinist (Igor Bezrodny)[64] and the hopeless music of Tikhon Khrennikov and Kara Karayev. It is incredible junk, but it was impossible for me to leave, especially because the previous day all these Soviet musicians came to visit me, we hosted them, and they invited me to celebrate my 80th birthday in Moscow next year (if I'm still alive), saying that I have never and nowhere been received as I will be received in Russia. It goes without saying that it's scary to think about all that, scary to look ahead to my eightieth birthday. Musical life in Russia is terrifying and it is terrifying to think that they have decided to honor "their venerable musician"; it is terrifying that I shall have to smile when I feel like throwing up. What can I do? These days the press and the radio have already been talking about nothing else. How horrible! I'm not prepared for this, I cannot believe that the invitation is a true act of repentance and an irrevocable change regarding me and my music. After all, Khrennikov is not Yudina, and the cult of Shostakovich is not a myth. So what am I to do about all this? What's to be done?

We are here until July. Leaving in August. . . .

When will you be in Switzerland? Will wait for news from you by return mail, if possible.

> I embrace you.
> Your I. Stravinsky

Of course, I knew Yastrebtsev—he was an awful dunce.[65]

4. Pyotr Suvchinsky to Igor Stravinsky

> Paris
> 16 June 1961

Dearly beloved Igor Fyodorovich,

Thank you for your wonderful letter (from 12 June). How I would like to embrace you warmly and give you a kiss right now, this very minute! The French newspapers have already written about your planned visit to Russia, of course.

I am not one to give you advice, of course, but I think, and I am convinced that you must accept this invitation, and see what happens a year from now.

If you like, it will be possible to find out through M. V. Yudina what sort of a meeting it will be. But who is really issuing the invitation—the Composers' Union or the government? Actually, it seems to me that this is *irrelevant*.[66]

Forgive the foolish word, but I see in this the metaphysics of your personality: this happened, and it couldn't not have happened. Someone in this terrible and inspired country finally came to his senses, and the Light of Reason—you know yourself what it is. You can't deny it to those who are asking for it. If dear Yudina had any influence on this at all—thanks to her!

But I am still surprised by this invitation of Khrennikov (whose "music" I know); everything has its hierarchy in Soviet Russia. I don't think that he would dare to act on his own initiative without the approval of Shostakovich, and the highest musical echelons. But your trip and the celebrations in your honor, will not be to Shostakovich's advantage. So what is going on?[67] Apparently there is something stronger than him and because of this affair—your trip may become a symbol of the liberation of a whole generation of Russian musicians.

But besides, your visit to Moscow is of course itself already a historical fact (I love "facts" and hate "processes"), an event of historical significance in the full sense of the word, and its consequences for the whole of Russian culture will have the most enormous consequences in every sphere. I am convinced of that and it should help you, dear Igor Fyodorovich, to overcome the emotion and reflexes of musical "vomiting," which I understand.

But, in general, spontaneous meetings and expressions of admiration, which always signify *gratitude*, are somehow typical of Russians and are part of the very *essence* of Russian *cultural* experiences.

Remember how Pushkin was received when he returned from exile and appeared at the Bolshoi Theater.[68] Remember how Dostoevsky was met at the unveiling of the Pushkin Monument in Moscow (people fainted!).[69] Remember what went on at the train station when Tolstoy left Moscow![70] All that is frightening, but it calls for respect——

How happy I am that we can see each other in Brussels, or in London, perhaps in Paris![71]

Around 5 June we will be in Saint-Maurice.

I think you can write a few words to Balmont's daughter and send them to M. V. Yudina's address. . . .

What do Vera Arturovna and Bob[72] think about the invitation from Moscow?

I embrace you warmly, dear Igor Fyodorovich, with all my heart and thoughts.

Yours truly
P. Suvchinsky

5. Union of Soviet Composers to Igor Stravinsky

Moscow
17 June 1961

Honorable Igor Fyodorovich!

Allow me in the name of all Soviet musicians to extend my heartfelt congratulations on your birthday.[73] We wish you great health and new creative triumphs. We hope to celebrate your eighty-year anniversary with you a year from now in our dear homeland, in Moscow. With you with all our hearts.

The Secretariat of the Union of Soviet Composers:
Khrennikov, Shostakovich, Khachaturian,[74] Shaporin,[75] Kabalevsky[76]

6. Igor Stravinsky to the Union of Soviet Composers

[Hollywood]
[after 17 June 1961]

My honorable colleagues, I am profoundly touched by your kind greetings and nice wishes. I am planning with great pleasure to be with you in Moscow a year from now. Please give my heartfelt regards to all Soviet musicians.

Igor Stravinsky

7. Igor Stravinsky to Maria Yudina

Hollywood
19 June 1961

My sincerest greetings, most kind M. V. Yudina. I am sending you these lines of gratitude for your nice greetings and birthday wishes, and also because thanks to you I received this bibliographical rarity (with Balmont's signature)—the eighth volume of Balmont's poems with "Zvezdolikiy" ["Roi des étoiles"], which his daughter sent me with a very touching inscription. How can I thank you for all this? I kindly ask you to give to Balmont's daughter the note that I have included.[77]

A week ago, Khrennikov, Karayev, Yarustovsky,[78] and Bezrodny were here, and three days ago they and the Union of Soviet Composers sent me their heartfelt congratulations and an invitation to come to Moscow next year for my eightieth birthday, signed by Khrennikov, Shostakovich, Khachaturian, Shaporin, and Kabalevsky. I telegraphed my gratitude and said I would be pleased to be with them in Moscow a year from now.

If all goes well, I will make this pleasure a reality and amplify it by meeting with you.

Sincerely yours,
I. Stravinsky

8. Igor Stravinsky to Pyotr Suvchinsky

Hollywood
19 August 1961,
the day of Diaghilev's
death in 1929

Dear Pyotr Petrovich!
I was happy to receive your letter from 15 August [and to hear] what you tell me about Yudina.

Of course, if Yudina can correspond with Morton (in what language?) that is the easiest and safest thing to do: he is reliable and well informed.

It would also be good for me to see her in Helsinki, if they let her leave.[79] What a country! On the one hand, Stockhausen and the pianist,[80] Nadia Boulanger (why should she go there?),[81] my festivals, and on the other hand they refuse to let Yudina leave and confiscate Pasternak's portraits.[82] Some kind of madhouse, a nightmare. Is it really possible that there is some order to all this that we just do *not see*?

The older I get the harder it is for me to accept ceremonies, honors, etc. That's why this whole unexpected Russian story is extremely vexing, all the more because I *do not believe* it. Is it really possible that they will honor me, the composer of *Canticum Sacrum*, *Agon*, *Threni*, and *Movements* with performances of *The Firebird* and *Petrushka*? Dear Lord, do I really have to go through all this?

Your I. Stravinsky[83]

9. Maria Yudina to Marianna and Pyotr Suvchinsky

Moscow
20 September 1961

Dear, kind, remote, esteemed Mariannochka Lvovna and Pyotr Petrovich!

. . .[84] Your lovely note about how desirable it is that I meet my great friend is a wonderful example of your purity of soul and spiritual abstraction in the spirit of—— Webern—— Forgive me for saying this, but that came from the heart—and it was "salt into the wounds"—— "The elbow is near, but you can't bite it," dear Pyotr Petrovich!! Did you truly think that going to Helsinki—is a matter of "up and away"??!! . . .

MVY

10. Igor Stravinsky to Pyotr Suvchinsky

Hollywood
10 December 1961

We are back! Phew!!!

Off to Mexico in a week! Phew!!![85]

. . . How did my DOMAINE MUSICAL concert with Boulez go?[86] Please, let me know.

When (if) I have time, I will write about my impressions of Cairo, Australia, New Zealand, and Tahiti, and in the meantime I embrace you both.

Your I. Stravinsky

How about those mugs?![87] It's the Soviet *mrakobesï* [88] who are inviting me to this country! And they *did not give* Yudina a passport so she could travel to Helsinki to see me.[89]

Thank you. I am *not* going there.

11. Pyotr Suvchinsky to Igor Stravinsky

Paris
16 December 1961

Dear Igor Fyodorovich,

I am so grateful for your letter, I cannot even tell you! You say "phew," but I say thrice 33 times—"Thank God!"

The thing is, Dr. M. *Gilbert* in Zurich[90] scared me very much, because he thought that your trip would be a very difficult one, due to the *quick transitions* between different climates, temperatures, and pressure levels.

Did you receive the program of the concert "*Domaine musical*," which was dedicated to you? It was a true triumph! An overcrowded hall, Boulez — *en pleine forme*, all the musicians and singers, who played and sung as if it were a holiday! I haven't seen such overall enthusiasm in a long time!

But I think that Catherine *Gayer*[91] can't sing what she tries to. With the exception of the "Japanese Lyrics," her voice was not strong enough for anything else——

As far as the second concert—which was devoted to Schoenberg—is concerned, it was less successful. . . .[92] Only the Serenade op. 24 was performed outstandingly. By the way, about this Serenade: I don't know if anyone has pointed this out: the presence of *L'Histoire du soldat* strikes the eye and ear. It generally seems to me that one should truly reconsider all of Schoenberg (and not only him!) in terms of the influence that *you* had on him. Boulez agrees with me on this. Listening to the Serenade, I am completely convinced that Schoenberg, in spite of his polemical attacks on you, never lost sight of your music and *knew* it more and better than the "Schoenbergians" think.

Schoenberg himself, of course, did not admit it, even though there is nothing shameful about this fact. But the truth should nevertheless be restored.

The "aesthetic fact," the aesthetic discoveries of the new musical era belong to you and no one else. This fact is *hierarchically* more important than all the theoretical discoveries and inventions of musical composition, which, of course, are by themselves extremely important. But there is and should be a hierarchy in everything.

Forgive me for writing so briefly about such important things, but to me this has become something *obvious*. I talked about it for an entire evening with Boulez and A. Schaeffner——

The academic M. V. Alpatov from Moscow was here.[93] He talked a lot about the preparations for the upcoming musical year, "the year of Stravinsky," as he put it. I told him to communicate with R. Craft and L. Morton about everything, or else those fools in Moscow will make many stupid mistakes. They apparently don't know what to play, what to stage—— Perhaps Balanchine will be able to give advice and instructions——

Yudina asked me to send you two programs.[94]

Best wishes to you, Vera Arturovna, and Bob for the upcoming holiday and a Happy New Year. . . .

Thank you for the clippings; terrifying Soviet mugs, or as Remizov[95] used to say: terrifying muzzles! Oh terrible world!

Yours truly,
P. Suvchinsky

12. Pyotr Suvchinsky to Igor Stravinsky

Paris
18 December 1961

Dear Igor Fyodorovich!

Forgive me for bothering you again, but in my last letter I forgot to tell you that Alpatov, from the Academy of Sciences, who visited me, invited me to come to Moscow. I told him that I decided once and for all never to ask myself this question. I—personally—will *never* travel to Russia.

The problem is not my pro-Soviet or anti-Soviet convictions, but that I don't like to and can't "go back" to the past. The past becomes "another state of being," and going back is to my mind as forbidden as looking into the future——

Besides, in 1929 Gorky offered me to return to Russia together with Count Sviatopolk-Mirsky. Both of them returned, and what came of it? Gorky was poisoned and Mirsky became an alcoholic who died in exile.[96] Of course, now that can't be repeated and there is no danger, but the Stalin era *deformed* the Soviet mind to such a degree that anyone arriving from Europe will not be treated as what he *actually is* (for example, I was never a "White" émigré). But to be suspected of anything is an unpleasant feeling and experience. All that, so to speak, is my *personal* drama, and I am not confusing it with my *general* conviction that the historical *center* of our epoch is located in Russia.

I might agree to visit Russia if it were occupied (God forbid!) by the Chinese or Negroes, but not by Russians; between them and me there is a real quarrel.

Forgive me for writing you all this, but to whom else would I write it if not you—— But I won't talk about this anymore.

Happy Holidays once more and a Happy New Year.

Yours very truly
P. Suvchinsky

13. Maria Yudina to Marianna and Pyotr Suvchinsky

Moscow
26 December 1961

. . . I am preparing a concert in honor of Igor Fyodorovich; the *first*, for the Leningrad House of Composers proposes no less than two chamber [concerts], as their hall is small. And maybe more than two. The first will probably include: 1) the Septet; 2) *In Memoriam Dylan Thomas*;[97] 3) Concerto for two pianos; 4) *Duo Concertante* for violin and piano or the Sonata for two pianos (1943–44); 5) Serenade for piano (I just recorded it, without waiting for an opportunity to exchange questions and answers with Igor Fyodorovich—it should have been recorded in 1961, so I already waited for a long time!——);[98] 6) *Pastorale, Pribaoutki* and also some other early vocal pieces by Igor Fyodorovich.[99] It seems like a diverse program and everything promises to be festive. The *Duo* depends on the violinists; hardly anybody knows it; some are preparing for the Tchaikovsky Competition,[100] others are on tour——

("This one silently prepared for the Trinity Fair,
That one, loudly whistling, fashioned a crossbow!!——")[101]

and still others aren't suitable. That will be decided in a short while. If the Leningrad tenor can sing [*In Memoriam Dylan Thomas*] in English—good, but I doubt it. . . . They are already rehearsing *Orpheus* at the Maly Opera.[102] Alas, for a number of reasons, it seems we won't be able to invite Kasyan Yaroslavich Goleizovsky. . . .[103] Yes, and thank you for both symphonies by Igor Fyodorovich. The one in three movements was performed here, by some conductor from London, but I couldn't be there—— On January 27 I am supposed to play Stravinsky's first concerto[104] with the Radio Orchestra, in a strange program with Sibelius and—— Dvořák!!![105]—How horrible! . . .

Dieu vous garde! —Kisses.

TaV–Votre–
Rossinante——[106]

14. Igor Stravinsky to T. N. Khrennikov

[Hollywood]
31 December 1961

I received your letter from September after returning from concerts around the world.[107] My interrupted composition requires my presence here in June. I deeply regret being unable to come to Moscow, having declined all concerts in June, but I may visit you in late September[108] after all the concerts and festivals. Best wishes for the holidays.

Stravinsky

On 18 January 1961, Stravinsky, Vera, and Robert Craft were guests of President and Jacqueline Kennedy at a dinner held in Stravinsky's honor at the White House. A few weeks earlier, on the eve of the new year, Kennedy and Khrushchev had exchanged New Year's greetings, and two days earlier Stravinsky had received the State Department's medal. The dinner of filet of sole mousse and lamb was hastily organized and attended by Leonard Bernstein, Nicolas Nabokov, Goddard Lieberson (head of Columbia Records), and others. Robert Craft reported laconically on the president's comments at the event in his diary:

> *"We have been honored to have had two great artists," [the President said]—I am wondering if I. S. realizes that [Pablo] Casals is meant by the other—"here with us in the last months. As a student in Paris, my wife wrote an essay on Baudelaire, Oscar Wilde, and Diaghilev" (I. S. later: "I was afraid he was about to say his wife made a study of homosexuality.") "I understand that you, Mr. Stravinsky, were a friend of Diaghilev. And I was told that rocks and tomatoes were thrown at you in your youth." The President's speech is based on [Vera's] briefing during dinner, and the story of the* Sacre *première amazed him and even made him laugh aloud. Rocks and tomatoes, I explain later—I. S. has understood the phrase literally—is an American interpretation; they are thrown at baseball umpires. But the speech is short and—because an American President is honoring a great creative artist, and that is so absolutely unheard of in American history—it is moving.*[109]

Arthur Schlesinger, in contrast, remembered Stravinsky as "an amiable man, very tiny, with a manner of twinkling gravity" and totally drunk. When the President toasted him, "Stravinsky, obviously moved, responded with immense charm."[110] *The event was highly publicized.*

15. Igor Stravinsky to Pyotr Suvchinsky

Hollywood
14 February 1962

Dearest Pyotr Petrovich. With these lines I'm sending a picture of our visit to the President. At this *small dinner party* there was an atrocious selection of 25 people who had nothing in common with me. There was a lot of drinking and everyone (especially I) drank too much. When the President's secretary[111] asked me, "How do you feel, Maestro?" the maestro answered, "drunk," and we went home early, because what are we to do at such parties other than drink. She is very striking and charming, he is quick-witted, but both have very little to do with art. I think I was not invited for my music so much as for my age (and, I think, to be ahead of the Russians, *whom I will not visit*. To hell with them!—It is the *mrakobesie*[112] that invited me, and not those who interest me and who need me—they will not let me see them!!!)

I have begun working here until April 15. . . .
Write!!!

16. Pyotr Suvchinsky to Igor Stravinsky

Paris
21 February 1962

Dear Igor Fyodorovich!

Thank you very much for your letter! It is an utter joy for me. . . .

What you write about *mrakobesï* and the youth in Moscow is confirmed by the stories of Nathalie Sarraute (she is the "leading" writer in the group of M. Butor, A. Robbe-Grillet, a Russian Jew by descent, and a very nice and intelligent sixty-year-old lady).[113]

N. Sarraute was invited to Moscow and Leningrad as part of a "cultural exchange" and spent two weeks in Russia. . . . The youth is wonderful, interested in everything, ready to retype books and manuscripts on a typewriter, but—according to Nathalie Sarraute—when she was alone, she was seized by a feeling of horror: no matter what, the world around her seemed alien and incomprehensible. She told me all of this more or less confidentially, so I am writing to you about this "between the two of us." Of course, she is not you and "concealing" you is impossible, but *mrakobesï*, whether literary or musical ones, are always on guard and they are the bosses on their turf. But most important, is it really worth it for you, you in particular, to begin to argue and debate with all of these *mrakobesï* and all of these fools?—— Of course, I believe and know that an entire generation of musicians is expecting you there, but—— let them figure things out themselves and find their own way. When a real musician finally appears in the Soviet Union, he should come visit you, despite all obstacles.——

Of course, poor Maria Veniaminovna will be in despair and horror, but—I ask myself this question—are there people (musicians) in Moscow right now, worth the moral effort this trip will cost you? . . .

I embrace you with all my heart.

Yours truly
P. Suvchinsky

17. Igor Stravinsky to Maria Yudina

26 February 1962

My deepest respects and heartfelt thanks to M. V. Yudina for sending the drawings and the books about my father.[114]

Happy New Year.

Sincerely,
I. Stravinsky

18. Pyotr Suvchinsky to Igor Stravinsky

Paris
9 March 1962

Dear Igor Fyodorovich!

The day before yesterday M. V. Yudina called me from Moscow. She heard rumors that you are not going to Moscow and, completely in despair, she turned to me regarding this rumor. I of course answered that I don't know anything definite and suggested that she write you frankly and in detail.

Don't think that I am deciding and allowing myself to get involved in this enterprise which is so complicated for you, but I tend to think about it as follows: it seems to me that the *anniversary year (1962)*—is the year *least suited* for your trip: how many empty, official and bombastic words will be said! On the other hand, this year will show (in the quantity and quality of concerts and performances dedicated to you, as well as lectures, articles, books——) to what extent and degree Soviet musicians (and the public) have understood *who you are* and *what* your entire oeuvre represents?

If the results should *actually* turn out to be positive and impressive, then the ground will be prepared for a visit in 1963 during which you will be able to, as it were, forever "enshrine" in the minds of young musicians and the Russian musical world your principles, ideas, and traditions. Besides, this year will also clear up very many things in terms of the relationships between Russia and the West and the USA.

Once again, I implore you not to read these words as an attempt, even the tiniest one, to interfere in an already very complicated situation.

Perhaps "my thoughts" will be of use to you one way or another—— If Russian musicians have come to their senses due to your birthday, then before they invite you, they will *prove* that they are worthy of such a visit.

In that case, your visit in 1963 will be an *answer* to their efforts, will take on a different aspect, and will be carried out in the best of circumstances.

I don't think that such a postponement could offend Soviet musicians, even though M. V. Yudina was extremely concerned ("all our work will be lost!"——) with the rumors that reached her. In addition, she had time to tell me about the interview you gave, but I didn't quite understand what was the matter, where, how, and why.

Forgive me for bothering you with all these *propos*, but I couldn't not write about this. Maybe I am thinking and reasoning incorrectly——

I'm sending you the text of my presentation, which I read on Radio Cologne.[115] Forgive me and don't be angry if something in it should not be to your liking.

Yours truly
P. Suvchinsky

P.S. Perhaps I'm expressing myself poorly, but it seems to me that it is important now to show how much more difficult your historical task was than the task of Schoenberg, and that the *aesthetic fact* of your music is immeasurably higher and more deserving than the *aesthetic* contribution of Schoenberg.

19. Pyotr Suvchinsky to Maria Yudina

Paris
12 March 1962

. . . Now about our dear I. F. Str.

Remembering my last meeting with him in Zurich and judging from his letters—I am beginning to think that it might be better to *postpone* his visit to Moscow *by one year*. I fear that his visit (this year) will do more harm than good. That's my *personal* opinion.

I. F. has become very nervous and is not careful in his views and conversations.

His point of view is the following: I want to see Yudina and the youth in Moscow, but since I'm invited by officials I will *not* be allowed to see them, and I don't want to argue and speak with musical *mrakobesï* I have neither the time nor health for that.

Aside from that, he is of course afraid of "shock." After all, in spite of everything, for him Russia and the Russian language are values and facts of which he was deprived (through no fault of his own, as he probably thinks) and without which he was forced to live his entire life and with which he was always very *intimately* and inwardly connected. And this deprivation has become to him a personal offense, for which "someone" is responsible.

Don't forget that, despite the surprising and perhaps only seeming rationality of his work, I. F. is not an intellectual, but a sensitive, emotional, and I would say *artistic* soul, in the widest sense of that word. It takes very little to offend and enrage him, and then communication becomes impossible.

To converse with I. F. is the greatest delight. He is brilliantly witty in his every word, but there are topics that must not be touched, since he simply *doesn't understand and acknowledge them*. Exactly that is what I am afraid of.

It seems to me that *in a year*, when the "anniversary year" will end and it will become clear *how* they truly feel about him in Russia, his trip will be advisable.

Besides, don't forget that there are all sorts of people flocking around I. F. and from a distance I find it very difficult to discuss all the "pros" and "cons" of his visit. In any case, write to him again, in detail and frankly.

May I send you the text of my talk about I. F. which I read on Radio Cologne? I would very much like to hear your opinion about this talk. . . .

Don't be upset with me if I am of a slightly different opinion than you in some regards. I know I. F. too well, I know his sharp polemical pronouncements too well not to warn you about it. But of course, he has to decide for himself. I repeat, in a year, when the "anniversary" period will be over, which he *hates* (he recently wrote me: "I am invited everywhere not because of my music, but because I'm 80 years old!") it will be easier and more sensible for you and everyone to meet with him.——

Always devoted and
loving you,
P. S.

From your last letter I see that you have fairly "complicated" relations with the Composers' Union. This fact worries me for two reasons: 1) Won't you get in trouble when I. F. S. comes to visit; and 2) How will you "share" him (that is, I. F.) between you, his friends, and the officials? For he is invited, unless I am mistaken, specifically by the "Soviet Composers Union"? Write me about this.

20. Igor Stravinsky to Pyotr Suvchinsky

> Hollywood
> 17 March 1962,
> at night

Dear Pyotr Petrovich!

I received your wonderful article about *Spring* and read it voraciously and with gratitude. Who crossed out in pencil on page nine what you wrote about the influence of *L'Histoire du soldat* on Schoenberg's Serenade?

Thank you also for your letter. Overall I agree with its reasoning about my planned visit to Russia, but it seems that I will nevertheless have to make an appearance there (in late September; earlier that month I will be in Israel by invitation of the government).[116] To tell you the truth, I don't see a big difference in visiting in September of this year or in 1963. Either way I won't see anything new in one year, in terms of their relationship toward my music. And if I don't go, I will upset many (which I don't want), for whom my appearance there is essential (and not just desirable—Yudina)[117]. . . .

I will be so pleased to see you, if only briefly.

I embrace both of you. WRITE ME.

> Your I. Stravinsky

21. Igor Stravinsky to Pyotr Suvchinsky

> Hollywood
> 12 April 1962

Dear Pyotr Petrovich!

I'm sending you this hysterical, 25-page letter by dear Yudina.[118] Once again I'm simply becoming afraid to travel there. I fear that I have neither enough strength nor nerves to bear this mixture of *admiration, provincialism, and* "cultural exchanges" with Western Marxists "who rise up against the formal and inhuman decadent art of the bourgeois world" (I am copying this out of the *Le Monde* article you sent me about the USSR.)[119]

Read this never-ending letter, and return it to me in Paris, when, I hope, I will be able to embrace you in the first half of May, as I am doing now mentally.

Your
Stravinsky

22. Pyotr Suvchinsky to Maria Yudina

Paris
16 April 1962

. . . Over the last years, Stravinsky's prestige and significance has increased immeasurably. He is of course the genius of our time. His creative biography is unmatched. Everything I'm writing here—so disorderly and brief—is not just my personal opinion. All my young friends think so too.

Stravinsky's interaction with Boulez and Stockhausen is quite significant. . . .

I deeply believe in the cyclical structure of life, and that the transition from one cycle to another is a transition into "otherness," and the otherness of the new cycle prohibits returning to the previous one.

In any case, thank you, dear, sweet Maria Veniaminovna, for thinking that I might visit together with I. F. But I am not needed by anyone and not interesting to Russia; whereas you, after B. L. P.,[120] personify all that is necessary and dear to me out of what is "there." That is all I need——

The other day I received the book *Balakirev: Issledovaniya i stat'i*, Gos. Muzïkal'noye izd-vo, Leningrad, 1961. Regarding the article of some Gozenpud, they write that I. F. is a "composer, ideologue (!?) of formalism and cosmopolitanism (?!)."[121] What wretchedness; it is time to wise up. . . .

I have long wanted to tell you: keep in mind, just in case, that I. F. does *not* like the music and aesthetics of O. Messiaen. This "distaste" is one-sided on the part of I. F., since Messiaen does wonderful analyses of Stravinsky's music in his class at the conservatory. I don't understand why the Russian "dandies" [*stilyagi*] are attacking Stravinsky "from the left" in the name of John Cage. Cage is a wonderful creature and I love him. Boulez, on the other hand, feels "ambivalently" about him.[122]

Send me, if possible, clippings from Soviet newspapers about the ballet performance of Stravinsky.[123] *He is very interested in it. . . .*

P. Suvchinsky

23. Pyotr Suvchinsky to Igor Stravinsky

Paris
17 April 1962

Dear Igor Fyodorovich!

Indeed, one can only withstand such a Russian force of nature in the Russian way: by grabbing the back of one's neck and scratching one's ears!

All that is clear is that M. V. Yudina is an awfully talented, temperamental personality, who finally rushed greedily toward her happiness and is choking on it, if she hasn't choked yet!——

I am very afraid that her enthusiasm and the joy of the many young musicians, who are of course expecting you in the state of a completely justified and understandable ecstasy, does not allow her and them to consider all the circumstances of your visit. For example, in her last letter to me, M. V. Yudina asks me to send her various scores "which the Union of Soviet Composers *has*, but I am not able to and do not want to ask them for anything."—— It follows that Yudina is on bad terms with official music circles. . . . [124]

I will also ask her to send press reviews about the "ballets of Stravinsky." It will be interesting to read how your music is being received and treated *now*. It seems to me, dear Igor Fyodorovich, that you already can't change the decision you have made: everyone knows that you are going to Moscow and, I should say, everyone is *unanimously* excited. You and Vera Arturovna will have to "chloroform" your sensitivity and impressionability and to sink to the bottom, as though down into a coal mine. But I'm also convinced that there will be many unexpected good things. After all, the country, nation, people—all that cannot be compared with anything else!

Whatever the case might be—now, at this time, "the cultural migration" is turning in this direction. Your visit will be a historical fact. . . . I embrace you warmly and look forward to seeing you—— like Yudina!

Faithfully
P. Suvchinsky

24. Pyotr Suvchinsky to Maria Yudina

[Paris]
21 May 1962

Dear, kind, esteemed Maria Veniaminovna,

The day before yesterday I sent off I. F.—to South Africa (Johannesburg, Pretoria, Le Cape——)![125] This trip, which to many seems like a form of madness, fills him with such enthusiasm. When he isn't writing music, he is terribly bored. Such travels are not only an amusement, a diversion for him but also, how to put it, an "escape forward." Besides, he says that he prefers spending money on all sorts of tours[126] rather than giving it to the American treasury. His health is very good; he was cheerful and affectionate, and apparently very pleased by his usual stay in Paris.

The misunderstanding with your phone call *upset* him *terribly*. Here is how it all happened: after his illness, I. F. had been having difficulty walking, for 3 years now; so that he wouldn't have to walk downstairs, they redirected the call to his room; he was busy and asked them to wait for *two minutes*; [but] when he picked up the phone the connection with Moscow was interrupted—— He apologizes very, very much to you.

I talked to him about the typographical errors in the Concerto, Serenade, and Sonata. He asked me to tell you that there is such a list of typos, but that he doesn't know where to find it. I. F. asked you not to worry about it: "A good musician knows everything himself and can play with errors, that isn't important." . . .[127]

Yours truly
P. Suvchinsky

25. Maria Yudina to Marianna and Pyotr Suvchinsky

Moscow
5–15 June 1962

. . . I am writing only the most important things: the center of my life is now not the "Warsaw autumn"—I still haven't planned the trip but will soon—but Igor Fyodorovich, his colossal figure, his path and—our Exhibit.[128] It is already time to start "tying up loose ends," but in my view the material is still insufficient. A lot of different things, especially about his years before America, and very few things about that. . . .

Alas, it is too late for me to correct the typos in the Stravinsky. I hope that they will not distort Igor Fyodorovich's works too much. Given his high standards, strictness, and accuracy, it isn't entirely clear to me *how he could allow* these errors and why the publishers would "*overlook*" them. . . .

Igor Fyodorovich will probably never understand our fates—— And you, dear friends, all understand them, of course. *I implore and beg you to come together with him.* I implore and beg you to start working on the visa. Valerian Mikhailovich Bogdanov-Berezovsky, author of the book about Ig. Fyod-ch's father and the vice chairman of the Leningrad Union of Composers, *an excellent gentleman*, asks the same. And many other people, musicians, scientists, and, of course, *M. V. Alpatov.* (I was at their place yesterday.) You are not only *NOT!!* "not needed by anyone"!! (nonsense, I am sorry!), but *needed by all of us both on your own and as the best friends and companions of Igor Fyodorovich.* Only with you will this trip truly be on its proper tracks. You are inimitable and irreplaceable, and I don't see anyone here who could comment on everything and explain it to him *truthfully.* I am likely insufficient in this sense and do not belong, as you know, to our "notables"—— Vera Arturovna has also been out of

Russia for "a hundred years" and will "float" outside of earthly life etc. *and cannot be compared to you, obviously.* Make this sacrifice, if it is a sacrifice, in the name of what is really important, Stravinsky's visit. *And why would it be a "sacrifice"?*—— You will see and experience, without doubt, many wonderful things—— The Trinity Lavra of St. Sergius (now Zagorsk),[129] Leningrad, our very own Moscow, the beauty of our autumn, a multitude of kind people, and *much, much more both for you and Mariannochka Lvovna—new and interesting,* and it is possible that many things here will make you ecstatic! . . . To be here—with Stravinsky—it is your mission, forgive me! . . .

Yours,
M. V. Yudina . . .

26. Pyotr Suvchinsky to Maria Yudina

[Paris]
4 July 1962

. . . Dear, kind Maria Veniaminovna,—thank you, M. V. Alpatov, and V. M. Bogdanov-Berezovsky for your invitation, but at this time my (our) visit is out of the question. I already wrote you: this is a very complicated matter for me.

Of course, Igor Fyodorovich does not understand many things about today's Soviet Russia, but he, always and in everything, makes up for it with unusual experience and gumption. Don't worry—everything will turn out well. . . .

Yours truly, P. S.

Stravinsky arrived in Moscow on a flight aboard a Soviet TU-104 from Paris on 21 September 1962, accompanied by Robert Craft and Vera Stravinsky. In his widely read account of the event (first published in Encounter*), Craft describes the welcome they received at the airport and the pride he felt in his ability to understand the linguistic Babylon he, Stravinsky, and Vera faced there. Craft also incessantly objectifies women in his account of the event, and expresses a deep sense of alienation and condescension toward the appearance and attitudes of his Soviet contemporaries. He recognized the "familiar faces" of Tikhon Khrennikov and Kara Karayev. He also recognized people "familiar-by-resemblance: a woman with the slant eyes Picasso saw in I. S., singing to me in a high voice 'Je suis la nièce de Monsieur Stravinsky.' Another short and stout woman, whom I mistake for Jacob Epstein, says 'Ich bin Yudina,' and plants a wet kiss. Someone else hands me a birch bark basket containing moss, a twig, a blade of wheat, an acorn, a leaf, telling me (in English) she is the daughter of the poet Konstantin Balmont. Inside the terminal we shake scores of hands and hear* dobro pozhalovat *over and over, from large, round, smiling faces."[130] The party arrives at the National Hotel, where they drink vodka and sweet champagne, and marvel at the miracle of Stravinsky's arrival. When Stravinsky reads Shostakovich's telegram (letter 27, below) aloud for the group, "national sentiment flows with the national champagne, and gets even thicker."*

27. Dmitry Shostakovich to Igor Stravinsky

Leningrad
21 September 1962

The 100-year anniversary celebration of the Conservatory has kept me in Leningrad. I regret very much that I could not meet you. I am sending you my very best wishes.

Dmitry Shostakovich

The Stravinskys remained in the Soviet Union from 21 September to 11 October. The visit pushed to the extreme the lifelong tension Stravinsky felt between his private life and public persona. On the one hand, he shone in his role as an icon of twentieth-century music and prodigal son. He gave concerts on 26 September (described in Jonathan Cross's essay in this volume, "Stravinsky in Exile"), 28 September, 2 and 8 October, in which he conducted his old Russian favorites with a smattering of neoclassicism: Petrushka, The Rite of Spring, Feu d'artifice, *Capriccio,* Ode, Symphony in Three Movements, Orpheus, *and* The Firebird Suite. *He also dutifully attended an endless stream of official meetings, receptions, and events. On 25 September, Stravinsky and his entourage paid an official visit to Yekaterina Furtseva, the Minister of Culture. There the question of his public bad-mouthing of the Soviet Union came back to haunt him again. "After the greetings and honors," Karen Khachaturian, the famous composer's nephew and a composer in his own right, wrote in his diary, Furtseva "suddenly said, 'Well, there were times in your life when you really disapproved of us.' She read him a whole reprimand. I almost fainted. Stravinsky got up and said: 'I am a Russian, I left Russia before all the events because I was busy with work in Europe. I felt very oppressed by the atmosphere in Russia.' And he took out a small set of keys: 'But now you tell me: I had an estate, a family estate, and my things were there, among them a small box of my father's that I treasured very much. Musorgsky's letters to my father were in it. All that disappeared, where is all that—are you going to tell me? Yes, I look critically at certain things that I don't like in Russia, but this is my homeland and I have the right to criticize it, just like my wife. But if a stranger admonishes her I will beat him. So don't you admonish me, my relationship is not with you but with my homeland.'"[131] After this confrontation the visits continued unabated, culminating in a private meeting with Khrushchev on 11 October.[132]*

The Union of Soviet Composers dominated Stravinsky's itinerary; visits and activities with them were organized almost every day of his trip. He discussed twelve-tone technique with composers there on 5 and 7 October; listened to works by Georgy Sviridov, Vadim Salmanov, Galina Ustvolskaya, and Edvard Mirzoyan, and met Boris Tishchenko and Sergey Slonimsky, who remembers him as more interested in talking about himself than examining the scores of Soviet composers.[133] During a discussion with young composers on serialism after a rehearsal on 8 October, he apparently quipped to Khrennikov, to everybody's general amusement, "You too, Tikhon Nikolayevich, will be trying it soon."[134] The mood became more serious when the composers asked why Stravinsky wanted to "visit his homeland."[135] "I decided to come because it seemed to me that my arrival will help revitalize your music, which is—although perhaps already to a lesser degree now—oriented toward the nineteenth century. That's horrible, it's reactionary—after all, in the first half of the century Russian art rushed out to the forefront. The Russian people have an enormous hidden potential that was artificially restrained and hindered—— My arrival is supposed to help musicians get past this impasse with greater determination. I am not a politician, I did not come to my homeland to give political speeches. I am a musician, and through my music I want to help you, so that your music will be turned not toward the past but the future. In that I see my mission, my duty."[136]

Behind the façade of public pronouncements and official obligations, Stravinsky experienced his visit as a profoundly private and emotional event, the intensity of his feeling magnified by the pain of his almost fifty-year absence: he visited his old haunts, relished newfound attachments to all things Russian, and reminisced nostalgically about the past. His niece Xenia (the daughter of his older brother Yury, who had died in 1941) restored a lost sense of family connection; the two shared stories of their family history during a visit to her apartment on the Kryukov Canal. Stravinsky was also surrounded by old acquaintances: Lina Prokofiev[137] came to vist, among many others. Rozhdestvensky gave Stravinsky the gift of a score he had bought—a copy of Debussy's Préludes with Debussy's dedication to Stravinsky on the cover—thereby indirectly informing him for the first time that his library at Ustilug had indeed been plundered and his books sold.[138] By all accounts, Stravinsky and Vera were profoundly moved by these personal encounters, and by the reacquaintance with their home. Craft reports how they were already feeling pro-Soviet after one day there, and how they started to discuss false images of the Soviet Union propagated in the United States. "They are at home," he realizes. "The schizophrenic U.S./U.S.S.R situation does not bother them at all, and forty-eight years abroad have not brainwashed them in the least. Their abiding emotion is an intense pride in everything Russian."[139]

Yet the Russia Stravinsky characterized in French to Robert Craft as their plane was descending over Moscow as "caviar and shit" aroused in him immensely ambivalent feelings.[140] This ambivalence crystalized around the figure of Shostakovich, whom he was now eager to meet. Karen Khachaturian remembered how he kept asking from the moment he arrived, "Where is Shostakovich?"[141] The two composers had an opportunity to play out their differences when they sat next to each other at an elaborate reception hosted by Minister of Culture Furtseva on 1 October. Shostakovich "chews not merely his nails but his fingers," Craft wrote condescendingly, "twitches his pouty mouth and chin, chain-smokes, wiggles his nose in constant adjustment of his spectacles, looks querulous one moment and ready to cry the rest." Although Craft did not speak Russian and experienced the event through his translator Alexandra Alexandrovna Afonina, he remembered Stravinsky standing up and declaring, "A man has one birthplace, one fatherland, one country—he can have only one country—and the place of his birth is the most important factor in his life. I regret that circumstances separated me from my fatherland, that I did not bring my works to birth there and, above all, that I was not there to help the new Soviet Union create its new music. But I did not leave Russia only by my own will, even though I admit that I disliked much in my Russia and in Russia generally—but the right to criticize Russia is mine, because Russia is mine and because I love it. I do not give any foreigner that right."[142] Karen Khachaturian described the same dinner far less dramatically, and could recall only that Stravinsky and Shostakovich tried in vain to strike up a conversation about Puccini.[143] At a farewell dinner on 10 October,

Shostakovich sat at Stravinsky's side, "looking even more frightened and tortured than at the first conclave, probably because he thinks a speech is expected of him," according to Robert Craft. Shostakovich apparently told Stravinsky he was "overwhelmed" by the Symphony of Psalms *and had completed his own piano score, to which Stravinsky deviously responded that he shared Shostakovich's high regard for Mahler. "Poor Shostakovich starts to melt," Craft reports, "then quickly freezes again as I. S. continues with 'But you should go beyond Mahler.'" Craft again: "Toward the end of the evening, and after drinking several* zubrovkas, *Shostakovich pathetically confessed that he would like to follow I. S.'s example, and conduct his own music, 'But I don't know how not to be afraid.'"[144] Shostakovich, for his part, may not have been as frightened and starstruck as Craft claims. Later Shostakovich remarked "Stravinsky the composer, I worship. Stravinsky the thinker, I despise."[145]*

Maria Yudina fell through the cracks of Stravinsky's high-profile visit. Neither Stravinsky's close friend, nor a valued male competitor, nor an official representative of the state, and disrespected by Craft, she found herself excluded from Stravinsky's social calendar. Craft noted that she didn't "sit smoothly with the powers of the Composers' Union." When she "pops a book from under the table and attempts to make them listen to her read religious philosophy from it" during a luncheon at the Composers' Union on 6 October after her performance of Stravinsky's Septet and a student performance of the Octet, "strong expressions of dislike are exchanged on both sides." Stravinsky acted oblivious to her suffering and cautious in his contact with her. He left the Soviet Union on 11 October 1962. Four days later, the Cuban Missile Crisis began.

28. Maria Yudina to Marianna and Pyotr Suvchinsky

Moscow
October 1962

Dear, dear Marianna L'vovna and Pyotr Petrovich!

I am returning to life as if after a typhoid fever, after an adventure on a stormy sea, after dreams of the most fantastical nature from which I couldn't awake——
——Yes, this was Stravinsky, living and breathing, in the flesh, the great Master and at the same time—the sweetheart Igor Fyodorovich, the wit, the tender familiar friend, endlessly close—— But he was surrounded by a multi-person entourage the barbed wire of which was impossible to penetrate; add to this countless paparazzi, reporters, and also simply onlookers insolently barging in (to rehearsals), pseudo-artists, insolent musicians with stupid things to say, ladies of various ages with bouquets; the main thing is that I was in Leningrad almost the whole time preparing the exhibit, and when he was there himself—I was feverishly learning the Septet—— But I went back and forth 4 times during this period, I met him [upon his arrival], went to 3 rehearsals (in Moscow), his and Craft's, and one in Leningrad, went to 1 (the main) program, saw him 2 times (briefly) at the "National,"[146] at our completely ruined ballets,[147] when he—alas—went to see them—— The entourage was composed of Craft's translator, Tikhon and his wife, Karen Khachaturian (he

is actually cute), Stravinsky's niece Xenia Yuryevna, she's nice—— Everything I planned didn't work out—i.e. Zagorsk, the Rublev Museum—the most serene place in Moscow itself (the restored Andronikov Monastery, where Rublev is buried),[148] a modest tea at my place with the Alpatovs and Lina Ivanovna with her sweetest youngest son Oleg, a visit to a spiritual person, a very educated individual—— etc. Even a visit to the Scriabin Museum, mainly for the sake of the new instrument. . . . Once in Leningrad, Igor Fyodorovich himself sent for me to eat lunch with him, but I did not succeed in steering the conversation onto more substantial tracks, the same thing as happened in Leningrad after the concert—— The whole time I had the impression it was going in one ear and out the other—— Craft was on the run the whole time too, and Vera Arturovna produced a strange effect, as if she was exhausted to the point of collapse, as she apparently was!! It's likely, as she isn't so young!!—— Only once did she say to me, "You are truly something out of a fairy tale!"—— I could not (and wouldn't have wanted even if I could, as I am completely in debt, and there are poor, extremely poor people!) give them expensive presents, but I gave them all some of my best books (even that old one about Peter I's cabinet of curiosities), that honey which I. F. loves, jam from the blackthorn in my garden—— But they were showered, it seems, with expensive and flashy gifts. They delighted in everything, as if they were big children, and that was charming. But all this is "menschliches"[149]—— When it comes to art, I. F. amazed everyone with his conducting, especially *Firebird* in Leningrad; this was the peak of his might, so to speak—— But in the end, *Orpheus* came alive during the 1st concert and was grandiose; in rehearsal it had been somewhat dead; I don't dare ascribe anything to myself, but in the intermission I chatted with many of the musicians, with the concertmasters, showed them photographs of stagings (Balanchine, Munich, and others) and sparked their imagination; maybe this helped a little bit—— Don't be angry with me for writing this, but ah, the musicians are so far from myth—— I even said this to them; about the Ode to Natalia Koussevitsky Igor Fyodorovich spoke (very well and clearly), but apparently thought that everyone knew everything about Orpheus already—— Or his genius hands (and not my modest words) awoke at least artistic pride in the musicians, [the inspiration] to play without fluttering their bows, by gliding across the instrument——

It's a terrible shame that they did *The Fairy's Kiss* in Leningrad, poor Craft got stuck in it, that composition does not flatter Stravinsky. For some reason, the symphony *In Memoriam Debussy*[150] disappeared. . . . I was satisfied with Craft the conductor; I don't need "temperament," gestures, sparkle. . . . I thought he conducted the *Sacre* magnificently. But 90% of people prefer Markevich——[151] I have to tell you, however, as a phenomenally close friend, that I think Robert committed a faux pas when after the *Sacre* and the first bows, he turned to the loge where I. F. and V. Art. were sitting and blew kisses in that direction—— Here, such tricks are [considered] unpleasant and primitive; it doesn't go well with his abstractness; I became very embarrassed for him, but did not tell him that, naturally; I pushed through all the admiring rabble to him with 2 bouquets of genuine small roses from one of the local greenhouses and a crystal goblet full of truffles for Robert; and the next day—again to Leningrad, and so on. . . . I was at the rehearsal in Leningrad; during intermission, in the Philharmonia's Red Salon there was a wonderful lecture with the "scientific-student" community, there were about 50 young people, conductors, by the way—Gennady Rozhdestvensky tagged along behind Igor Fyodorovich—and older composers; they asked smart and stupid questions, but Igor Fyodorovich—as always, spoke grandiosely: simply, sharply, "incisively," as he himself said about something else, when necessary—cagey, when necessary, "head-on" (Meyerhold's expression). He praised Boulez, and partly praised Stockhausen, recommended the serial and dodecaphonic technique, its discipline, explained its role in music history (the changing eras). Everyone was shocked, stunned, happy; *moi-même*[152]—in particular; toward the end, when everyone was leaving, I greeted him with my favorite quote "spiritus flat ubi vult,"[153] i.e. he has now told us what is most important, he broke into smiles and answered: "ubi, ubi[154]—in Leningrad!!"—Of course, I didn't get to Oranienbaum and Peterhof![155] The exhibit was mounted half an hour before its opening; the fact that I. F. shortened his stay in Leningrad by 2 days was particularly torturous, especially for me, I was already sleeping only 2–3 hours a night, couldn't be at the most *simpatico* reception of the Leningrad composers, where there were serious conversations, where there are outstanding people (and he himself [was] particularly pleased with the reception!); during my workday, I would suddenly fall asleep for 3 minutes and ask myself, "Where am I, Moscow or Leningrad?"—— It's likely that they told delightful tales of Peterhof and Oranienbaum. The autumn was divine, almost without rain, *wie gerufen*!![156]—— It was lovely at the aerodrome upon his arrival, although the departure for some reason carried an Arakchevian[157] (now outdated) character. I am still taken aback, how some have gone and some remain—— Well, we left quickly, me, Balmont's daughter, Alpatov, the Radio editor, the old sculptor Kepinov,[158] an old admirer of Vera Art[urovna]. Someone had heard Tikhon saying to someone else: "Pare people down!"—— And I cherished: "The hour of departure is more alive than the meeting itself"——[159] God judged otherwise . . . —My quill won't write— I'll end this letter. *I will write more soon. Write to me, I beg you.* . . .

Always yours,
M. V. Yudina

29. Maria Yudina to Yelena and Mikhail Bakhtin[160]

Moscow
21 November 1962

. . . I asked [you] for the last 100 rub. since I could no longer defer payment for the photographers, whom I also paid *myself*; that was the *Stravinsky exhibit* at the House of Composers with which I was tasked. And it was very successful—— I put in about 1,500 rubles (in the new currency!——) i.e. more than I will now put into the new house—— In addition to everything else, I traveled from Moscow to Leningrad and back 5 times for the materials, to meet Stravinsky, to sit in on his rehearsals and meetings. When I was invited to the banquets, I did not have time to go, so I ate only a few official caviar sandwiches the evening he arrived!—— Some partied—the majority—the orchestras rehearsed, which is what they should do, some worked day and night, among those—chiefly—your humble servant. *Comme toujours*——[161] I have been corresponding with him for 4 years! He is charmingly youthful, agile, wise, witty, resourceful, sarcastic, educated, a polyglot, has seen the whole world, but at the same time he is an old slave of God, dreaming about eternity. In his art, his compositions, and in his conducting there isn't the slightest trace of decline—— Now I am moving on to the late Schoenberg, who is also a grandiose figure—but of a different order. . . .

If it will be possible to translate the "Stravinsky–Craft Dialogues" it will be "marvelous"—— His *Autobiography* was translated by Lyubov Shaporina, who is 82 years old, how about that!![162] Craft is Stravinsky's assistant, a magnificent example of an absolutely abstract person: extremely educated, but perhaps a touch too remote from all that is living. He is indispensable to Stravinsky, as a son, helper, commentator; his three adult children[163] live in different cities and countries, they have their own life. He helps them, and is generally very family-oriented. His wife is a former beauty, an artist, who somehow effaces herself, but is one and a half times as tall as her already tall husband. . . .

M. V.

30. Pyotr Suvchinsky to Maria Yudina

[Paris]
7 January 1963

. . . Thank you for the program of the premiere of Shostakovich's 13th Symphony. Everything you write about it (the symphony) and him (Shostakovich)—is deeply intelligible to me if I use my imagination and put myself in your place. But what am I to do if this music, awfully talented and historically validated in the Russian "place of development" (using a translation of the term "Entwicklungsort" from the field of geopolitics)—drives me to mental and nervous despair!? It seems to me that Shostakovich is simultaneously hero and victim; in his music and in his fate all the fundamental contemporary problems of music, art, aesthetics meet. Someday, someone will write about him (about his intention)—a real treatise on the psychology and culture of our (transitional) epoch. . . . Yesterday I received a long Christmas letter from I. F. He is surprised that he hasn't seen a single line from you since his visit to Moscow.

About I. F.—I would like to tell you the following: it is just as easy to "*over*love" as it is to "*under*love" him. Actually, in all relations with him exclude all *psychology* once and for all. The supreme level of his artistic persona and the always surprising contradictions of his character (the seismographic sensitivity of certain centers and the paralyzation of others) determine all "contact" with him. He should be loved above all (and only) as a miracle. That is not so easy, of course, since a "miracle," precisely because of its "foreign-ness"—doesn't evoke *feelings* of love, but more likely feelings of gratefulness of a higher order, which is related to surprise and delight. . . .

Forever faithful
to you, P. S.

Write! Faithful
and loving you, P. S.

In spring 1963, Yudina began to feel more severe consequences of her advocacy of Stravinsky and contemporary music. She had been playing a delicate balancing act with the powers that be for decades and her luck was about to turn. After returning from a tour in March, she was denounced by teachers at the Khabarovsk Music School who were upset that she talked for hours about Berg, Hindemith, Schoenberg, and Stravinsky, rather than performing a concert, and that she praised Volkonsky but would not speak about Shostakovich's music. Concert organizations of the Soviet Union were ordered to stop programming her and she returned to concertizing only in 1966.[164]

31. Maria Yudina to Marianna and Pyotr Suvchinsky

Moscow
8 June 1963

. . . They wrote a "letter" (in fact it's called something a little different!—) about me from Khabarovsk to the ministry about the "incorrect illumination of contemporary music"—— I answered that I still think Stravinsky is a genius, Pasternak's poetry is genius, Volkonsky is on the verge of genius, Shostakovich's XIII Symphony is remarkable, Rachmaninoff is a hopelessly dated composer,

Figure 1. Maria Yudina meets Igor Stravinsky, 6 October 1962.

etc. Seeing as how these facts are fully official, I have the moral opportunity to write about them to you in Paris. . . . I finally overcame myself and sent Rufina Vsevolodovna Ampenova[165] a list of fifteen musical scores by Igor Fyodorovich. The thing is that except for the *Symphony of Psalms*, the Mass, and *Oedipus*, I gave everything away. After all, we all live through the gifts of others and this is the most essential law of existence, I think—so I did the right thing. Just think, I even gave away my beloved *Threni, Perséphone*!! That's why I asked her for all of this, making reference to Igor Fyodorovich himself and —— to you, too, dear Pyotr Petrovich! Don't be too hard on me, but I didn't even have *Spring* and *Renard*, I was ashamed to admit it! . . . .

Of course, I will write to Igor Fyodorovich, but he's not someone to listen to your problems. He is "in the empyrians." And Vera Arturovna— God forgive me!—it seems to me that she thinks all strangers are *unnecessary, wearying, incomprehensible*. And Craft-cipher[166]—how can anybody be friends with him? How aptly you described him! Exactly, he has everything, internally, and is somehow utterly out of place—— But I only sung his praises to strangers. . . . One has to spare others' sense of honor and all of this *does not concern me*, whether it is in place or not, but all together—but still it is sad that I didn't really get to exchange even two words with Igor Fyodorovich. . . .

Your M. V. Yudina

32. Maria Yudina to Marianna and Pyotr Suvchinsky

Moscow
22 July 1963

. . . *About I. F.*—— Perhaps the only correct way of living is: "not to get offended"—— But it is impossible *not to be upset*—— I phoned Milan twice, at the Hotel Continental. At first I was told: "We are expecting them, but they haven't arrived yet" (June 18); the second time: "They have arrived but are rehearsing" (June 19); then I sent a telegram letter (because of the cheaper price), those take *twenty-four hours, no longer*, that was on the 20th or 21st [of June]. It was not returned to me—— that means *they received it*—— In it were congratulations, respects, and kisses *to all three*,[167] a request for a "little message" and my new address—all very detailed—— Until now he (I. F.) has always answered me. For example, he received Rublev[168] from me in Italy and responded immediately—— I know from Xenia Yuryevna—no, no, that's wrong, from Lina Ivanovna Prokofiev, who is on good terms with Khrennikov and his wife, Klara, that Khrennikov received a lengthy congratulatory telegram on his fiftieth birthday from I. F. and Ks. Yur. Stravinsky[169] (his niece) wrote me about how Khrennikov called him (I. F.) to invite him to Moscow and how I. F. "recognized Khrennikov's voice"[170]—— So, he "exchanged" me with those who are at the helm—— I did everything that was possible and impossible—— and am no longer needed and, ergo, can be *disregarded*. *When something like this happens to another, one can talk a lot; when it happens to oneself, one can only step aside and be silent*—— To be honest, there were analogous touches when he was here, too, but I looked at them "over the barriers,"[171] but now I have some-how—— lost all desire—— no one should have to *aufbinden*[172] one's friendship and one's—— understanding—— His brilliance and overall charm remain, of course.

> And the heart forgave
> But the heart cooled——[173] . . .

It is almost no secret to anyone that for the expenses for the exhibit about Igor Fyodorovich I had to put in very large sums myself, or borrow them from others, since the House of Composers couldn't exceed its limit and there was neither time, nor help, nor money. I was helped by artists, workers of the Hermitage, and just friends from my days in university. I invited everyone, except for Valerian Mikhailovich Bogdanov-Berezovsky; I even paid for Nina Konstantinovna Bruni's trips. But the House of Composers—*no matter how much I insisted!*—did not orga-nize a guestbook, did not photograph the exhibit, and spoiled a few things—— The *Melos* correspondents didn't even mention me—— The Polish *Ruch Muzycny* correspondents did, but did not understand (or want to understand) the key to everything. Only Ralph Albertovich Parker[174] wrote in his report to London about I. F.'s visit to the U.S.S.R., briefly, but accurately—— And I created the exhibit at the Maly Opera Theatre in advance, calmly, and then I gave it into the knowing hands of their museum—I. F. saw that I could not even come to the (actually pleasant and modest) dinner with him and the composers, since I was still rehearsing the Septet at night, and in the evening we were finishing everything: hanging, gluing, labeling—— I met him in my "working gear" and that is how we were photographed—— *Forgive me for returning to things that have been suffered through and forgotten*—— But his indifference, his orientation toward the powerful people out of those whom he saw in his homeland—alas, slightly upset old wounds—— Of course, only the Lord God passes judgment and it is not my place to judge our—universal master. . . .[175]

Your MVY . . .

33. Pyotr Suvchinsky to Maria Yudina

Saint Maurice
5 August 1963

. . . I also received a long and very touching letter from our dear, lovely, unique Igor Fyodorovich. He is now in Santa Fe, New Mexico.

I understand everything that happened between him and you, and sympathize very, very much. But, believe me, he knows perfectly well who and what you are, he always speaks about you with great interest and affection, but—he really must be understood and forgiven. He doesn't *really* correspond with anyone (apparently only with me, according to Vera Arturovna), and life (I mean day-to-day life) is very difficult for him, for various reasons. That's why he "slips away" from many things and many things "slip away" from him.

It's difficult to write about this, but you *must* understand.

By the looks of it, his life continues on in the happiest, most indifferent, and I would even say banal, manner——

But inwardly—this is a man (in spite of his genius, or perhaps because of it)—who lives a deep, *secret and tragic* life. None of those around him understand this. At some point I will try again to tell you about his typology, which is very strange, contradictory, and, I would say, doomed—— . . .

Devoted and
loving you
P. Suvchinsky

NOTES

Svetlana Savenko suggested the publication of these letters in this volume, and prepared the first draft of an introduction and their selection. She provided crucial input on the Russian sources and on information she wanted included in the introduction. The notes profited from her input and from Anatoly Kuznetsov's notes in the published edition of Yudina's letters, and from the draft notes Viktor Varunts originally planned for his edition. I am deeply indebted to her scholarly groundwork and productive collaborative efforts in completing this edition.

The letters were translated by Philipp Penka. Alexandra Grabarchuk contributed significantly to these translations by reviewing and checking them against the originals. She also translated major additions to the letters in the second round of editing, as well as all of letter 28.

1. The "Nansen passport" was developed by Fridtjof Nansen as part of a League of Nations initiative for stateless refugees. Vera Sudeikina still had her Nansen passport when she arrived in the United States to marry Stravinsky in 1940.

2. See Tamara Levitz, *Modernist Mysteries:* Perséphone (New York: Oxford, 2012), 304–5, 329–30.

3. "Stravinsky auf der Probe," *Neues Wiener Tageblatt*, 18 March 1926.

4. For an extensive examination of this friendship in the 1930s, see Levitz, *Modernist Mysteries:* Perséphone, 117–81, 290–395. For broader insight into Suvchinsky's intellectual and musical life see Irina Akimova, *Pierre Souvtchinsky: Parcours d'un Russe hors frontière* (Paris: L'Harmattan, 2011).

5. On Suvchinsky's possible dealings with agents in the Soviet Union, see Dmitry V. Shlapentokh, "Eurasianism: Past and Present," *Communist and Post-Communist Studies* 30/2 (1997): 136–44. For a list of Suvchinsky's political writings, see Eric Humbertclaude, *La Liberté dans la musique* (Château-Gontier: Edition Aedam Musicae, 2012), 83–98.

6. See Valérie Dufour, The *Poétique musicale*: A Counterpoint in Three Voices," in this volume.

7. See Stravinsky to Ernest Ansermet, 4 April 1935, in *Correspondance Ansermet-Strawinsky (1914–1967)* (Geneva: Georg, 1992), 3:50. In this same letter to Ansermet, Stravinsky compares the reception of *Lady Macbeth* to that of Kurt Weill's *Kleine Dreigroschenmusik* and *Mahagonny* in Paris in June 1933, complaining about the audience's snobby affection for leftist art on both occasions.

8. "Sumbur vmesto muzïki" (Muddle instead of music), *Pravda*, 28 January 1936. Suvchinsky remarked in the letter accompanying this article, "I am sending you a curious clipping from *Pravda* about Shostakovich. Apparently, this notice was written under the direct instruction of Stalin!" See Suvchinsky to Stravinsky, 1 February 1936, in *I. F. Stravinskiy: Perepiska s russkimi korrespondentami. Materialï k biografii*, ed. Viktor Varunts (Moscow: Kompozitor, 2003), 3:597 (hereafter *SPRK*).

9. See "Igor Stravinsky Talks About the Future Directions of His Music and His Art" in "Stravinsky Speaks to the Spanish-Speaking World," in this volume.

10. Stravinsky had first expressed exaggerated affection for the United States during his tour there in 1925. See, for example, Charles Ludwig, "'I Love America,' Composer Declares," *Cincinnati Times-Star*, 4 March 1925.

11. Stravinsky, quoted in "Stravinsky, Russ Composer, Will Become U.S. Citizen," *Minneapolis Star-Journal*, 16 December 1940.

12. G.D.G., "Stravinsky Bares Aversion to Canned Music on Radio: Famous Composer, Conducting Here Tomorrow, Seeks U.S. Citizenship," *Washington Times-Herald*, 7 January 1941.

13. "Russian Music Declared in State of Transition," *Rochester Democrat and Chronicle*, 26 February 1945.

14. Stravinsky, quoted in Jean-Louis Roux, "Igor Stravinsky," *Le Quartier Latin* (Montréal), 23 March 1945.

15. Marjory M. Fisher, "Stravinsky Sees Freedom as Inspiration for Music," *San Francisco News*, 21 March 1946.

16. See Leslie Sprout, "The 1945 Stravinsky Debates: Nigg, Messiaen, and the Early Cold War in France," *Journal of Musicology* 26/1 (Winter 2009): 85–131.

17. As Sprout documents, Messiaen admired the *Rite*, but rejected Stravinsky's neoclassicism. See Sprout, "The 1945 Stravinsky Debates," 110–16.

18. Pyotr Suvchinsky, "Igor Strawinsky," *Contrepoints* 2 (February 1946): 19–31; included in *Un Siècle de musique russe (1830–1930)*, ed. Frank Langlois (Paris: Actes Sud, 2004), 195–208.

19. See André Schaeffner to Stravinsky, 1 September 1946, and Stravinsky to Schaeffner, 12 September 1946, microfilm 102.1, 2744–46, Paul Sacher Stiftung (hereafter PSS).

20. See "Foreign Relations: Tumult at the Waldorf," *Time*, 4 April 1949; "Red Visitors Cause Rumpus," *Life*, 4 April 1949, 39–40. The "Prague Manifesto" is the name given to the resolutions promoting national, accessible music in the tradition of socialist realism that emerged from the Second International Congress of Composers and Music Critics in Prague from 20 to 29 May 1948. Suvchinsky became involved in the debate about these issues in France.

21. Stravinsky, quoted in Franz Myers, "Stravinsky Likes Money, But 'Only With Pleasure,'" *News-Gazette* (Illinois), 3 March 1949. Stravinsky also commented in this interview on how "tactless" it was for Walter Gieseking's agents to invite him to the United States when he was "too much mixed up with the Nazi Party."

22. In his file on "Olin Downes/Shostakovich 1949," Stravinsky kept a note from the Communist Party USA in which he underlined the statement "American communists would support Russia in the event of a war," and wrote in the margins "The U.S. needs more *Patriots* like Stravinsky." See Charles M. Joseph, *Stravinsky Inside Out* (New Haven: Yale, 2001), 18–20.

23. Stravinsky wrote Eisler on 5 October 1947 to congratulate him on *Leben des Galilei*, and subsequently agreed to put his name on a concert of Eisler's music. But when his attorney Aaron Sapiro told him on 6 December 1948 that the invitations being sent out for that concert were accompanied by Martha Gellhorn's leftist article "Cry Shame…!" (*The New Republic*, 6 October 1947, 20), Stravinsky wrote a letter of protest to the *Los Angeles Times* (subsequently not published), in which he insisted his interests were apolitical. Robert Craft misleadingly implies that Stravinsky supported Eisler in this affair, although there is no evidence to support this thesis. See Robert Craft and Vera Stravinsky, *Stravinsky in Pictures and Documents* (New York: Simon & Schuster, 1978): 557 (hereafter *SPD*).

24. See Stravinsky to Craft, 16 March 1949, in *Stravinsky: Selected Correspondence*, ed. Robert Craft (New York: Alfred A. Knopf, 1982), 1:358n71. Craft embellishes this story in ways I could not corroborate.

25. The House Committee on Un-American Activities reviewed this conference on 19 April 1949.

26. Herbert Kupferberg, "Shostakovich Hits Stravinsky as 'Betrayer,'" *New York Herald Tribune*, 28 March 1949. See also Olin Downes, "Shostakovich Bids All Artists Lead War on New 'Fascists,'" *New York Times*, 28 March 1949.

27. Shostakovich, quoted in Irving Kolodin, "Shostakovich vs. Stravinsky: Russian Composer Takes Modernist to Task for Betraying Native Land," *New York Sun*, 28 March 1949. Olin Downes quotes Shostakovich slightly differently in "Shostakovich Bids All Artists Lead War on New 'Fascists.'"

28. Kolodin, "Shostakovich vs. Stravinsky." See Mark Carroll, *Music and Ideology in Cold War Europe* (Cambridge: Cambridge University Press, 2003), 25–36; and Elizabeth Wilson, *Shostakovich: A Life Remembered* (Princeton: Princeton University Press, 1994), 238–39.

29. See Robert Craft's comments and selection of correspondence between Stravinsky and Nabokov in *Stravinsky: Selected Letters*, 2:364–420.

30. On these politics, see Carroll, *Music and Ideology in Cold War Europe*, 69–86; and Ian Wellens, *Music on the Frontline: Nicolas Nabokov's Struggle Against Communism and Middlebrow Culture* (Aldershot: Ashgate, 2002), 49–56.

31. On the CIA's involvement in the festival, see Wellens, *Music on the Frontline*, 47–49. This *Rite of Spring* apparently cost the CIA $166,359 (page 61).

32. Craft documents their social activities in Paris, without mentioning the politics of Nabokov's festival, in *Stravinsky: Chronicle of A Friendship* (Nashville: Vanderbilt, 1994), 75–85.

33. Stephen Walsh postulates that Stravinsky did not see Suvchinsky because he resented the latter's friendship with Pierre Boulez, with whom Suvchinsky founded the Domaine musical a

year later. See Stephen Walsh, *Stravinsky: The Second Exile, France and America, 1934–1971* (Berkeley: University of California Press, 2006), 290, 349–53.

34. Peter Schmelz offers an astonishing, meticulously researched account of modern and contemporary music culture behind the scenes in the Soviet Union in this period in *Such Freedom, If Only Musical: Unofficial Soviet Music During the Thaw* (New York: Oxford University Press, 2009).

35. Boris Schwarz, "Stravinsky in Soviet Russian Criticism," *The Musical Quarterly* 48/3, *Special Issue for Igor Stravinsky on his 80th Anniversary* (July 1962): 350–61. Schwarz claims Soviet critics took offense at Robert Craft and Igor Stravinsky's "35 Antworten auf 35 Fragen," *Melos* 24/6 (June 1957): 161–76, published in English as "Answers to 34 Questions: An Interview with Igor Stravinsky," *Encounter* 9/1 (July 1957): 3–7. In this interview, Stravinsky discussed serialism, expressed his love of Webern, and praised Boulez's *Le Marteau sans maître*. He sharply criticized the Soviet Union, speaking of "Russia's musical isolation" of the last thirty years, the backwardness of their orchestras, and how his music and that of the Second Viennese School was not available in Russia.

36. Viktor Varunts intended to publish the correspondence between Stravinsky and Suvchinsky in the fourth volume of his edited collection of Russian letters, *SPRK*. Tragically, Varunts passed away suddenly in New York City in 2003. Svetlana Savenko is now preparing the fourth volume of his edition for publication in Russian. The originals of most, but not all, of this correspondence, as well as Heidi Tagliavini's German translations of Suvchinsky's letters to Stravinsky, are kept at the Sammlung Paul Sacher and Stravinsky Nachlass in the PSS, though they are currently closed to the public. Alla Bretanitskaya previously edited a selection of the correspondence between Yudina and Suvchinsky in *Pyotr Suvchinskiy i yego vremya* (Moscow: Kompozitor, 1999), 321–83; and Anatoly Kuznetsov edited a new edition of Yudina's letters that includes the correspondence with Maria Yudina reproduced here. See Mariia Yudina, *V iskusstve radostno byt' vmeste: perepiska 1959–1961* (Moscow: Rosspen, 2009); and Mariia Yudina, *Dukh dishit, gde khochet: Perepiska 1962–1963* (Moscow: Rosspen, 2010). Hereafter *VIR* and *DD* respectively. The translations here have benefited from Stephen Walsh's excellent translations of short excerpts from several of these letters in *Stravinsky: The Second Exile*. The organization of the letters is based on Varunts's original selection.

37. Robert Craft, "Stravinsky's Return: A Russian Diary," *Encounter* 117 (June 1963): 33–48; reprinted in Igor Stravinsky and Robert Craft, *Dialogues and a Diary* (Garden City, NY: Doubleday, 1963), 224–65.

38. Documents relating to Suvchinsky's attempts to found a "Centre d'Etudes Igor Strawinsky" are kept in the Sammlung Paul Sacher, PSS. The story of Suvchinsky's intended role in administering Stravinsky's posthumous legacy remains unclear. See Walsh, *Stravinsky: The Second Exile*, 530–63.

39. In a letter to Suvchinsky, Yudina confessed that she was Jewish but had converted to Orthodoxy at age nineteen because she felt she "had come to live so closely with the Russian people, *specifically the people . . .*" She cautiously observed that Suvchinsky's connection to Schoenberg and Pasternak "seemed sufficient proof of the unthinkableness of you having any antipathy toward my people. Not to mention your most high spiritual culture." Suvchinsky replied that she didn't have to tell him about her Jewishness. "First," he wrote, "I really love Jews and have ever since my childhood in Kiev province; I have always had an 'attraction' to Jews and Jewishness." He described hearing music in the Karlsbad Synagogue, and the Jewish orchestras in Ukraine that he thought influenced *L'Histoire du soldat*. "You would not be M. V. Yudina without that bloodline, as Pushkin would not be Pushkin if he did not have Abyssinian blood flowing in his veins. The historical connection of the Russian people (and the Russian Revolution) with Jewishness is a providential fact. I deeply believe that the Russian people are a second Israel, and this realization has always deeply shaken and shakes me." Yudina responded by expressing her own doubts about Jews. See Yudina to Suvchinsky, 13/16/19 March 1961; Suvchinsky to Yudina, 27 March 1961; and Yudina to Suvchinsky, 16 April 1961, in *VIR*, 499–512, 525.

40. Schmelz, *Such Freedom, If Only Musical*, 90.

41. See Yudina to Suvchinsky, 16 September 1959, *VIR*, 111–12. On the notion of "professionalism" in Soviet musical life and the possibilities for composing and performing modern and avant-garde music, see Kiril Tomoff, *Creative Union: The Professional Organization of Soviet Composers, 1939–1953* (Ithaca, NY: Cornell University Press, 2006), 203–13.

42. Peter Schmelz discusses the dramatic influx of scores and recordings by Western modernist composers into the Soviet Union after 1960 through both legal and illegal channels in *Such Freedom, If Only Musical,* 45.

43. See Yudina to Suvchinsky, 19 October 1959, *VIR,* 161.

44. Arthur Berger's "Some Conversations on Life and Work and Art," *The New York Times Book Review,* 11 March 1962. This article consists of a fascinating review of Craft's and Stravinsky's third book of published conversations, *Expositions and Developments.*

45. To indicate Yudina's (and to a lesser extent Suvchinsky's) faltering or uncertain speech patterns we have introduced the rather indiosyncratic use of double em-dashes here. Anatoly Kuznetsov had placed three ellipsis dots when he edited Yudina's letters for publication, but to follow him would preclude our presenting a clear distinction between uncertain speech and editorial ellipses.

46. Stravinsky's close friend Lawrence Morton was a pianist, composer, and impresario. He was executive director of the Monday Evening Concerts in Los Angeles (1954–71), several times director of the Ojai Festival, and curator of the Bing Concerts at Los Angeles County Museum of Art after 1965. He met Stravinsky in 1941, but became close with him in the late 1950s.

47. Suvchinsky voiced similar ideas in "Stravinsky as a Russian," *Tempo* 81 (Summer 1967): 5. He had first begun speaking about the Russian typology of Stravinsky's character in the 1930s; see Levitz, *Modernist Mysteries:* Perséphone, 160–65, 324. Suvchinsky had earlier written to Yudina, "I was never a 'nationalist,' but can't help being proud of the fact that [Stravinsky] is Russian. If you only knew to what extent he remained it (Russian!) How amazingly he speaks Russian." Suvchinsky to Yudina, 28 October 1959, *VIR,* 166.

48. Suvchinsky frequently quotes this passage from Gogol's *A Terrible Vengeance* (1832).

49. Morton was planning to travel to the Soviet Union to gather biographical materials about Stravinsky for a proposed monograph. Suvchinsky somewhat questioned Morton's ability to do this research in a letter to Yudina, 14 April 1960, *VIR,* 284–85. Yudina and Suvchinsky frequently discussed in their correspondence Morton's research and travel plans, which never materialized.

50. The letter includes a carte-de-visite dated 7 May 1960 from Stravinsky to Yudina in which he thanks her for her letter and asks her to write.

51. Stravinsky is referring to a letter from Yudina dated 29 April 1960, in which Yudina praised his music and writings in heightened and rhapsodic prose. She spoke abjectly of communicating with him only "from a place of poverty, and humility, from positions of life, the world, which are likely unknown to you." "What can I do? Only thank Providence for the fact that you exist on earth, that I am your co-citizen and contemporary, and that I have the honor and happiness to be acquainted with you even from afar and sometimes have the opportunity to play your compositions (I would play them constantly, but this does not depend on me!)" See *VIR,* 295–96. In a letter from 28 November 1960, Yudina calls Stravinsky a "genius of geniuses" and suggests she ought to write him in Latin or Greek verse, given his stature, rather than in simple prose. See Yudina to Stravinsky, 28 November 1960, *VIR,* 388–89.

52. Marianna Suvchinsky (1910–1993) was married to Pyotr Suvchinsky. She was the daughter of Lev Karsavin (1882–1952) and niece of the Ballets Russes dancer Tamara Karsavina (1885–1979).

53. "Stravinsky Shakes a Stick at Red Music," *Washington Post,* 24 December 1960, quoted in Walsh, *Stravinsky: The Second Exile,* 440–41.

54. Stravinsky to Yudina, 16 January 1961, *VIR,* 454.

55. See Yudina to Suvchinsky, 13–19 March 1961, *VIR,* 502–3.

56. See Svetlana Savenko, "Stravinsky: The View from Russia," in this volume. Tikhon Khrennikov (1913–2007) was secretary of the Union of Soviet Composers from 1948 to 1991.

57. Franz Waxman founded the Beverly Hills Music Festival in 1947, and renamed it the Los Angeles Music Festival two years later.

58. Craft, *Chronicle of a Friendship,* 240.

59. See Albert Goldberg, "Soviet Night," *Los Angeles Times,* 13 June 1961.

60. Walsh, *Stravinsky: The Second Exile,* 440.

61. Simon Morrison has access to the records on Stravinsky at the VOKS archive at the State Archive of the Russian Federation in Moscow, and promises to provide insight into the politics of this invitation in his research on this subject.

62. Tikhon Khrennikov, "Serdechnïy privet ot Stravinskogo," *Ogonyok*, August 1961, quoted in Walsh, *Stravinsky: The Second Exile*, 441. See also "'On umer drugom svoyey rodiny': Beseda S. Savenko s T. N. Khrennikovym" *Muzïkal'naya akademiya* 4 (1992): 218.

63. Yudina had arranged to have Konstantin Balmont's daugther Nina Bruni-Balmont send Stravinsky a copy of the 1911 edition of Balmont's poems which Stravinsky had used when setting "Zvezdolikiy" ("Le Roi des étoiles"). See Tatiana Baranova, "Stravinsky's Russian Library," in this volume. Stravinsky does not mention here and may not have known that Yudina had just given two groundbreaking concerts at the Concert Hall at the Finland Station in Leningrad and Leningrad House of Composers on 11 and 12 May 1961, in which she had performed Volkonsky's *Musica Stricta* (1956–57) and his own Sonata for Two Pianos (1944), among other works.

64. Igor Bezrodny (1930–1997) was a gifted violinist, member of the Moscow Trio, and conductor of the Moscow Chamber Orchestra (1976–81) and Turku Philharmonic Orchestra in Finland (1986–90).

65. Vasily Yastrebtsev was a faithful student and admirer of Rimsky-Korsakov and wrote *Reminiscences of Rimsky-Korsakov*, ed. and trans. by Florence Jonas (New York: Columbia University Press, 1985).

66. Savenko argues that this was indeed irrelevant in that the Union of Soviet Composers was a state organization.

67. Savenko believes Suvchinsky, who was in general well informed about the Soviet Union, shows his apparent lack of understanding of the situation here. Khrennikov occupied a higher position in the Soviet hierarchical ladder than Shostakovich (who had incomparably more professional and moral authority).

68. Nicolas I, who was coronated on 22 August (3 September) 1826, allowed Pushkin to return from exile in early September 1826. He was greeted with great enthusiasm.

69. Dostoevsky spoke on 8 June 1880 as part of the lavish ceremonies accompanying the unveiling of Alexander Opekushin's monument to Pushkin in Moscow. Stravinsky scholars and friends frequently refer to this speech in relation to Stravinsky's exile from Russia.

70. Suvchinsky is referring to Leo Tolstoy's last visit to Moscow on 18–19 September 1909 and to the crowd that gathered at Bryansk Station.

71. Stravinsky traveled to Sweden and Berlin in September; Zurich, London, and Cairo in October; and Australia and Tahiti in November–December 1961.

72. Robert Craft.

73. Stravinsky turned seventy-nine on 17 June 1961.

74. Aram Khachaturian (1903–1978) was a celebrated Soviet Armeniam composer.

75. Yuri Shaporin (1887–1966) was a Soviet composer and Professor at the Moscow Conservatory.

76. Dmitry Kabalevsky (1904–1987) was a Soviet composer and major figure in the Union of Soviet Composers, and famous for his music for children. Karen Khachaturian told Svetlana Savenko in an interview in 1992 that Kabalevsky and others in the Union of Soviet Composers had energetically opposed Stravinsky's visit with comments like "How can it be that the leader of avant-gardism, the representative of bourgeois art, is visiting us and we are receiving him?" Shostakovich's staunch support of Khrennikov's invitation and of Stravinsky had proved crucial in convincing the Union to proceed with the visit. See "'Ya bïl rozhdyon dlya muzïki': Beseda S. Savenko s K. S. Khachaturyanom," *Muzïkal'naya akademiya* 4 (1992): 221.

77. Anatoly Kuznetsov notes that Stravinsky included his carte-de-visite, on which he had written: "To N. Bruni-Balmont, the daughter of the great poet, my heartfelt gratitude for her wonderful gift. With sincere respect, I. Stravinsky." It is kept at the Research Division of Manuscripts at the Russian State Library in Moscow (NIOR RGB).

78. Boris Yarustovsky (1911–1978) was a musicologist and director of the cultural division of the Central Committee of the Communist Party of the Soviet Union from 1948 to 1956, famous

for his hounding of Shostakovich. He later published *Igor' Stravinskiy: Kratkiy ocherk zhizni i tvorchestva* (Moscow: Muzïka, 1963; rev. 1969).

79. Stravinsky planned to be in Helsinki 10–14 September 1961.

80. Through Yudina as intermediary, Stockhausen had spoken with Shostakovich and the Union of Soviet Composers about a concert tour of the Soviet Union including David Tudor and percussionist Christoph Caskell. The official invitation with Shostakovich's signature arrived in 1963, but was later annulled. See Yudina to Suvchinsky, 6 August 1961, in *VIR*, 618–26.

81. Yudina claims that Nadia Boulanger wrote the Union of Composers to tell them of her desire to conduct in the U.S.S.R. Boulanger sat on the jury for the third Tchaikovsky Competition in Moscow in June 1966 and visited the Leningrad Conservatory. See Yudina to Suvchinsky, 6 August 1961, in *VIR*, 618–26; and Schmelz, *Such Freedom, If Only Musical*, 55.

82. Stravinsky is referring to the photographs Yudina had sent Suvchinsky of Pasternak's funeral on 2 June 1960, which never reached him. Pasternak played a unique role in Yudina's avant-garde performances. See Schmelz, *Such Freedom, If Only Musical*, 94–95.

83. At the end of this letter, Stravinsky lists his travel plans from 25 August to 25 September 1961.

84. In the first part of this letter, Yudina discusses a concert she will give in Moscow's Dom uchyonïkh (House of Scholars) on 29 September 1961, in which she plans to perform Stravinsky's Sonata, Sonata for Two Pianos, and Concerto for Two Pianos, among other works.

85. Stravinsky conducted a concert in Mexico City on 20 December 1961, for which he prepared a wind-band arrangement of his tango from *Cinq doigts* (1921), and Robert Craft conducted the *Scènes de ballet*.

86. A "Stravinsky Retrospective: In Honor of His Eightieth Birthday" concert took place at the Domaine musical on 8 November 1961. Boulez conducted a wide range of Stravinsky's songs, as well as the Concertino, *Symphonies d'instruments à vent*, *In Memorium Dylan Thomas*, Three Pieces for String Quartet, and *Renard*.

87. This letter included newspaper clippings with a photograph of Vyacheslav Molotov (1890–1986) and Vladimir Semichastny (1924–2001). Molotov was Minister of Foreign Affairs (1939–49 and 1953–56) and Stalin's closest collaborator, but Khrushchev dismissed him from the Politburo of the Central Committee in 1957. Semichastny had just been named chairman of the KGB, a position he kept from 13 November 1961 to 1967.

88. *Mrakobesï*: obscurantist (literally "demon of darkness")—a popular derogatory term used in the Soviet Union to disparage political reactionaries and religious fanatics, here applied to the reactionary Soviet leadership.

89. Stravinsky does not mention here and may not have known that Yudina performed his Concerto for Piano and Wind Instruments for the first time with Roman Matsov conducting the Estonian Radio Symphony Orchestra on 27 October 1961.

90. Stravinsky had known Dr. Maurice Gilbert in Geneva since visiting his son Théodore there in 1952, and Dr. Gilbert treated him when he suffered a stroke while on tour in Switzerland and Germany in 1957.

91. Catherine Gayer (b. 1937) is a U.S. coloratura soprano who sang at the Deutsche Oper Berlin after 1961. She performed Mozart, Donizetti, Strauss, jazz, and cabaret, as well as contemporary music.

92. A Schoenberg festival took place at the Domaine musical on 6 December 1961.

93. Mikhail Alpatov (1902–1986) was a Soviet art historian and member of the USSR Academy of Arts after 1954, and Yudina's close friend.

94. Yudina sent the program of her concert on 29 September 1961.

95. Aleksey Remizov (1877–1957) was a Russian writer who emigrated to Paris in 1921. See Tatiana Baranova, "Stravinsky's Russian Library," in this volume.

96. Maxim Gorky (1868–1936). Suvchinsky traveled with Sviatopolk-Mirsky to visit Gorky in Sorrento, Italy, over Christmas 1927. Dmitry Sviatopolk-Mirsky (1890–1939) was a Russian political and literary historian, and founding member of the Eurasianist movement. He lived in England

after 1917 but returned to the Soviet Union in 1932. The NKVD arrested him in 1937 and he died in a gulag near Magadan in 1939.

97. This piece was not performed in the concert.

98. Yudina's recording of Stravinsky's Sonata and Serenade were released on the Soviet label Melodiya Blue Torch in 1962, and reissued by harmonia mundi in 1986.

99. This program, with some changes, took place on 10 January 1962 at the Leningrad House of Composers. Yudina repeated it on 6 October 1962 in the presence of Stravinsky, but played only the Septet on the latter concert.

100. The second International Tchaikovsky Competition took place in Moscow in spring 1962.

101. Boris Pasternak, "Marburg," 1916; rev. 1928. The line actually reads: "Someone whistling loudly fashioned a crossbow/and someone planned silently for Trinity Fair."

102. The ballet company of the Leningrad State Academic Maly Opera Theater performed Konstantin Boyarsky's choreography of Stravinsky's *Orpheus* on 26 March 1962. Yudina discusses the choice of *Orpheus* in a letter to Suvchinsky, 5 November 1961, *VIR*, 702–706.

103. Kasyan Yaroslavich Goleizovsky (1892–1970) was a Russian avant-garde choreographer who staged dances for *The Bat* (*Chauve-Souris*) after 1916. He also established an important dance studio in the Soviet Union in the 1920s.

104. Yudina consistently refers to Stravinsky's Concerto for Piano and Wind Instruments as his "First Concerto." This was one of her favorite pieces of his. See Yudina to Suvchinsky, 10 November 1959, *VIR*, 171–74. Suvchinsky once told her amusingly about his experience of the premiere of this work in Paris in 1924, when he had the unenviable task of "hiding" Stravinsky from Maximilian Steinberg, whom he did not like and did not want to see. See Suvchisnky to Yudina, 17 January 1961, ibid., 455–57.

105. Yudina recorded Stravinsky's Concerto for Piano and Wind Instruments with Gennady Rozhdestvensky conducting the State TV and Radio Committee Grand Symphony Orchestra on 5 August 1962.

106. *Dieu vous garde!* translates as "God bless you!" and "T[out] àV[ous]–Votre *Rossinante*" translates as "All the best, your Rocinante." Rocinante was Don Quixote's horse.

107. Stravinsky responds here to Khrennikov's second invitation of 11 September 1961.

108. Stravinsky may not have wanted to travel to the Soviet Union for his eightieth birthday for the same reason that he did not want to meet President Kennedy on that day—as he wrote Nicolas Nabokov on 3 January, he wanted to celebrate with family and friends. It appears he may have been wary of his birthday being used by either side to political ends. See Walsh, *Stravinsky: A Second Exile*, 447, 449.

109. See Craft, *Dialogues and a Diary*, 199–200. See also Jay Mulvaney and Paul De Angelis, *Dear Mrs. Kennedy: The World Shares Its Grief, Letters November 1963* (New York: Macmillan, 2010): 134–35; and Walsh, *Stravinsky: A Second Exile*, 448, 551.

110. Arthur M. Schlesinger, *Journals: 1952–2000* (London: Penguin, 2007), 146.

111. Stravinsky is referring here to Arthur Schlesinger, who had also helped to arrange Stravinsky's visit to the White House through the intermediary of his close friend Nicolas Nabokov.

112. Here Stravinsky uses the noun *mrakobesie* (obscurantism) rather than the name for persons *mrakobesï* (obscurantists). This postcard is unsigned.

113. Nathalie Sarraute (1900–1999), Michel Butor (b. 1926), and Alain Robbe-Grillet (1922–2008) were representatives of the 1950s literary trend of the nouveau roman.

114. Stravinsky sent this card to thank Yudina for sending a copy of Valerian Bogdanov-Berezovskiy, *Fyodor Stravinskiy* (Moscow: Muzgiz, 1951).

115. Pierre Souvtchinsky, "Le Miracle du *Sacre du printemps* (Tradition et inspiration)," unpublished text in French taken from the draft of *Un Siècle de musique russe*, and read on the "Stravinsky-Zyklus" on Radio Cologne, 2 February 1962. This text was published in part in Jean-Pierre Wilhelm's German translation as "Das Wunder des *Sacre du printemps*: Tradition und Inspiration," in *Igor Stravinsky: Eine Sendereihe des W.D.R. zum 80. Geburtstag*, ed. Otto Tomek (Cologne: Westdeutscher Rundfunk, 1963).

116. Stravinsky traveled to Israel from 29 August to 7 September 1962.

117. In contrast to Stravinsky's minimizing of Yudina's influence on his decision to travel to the Soviet Union (he sees her as less important than the officials he will anger), Suvchinsky wrote Yudina on 26 March 1962 that Stravinsky had decided to travel to Moscow precisely because she had made him realize the significance of his trip. See *DD*, 72.

118. This letter is included in *DD*, 177–84. Svetlana Savenko believes it is misdated 30 April 1962.

119. Stravinsky writes this sentence in French: "'Les échanges culturels' avec les marxistes occidentaux 'qui se dressent contre l'art décadent formaliste et inhumain du monde bourgeois.'"

120. Boris Leonidovich Pasternak (1890–1960).

121. Suvchinsky is referring to how Stravinsky is described in the index of E. L. Frid's *Miliy Alekseyevich Balakirev: Issledovaniya i stat'i* (Leningrad: Gos. Muzïkal'noye izd-vo, 1961), 443, in reference to where his name appears in the book in Abram Gozenpud's article "Neosushchestvlyonnïy opernïy zamïsel."

122. Suvchinsky uses the derogatory term *stilyaga*, which refers to fashion-conscious people (*stilyaga* comes from *stil*, style), wore flared jeans and colored vests, and listened to jazz. Suvchinsky uses the term figuratively to describe young, Western-oriented Soviet composers for whom Stravinsky was an obsolete figure.

123. Suvchinsky is referring to the Leningrad State Academic Maly Opera Theater's production of Stravinsky's *Orpheus* on 26 March 1962.

124. Here Suvchinsky repeats the very questions he asked Yudina about the Union of Soviet Composers at the end of his letter of 12 March 1962 (letter 19).

125. Stravinsky travelled to South Africa on 18 May 1962 as a guest of the South African Broadcasting Corporation. "Le Cape" refers to Capetown.

126. Suvchinsky uses the French word *tournées*.

127. At the end of this letter, Suvchinsky discusses the importance of Lawrence Morton's article on Stravinsky in *Encyclopédie de la musique* (Paris: Fasquelle, 1959–61).

128. Yudina was using her own resources and finances to create "Stravinskyana," an exhibit of photographs documenting Stravinsky's life and works at the Leningrad House of Composers. She requested materials for the exhibit from Suvchinsky in a telegram dated 12 May 1962. *DD*, 198–99.

129. Zagorsk, today called Sergiyev Posad, is a town on the outskirts of Moscow and home of the Russian monastery Trinity Lavra of St. Sergius.

130. Xenia Stravinsky says in French, "I am the niece of Mr. Stravinsky," and Maria Yudina says in German, "I am Yudina." Jacob Epstein was an American-born British sculptor, and *dobro pozhalovat* means "welcome" in Russian. See Robert Craft, *Dialogues and a Diary*, 225–26.

131. "'Ya bïl rozhden dlya muzïki': Beseda S. Savenko s K. S. Khachaturyanom," 222.

132. Craft, *Dialogues and a Diary*, 262–65, also published as Robert Craft, "Stravinsky talks with Khrushchev," *Vogue* 142/8 (1 November 1963): 134–35, 184–85, 187–89.

133. Schmelz, *Such Freedom, If Only Musical*, 60–61.

134. Craft, *Dialogues and a Diary*, 257–58. For Khrennikov's account of Stravinsky's visit, see "'On umer drugom svoyey rodiny.'" For an official Soviet view of these events, see Izrail' Nest'yev, "Vechera Igorya Stavinskogo," *Sovetskaya muzïka* 12 (December 1962): 92–95.

135. Stravinsky had underlined the word *homeland* twice in a letter he received from Yudina back on 29 April 1960. A bit later in the letter, after the word *visit*, he had written in the margin: "How strange—'visiting' the 'Homeland.' That is our tragedy, that we can only be invited to visit this 'Homeland.'" Yudina, *VIR*, 297. Stravinsky had shared this comment with Suvchinsky, who had found it so remarkable that he had repeated it in somewhat modified form in a letter to Yudina, 12 May 1960, *VIR*, 309.

136. "'Ya bïl rozhdyon dlya muzïki': Beseda S. Savenko s K. S. Khachaturyanom," 222. Stravinsky had commented similarily to the press months before his visit to Russia that "nostalgia has no part in my proposed visit to Russia. My wish to go there is due primarily to the evidence I have received of a genuine desire or need for me by the younger generation of Russian musicians. No artist's name has been more abused in the Soviet Union than mine, but one cannot achieve the

future we must achieve with the Russians by nursing a grudge." "Stravinsky at 80," *Newsweek*, 21 May 1962, 54. Stravinsky appeared on the cover of this issue.

137. Lina Prokofiev (1897–1989), maiden name Kodina, also used the artist name Lina L'yubera. She was Prokofiev's first wife.

138. Craft, *Dialogues and a Diary*, 234. Stravinsky could not return to Ustilug because it was closed to foreigners.

139. Ibid., 230.

140. "Caviar et merde," quoted in ibid., 224.

141. Karen Khachaturian in conversation with Elizabeth Wilson, quoted in *Shostakovich: A Life Remembered*, 375; and in Walsh, *Stravinsky: A Second Exile*, 467.

142. Craft, *Dialogues and a Diary*, 246.

143. See Khachaturian's remarks in Wilson, *Shostakovich: A Life Remembered*, 375–76.

144. Craft, *Dialogues and a Diary*, 262. Craft's judgmental portrayal of Shostakovich mirrors that of the U.S. reporters in 1949.

145. Shostakovich in a letter dated 9 September 1971, quoted in Wilson, *Shostakovich: A Life Remembered*, 377.

146. The National is a famous hotel in Moscow, built in 1903.

147. Yudina is referring to the Leningrad State Academic Maly Opera Theater's staging of *Petrushka*, *Orpheus*, and *Firebird* in the Kremlin Palace of Congresses on 25 September 1962. Stravinsky was not pleased with the performance, and the next morning told his niece Xenia, "You have no idea how unhappy I was yesterday!" Quoted in Kseniya Stravinskaya, *O I. F. Stravinskom i ego blizkikh* (Leningrad: Muzïka, 1978), 116. See also Walsh, *Stravinsky: A Second Exile*, 464.

148. The Andrey Rublev Museum of Ancient Russian Art is housed in the Andronikov Monastery in Moscow.

149. "Human"; perhaps a reference to Nietzsche's *Menschliches, Allzumenschliches* (1878).

150. *Symphonies d'instruments à vent.*

151. Igor Markevich was a Ukranian composer and conductor, and old acquaintance of Stravinsky's and Suvchinsky's from the Ballets Russes days. He conducted works by Stravinsky in the USSR numerous times after 1959.

152. In English, "me personally."

153. Latin: "The spirit blows where it will."

154. Latin: "Where, where."

155. Peterhof is a residence/imperial palace about 30 kilometers outside of Petersburg. Stravinsky was born in Oranienbaum, on the outskirts of the city. The composer went on excursions to both places while in Russia.

156. German: "as if made to order."

157. *Arakcheyevshchina*, named after Aleksey Arakcheyev, is a derogatory term to describe a military state or oppressive regime.

158. Grigory Kepinov (1886–1966) was an Armenian sculptor.

159. A quote from Pushkin's "Flowers of Autumn" (1825). The original reads: "Just as the pain of separation is stronger than the sweet of date."

160. Mikhail Bakhtin (1895–1975) was a Russian philosopher and literary critic who had been active in the Soviet Union since the 1920s but became widely known after the 1960s.

161. "As always."

162. Lyubov Shaporina (1879–1967) translated Stravinsky's *Autobiography* into Russian as *Khronika moyey zhizni* (Leningrad: Gozmuzizdat, 1963).

163. Stravinsky had two adult sons, Soulima and Théodore, and one living daughter, Milena.

164. See Pedagogues of the Khabarovsk Music School to *Izvestiya*, 7 March 1963, in *DD*, 442–46. See also Peter Schmelz, *Such Freedom, If Only Musical*, 89n63, 90n67.

165. Ampenova worked at Boosey and Hawkes.

166. Yudina writes "Craft-*chislo*." *Chislo* is the Russian word for numeral or integer, and is a synonym for *tsifra*, which shares the same root as "cipher." This word conveys Yudina's impression of Craft as "an absolutely abstract person" in her letter to Yelena and Mikhail Bakhtin (no. 29).

167. Igor, Vera, and Robert Craft.

168. Yudina sent Stravinsky Viktor Lazarev's *Andrey Rublev: Al'bom reproduktsiy* (Moscow: Sovetskiy khudozhnik, 1960).

169. Xenia Yuryevna Stravinsky.

170. See Xenia Stravinsky to Yudina, 8 June 1963, in *DD*, 527–28.

171. *Over the Barriers* is a 1917 collection of poetry by Pasternak.

172. *Aufbinden,* in the sense of forcing something onto someone.

173. Yudina quotes this line from Konstantin Balmont's poem "Wordlessness" (1900). The line actually reads "Your heart did forgive / but your heart became lifeless."

174. See Ralph Parker, "Stravinsky in Russia," *The New Statesman*, 2 November 1962.

175. In a letter to Marianna and Pyotr Suvchinsky from 24–29 September 1963, Yudina explained further that Stravinsky had sensed her lack of official position and stayed far away from her in Russia, and that she didn't want to complain about him but her "heart has cooled" and she no longer wanted to write either him, the "wilted" Vera, or the "cipher-Craft." See *DD*, 597–600.

"The Precision of Poetry and the Exactness of Pure Science": Nabokov, Stravinsky, and the Reader as Listener

LEON BOTSTEIN

Parallel Lives

In his meticulously prepared compendium of interviews, *Strong Opinions*, Vladimir Nabokov reprinted a 1970 response to a question posed by Alfred Appel about whether he knew Igor Stravinsky, "another outspoken émigré." Nabokov replied, "I know Mr. Stravinsky very slightly and have never seen any genuine sample of his outspokenness in print."[1] Nabokov's response to Appel, one of the first and most respected of Nabokov scholars, revealed an uncanny but not unexpected doubt about Stravinsky's role in the authorship of the (by then) extensive accumulation of Stravinsky-Craft volumes of conversations. The questions about Robert Craft's role and who was responsible for what appeared in print as Stravinsky's words remain matters of controversy.[2] Craft's contribution was, if not decisive, then certainly substantial. He confessed to Stephen Walsh, with pride, that one reviewer of the 1959 *Conversations* expressed the opinion that "the two finest writers of English prose" were Russians: Nabokov and Stravinsky.[3]

The idea that Stravinsky was considered a "fine writer" surely irritated Nabokov. Such a notion revealed a familiar philistinism and stupidity, not entirely unrelated to the evils of *poshlost'*, Nabokov's term for the fake suggestion of genuine art, refinement, and judgment so rampant in so-called civilized society.[4] Nabokov's subtly worded skepticism about the authorship of the volumes anticipated what has remained for scholars a source of ambiguity with respect to understanding Stravinsky, particularly in his American years. It seems that everything Stravinsky published, from his *Autobiography* of 1935 and 1936 to the 1939 Charles Eliot Norton Lectures and the volumes with Craft was, if not ghostwritten, then the work of close collaboration.[5] This does not disqualify the utility of what was published under Stravinsky's name as sources for understanding Stravinsky. But there are no grounds for elevating the composer to the stature of Nabokov as a writer.[6]

Nabokov's aside about Stravinsky also needs to be read within the context of the writer's persistent comments about his own weak relationship to music.

Even if we accept Nabokov's humorous descriptions of his imperviousness to music, the contact between these two prominent émigrés during the American exile they shared was unexpectedly minimal, as many have noted.[7] They appear to have barely known each other. Stravinsky seems not to have read Nabokov, neither during the 1930s in Russian, nor in English in the 1950s and 1960s. After 1940 Nabokov took pains to protest his lack of musicality, even though he took ironic pride in being a descendant of Carl Heinrich Graun, a minor but well-regarded eighteenth-century composer, and took genuine pleasure that his only son, Dimitri, became an opera singer. "I have no ear for music—a shortcoming I deplore bitterly," he confessed in a 1964 *Playboy* interview.[8] Nabokov admitted to retaining a memory of unwanted attendance at operas during his childhood and having once translated Schubert song texts into Russian, but officially the art of music was foreign to him. "Music, I regret to say, affects me merely as an arbitrary succession of more or less irritating sounds," he wrote in *Speak, Memory*. In underscoring his distance from most modern poetry in 1969, he quipped: "I know as little about today's poetry as about new music."[9] Nonetheless, Alfred Appel suggested in 1967 that Nabokov was perhaps protesting too much about his lack of connection to music, an idea now increasingly supported in the critical literature.[10] Appel argued that Nabokov's obsessions with memory, consciousness, time, and the structure of the novel all took on explicitly musical metaphors and analogies; perhaps Nabokov, by dismissing his connection to music, was following a time-honored tradition of intentionally throwing off his would-be interpreters.

Stravinsky was, by all accounts, an avid reader. But he seems to have taken no interest in Nabokov the writer. The absence of any real contact between him and Nabokov, who both arrived in America from France within two years of each other and shared common cultural and historical origins, is even more remarkable given the tight interconnections (so vividly described in *Pnin*) within Russian émigré circles. True, Nabokov resided in the East, and Stravinsky on the West Coast, until the mid-1960s, when he was already quite ill. But the two men seem also never to have met in Berlin or Paris, where both found themselves with some frequency, and were in contact with Russian émigrés in those cities.

Nabokov and Stravinsky had one significant friend in common, perhaps the only person to be in attendance at the funerals of both men, Nicolas Nabokov, the composer and controversial cultural impresario. Nicolas was a first cousin of the writer. His help for Nabokov extended to arranging lodgings (his ex-wife provided Vladimir and Vera Nabokov with their first home in America in 1940), and Vladimir was in intermittent social contact with him until his death.[11] Stravinsky knew Nicolas from his Paris years, and throughout the American years he was among those closest to Stravinsky and worked hard to promote his music.[12] Bringing Nabokov and Stravinsky together would have been easy. It appears that they may actually have avoided each other.[13]

Considering Stravinsky and Nabokov together for the mere fact of shared birthplace and common exile—first in Europe and then America—possesses a basic historical logic. There are obvious parallels in their lives, as well as key divergences that help explain the absence of contact. Despite the social distance between them, striking connections emerge between Stravinsky's music and Nabokov's prose when one compares their careers and work. They shared parallel premises and prejudices in their views on art. And their respective places in the history of modernism bear comparison.

Upon closer inspection, the contrasts in biography stand out. The writer was seventeen years younger. Nabokov was born into a family of high aristocracy and great wealth. Stravinsky, in contrast, descended from petty aristocracy.[14] He did his best to assert his aristocratic origins and prized his provenance of privilege and exclusivity, but the social gulf between them was marked. In their American years, Nabokov seems never to have complained about his loss of status and wealth and he did not try to impress Americans with his ancestry. Stravinsky, in contrast, exaggerated his vanished social distinction and was notoriously obsessed about money. Both men had famous fathers, but Vladimir Nabokov idealized and idolized his whereas Igor Stravinsky seems only to have harbored resentment against his distinguished father, Russia's finest operatic bass before Fyodor Chaliapin.[15] Nabokov's parents, music lovers, were in the patron class. Chaliapin and Serge Koussevitzky performed in the Nabokov home, and perhaps so too did Igor's father.[16]

Both the writer and the composer spent the interwar years in exile in Europe. Both lived at one time in Switzerland, a country for which each had a particular fondness. Stravinsky spent most of the years between 1917 and 1939 in France, whereas Nabokov chose Berlin. In Berlin Nabokov kept close to the Russian émigré community. Stravinsky had many Russian friends and colleagues in France, but he became a French citizen and emerged by the 1930s as the leading and most influential composer among the French. Ironically, Stravinsky's best foreign language from childhood was German. His French developed later, during his many years in France and in French-speaking Switzerland. Nabokov (for whom English was a childhood language and his second language) preferred French, his years in Berlin notwithstanding. He read German and spoke it, but never used it as a language of writing, even though he wrote most of his early novels in Germany. Stravinsky shifted from an initial hostility to the German cultural tradition in music to an increasing admiration and consideration of it as normative.[17] He never could quite accommodate Wagner, but in his later years Beethoven and Schubert became important to him in a manner they had not been early in his career. By the mid-1930s he was most eager, despite the Nazi seizure of power, to gain acceptance in Germany. Nabokov was repulsed by things German, except for scientific works. His novels—particularly *King, Queen, Knave* and *The Gift*—are peppered with contempt and parody of German habits and culture. For

Nabokov, the Germans came to be emblematic of the worst of pseudo-culture, prime purveyors of a particularly pretentious tradition of *poshlost'*.[18]

Nabokov, like his father, was an ardent foe of anti-Semitism. He despised not only the Nazi variety but also the anti-Semitism so commonplace within the Russian intelligentsia. Nabokov hated the fascists, and indeed all tyranny. The same cannot be said of Stravinsky. Stravinsky admired Mussolini; in 1936 he was annoyed only that Il Duce had no time for him.[19] The text of Stravinsky's 1939 Norton Lectures, *The Poetics of Music*, is marked by an obsessive assertion that the centrality of "the stern auspices of order and discipline" in modern life and art were being neglected. Stravinsky declared, "Modern man is progressively losing his understanding of values and his sense of proportion." This was "serious" since it challenged the "fundamental laws of human equilibrium." Whether intentionally or not, Stravinsky evoked the pseudo-historical justification peddled by purveyors of fascist ideology as the proper antidote to chaos and degeneracy. Stravinsky thought that the errors of contemporary culture revealed that "the mind itself is ailing." Much of the music of the time, Stravinsky told his audience, "carries within it the symptoms of a pathologic blemish and spreads the germs of a new original sin."[20] His rhetoric possessed an uncanny and perhaps unintended family resemblance to the aesthetics favored by fascist regimes that defined "degenerate art." Despite Stravinsky's unambiguous dislike of the Soviets in the 1930s, the Eurasiansim he subscribed to led him to a critical skepticism in 1939 more implicitly consonant with the Stalinist dogma of the mid- and late 1930s that ostracized Dimitry Shostakovich and Gavriil Popov. The criticisms shared a tone of moral disapproval.

In exile, Stravinsky not surprisingly developed an overt commitment to religion, in particular Russian Orthodoxy. And by the mid-1920s he assumed, under the guise of neoclassicism, a stark anti-modernist stance. Stravinsky had no use for socialist realism, but his problem with Russia under Communism was comparatively nuanced. During the years he flirted with Eurasianist notions, Stravinsky observed, "Now Russia has seen only *conservatism*, without *renewal* or *revolution* without *tradition*."[21] Nabokov shared none of this. Organized traditional religion remained foreign to him. He maintained the same strict and unwavering contempt for post-revolutionary Russia, the Soviets, as he did for the fascists. He kept his distance from all "isms." His views on human history and progress were linked to his own lifelong encounter with the detailed scientific observation of nature. Individuality and freedom in art and thought were endangered by the politics and culture of modern times. In 1937 Nabokov wrote, "The symmetry in the structure of live bodies is a consequence of the rotation of worlds . . . and that in our straining toward asymmetry, toward inequality, I can detect a howl for genuine freedom, an urge to break out of the circle."[22] For all his snobbery about writers past and present, Nabokov never strayed from the modernism he came to admire early in his career, that of Andrey Bely, Franz Kafka, the Proust of *Swann's Way*, and the Joyce of *Ulysses*.[23]

Although both men were anti-communist, Nabokov's pessimism about modernity never led him down the more reactionary path taken by Stravinsky in the years between 1922 and the mid-1950s. Nabokov feared the populist embrace of the despotic imposition of order and discipline in political life—including the sort of uniform assertion of a "healthy" social utilitarian aesthetic promoted by Hitler and Stalin. He also did not romanticize autocracy, including that of the czars before 1917. The trap faced by Adam Krug, Nabokov's protagonist in *Bend Sinister*, is the futility and self-destructiveness of any struggle to hold on to a shred of individuality, genuine refinement, originality, and morality—particularly by engaging with language, thought, literature, and culture—in the context of modern dictatorship. The pretense of value on behalf of culture and the making of art itself are complicit in concealing this trap—a truth grasped by Ember, the Shakespeare translator and Krug's friend in *Bend Sinister*.[24]

The cult of self-improving culture displayed in *Lolita* by Dolores Haze (consider the meaning of the name) and the sort of bad art associated with middle-class, semi-educated taste for the sentimental and the emotionally illustrative provide no protection against barbarism and violence. Humbert Humbert's highly cultivated and persuasive tastes in literature, music, and art, his evidently learned superiority over the Americans he meets seduces the reader; Humbert's aesthetic sensibility, even his capacity for poetic eloquence, makes the case for his defense hard to resist. Yet connoisseurship does not prevent his crimes. It merely softens the cruelty and deepens the plausibility of rationalization. Whether delivered by would-be individualists like Humbert or bureaucrats and dictators who create concentration camps, aesthetic gifts and cultural sensibilities fail, for Nabokov, as antidotes to the evil in modern life.[25]

When Humbert Humbert chases Clare Quilty, attempting to shoot him, his victim "sat down before the piano and played several atrociously vigorous, fundamentally hysterical, plangent chords, his jowls quivering, his spread hands tensely plunging, and his nostrils emitting the soundtrack snorts which had been absent from our fight. Still singing those impossible sonorities, he made a futile attempt to open with his foot a kind of seaman's chest near the piano."[26] Nabokov could not have evoked a more effective caricature of the pretensions of the modern piano virtuoso and the cheap, illustrative Romanticism of the kind Stravinsky also despised, and the futility of a tradition of cultural consumption (the seaman's chest) as means of escape from a fatal barbarism that threatens the survival of morality, civility, and the humane—much less that of talent, originality, beauty, and learning.

For Nabokov, the Russia of his youth was personal; it vanished and lived only in his memory. The pretense of finding in the past a legitimate basis for nostalgia held no allure. In his adult life Nabokov remained resistant to organized causes and ideologies, including patriotism and cultural chauvinism. Although Russian was his primary language, the Russia that continued to occupy him was his own invention, and bore little, if any relation to the Russia that existed after 1917.

He never sought to return to Russia or to maneuver to gain access to readers in Soviet Russia. Stravinsky on the other hand held on to the idea of an ongoing residual national solidarity, while rejecting a narrow nationalism. He saw himself as a supranational, universal figure above politics. Yet he subordinated his distaste for Communism and joined with other émigrés in taking some pride in the Soviet part of the Allied war effort in the 1940s. Stravinsky may have been ambivalent about returning to Russia, but he calculated correctly that if he did, he would return in triumph—which happened in 1962, after an absence of fifty years. He embraced the Russia he encountered on that trip; it evoked not only nostalgia but also a renewed sense of connection.

Stravinsky rose to fame in 1913 with *The Rite of Spring* not as an exile, but as a Russian composer on a voluntary, temporary sojourn from Russia, the sort of visit to the West commonplace in the history of Russian music and literature, as seen in the examples of Pyotr Tchaikovsky, Nikolay Gogol, Alexander Scriabin, and Ivan Turgenev. In contrast, Nabokov's great fame occurred in the context of involuntary exile. He always resented comparison with Joseph Conrad. Conrad was not an exile. He had no career as a Polish writer. Nabokov was a respected writer of Russian poetry and prose. Like Conrad, he achieved worldwide fame as a writer in English. But Nabokov did so while maintaining an explicit commitment to a particular tradition of Russian literature. His harsh loyalty to the virtue of literal translation (and skepticism about any other sort) was rooted in a view of the indivisible uniqueness of language. Its meanings were contingent on specificity, on time and place.

In the end, however, Nabokov's origins as a Russian did not define him in America, despite his teaching of Russian language and literature in a manner that suggested an indisputably superior knowledge and authority. The works that made him famous—*Lolita, Pnin*, and *Pale Fire*—were all novels located in America. In Stravinsky's case, the explicitly Russian aspects of his music never disappeared, no matter how subtly altered and camouflaged, and actually helped shape some of his finest music written in America. With his Russian influences intact, Stravinsky influenced decisively the direction of French music between the early 1920s and 1940. The role he played in French musical life as a lionized personality was analogous to the place Nabokov came to occupy as a writer in America from the late 1950s until his death in 1977.

If Stravinsky's breakthrough came in 1913, Nabokov's occurred between 1955 and 1958 with the publication of *Lolita* in Paris and New York. Both artists experienced—at different stages of their careers—a sudden burst of worldwide notoriety because of the scandal associated with a single work. Stravinsky became world-famous at age thirty. He arrived in America a well-known, influential, and admired figure, which led to the invitation to give the prestigious Norton Lectures at Harvard. Stravinsky complained constantly about money, but he came to America without the sort of dire financial worries common among émigrés (consider the fate of the Austrian composer Alexander Zemlinsky, who died in penury and obscurity in 1942 in Larchmont, New York). When Nabokov arrived in 1940, he brought with him at best an arcane reputation limited to émigré circles. He was in desperate straits. Among those prepared to help him were Sergey Rachmaninoff and Serge Koussevitzky, who provided the affidavit. Nabokov's rise to the status of a superstar came when he was in his late fifties. As Stravinsky with the *Rite*, Nabokov was made famous by the surface of a single work, *Lolita*, rather than by the work's greatness and importance as ultimately identified by a common critical consensus. With respect to the *Rite*, the choreography and the spectacular orchestral sonorities and effects generated the scandal. In the case of *Lolita*, the predictably reductive account of the plot and overt subject of the novel, the sexual passion for a "nymphet," made the writer rich and famous—not its language and structure or its many tantalizing asides.

Stravinsky's renown when he arrived in America came about partly through the proselytizing of Nadia Boulanger, with whom Aaron Copland, Virgil Thomson, and many others had studied, and this identity he retained. Nevertheless Stravinsky, like Nabokov, faced the problem of how to establish himself in America. Robert Craft was central to this process, helping to reinvent the composer's image. Stravinsky was always keenly attuned to the winds of fashion and the critical reaction to his own music. His disappointment at the reception of his 1951 opera *The Rake's Progress*, a work that many have regarded as the culmination of the composer's romance with the "order and discipline" of neoclassicism—understood strictly as evocative of eighteenth-century practices—motivated him to explore serialism, with Craft's help and Ernst Krenek's guidance. The major works of his final serial period, along with Craft's deft handling of the composer as a personality, helped place Stravinsky within the center of American classical musical life. Craft's role made the output of new music possible. Yet despite this remarkable late period, the repertoire that defined the composer's public persona to the end of his life was that written before the American years.

Nabokov did not have a past visible to his new American public. And he did not require a Craft to assist him. Yet, as Nabokov freely admitted, his entry into the American literary world would certainly have been even more difficult than it turned out to be without the critic Edmund Wilson. In the end, however, Nabokov achieved his own carefully crafted iconic status as an American writer through the works he wrote in English. The supposed poetic masterpiece around which *Pale Fire* is constructed is evidence of Nabokov's deep immersion into American life and letters. Nabokov's Russian novels gained a wide reading public only in retrospect after *Lolita*—a pattern between old and new work that is the exact reverse of Stravinsky's.

Nabokov used his American success to withdraw, in part, from America. Living in Montreux for his final sixteen years, he continued to assert his affection and allegiance to America; he maintained his prominence in the world of letters from afar and continued to write in English. "I am trying to develop, in this rosy exile, the same fertile nostalgia in regard to America, my new country, as I evolved for Russia, my old one."[27] His move was only in a minor way a move "back." It ought not be compared to the return to Europe of Thomas Mann, Theodor W. Adorno, or Paul Hindemith—none of whom ever considered America a plausible second home. Craft may have briefly considered getting Stravinsky to move back to Switzerland in the 1960s, but Stravinsky never truly considered returning to Europe after 1945. When he decided to leave the West Coast in the 1960s, he settled in New York. He managed, like Nabokov, to balance his own construct of a lost homeland with affection for his new American home. In the end, however, he was buried in Venice, near Diaghilev.

Method and Influence

Richard Taruskin, in his brilliant, definitive, and exhaustive two-volume account of Stravinsky's career through to the composition of *Mavra* in 1922—with its epilogue on the composer's final masterpiece, the 1964 *Requiem Canticles*—has painstakingly and persuasively described the defining early phases of the composer's career.[28] These modes of engagement with Russian traditions and contemporaries shaped the composer's method and aesthetic. Stravinsky's music, from the 1920s to the 1960s, reveals a lasting debt to Russian sources, the Russian context in which he came of age, and the manner in which he transformed Russian elements in the first years of exile in Switzerland.[29]

Feu d'artifice and *The Firebird* display the young composer's initial debt to a late nineteenth-century aesthetic, an older Romantic nationalism in which folklore was adapted into music for the stage and domestic use—the Kuchkist heritage of the so-called Mighty Five. Stravinsky, as his comments on Tchaikovsky suggest, also sought to prove himself within the Rimsky-Korsakov circle by demonstrating his command of the craft of composition defined in the German-centered "Western European" terms of Glazunov's more conservative formalism. That craft involved the display of symphonic thinking, in which a dynamic if not self-declared organic logic drives the use and transformation of harmony and melody. There, harmony serves a functional purpose in shaping musical time and structure, providing context for the process of thematic transformation, development, and recapitulation. These in turn generate audience expectations and the mechanisms by which instrumental music can appear to mimic narrative patterns in prose. These strategies made it possible for composers successfully to occupy duration and recalibrate long stretches of time.

The Russian music of the 1880s and '90s was Stravinsky's initial formative aesthetic environment. It can be taken, with its nationalist colorings, as the musical equivalents of the literary realism that dominated Russian literature, if not into the early 1900s, then, at minimum, until the mid-1880s, after the death of Czar Alexander II.[30] Social and political content and straightforward narrative and plot structure dominated, whereas matters of style, the self-conscious awareness of form, or any pretense to rendering prose closer to the poetic were subordinated. Literature, notably in the case of Dostoevsky and the later Tolstoy, became a prose forum for ideas—mostly on behalf of social and political changes that could elevate the moral significance and worth of all human beings. Method and form were contingent on a commitment to realism. The spiritual betterment of the reader became a goal. Ideas were rendered through action, description, and dialogue. The reader was drawn in by the writer's manipulation of the illusions of sequential time and pictorial realism. Not surprisingly, one of Nabokov's father's favorite novelists was Charles Dickens.

Although Nabokov was considerably younger than Stravinsky, they both confronted these qualities, colored by nationalist sentiment, as the dominant aesthetic credo of their parents' generation. Whether in prose or in music, the objective was to use aesthetic conventions to master the suggestion and evocation of content whose plausibility was located in methods of persuasion tied to realist criteria. Stravinsky, even when he abandoned the Rimsky-Korsakov model, sustained a nationalist impetus by drawing on more ethnographically authentic sources of Russian folk music. But he located new formal possibilities for music in their melodic and rhythmic elements and articulated a nationalist sensibility less defined by the aesthetics of Romanticism and at once more novel and authentic. His means deviated from the program music tradition and were influenced by the ideas of contemporaries, several linked to the *Mir iskusstva* (World of Art) circle—Serge Diaghilev, Léon Bakst, and Alexandre Benois in particular. The last two were themselves part of the circle of artists around the Nabokov family. The vogue for symbolism and synesthesia, particularly in the work of Bely and Scriabin, also played a role in shaping the path Stravinsky took.

In the *Rite*, Stravinsky used abstraction of the archaic Russian materials he appropriated to achieve an "architectural" rather than "anecdotal" use of musical time. Repetition in the form of sustained rhythmic pulsation was juxtaposed with abrupt harmonic shifts and changes in sonority at odds with the tradition of the symphony. The combinatorial ingenuity Stravinsky revealed (meant here not strictly in the sense defined by Milton Babbitt) employed the octatonic scale and intervallic cells—"a syntax of subsets and super-sets" derived from them.[31] With that as a base he pursued intentional "simplification"—the abstraction of genuine folk melodic and rhythmic usage. This led Stravinsky to achieve what Taruskin describes as "a hard-nosed esthetic modernism."[32] Harmony was no longer directional and dynamic, but static. The effect was not unlike the visual aesthetic pursued by Nicholas Roerich, the designer of the first *Rite* production. Roerich, working from the suggestion of authentic national antique sources, produced flat, static, frozen imagery further abstracted from any form of realism by the stark uninflected use of color and the reduction of perspective; juxtaposed geometric patterns in the visual frame undercut the nominal suggestion of narrative meaning.[33]

By the time he composed the *Rite* Stravinsky, distancing the experience of musical time from traditional expectations, had shifted the relationship of the listener to a musical work away from an analogy with that of a reader following a narrative. In the realist novel, opera, and Romantic symphony, the plausibility of an imagined past, present, and future, occurring in a logical sequence had been enhanced by the realist plainness (or naturalistic resemblance) of prose style (including dialogue) and the manipulation of the narrative voice. In music, these expectations among listeners had been amply met by the techniques of musical usage of both sides of the apparent divide between the circles around Tchaikovsky and Rimsky-Korsakov. But with the *Rite*, anticipation and release as well as recollection during the act of listening were subordinated to the intensity of the momentary encounter with sound and the unprepared contrasts in the sharply delineated sequence of events. Music intensified the experience of time in the immediacy of its encounter, emancipating it from any dependence on recapitulation and foregrounding accumulation. Stravinsky's *Rite* appeared in direct conflict with musical realism's most skilled practitioner of the fin de siècle, Richard Strauss, notably his two last symphonic works, the *Sinfonia Domestica* and the *Alpine* Symphony.

However fierce the antipathy may have been between the Kuchkists and their opponents (or between the Wagnerians and anti-Wagnerians), the advent of modernism circa 1913 in Stravinsky unmasked what all of these separate camps held in common in terms of the function of harmony and the character of form, and therefore the construct of musical time. Whether formalist (in the sense of Eduard Hanslick and later Stravinsky himself, who in his autobiography never tired of underscoring the idea that music expressed nothing except itself), or blatantly illustrative, as in Wagner's, Liszt's, and Strauss's compositions, musical time had been controlled by convention so as to confirm the apparent reality of a past and present moment, and the existence of a causal nexus analogous to the empirical experience of events or its linguistic representation. Art sought to engender either a remembered, imagined, or implied narrative.[34]

Stravinsky's achievement in the 1913 *Rite* and more strikingly in 1917 with *Les Noces*—a distillation of a modernist aesthetic out of neo-nationalist material using simplification and abstraction that recalibrated the experience of time and defined a style—can be compared with the project that Nabokov undertook as a novelist in his twenties, after his years at Cambridge and his move to Berlin. Nabokov shared sources of inspiration with his older composer compatriot, notably the *Mir iskusstva* movement that argued the autonomy of the aesthetic and the primacy of matters of style and form against the inherited utilitarian aesthetics of realism. Symbolism and the World of Art movement motivated Stravinsky and Nabokov to question the claim of a correspondence between aesthetic experience and the quotidian encounter with experienced time, both measured and remembered. This challenge to the traditional logic of art extended to a critique of the late Tolstoy's insistence that there be an evident moral and, by implication, redemptive justification beyond a purely aesthetic one. Stravinsky and Nabokov experimented not only in terms of their engagement with their respective traditions in Russian music and literature, but in terms of the fundamental character, function, and purpose of the work of art and its relationship to its audience, the link between literature and reader or music and listener.

The Gift, Nabokov's last novel from his Berlin years (and for some his finest) is in part framed by two exchanges between the two most sympathetic figures in the book: Fyodor, the nominal protagonist, who writes a satirical, almost Gogol-like biography of Nikolay Chernyshevsky (the arch-realist of the nineteenth century and a favorite of Lenin and the Soviets), and Koncheyev, the poet. In the first exchange Fyodor asserts, quoting Koncheyev, "Yes, some day I'm going to produce prose in which 'thought and music are conjoined as are the folds of life in sleep.'"[35] Thinking in words is idealized by language's musical properties—its sounds and rhythms—not meanings that might be detached from sound and form. For the young Nabokov, the writing of literature was framed by language that revealed a nonlinear temporal logic outside of ordinary time, comparable to the distortion of time in dreams, yet possessed of a precision reminiscent of science and susceptible to being captured in works.

In the second exchange Fyodor picks up this theme (one Nabokov would return to explicitly at the end of *Ada, or Ardor*):

> It would be a good thing in general to put an end to our barbaric perception of time. . . . Our mistaken feeling of time as a kind of growth is a consequence of our finiteness which, being always on the level of the present, implies a constant rise between the watery abyss of the past and the aerial abyss of the future. Existence is thus an eternal transformation of the future into the past—an essentially phantom process—a mere reflection of the material metamorphoses taking place within us. . . . The theory I find most tempting—that there is no time, that everything is the present situated like a radiance outside our blindness—is just as hopeless a finite hypothesis as all the others.[36]

Nabokov attempted to find the "radiance outside our blindness" by writing a poetic prose that treated language as music—shattering the inherited narrative and structural conventions of the novelistic form of realism and locating in its place an alternate sensibility that transcended the mundane. Despite the evident contrasts, this project took shape in a manner comparable to Stravinsky's evolution from the 1907 Symphony in E-flat to the 1917 *Les Noces*. Nabokov experimented not only with language at every point in a novel (or short story)—each unit of which was ultimately contained on index cards—but in the overall structure, routinely divorcing each novel from following an inherited model as a sequential narrative marked by character development and a clear demarcation of past, present, and future. Stravinsky, by rejecting the symphonic model and the conventions of late nineteenth-century musical continuity, formed what Edward T. Cone identified as a "method" in three parts: stratification, interlock, and synthesis.[37] These three terms could also be applied to Nabokov's novels from the 1930s, particularly *The Gift* and *Invitation to a Beheading*, and those from the 1950s, particularly *Lolita* and *Pnin*.

The privileging of the aesthetic pioneered by the World of Art movement and the symbolists of the Silver Age in Russia offered both Stravinsky and Nabokov ideological bases for shifting the criteria of an artwork from matters of content to those of structure and form. Within formal criteria, style and method were foregrounded. Cone identified the use of successive "time-segments" in the 1920 *Symphonies d'instruments à vent*.[38] Each of these is suspended, creating opportunities for their employment in contrapuntal usage. The synthesis comes not in a climax, but in the reduction or the assimilation of one element into another. Bridges and divergences are common. Stratification using discrete musical variables defines Stravinsky's compositional procedure well into the music of the 1940s; in Cone's view, it also describes the way in which the strong tonal components of the 1930 *Symphony of Psalms* are organized. Another way of imagining Stravinsky's method in the *Symphonies d'instruments à vent* is, as Louis Andriessen and Elmer Schönberger have argued, to apply the metaphors of montage and collage in which the structural relationship and identity of disparate fragments are altered and manipulated, generating an overarching unified framework in which the discrete elements remain visible.[39] Taruskin has perhaps the most elaborate and persuasive way of characterizing Stravinsky's novel approach to form, for which he uses the Russian term *drobnost'*, or "splinteredness," a "sum of parts."[40]

The parallels to such procedures can be found in Nabokov in the fragmentation of time, the subtly arranged but sudden shifts in voice, and in the inconsistent presence of the narrator. Nabokov's "time fragments" are deployed so as to create ambiguities between the real and imagined. The reader is continually alert to the persistent shedding of the illusions of realist narration; just as the listener to Stravinsky is struck by the distinct substance of each musical moment apart from any functional implication backward or forward, Nabokov's reader is forced to confront sentences and paragraphs as stylistic entities, with significance apart from any overarching narrative frame. Literature, insofar as it is part of "the forces of imagination," is a "force of good," Nabokov observed in 1965. Translating *The Eye* more than three decades after its publication, Nabokov confessed he was in search of the "reader who catches on at first"; this reader will derive "genuine satisfaction," but from more than a story.[41] Nabokov's ideal reader is asked to jettison the commonsense notion of language as representational or corresponding to an external reality. A different sort of precision is required. Stylistic self-awareness of how observation can be discussed alters the perception of elapsed time and preserves it in memory. The more detailed, the more unusual and poetic, the more vivid. Through writing fired by the poetic imagination a new reality comes into being that is more real than the "real" itself.

The framing of the novels—visible in the cloaked identity of the narrator in *Pnin*; in the construction of *Pale Fire* out of segments of commentary that follow a text and scramble past, present, and future and the multiple identities of its protagonist Kinbote; in the form of *Lolita* as an account by a man awaiting trial; or in the uncertain connection to dream life and everyday existence in *Despair*, *Invitation to a Beheading*, and *Bend Sinister*—suggest parallels to Stravinsky's procedures of stratifying elements that have been abstracted from otherwise familiar patterns. In music, pitch and rhythm are the elements in play; in prose they are words, plot, time, and character. Nabokov's method of collage and montage is clearest in his use of time, his layering of perspectives using fragments of memory and distortions of the way time is segmented into a sequence of past, present, and future.[42] Nabokov's syntactic inventiveness, his virtuosic use and invention of words, his nearly Shakespearean synthesis of word use and thought, as well as his assemblage of the novel by the ordering of completed units (his beloved index cards) show his literary method as not dissimilar from musical composition as practiced by Stravinsky. Stravinsky's meticulous habits in the process of composition, as understood by theorists and as evident in the manuscripts of *The Rake's Progress* and the *Requiem Canticles* (to cite just two often reproduced examples), suggest that Nabokov and Stravinsky shared an innovative combinatorial genius.[43]

Consider, for example, the elegance, variety, and ingenuity in the disposition of intervals and sonorities in the *Requiem Canticles* as analogous to the illusory simplicity of the relationship of poem to commentary in *Pale Fire*. Kinbote, with knowing irony, speaks early of the one line that "would have completed the symmetry" of Shade's poem. Nabokov has him end this thought by writing "damn that music. Knowing Shade's combinatorial turn of mind and subtle sense of harmonic balance, I cannot imagine that he intended to deform the faces of his crystal by meddling with its predictable growth."[44] Yet deformation precisely describes what he as a novelist and Stravinsky as composer, in their relationship to the traditions in their respective arenas, actually accomplished. The deformation and meddling were directed at the narrative conventions of form and continuity that derived their power from a presumed correspondence to lived experience that was ultimately banal.

Nabokov was fabled for his visual acuity. His love of Sherlock Holmes rested less on the detective's deductive powers than on his eye for detail. Nabokov's meticulous work on butterflies, his fanatical concern for the accuracy of descriptive detail, his poetic response to landscape in his novels all attest to the primacy of attention to the smallest detail in a work of art and the imagination. "I discovered in nature the nonutilitarian delights that I sought in art. Both were a form of magic, both were a game of intricate enchantment and deception."[45] No wonder he derided novelists of "general" ideas who penned prosaic sentences filled with the vocabulary of abstraction. In *Speak, Memory* Nabokov pointed to the moment of intense sight as the means by which the finest that is human can stake its claim:

> It is certainly not then—not in dreams—but when one is wide awake, at moments of robust joy and achievement, on the highest terrace of consciousness, that mortality has a chance to peer beyond its own limits, from the mast, from the past and its castle tower.[46]

In Nabokov's writing, the aural experience in the present moment, not only the visual, mirrors "the heightened terrace of consciousness" that can be set to words. At stake is not a talent for synesthesia (as with the Lithuanian composer Mikalojus Čiurlionis, who perceived color and sound at one and the same time) or its ideology (as developed by Scriabin).[47] Nabokov did, however, recall that the imagining of the outline of a single letter of the alphabet produced a "fine case of colored hearing."[48] But Nabokov's memories were framed not only by sight but by sounds—a "throbbing tambourine," "trilling" nightingales, the sounds of village musicians, the rhythm of Mademoiselle's speech.[49] King Charles in *Pale Fire* was a musician. Nabokov routinely praised poetry in terms of music (its "contrapuntal pyrotechnics"), and for its music ("that dim distant music").[50] Cincinnatus C. recalls the world being "hacked" into "great gleaming blocks" by the "music that once used to be extracted from a monstrous pianoforte."[51]

Indeed, for Nabokov, the power of music and of sound—beyond all its links to memory—was that it intensified the ordinary consciousness of time understood as a continuum along the lines of the quotidian.[52] The short story "Music" revolves around the perception that music easily links present with past.[53] At the same time Nabokov grasped the need to deviate from a sense of time located in nature. Music was an art that, like poetry, could expand time. Kinbote, defending his friendship with Shade, credited his short acquaintance with the capacity of the aesthetic to defy the calendar, creating "inner duration," "eons of transparent time" independent of external "rotating malicious music."[54] Nabokov's view is not entirely dissimilar to Stravinsky's. The composer wrote in his autobiography, "Music is the overarching domain in which man realizes the present." Music's sole purpose was to establish "an order in things" and especially "the coordination between *man* and *time*." Music redefines time in the present and gives "substance" and "stability" to "the category of the present."[55]

Art and Time

Stravinsky and Nabokov shared an obsession with how the aesthetic realm might influence the phenomenon of time perception, despite a surface of divergence between the two: Nabokov struggled against the tyranny of a seemingly objective and uniform construct of time, whereas Stravinsky attempted to deepen the sense of the present through musical construction. For both, nostalgia and memory were tied to the experience of time, and both struggled to come to terms with the link between past and present. In their various speculations, both also drew on two common sources: Henri Bergson and Andrey Bely. Writing about Stravinsky in 1949, Craft mentions Stravinsky's having read Bergson.[56] Whether he actually did so or learned of Bergson's ideas from Pyotr Suvchinsky and Paul Valéry in the 1920s, the philosophical connection Bergson forged between the experience of time in the present and the expression of the human creative force left a lasting impression on the composer's beliefs about the character and function of music.[57] Music, by framing and in fact stopping the ordinary experience of time so that it appeared always in the present, rendered music "petrified" architecture and deepened the consciousness of human creativity. Nabokov, who had a more complex understanding of time, was also influenced by Bergson, whom he admitted reading avidly in the interwar years.[58]

With Stravinsky, musical time—defined as the extension and construction of the present moment—reappears as well in the late work, mostly as a result of his encounter with the music of Anton von Webern. Predominant in this music are silence as a component of compositional structure and the ascetic economic manipulation of sonority, mostly in units of short duration; the result is a heightening and deepening of time in the moment of listening. For Nabokov the issue of time, always present in the novels, took center stage in the 1960s in *Ada*. The "flowering of the present," as Van Veen in *Ada* put it, demanded the awareness that time is "vaguely connected to hearing"; the apprehension of time requires "the utmost purity of consciousness," which is not spatial and visual but aural.[59]

The key is that the "still fresh past" defines the present. The "present" slips in when we inspect "shadow sounds." The "dim intervals between the dark beats" of the authentic rhythm of time offer merely the "feel of the *texture* of Time." Nabokov concluded: "Our modest Present is, then, the time span that one is directly and actually aware of, with the lingering freshness of the Past still perceived as part of the nowness."[60] The synchronized flow of time as measured by clocks was itself an illusion, since the boundaries between past and present were if not fluid, interdependent, with the selective consciousness of the past defining the present and then subsequently the reverse, in which the past becomes circumscribed by the sense of the present moment.[61] This fluidity reveals itself in the movement back and forth in time in Nabokov's narrative voice. His characters take the same journey—often so deftly from the reader's perspective that the shifts become noticeable only after the act of reading, making the reader aware of the author's challenge to a reductive realism within his or her own time experience, not merely within the artificial time frame of the novel.

For both Nabokov and Stravinsky, the issue of time and its perception was more than an aesthetic problem. The experience of exile forced a many-sided dilemma with regard to memory and anticipation. First was the challenge of how to come to terms with the artistic heritage, public, and tradition of which the exile once expected to be part, and from which he was now separated. Second was the need to grapple with the tyrannies of memory—the lacunae, the willful and inadvertent distortions, and the fragments all heightened by discontinuity and distance, the forced separation from the familiar and the illusions of continuity that non-exiles take for granted. Third was the danger posed by the allure of nostalgia, the sentimental distortion of memory, and the exaggerated fear of forgetfulness. To forget was to destroy not merely the past but the possibilities of the present. Yet memory, the driving force of the present and essential to the artist, was constantly at risk in exile, where it became a purely mental property unaided by sight and sound.

A last dilemma for exiles, and a consequence of all the difficulties already alluded to was how to find an alternative to the tacit assumption of continuity—an effective means to forge an ongoing connection between past and present—something thoughtlessly possible for those not displaced. Indeed, the definition of the present—the temporal frame for the making and experience of art—became more complex since the significant past was ever harder to keep "still fresh," and its capacity to "slip" into the present and define it was steadily weakened. At risk was the very capacity to grasp the present, to intuit the texture of time sufficiently to allow the imagination to take flight.

Nabokov's approach to the issue of time was influenced by Bergson, but it was the thought of Bely that most directly shaped the way Nabokov considered his craft and vocation as a writer and his approach to aesthetic questions.[62] Writing in 1907, Bely argued against a "synthesis" of art forms (despite his early admiration for Wagner). Rather, the purpose of art reflected an underlying unity in the arts. "Is it simply so that we may transform a few hours into a dream, only to have the dream destroyed again by the intrusion of reality?" Bely asked. His answer was that the creative act was, in Kantian terms, "cognition for its own sake," an intuitive form of engaging time without any purpose or object. The "method of creation" becomes "an object in and for itself." The result was the "extreme form of individualization." The process of artistic creation demanded that each artist "become his own artistic form." The categories of time were artificial subjective conventions for framing reality and must be rethought. Bely termed new art as "the past that is reborn," where "we find ourselves at the mercy of the cherished dead." In a manner reminiscent of Nabokov's own speculations Bely argued, "We must forget the present. We must re-create everything and in order to do this we must create ourselves."[63]

The interconnection of a construct of the past—the task of reassembling the past, or in Bely's terms, re-creating it—requires that conventions about understanding the "present" be set aside. Forgetfulness is a prelude to the restoration of memory. The sense of time is not connected to a cognitive correspondence between external reality and consciousness but a function of a highly individualized creative act, using the aesthetic medium—the musical, the poetic, and the visual—to redefine consciousness and time. These claims connect directly to the innovations of both Nabokov and Stravinsky.

For Bely—as well as Nabokov and the mature Stravinsky—the key to escaping the notion that art was a mere illusory respite from an objective reality was the recognition that the form in which the creative act expressed itself generated an alternate reality, an experience of time located in the human possibility of individuality for the author and his public that vindicated life. In moral terms, the most significantly true reality came into being through the forms of art in a manner that transcended, with considerable precision, the mundane understanding of real time and experience. This mundane understanding was itself the result of an impoverished use of language. Placing art before any notion of "life," Bely concluded "in art, in life, things are more serious than we think."[64]

The most "serious" realization—one crucial to Stravinsky and Nabokov— was Bely's idea that "if words did not exist then neither would the world itself." Bely put forward a notion of "living speech," which was the "very condition of existence of mankind itself." And since "mankind's purpose lies in the living creation of life," by hearing speech that is "imagined" and "living" we are led to new words and word constructions that in turn lead to "the acquisition of new acts of cognition."[65] The next step was from words to music.

Bely's privileging of language as the mother of thought, as his Viennese contemporary Karl Kraus put it, was not new. But there was a metaphysical premise in Bely that justified a scientific precision in the use of language particularly dear to Nabokov. Language, especially poetic language, created the reality we define as "living" relationships, including the future creation of language. Within the linguistic realm, and within art, for example, the coincidence of vocabulary (as Bely discussed in the case of Kant and Hanslick) suggested that within this ever-expandable universe of linguistic invention were scientific criteria of truth, a "real dimension."[66] Nabokov's distaste for conceptual language, the vocabulary of ideologies—in Marx and Freud—derives from Bely's skepticism that there is false language, language that is wholly unreal, detached from the "direct expression of life." Naming becomes crucial since it creates that which would otherwise not exist. "The word is the sole real vessel on which we sail from one unknown to another—amidst unknown spaces (called "earth" "heaven" "ether" and so forth) and amidst unknown temporalities." The "firework" displays of words "fill the void surrounding me."[67] Bely's vision veers close to a method of musical composition using intervals and sonorities in a novel fashion, much like Stravinsky's procedures.

Poetry for Bely and Nabokov is the highest form of word usage; it is the source of the creation of language and the purely "imaginal combination of words." Indeed, in historical moments of decay, poetry's importance is at its highest, for it lets us "recognize the meaning of new magical words" by which to "conjure the gloom of night hanging over us." In moments of despair, "we are still alive, but we are alive because we hold on to words."[68] This thought succinctly described Nabokov's commitment to his vocation as a writer, particularly considering his keen sense of the darkness of the era in which he lived. For Nabokov, Bely's observation that "mankind is alive, so long as the poetry of language exists," was a genuine article of faith.[69]

For Bely, all this was contingent on a belief in the necessity of form and the capacity to locate objective criteria for understanding aesthetic form within all the arts. Formalism was not derivative of tradition or a distillation of historical practice—a deduction resulting from the imposition of norms of judgment onto an empirical base of past practice, such as the manner in which theorists establish norms of sonata form. Bely, an accomplished mathematician, was in search of a priori axioms. Predictably, his source was mathematics and physics. Bely's translation of scientific modes of thought into aesthetics was distinctive and may have provided the young Nabokov a suggestive model of how to link his fascination with nature and with butterflies to his ambitions as a writer.

For Bely there was no division between content and form: the way in which the concrete materials of art are considered constitutes the subject of form. Form was the "governing" principle in all art and protected art from descending into meaningless chaos and "tendentious encroachments."[70] Bely's principles were framed in terms of Newtonian laws. First came a hierarchy of the arts. He posited an "inverse proportion" between space and time in the ranking of the arts. This made music the highest of the arts, since in it all spatial and visual elements were abstracted. Music possessed no spatial dimension. It was the means by which pure temporality was expressed. Only through "vague" analogies could "visual and spatial" meanings be attributed to music. For Nabokov, as for Stravinsky, aesthetic judgment required the subordination of the spatial and visual to the temporal, for it strengthened the idea that art was autonomous and ought not be tied to a vulgar sense of the real, to any illusionism or pictorial realism. Music was the art of time, understood as the "art of pure motion," with a precise truth-value akin to science.[71]

For Bely, poetry came next after music. "Poetry views the visible world musically, like a veil over an unspoken mystery of the soul. . . . Music is the skeleton of poetry. If music is the common trunk of all creation, poetry is its leafy crown."[72] Although Nabokov derided his own connection to music, his notion of poetry and the nature of his prose, when considered in light of Bely's premium on word creation and the novel combinations of words, are like musical renderings of a world imagined. Painting, predictably, occupied the lowest rung of Bely's ordering of the arts.[73]

Bely's formalism was further understood in terms of the natural law of conservation, defined as the conservation of creative energy. In a proper artistic form that aesthetic energy needed to be expended in proportional manner to overcome "stasis" in the very materials of creation. The aesthetics of form possessed its own "law of equivalents" by which the creative energy of the result matched that of its components and creation. Bely's effort to establish a non-arbitrary parallel between the laws governing energy with those governing art led him to assert that aesthetics could be an "exact science" with unlimited competence in the sense of the natural sciences.[74] Here again can be found the sources of the conceits of Stravinsky and Nabokov, particularly Stravinsky's explicit appeal to the primacy of the "Apollonian" dimension in art. Indeed, Stravinsky's turn to the ideal of neoclassicism reveals a debt to Bely.

Using a single-minded emphasis on form, Bely formulated his own answer to the question of the connection between truth and beauty. Unlike the normative philosophical discourse of the eighteenth century that posited the link as between aesthetics and ethics, Bely's was a direct, unmediated link between the truth content in descriptive aesthetics and science.

In Nabokov's case the connection to Bely is even more striking. Using elaborate diagrammatic schemes, Bely argued that one could measure and describe the harmonious balance between content and form in a lyric poem; one needed a theory of rhythm and "instrumentation" so as to study word choices. Bely dissected a poem by Nikolay Nekrasov, separating its "experiential" from its "ideational" content.[75] He compared the rhythmic complexity of early and late Pushkin in order to grasp the "how" of words and sounds. An intensely descriptive science, including a taxonomy, was required to grasp the beauty of poetry, hence:

> Every lyric work demands a basic commentary. In commenting on a poem we are decomposing it, as it were, into its constituent parts and looking carefully at the means of representation, at the choice of epithets, similes, and metaphors in order to characterize the content. We feel the words and look for their mutual rhythmic and sonorous relations. In thus reorganizing the analyzed material into a new whole, we often can no longer recognize a familiar poem at all. Like the phoenix, it arises anew out of itself in a more beautiful form, or, conversely, it withers away. In this way we come to recognize that a comparative anatomy of poetic style is truly necessary, that it is the ultimate stage in the development of a theory of literature and lyric poetry, and finally that it represents a *rapprochement* between these two disciplines and the various fields of scientific knowledge.[76]

There could be no more persuasive source for Nabokov's *Eugene Onegin* project, his structural choices in *Pale Fire*, or his suspicion of anything but literal translation. The purpose for this exact analytical science rested first in precision in the variables of art—words, colors, and pitches—and second in the inherent objective logic of their use and elaboration. The pure aesthetic that such analysis could reveal was an authentic realism of the imagination beyond the realism of the visible. "Reality is not how it appears to us. . . . Reality as we know it is different from reality as it truly is," Bely concluded.[77]

In Bely's terms, Nabokov, by first approaching language as poetry, aspired to the state of music. "I have never been able to see any generic difference between poetry and artistic prose," Nabokov once observed.[78] Since all art shares features with music, and music "unites and generalizes" all art, owing to its status as purely about time, "the profundity and intensity of musical works give us, according to Bely, a hint" that through the aesthetic imagination, composer and listener, writer and reader can begin to remove "the deceptive veil" that covers the "visible world," and demolish the "deceptive picture" with which we live.[79] Nabokov's intensity of visual and oral observation, shorn from a conventional narrative or obvious temporal context, cast in rich and original poetic language (invented words and startling juxtapositions), invited his reader to lift the veil and penetrate beyond the deceptive picture.

Stravinsky's connection to Bely was certainly less direct, but equally significant. The influence of Bely's notions of form and his views on music—and indeed the centrality of art—were most powerfully communicated through the World of Art movement, by the painters and poets who were his contemporaries. But the link to Stravinsky's mature positions on the nature of music was profound. Perhaps the most oft-cited claim Stravinsky made can be found in his autobiography:

> For I consider that music is, by its very nature, essentially powerless to *express* anything at all, whether a feeling, an attitude of mind, a psychological mood and phenomenon of nature, etc. . . . *Expression* has never been an inherent property of music. That is by no means the purpose of its existence. If, as is always the case, music appears to express something, this is only an illusion and not a reality.[80]

A corollary of this formalist claim is the assumption that the formal character of a piece of music has an objective character that can be exactly described and rendered. Bely's synthesis of natural science and aesthetics was a source of Stravinsky's intense disparagement of the practice and justification of subjective interpretation by performers and his personal affinity first for the pianola, and subsequently for recording technology, through which exact and objective representations of a musical work could be transmitted.

Art and Consequences

Stravinsky shared with Nabokov the belief that the work of art held its value in its aesthetic and formal properties. Art was powerful to the extent it contested commonsensical notions of the real and categories of space, time, and causality.

Nabokov once observed, "Both memory and imagination are a negation of time."[81] Nabokov and Stravinsky held on to a belief in valid norms of aesthetic value that allowed for individuality while at the same time they mistrusted a view of art as mere subjectivity, of art without objective criteria of judgment. Precision and exactness were indispensable attributes. In the end, however, such exactitude and precision were inevitably compromised by Stravinsky's concession that even in music, the least "realistic" of the arts, something other than itself always seems to be expressed.[82] Stravinsky was aware that the actual social function of music—its reception—derived from the assignment of meaning on the part of the listener, intended or not: the listener ascribed to music meanings both symbolic and literal that, strictly speaking, did not reside in the work itself.

For Stravinsky, this was actually a convenient error, one with which, for practical reasons, he could readily reconcile himself. At best, a truly informed aesthetic response to art permitted the listener to make legitimate contact with a religious sensibility—a communion, as Stravinsky concluded in 1939, with a generalized notion of humanity, "our fellow man" and with the "Supreme Being." Thus for Stravinsky the formal power of art did in the end connect with faith through some perhaps quasi-mystical religious feeling not contained in the music itself. In this manner the theologian Jacques Maritain influenced Stravinsky in his Paris years. Maritain reconciled "art for art's sake" and the premium on form with ethics and the suggestion of content: art, by being just art, mirrored the divine. Despite Stravinsky's vigorous distaste for communal ideologies, his 1939 Maritain-inspired evocation of the divine recognition that derived from music had much in common with Romain Rolland's suggestion in the late 1920s of the possibility of "an oceanic" feeling that might be a force for good. Both mirrored in different ways the interwar search for spiritual solace in the wake of the Great War. Stravinsky had no use for Rolland. Neither did Nabokov or Nabokov's least favorite theorist, Sigmund Freud, in *Civilization and Its Discontents*. Nabokov's hostility to Freud rested in the writer's mistrust and contempt for a reductive causality about creativity, his denial of a deeper reality beyond the visible empirical world unmediated by the individual imagination, and therefore the freedom of the individual imagination. But Freud's criticism of Rolland did not redeem either Freud or Rolland for Nabokov. And for Nabokov, the religious issue—the stuff about an "oceanic" sensibility or a divine "Supreme Being"—was a matter of silence, beyond words.[83] For Stravinsky, however, a quite conventional appeal to religious justification remains buried beneath his denial of music's power to express.

For Nabokov the formal virtues of art, properly grasped by the reader, did more than lead the reader into a vague humanism or Stravinsky's moment of spiritual recognition. Implicit in the act of reading literature, particularly poetry and prose written in a modernist style defined by the attributes of poetry (as in Bely's *St. Petersburg* and Joyce's *Ulysses*) was a potency that could prevent the reader from denying the power of art. Art contested the utterly mundane, so that the aesthetic did more than merely conform to the ordinary experience of reality. Indeed the artwork, by its formal greatness, could stop readers in their tracks. True art in the medium of literature provided writer and reader an escape from the tyranny of experience that emanated from everyday life. Here was a form of deception: experience transfigured by the imagination, a reality consciously protected from barbarism and vulgarity. For Nabokov the making of art and its proper appreciation was at its best a purely inner moral act of rescue, a route for individuals to confront freedom and the paradox that human decency—culture notwithstanding—is endangered.

Nabokov undermines the act of reading as a passive experience in the same way Stravinsky demands the concentration of the listener. The recollection of details, the passage back and forth in the narrative, force the reader to reflect and piece together fragments, to reconsider and remember, creating within the present moment the allure of a complex interpretation. Nabokov and Stravinsky found comparable ways for an aesthetically generated control, distortion, and manipulation of elapsed time to define present experience.

Thus the structure of a Nabokov novel can be said to share formal aspects similar to those used in music, particularly Stravinsky's. Repetition, abrupt transitions, modulations, fragmentation, inversions, cross- references abound, as do excursions into intense counterpoint with multiple subjects placed in discrete units. Nabokov's methods resemble Stravinsky's insofar as the elements of the composition are not present or utilized as placeholders for other meanings or expressive of something other than themselves. Even when words are set to music, as in Stravinsky's settings of texts, from the *Three Japanese Lyrics* (1912) to *The Rake's Progress*, they are used as sound elements, with syllables manipulated as musical elements.[84] The attempt to "set" the meaning of the words or illustrate them in a Wagnerian manner reliant on ordinary diction is subordinated. Stravinsky's procedure in 1912 already bears comparison with the purpose and method of the relationship between text and music articulated by Arnold Schoenberg that same year in the essay "The Relationship to the Text."[85] Even when linguistic meaning is presumed—as in song or opera—the text is used musically and proceeds independently of any "meaning." The parallel in Nabokov occurs when the presumed reality of the narrative object of the novel—its setting and character—is put in question by the defiance of a single familiar perspective. The argument or plot of the novel is disconnected from a fabric of continuity and displaced from the reader's attention. Rather, the act of writing, the craft of writing, and the predicament of the writer take center stage within the text itself.

This approach elevates Nabokov's prose to the status of music. Nabokov, like Stravinsky, calls explicit attention to the craft and method of his compositions. In order to foreground the act of writing Nabokov asks for a reader more akin to the listener imagined by Stravinsky—a person who can follow the musical logic and smile, when necessary, at complex structures and the elegance with which past tradition becomes part of the present moment, as in the 1924 Concerto for Piano and Wind Instruments, and the 1931 Violin Concerto, with their evident allusions to Bach. Nabokov's writing is often about other writing, just as Stravinsky's music, particularly in the 1920s, has as its premise music from the past. Both Nabokov and Stravinsky, as exiles, used the aesthetic tradition in which they worked against itself, albeit respectfully, cloaking the new with evocations of the past.

It is not surprising that from their shared heritage both artists, skipping over the tastes of the previous generation, were particularly attached to Pushkin. The tradition they drew on was in that sense pre-modern, at the intersection of eighteenth-century classicism and early Romanticism. Furthermore, Pushkin, like Tchaikovsky later in the century, represented an ideal synthesis of the Russian and the Western. Yet his star began to fade even towards the end of his career. Those who regarded themselves part of the intelligentsia were, to quote D. S. Mirsky, "indifferent" or "hostile" after 1860; whatever surviving cult of Pushkin remained became "the religion of a paradise lost."[86] Nabokov idealized the poet who was neglected in the literary age of realism and social utility. He and Stravinsky identified with the very quality in Pushkin that outraged the older Tolstoy of the 1890s—the focus on an elite readership and the absence of a moralizing agenda. Pushkin's use of language defined what was distinctive about Russian poetry and the musical and expressive possibilities of Russian speech, even as he found a means for their expression in Western forms.[87] Stravinsky lamented that for "foreigners" Pushkin was little more than "a name in an encyclopedia." Yet for these two exiles of an aristocratic sensibility and inclination, Pushkin's "nature, his mentality, and his ideology" was "the most perfect representative of that wonderful line which began with Peter the Great . . . and has united the most characteristically Russian elements with the spiritual riches of the West."[88]

Stravinsky turned to Pushkin, first during the composition of *Les Noces* and then explicitly with *Mavra* in 1922.[89] Stravinsky sought to signal a shift away from the patterns of late nineteenth-century Russian musical nationalism. He reinvented a lineage for himself located in Glinka and Tchaikovsky—a lightness, economy, and elegance reminiscent of Mozart and explicitly defiant of Wagnerism and post-Wagnerian German modernism. Following Pushkin—and Tchaikovsky—he would attempt a synthesis of the Russian with the refined Western sensibilities derived from the era during which aristocratic patronage dominated musical culture, the age before the death of Beethoven. Stravinsky recalled with regard to *Mavra*:

> This poem of Pushkin led me straight to Glinka and Tchaikovsky, and I resolutely took up my position beside them. I thus clearly defined my tastes and predilections, my opposition to the contrary aesthetic, and assumed once more the good tradition established by these masters. Moreover I dedicated my work to the memory of Pushkin, Glinka, and Tchaikovsky.[90]

Nabokov did not share Stravinsky's enthusiasm for Tchaikovsky. He disdained Tchaikovsky's operatic version of *Eugene Onegin* for what he regarded as its mawkish sentimentality, "cloying banalities," and bowdlerization of Pushkin's text.[91] This disdain rested in the recognition, extensively argued by Bely, that in the streamlined elegance of Pushkin's verse the full power of Russian rhythm and usage was exploited.[92] (Well before Nabokov, Pushkin's work was known to resist proper translation.) Pushkin, by being tied to the West while remaining the greatest exponent of the distinctive qualities of the Russian language, emerged as a matter of some obsession for the exiled Nabokov and as a powerful anchor for the emigré Stravinsky.[93]

As Stravinsky observed, "the national element occupies a prominent place with Pushkin as well as with Glinka and Tchaikovsky."[94] In exile, Nabokov and Stravinsky found in Pushkin a mirror of their dual condition: in possession of a uniquely Russian instrument (language for Nabokov, source material and harmonic usage for Stravinsky) but trapped in a Western context. That "fortunate alloy,"[95] as Stravinsky termed Pushkin's synthesis, remained present in the work of both men to the end. It is even visible in Nabokov's American novels but dominant in his translations of his earlier works into English. The synthesis of the Russian and the Western is audible, for example, in three of Stravinsky's later works, the *Canticum Sacrum*, *Babel*, and the *Requiem Canticles*.[96]

Nabokov and Stravinsky called on their respective publics to confront the method and materials of their work—the self-conscious distinctive style they developed in the making of art. The listener to Stravinsky's music, from *The Rite of Spring* and *Les Noces* through the finest of the late works, was confronted with intense moments, abrupt changes in sonority without conventional preparation, and complex but unified contrapuntal combinatorial elaborations. All these were independent of a late-Romantic reliance on duration and structural devices based on habitual expectations or derived from practices dependent on easily located thematic expositions, repetitions, variations, recapitulations, and transitions.

Stravinsky's and Nabokov's initial sources were Russian but their audiences—certainly after 1940—were not. They embedded in their styles what for them was distinctly and irreducibly Russian—not the Russian of the late nineteenth century but of Pushkin and, in terms of humor, Gogol. By recasting that aspect of tradition they engaged in their own distinctive manner of nostalgia—a nostalgia that suggested a highly conservative but idiosyncratic and imaginary past, inherently critical of aspects of modernity and modernism fashionable during the mid-twentieth century. Stravinsky may have employed his own version of serialism, but after 1939 kept his distance from the radical experimentalism of Pierre Boulez (with whom Stravinsky had a complex relationship), Olivier Messiaen (whom Stravinsky disliked), or John Cage (whom Stravinsky dismissed), just as Nabokov, despite a commitment to modernism, disparaged most if not all of his contemporary "modern poets" (T. S. Eliot and Ezra Pound, for example).[97]

At the same time both men shunned populists, particularly the writers and composers in the Soviet Union. Stravinsky's appreciation for Schoenberg and Webern derived from his recognition that they too drew from an idealized pre-Romantic tradition located in Viennese classicism. Nabokov had contempt for the books sent to him in the 1950s and '60s and resisted the academic enthusiasm for and literary emulation of Joyce's *Finnegans Wake*.

The legacy Stravinsky and Nabokov shared helped inspire them to produce a body of work tied to a mythical past kept fresh in their minds in exile, yet stylistically modernist in an individualist manner. They remained independent of dominant modernist trends such as the derision of style per se, the devaluation of ornament, and the suspicion of complexity. Their distinctive modernism stood apart from any reactionary embrace of the strategies of narrative realism and Romanticism. Their appropriation of sources from a vanished past permitted them to develop formal strategies to turn the reader into the listener. The temporal frame of an encounter with music came to define the aesthetic experience of reading. Stravinsky put the idea of the reader as listener into succinct terms: "Music is based on temporal succession and requires alertness of memory."[98] Yet Stravinsky was never a literary composer in the Wagnerian sense. And Nabokov, his protestations to the contrary, turned the encounter with prose into an act of intense musical listening in which meaning derived from the formal properties and use of words that framed the reader's encounter, her perception of time, memory, and her construct of meaning—all sealed within the framework of a work of art, an imagined abstraction from the shared encounter with ordinary reality.

Yet, for all the common ground between them in method and procedure, key differences remain in the ethical substance implicit in their work—in how they, as artists, construed modernity. At stake were not merely the predicament of the artist, but the proper purpose and character of the intended response. The experience of exile, and the distance it created from any semblance of home, rendered ordinary history and even the fragments of biography—for both, based in Russia—ultimately as fanciful as Kinbote's Zembla. For Nabokov, that uprooted existential circumstance turned out to be the most reasonable vantage point from which to observe human nature and to write within the most noble and beautiful traditions of his craft. By moving back to Montreux, he secured the necessary distance vis-à-vis his new home, America. That distance found the possibility that, at best, he could sustain in his writing the "precision of poetry and the exactness of science."[99] The precision and exactness were located in the use of words, the acuity of observation, and his art's penetration beneath the surface to confront the moral circumstances of the individual.

Stravinsky shared Nabokov's allegiance to an art of precision and exactness and to an art located in a Russian tradition mediated through Western European practice. But he was rather impervious to the moral crisis represented by fascism and Communism, by the terror, barbarism, and slaughter they inspired.[100]

Nabokov (as he never tired of asserting in the face of the scandal surrounding *Lolita*) remained a moralist with eighteenth-century values located in the love of individual freedom, art, and science.[101] "Actually I'm a mild old gentleman who loathes cruelty," he told an interviewer in 1962.[102] He sought to engage his best readers in confronting, albeit indirectly, the threat evident in the course of twentieth-century history. Deftly woven within all his novels is the recognition of the nearly irresistible pressure on each individual, practical and psychological, to succumb and conform, and therefore the powerlessness of individuals to resist, escape, and reject the allure of entrapment and collaboration with cruelty. Only in the temporal realm of the imagination could the human possibility of decency find its voice.

This aspect of Nabokov helps illuminate the link between his writing and his work with butterflies. The butterfly, much like the nymphet, has a brief moment of detailed and uniquely differentiated beauty that emerges from the uncanny camouflage of the ordinary. The temporal frame of that beauty is brief, comparable to the act of writing, the act of listening, and the act of reading. It is a revealing coincidence that in concentration camps that held children, the children spontaneously drew on the walls pictures of butterflies as emblems of hope.[103] Reading Nabokov and perhaps listening to Stravinsky—despite the absence of any comparable admirable intentions on the part of the composer—permits us the same fleeting hint of hope and beauty expressed by the children as their own pasts were obliterated and the present brought them only nearer to their deaths.[104]

NOTES

1. Vladimir Nabokov, *Strong Opinions* (New York: Vintage Books, 1990), 171–72. Brian Boyd's two-volume biography, *Vladimir Nabokov: The Russian Years* and *Vladimir Nabokov: The American Years* (Princeton: Princeton University Press, 1990–91), is a necessary and indispensable source. The subject matter in this essay has been treated provocatively by Daniel Albright in the chapter on Nabokov in *Representation and the Imagination: Beckett, Kafka, Nabokov, and Schoenberg* (Chicago: University of Chicago Press, 1981), 52–94; and in his discussion of Stravinsky in *Untwisting the Serpent: Modernism in Music, Literature, and Other Arts* (Chicago: University of Chicago Press, 1999).

2. See Stephen Walsh's account of Craft's role. Although it contradicts Craft, it seems both balanced and persuasive, given Stravinsky's past practices in the publication of opinions and books. See *Stravinsky: The Second Exile, France and America, 1934–1971* (New York: Knopf, 2006), 398–99.

3. Ibid., 399.

4. See Sergei Davydov on *poshlost'* in *The Garland Companion to Vladimir Nabokov*, ed. Vladimir E. Alexandrov (New York: Routledge, 1995), 628–32.

5. See Valérie Dufour, *Stravinsky et ses exégètes (1910–1940)* (Brussels: Editions de l'Université de Bruxelles, 2006), 51–79; and Walsh, *Stravinsky: The Second Exile*, 397–98.

6. See Valérie Dufour, "The *Poétique musicale*: A Counterpoint in Three Voices," in this volume.

7. For Nabokov on music see, for example, *Strong Opinions*, 35. See also Charles Nicol, "Music in the Theater of the Mind: Opera and Vladimir Nabokov," and Nassim W. Balestrini, "Vladimir

Nabokov's *Invitation to a Beheading* and Igor Stravinsky's *Petrushka*," in *Nabokov at the Limits: Redrawing Critical Boundaries*, ed. Lisa Zunshine (New York: Garland, 1999), 21–42 and 87–110, respectively.

8. Nabokov, "*Playboy* (1964)," in *Strong Opinions*, 35.

9. Nabokov, *Speak, Memory: An Autobiography Revisited* (New York: Vintage Books, 1989), 35; and Nabokov, *Strong Opinions*, 151.

10. Nabokov approved of Appel's *The New Republic* review *of Speak, Memory*. See "Nabokov's Puppet Show: Parts I and II," *The New Republic*, 14 January 1967 and 21 January 1967.

11. Boyd, *Nabokov: The Russian Years* and *Nabokov: The American Years*, passim.

12. See Tamara Levitz, "Igor the Angeleno: The Mexican Connection," in this volume.

13. Vincent Giroud, unpublished drafts of a forthcoming biography of Nicolas Nabokov; Nicolas Nabokov, *Old Friends and New Music* (Boston: Little, Brown, and Co., 1951), 190–204, 209–11; Nicolas Nabokov, *Zwei rechte Schuhe im Gepäck: Erinnerungen eines russischen Weltbürgers* (Munich: Piper, 1975), 208–27, 357.

14. See Boyd, N*abokov: The Russian Years*; and Richard Taruskin, *Stravinsky and the Russian Traditions: A Biography of the Works through* Mavra (Berkeley and Los Angeles: University of California Press, 1996), 1:77–162.

15. Boyd, *Nabokov: The Russian Years*, passim; and Nabokov, *Speak, Memory*, 71.

16. Boyd, *Nabokov: The Russian Years*, 40; and Nabokov, *Strong Opinions*, 171.

17. See the discussion of Stravinsky's engagement with Tchaikovsky's work in Taruskin, *Stravinsky and the Russian Traditions*, 1:2–5, 2:1529–1618.

18. This was a favorite term of Nabokov's. It means "corny trash, vulgar clichés, Philistinism in all its phases, imitations of imitations, bogus profundities, crude, moronic, and dishonest pseudo-literature." *Strong Opinions*, 101.

19. See Robert Craft, "Jews and Geniuses" *The New York Review of Books*, 16 February 1989, and Richard Taruskin and Robert Craft, "Jews and Geniuses: An Exchange," *The New York Review of Books*, 15 June 1989. On Stravinsky's eagerness to curry favor with the Nazis, see the letters to Willi Strecker in *Stravinsky: Selected Correspondence*, ed. Robert Craft (New York: Alfred A. Knopf, 1985), 3:235, 236, 243, 244, 251, 265–66.

20. Igor Stravinsky, *Poetics of Music in the Form of Six Lessons*, trans. Arthur Knodel and Ingolf Dahl (Cambridge, MA: Harvard University Press, 1970), 61.

21. Ibid., 157.

22. Vladimir Nabokov, *The Gift* (New York: Vintage Books, 1991), 343.

23. Nabokov, *Strong Opinions*, 71–72, 85–86.

24. See Vladimir Nabokov, *Bend Sinister* (New York: Vintage Books, 1990).

25. See Will Norman's discussion in his book *Nabokov, History, and Texture of Time* (New York: Routledge, 2012), 104–29.

26. Vladimir Nabokov, *Lolita* (New York: Vintage Books, 1997), 302.

27. Nabokov, *Strong Opinions*, 49.

28. This essay is indebted to Richard Taruskin's brilliant and detailed analysis of Stravinsky, especially in *Stravinsky and the Russian Traditions*. His portrait of the history, his analytical accounts of the music and the biographical claims form an indispensable basis for anyone writing on Stravinsky.

29. In addition to Taruskin, see Pieter C. van den Toorn, "Octatonic Pitch Structure in Stravinsky," in *Confronting Stravinsky*, ed. Jann Pasler (Berkeley and Los Angeles: University of California Press, 1986), 154–56.

30. This comment uses realism as a general term from literary history. It is not being used in the specific sense in which Carl Dahlhaus and others speak of musical realism. For example, I am not referring to the analysis of Musorgsky as a model of musical realism. The idea here is more general, in that the relationship of the audience to the musical experience—the fundamental sense of syntax, continuity, shape, and the rhetorical parallels to emotion and illustration—ran in tandem with the expectations and tastes of readers at the end of the nineteenth century. The point in this sense is not a technical one within a scholarly debate about a category in music history. The other analogy would be between musical practice and genre and historical painting, and with the pictorial

illusions of realism at the end of the nineteenth century, as argued in my essay, "Music as Language of Psychological Realism: Tchaikovsky and Russian Art," in *Tchaikovsky and his World*, ed. Leslie Kearney (Princeton: Princeton University Press, 1998), 99–144. See also D. S. Mirsky, *Contemporary Russian Literature, 1881–1925* (New York: Alfred A. Knopf, 1926).

31. See Allen Forte, "Harmonic Syntax and Voice Leading in Stravinsky's Early Music," in Pasler, ed., *Confronting Stravinsky*, 129.

32. Taruskin, *Stravinsky and the Russian Traditions*, 1:950.

33. See the two-volume set *Nicholas Roerich*, ed. Yevgeny Matochkin and Lisa Korshunova (Samara: Agni, 2011); and Richard Taruskin, "From Subject to Style: Stravinsky and the Painters," in Pasler, ed., *Confronting Stravinsky*, 16–38.

34. See Pierre Souvtchinsky, "La Notion du temps et la musique (Réflexions sur la typologie de la création musicale)," *La Revue musicale* 20/191 (May–June 1939): 70–81; repr. in Souvtchinsky, *Un Siècle de musique russe, 1830–1930*, ed. Frank Langlois (Paris: Actes Sud, 2004), 239–52.

35. Nabokov, *The Gift*, 71.

36. Ibid., 342.

37. Edward T. Cone, "Stravinsky: The Progress of a Method," in *Perspectives on Schoenberg and Stravinsky*, ed. Benjamin Boretz and Edward T. Cone, rev. ed. (New York: W. W. Norton, 1972), 156.

38. Ibid.

39. Louis Andriessen and Elmer Schönberger, T*he Apollonian Clockwork: On Stravinksy*, trans. Jeff Hamburg (Amsterdam: Amsterdam University Press, 2006), 160–64.

40. On *drobnost'*, see Taruskin, *Stravinsky and the Russian Traditions*, 1:951–65 and 2:1677.

41. Nabokov, *The Eye* (New York: Vintage Books, 1990), introduction (n.p.).

42. See the analysis in Michael Wood's brilliant study of Nabokov, *The Magician's Doubts: Nabokov and the Risks of Fiction* (Princeton: Princeton University Press, 1997).

43. See, for example, Maureen Carr, *Multiple Masks: Stravinsky's Neoclassicism in His Dramatic Works in Greek Studies* (Lincoln: University of Nebraska Press, 2002).

44. Nabokov, *Pale Fire* (New York: Alfred A. Knopf, 1992), 10.

45. Nabokov, *Speak, Memory*, 95.

46. Ibid., 34.

47. On Čiurlonis and synesthesia, see Dorothee Eberlein, "Čiurlonis, Skrjabin und der osteuropäische Symbolismus," in *Vom Klang der Bilder: Die Musik in der Kunst des 20. Jahrhunderts*, ed. Karin v. Maur (Munich: Prestel, 1985), 340–45.

48. Nabokov, *Speak, Memory*, 21.

49. Ibid., passim.

50. Nabokov, *Pale Fire*, 194, 226.

51. Nabokov, *Invitation to a Beheading* (New York: Vintage Books, 1989), 93.

52. In *Pale Fire*, for example, the use of musical metaphors, references, and analogies abound. See esp. 10, 12, 13, 20, 21, 86–88, 100, 103, 105, 150–51, 153–55, 159, 165, 172, 188, 204, 219–20, and 226.

53. Vladimir Nabokov, "Music," in *The Stories of Vladimir Nabokov* (New York: Vintage Books, 1997), 332–37.

54. Nabokov, *Pale Fire*, 13.

55. Igor Stravinsky, *An Autobiography* (New York: W. W. Norton, 1962), 54.

56. Robert Craft, *Chronicle of a Friendship, 1948–1971* (New York: Vintage Books, 1973), 10.

57. Taruskin, *Stravinsky and the Russian Traditions*, 2:1125–26; Dufour, *Stravinski et ses exégètes*, 52–86 (Suvchinsky), 119, 138 (Valéry). See also Tamara Levitz, *Modernist Mysteries:* Perséphone (New York: Oxford University Press, 2012).

58. Leona Toker, "Nabokov and Bergson," in Alexandrov, *Garland Companion to Vladimir Nabokov*, 367–74.

59. Nabokov, *Ada, or Ardor* (New York: Vintage Books, 1990), 543–44. These are the words of Van Veen, whom I do not assume to be Nabokov.

60. Nabokov, *Ada, or Ardor*, 548, 550.

61. See Natalie Reitano, "Our Marvelous Mortality: Finitude in *Ada, or Ardor*," *Criticism* 49/3 (2007): 377–403.

62. See Vladimir E. Alexandrov, "Nabokov and Bely," in Alexandrov, *Garland Companion to Vladimir Nabokov*, 358–66; on Bely, see Ada Steinberg, *Word and Music in the Novels of Andrey Bely* (Cambridge: Cambridge University Press, 1982); Roger Keys, "Bely's Symphonies," in *Andrey Bely: Spirit of Symbolism*, ed. John E. Malmstad (Ithaca, NY: Cornell University Press, 1987), 19–59; Vladimir E. Alexandrov, *Andrei Bely: The Major Symbolist Fiction* (Cambridge, MA: Harvard University Press, 1985); and John E. Bowlt, *Moscow and St. Petersburg 1900–1920: Art and Culture* (New York: Vendome Press, 2008), 89–91, 208–13.

63. Andrey Bely, "The Art of the Future (1907)," in *The Selected Essays of Andrey Bely*, ed. and trans. Steven Cassedy (Berkeley: University of Chicago Press, 1985), 198–202.

64. Ibid., 202. Two Years later, in "The Magic of Words," Bely wrote "either life must be transformed into art or art must be made living." In Cassedy, *Selected Essays of Andrey Bely*, 100.

65. Bely, "The Magic of Words," 93–96.

66. Ibid., 100. On art and science in Nabokov, see Leland de la Durantaye, "Artistic Selection: Science and Art in Vladimir Nabokov," in *Transitional Nabokov*, ed. Duncan White and Will Norman (New York: Peter Lang, 2009), 55–66.

67. Bely, "The Magic of Words," 103.

68. Ibid., 110.

69. Ibid.

70. Bely, "The Principle of Form in Aesthetics (1906)," in Cassedy, *Selected Essays of Andrey Bely*, 205.

71. Ibid., 208.

72. Ibid., 208–9.

73. Ibid., 209–10. Bely's writing on Pushkin and on rhythm in Pushkin's poetry appear to have been influential. See "Lyric Poetry and Experiment (1909), in Cassedy, *Selected Essays of Andrey Bely*, 222–73; and Bely, *Ritm kak dialektika i "Mednïy vsadnik"* (Moscow, 1929)—this book makes a cameo appearance in *The Gift*.

74. There are parallels between Bely and Bergson's notion of "vital" creative moment and both men's engagement with science. Bely, "Lyric Poetry and Experiment," 225. A telling example of Nabokov's obsession with the precision of language and its parallels in the conduct of science is the episode about Fyodor's father in chapter 2 of *The Gift*. Nabokov writes there of the dangers of "secondary poetization which keeps departing from that real poetry with which the live experience of these receptive, knowledgeable and chaste naturalists endowed their research" (139).

75. Ibid., 232.

76. Ibid.

77. Andrei Bely, "The Forms of Art," in *The Dramatic Symphony, a Novel, with an Essay: The Forms of Art* (New York: Grove Press, 1986), 175. *Dramatic Symphony* is translated by Roger and Angela Keys, the essay by John Elsworth.

78. Nabokov, *Strong Opinions*, 44.

79. Bely, "The Forms of Art," 178.

80. Stravinsky, *An Autobiography*, 53.

81. Nabokov, *Strong Opinions*, 78.

82. Stravinsky, *An Autobiography*, 53–54.

83. Nabokov, *Strong Opinions*, 45.

84. See the discussion in Taruskin, *Stravinsky and the Russian Traditions*, 1:820–48. See also Peter Dayan, *Art as Music, Music as Poetry, Poetry as Art, from Whistler to Stravinsky and Beyond* (Burlington, VT: Ashgate, 2011), 119–46.

85. In Arnold Schoenberg, *Style and Idea*, ed. Leonard Stein, trans. Leo Black (London: Faber & Faber, 1975).

86. D. S. Mirsky, *A History of Russian Literature: From Its Beginnings to 1900*, ed. Francis J. Whitfield (Evanston, IL: Northwestern University Press, 1999), 102; see also Mirsky, *Contemporary Russian Literature*.

87. There are many sources for Nabokov's veneration of Pushkin; see for example, in *The Gift*, 148–49. See also Sergei Davydov, "Nabokov and Pushkin," in Alexandrov, *Garland Companion to Nabokov*, 482–95. It should be noted that Nicolas Nabokov's elegy in three movements for high voice and orchestra of 1964, *The Return of Pushkin*, used poems translated by Vladimir Nabokov. See Nicolas Nabokov, *The Return of Pushkin* (Bonn: M. P. Belaieff, 1966). The texts are given in Russian, German, and English. The presumption is that both the German and the English versions are credited to Vladimir Nabokov.

88. Stravinsky, *An Autobiography*, 97. See also Jonathan Cross's essay in this volume.

89. See Simon Karlinsky, "Igor Stravinsky and Russian Preliterate Theater," in Pasler, ed., *Confronting Stravinsky*, 5; Martha Hyde, "Stravinsky's Neoclassic," in *The Cambridge Companion to Stravinsky*, ed. Jonathan Cross (Cambridge: Cambridge University Press, 2003), 107–9; Taruskin, *Stravinsky and the Russian Traditions*, 1:1549–585.

90. Stravinsky, *An Autobiography*, 98. See also Stravinsky's unpublished program note about *Mavra* in "Who Owns *Mavra*? A Transnational Dispute," in this volume.

91. Nabokov, *Strong Opinions*, 266.

92. See Bely, "Lyric Poetry and Experiment."

93. See Yuri Leving, "Singing *The Bells* and *The Covetous Knight*: Nabokov and Rachmaninoff's Operatic Translations of Poe and Pushkin," in White and Norman, *Transitional Nabokov*, 205–25.

94. Stravinsky, *An Autobiography*, 97.

95. Ibid.

96. Karlinsky, "Igor Stravinsky and Russian Preliterate Theater," 15.

97. Boyd construes John Shade's poem in *Pale Fire* as "a deliberate challenge to Pound and Eliot." Boyd, *Nabokov: The American Years*, 439, and Nabokov, *Strong Opinions*, 43. See also Igor Stravinsky and Robert Craft, *Dialogues and a Diary* (London: Faber, 1968), 58–59, 69; Stravinsky and Craft, *Conversations with Igor Stravinsky* (Berkeley: University of California Press, 1980), 127–30; Stravinsky, *Themes and Conclusions* (Berkeley: University of California Press, 1982) 30–31, 109. See also Walsh's discussion of Stravinsky's relationship to Boulez in his *Stravinsky: The Second Exile*, passim.

98. Stravinsky, *The Poetics of Music*, 37.

99. See the interview "Nabokov and the Moment of Truth," available on YouTube, http://www.youtube.com/watch?v=p3fsSL4Bw9w.

100. See the nostalgic aside in *Pale Fire*, 188.

101. See Norman, *Nabokov, History, and Texture of Time*, esp. 118–29.

102. Nabokov, *Strong Opinions*, 19.

103. Elisabeth Kübler-Ross, lecture at the University of Zurich. See *Elisabeth Kübler-Ross: Dem Tod ins Gesicht sehen*, a film by Sefan Haupt, Edition Salzgeber DVD D256.

104. As the Stravinsky letters reveal, he wanted his works performed in Germany until 1940, after the invasion of France. He, like Richard Strauss, thought of himself as better than any regime, and all he appeared to care about was getting his works performed and earning money from them. Stravinsky apparently reacted to America's entry into the war in 1941 by thinking only about himself and where else he might be able to move. See comment in Tony Palmer's film *Stravinsky: Once, at a Border . . .* ,TP-DVD126, Voiceprint Records, 2008.

Index

Page numbers followed by n indicate notes; italicized page numbers indicate material in tables, figures, or musical examples.

Index to Igor Stravinsky's Works

Name and Subject Index

Notes on Contributors

Tatiana Baranova Monighetti graduated from the Moscow Conservatory. Later, while working in the conservatory's music theory department, she organized the first international conference held in Russia on music of the pre-Classical period. She has lectured extensively in Europe and the United States, and published over fifty articles in scholarly journals. After leaving Russia Dr. Baranova Monighetti worked at the Escuela Superior de Musica Reina Sofia in Madrid, and in recent years has conducted research at the Paul Sacher Stiftung in Basel.

Bridget Behrmann (translator) graduated from Bard College and is completing a PhD in French and Italian at Princeton University. Her dissertation focuses on the poetic movement *le Parnasse* and relationships between poetry and science. Currently she is working on a translation of selections from Sully Prudhomme's poetry.

Leon Botstein is president and Leon Levy Professor in the Arts of Bard College, author of several books and editor of *The Compleat Brahms* (1999) and *The Musical Quarterly*. The music director of the American Symphony Orchestra and conductor laureate of the Jerusalem Symphony Orchestra, he has recorded works by, among others, Szymanowski, Hartmann, Bruch, Dukas, Foulds, Toch, Dohnányi, Bruckner, Chausson, Richard Strauss, Mendelssohn, Popov, Shostakovich, and Liszt.

Jonathan Cross is professor of musicology at the University of Oxford, and Student in Music (fellow) at Christ Church, Oxford. He has written extensively on Stravinsky, including the acclaimed monograph *The Stravinsky Legacy* (1998), and as editor of *The Cambridge Companion to Stravinsky* (2003). He is currently completing a "critical life" of the composer for Reaktion Press. He has worked widely on issues in modernism and contemporary music and is an associate editor of *Grove Music Online*.

Valérie Dufour is an advanced research scholar at the Belgian Fonds National de la Recherche Scientifique and teaches musicology at the Univeristé libre de Bruxelles. She has written and edited several articles and books on Igor Stravinsky—most recently *Confidences sur la musique: Ecrits et entretiens d'Igor Stravinsky* (2013)—and on the history of intellectual discourse around music in the nineteenth and twentieth centuries. With Michel Duchesneau and Marie-Hélène Benoit-Otis she edited the collection *Ecrits de compositeurs: Une autorité en questions* (2013). Dufour is currently interested in questions of urban geography and the role of metropolitanization in the development of musical life.

Katya Ermolaev (translator) is a PhD candidate in musicology at Princeton University where she is writing her dissertation on Sergey Prokofiev's film score

Ivan the Terrible (directed by Sergei Eisenstein). For a concurrent second PhD from the Royal Conservatoire of Scotland, she is co-editing the critical edition of Prokofiev's opera *War and Peace*.

Laurel E. Fay (translator) is an independent scholar and author of *Shostakovich: A Life* (2000), which won the Otto Kinkeldey Award of the American Musicological Society. She also edited *Shostakovich and His World* (Bard Music Festival/Princeton University Press, 2004).

Mariel Fiori (translator) is a journalist, co-founder and managing editor of the Bard-sponsored Spanish-language magazine *La Voz*. She holds an MBA from New York University and a BA from Bard College. Fiori has received the Dutchess County Executive Arts Award and is a board member of Somos la Llave del Futuro, SLF, Inc., a non-profit organization that seeks to build leadership in immigrant communities.

Alexandra Grabarchuk (translator) is a PhD student in the Department of Musicology at the University of California Los Angeles. She is currently writing a dissertation on popular music aesthetics and cultural production in the Brezhnev-era Soviet Union. In addition to studying Soviet *estrada*, she is an avid performer of early repertoire both as singer and instrumentalist.

Gretchen Horlacher is professor of music at the Jacobs School of Music at Indiana University. She holds a BA from Cornell and a PhD from Yale University, and as a pianist received the *Prix d'excellence* from the Ecole américaine de musique in Fontainebleau, France. She is the author of *Building Blocks: Repetition and Continuity in the Music of Stravinsky* (2011), and has published widely also about Steve Reich, theories of rhythm and meter, and sketch studies.

Yasha Klots (translator) holds a PhD from Yale University. He has worked on émigré literature, bilingualism and literary translation, Gulag narratives, and the mythology of St. Petersburg. He is the author of *Joseph Brodsky in Lithuania* (2010; in Russian), co-translator of two recent nonfiction books, and is currently working on an anthology of Russian poetry about New York City.

Tamara Levitz is professor of musicology at the University of California Los Angeles. She has lectured and published widely on musical modernism and her work has appeared in numerous venues. Combining extensive archival research with critical interpretation, Dr. Levitz explores the intentions, motivations, sexual and gender identifications, and intricate social relations of musicians, composers, critics, ethnographers, performers, and audiences. Much of her work has focused on Ferruccio Busoni, Igor Stravinsky, and André Gide, and she recently completed the monograph *Modernist Mysteries:* Perséphone (2012), a microhistorical analysis of the 1934 premiere of André Gide's and Igor Stravinsky's melodrama.

Klára Móricz is Joseph E. and Grace W. Valentine Professor of Music at Amherst College. With Christopher Hailey she is editor of *Journal of Musicology*. Her articles have appeared in *JAMS, twentieth-century music, Notes, Cambridge Opera Journal, Pushkin Review,* and *American Music*. Her book *Jewish Identities: Nationalism, Racism and Utopianism in Twentieth-Century Art Music* was published in 2008. With Simon Morrison she is presently editing a volume of essays entitled *Funeral Games in Honor of Arthur Lourié.*

Philipp Penka (translator, Bard '08) is a PhD candidate in the Department of Slavic Languages and Literatures at Harvard University. He is currently working on a dissertation about Russian modernism in the context of sound recording and transmission. He lives in Berlin and Cambridge.

Leonora Saavedra studied performance and musicology in Mexico, France, Germany and the USA and is currently associate professor at the University of California Riverside. She has served as the director of the National Center for Music Research (CENIDIM) in Mexico City and her research interests include the music of Manuel M. Ponce, Carlos Chávez, Silvestre Revueltas, Ernesto Elorduy, Aaron Copland, and the musical relations between Mexico and the United States. She was one of the founders of the Mexican music journal *Pauta* and her work has appeared widely in other periodicals and publications. As an active performer of new music from 1980 to 1985 she gave the first performances of numerous works by Mexican composers.

Svetlana Savenko graduated from the Moscow Conservatory where she is currently professor of Russian music. She is the author of more than 100 publications in Russian, English, and German including the monograph *Mir Stravinskogo* (Stravinsky's world; 2001), a biography of Stravinsky (2004), and the annotated Russian-language editions of Stravinsky's *Chroniques de ma vie* (2004) and *Poétique musicale* (2nd edition 2012).

Boris Wolfson teaches Russian culture at Amherst College. He has published on nineteenth- and twentieth-century Russian cultural history and is completing a study of theater, performance, and modes of self-understanding in the Soviet 1930s.

OTHER PRINCETON UNIVERSITY PRESS VOLUMES PUBLISHED
IN CONJUNCTION WITH THE BARD MUSIC FESTIVAL

Brahms and His World
edited by Walter Frisch (1990)

Mendelssohn and His World
edited by R. Larry Todd (1991)

Richard Strauss and His World
edited by Bryan Gilliam (1992)

Dvořák and His World
edited by Michael Beckerman (1993)

Schumann and His World
edited by R. Larry Todd (1994)

Bartók and His World
edited by Peter Laki (1995)

Charles Ives and His World
edited by J. Peter Burkholder (1996)

Haydn and His World
edited by Elaine R. Sisman (1997)

Tchaikovsky and His World
edited by Leslie Kearney (1998)

Schoenberg and His World
edited by Walter Frisch (1999)

Beethoven and His World
edited by Scott Burnham and
Michael P. Steinberg (2000)

Debussy and His World
edited by Jane F. Fulcher (2001)

Mahler and His World
edited by Karen Painter (2002)

Janáček and His World
edited by Michael Beckerman (2003)

Shostakovich and His World
edited by Laurel E. Fay (2004)

Aaron Copland and His World
edited by Carol J. Oja and
Judith Tick (2005)

Franz Liszt and His World
edited by Christopher H. Gibbs and
Dana Gooley (2006)

Edward Elgar and His World
edited by Byron Adams (2008)

Prokofiev and His World
edited by Simon Morrison (2008)

Brahms and His World (revised edition)
edited by Walter Frisch and
Kevin C. Karnes (2009)

Richard Wagner and His World
edited by Thomas S. Grey (2009)

Alban Berg and His World
edited by Christopher Hailey (2010)

Jean Sibelius and His World
edited by Daniel M. Grimley (2011)

Camille Saint-Saëns and His World
edited by Jann Pasler (2012)